MASS COMMUNICATION ETHICS

5/1 abs Bill + Meghan
Whitney, Jared, Lori, Jenn

5/6 abs Lori, Whitney

MASS COMMUNICATION ETHICS

Decision Making in Postmodern Culture

Larry Z. Leslie
University of South Florida, Tampa

HOUGHTON MIFFLIN COMPANY   Boston   New York

Senior Sponsoring Editor: George Hoffman
Assistant Editor: Jennifer Wall
Senior Project Editor: Fred Burns
Production/Design Coordinator: Jennifer Meyer Dare
Assistant Manufacturing Coordinator: Andrea Wagner
Marketing Manager: Pamela Laskey

Cover Design: Minko T. Dimov, MinkoImages.
Cover Images: Kandinsky, *Yellow, Red, Blue.* Vasily Kandinsky (1866–1944)
Gelb, Rot,Blau. Oil on canvas, 127 × 200 cm. Musée National d'Art Moderne,
Centre Georges Pompidou, Paris.

Printed in the U.S.A.

Library of Congress Catalog Card Number: 99-71945

ISBN: 0-395-90490-0

1 2 3 4 5 6 7 8 9 –EB – 03-02-01-00-99

To my parents, Harry and Jean
and to my daughter, Kelly

CONTENTS

Preface   xv

Section I   Introduction and Historical Context   *1*

Chapter 1   **Postmodern America**   *5*

    Postmodernism Defined   *5*

    A Backward Look   *6*

    Postmodernism Explained   *7*

Chapter 2   **Ethics in America**   *15*

    Current Concerns   *15*

    Ethics Defined   *16*

    Ethics in Journalism/Mass Communication Programs   *18*

    Some Basics   *19*

Section II   Philosophical Foundations   *21*

Chapter 3   **The Greek View**   *25*

    Plato   *25*

        The Life   *25*

        The Philosophy   *26*

        Decision-Making Tool   *28*

        Suggested Media Application   *28*

        Recommended Case Studies   *29*

    Aristotle   *29*

        The Life   *29*

        The Philosophy   *30*

        Decision-Making Tool   *32*

        Suggested Media Application   *32*

        Recommended Case Studies   *33*

Chapter 4   **Transition Figures**   *37*

    Abelard   *38*

        The Life   *38*

        The Philosophy   *39*

Decision-Making Tool   *40*

Suggested Media Application   *40*

Recommended Case Studies   *40*

St. Thomas Aquinas   *40*

The Life   *40*

The Philosophy   *41*

Decision-Making Tool   *42*

Suggested Media Application   *42*

Recommended Case Studies   *42*

Francis Bacon   *32*

The Life   *42*

The Philosophy   *44*

Decision-Making Tool   *45*

Suggested Media Application   *45*

Recommended Case Studies   *45*

Chapter 5   **Rebels**   *47*

Niccolò Machiavelli   *48*

The Life   *48*

The Philosophy   *50*

Synthesis   *52*

Decision-Making Tool   *52*

Suggested Media Application   *52*

Recommended Case Studies   *53*

Thomas Hobbes   *53*

The Life   *53*

The Philosophy   *54*

Decision-Making Tool   *55*

Suggested Media Application   *56*

Recommended Case Studies   *56*

François Marie Arouet Voltaire   *56*

The Life   *56*

The Philosophy   *58*

Decision-Making Tool   *59*

Suggested Media Application   *59*

Recommended Case Studies   *59*

Jean Jacques Rousseau   *59*
   The Life   *59*
   The Philosophy   *61*
   Decision-Making Tool   *62*
   Suggested Media Application   *62*
   Recommended Case Studies   *62*

Chapter 6   **Traditionalists**   *67*

Benedict Spinoza   *68*
   The Life   *68*
   The Philosophy   *70*
   Decision-Making Tool   *72*
   Suggested Media Application   *72*
   Recommended Case Studies   *72*
Immanuel Kant   *72*
   The Life   *72*
   The Philosophy   *76*
   Decision-Making Tool   *77*
   Suggested Media Application   *78*
   Recommended Case Studies   *78*
John Stuart Mill   *78*
   The Life   *78*
   The Philosophy   *81*
   Decision-Making Tool   *82*
   Suggested Media Application   *82*
   Recommended Case Studies   *82*

Chapter 7   **The Continental Connection**   *87*

Arthur Schopenhauer   *88*
   The Life   *88*
   The Philosophy   *91*
   Decision-Making Tool   *93*
   Suggested Media Application   *93*
   Recommended Case Studies   *93*
Émile Durkheim   *94*
   The Life   *94*
   The Philosophy   *94*

Decision-Making Tool   *97*
Suggested Media Application   *97*
Recommended Case Studies   *98*

Chapter 8   Modern Influences   *101*

Jean-Paul Sartre   *102*
The Life   *102*
The Philosophy   *106*
Decision-Making Tool   *109*
Suggested Media Application   *109*
Recommended Case Studies   *109*

Ayn Rand   *109*
The Life   *109*
The Philosophy   *112*
Decision-Making Tool   *114*
Suggested Media Application   *114*
Recommended Case Studies   *115*

Lawrence Kohlberg   *115*
The Life   *115*
The Philosophy   *116*
Decision-Making Tool   *118*
Suggested Media Application   *118*
Recommended Case Studies   *119*

Judeo-Christian Tradition   *119*
The Rationale   *119*
The Jewish Tradition   *120*
The Christian Way   *121*
Decision-Making Tool   *122*
Suggested Media Application   *122*
Recommended Case Studies   *122*

Chapter 9   Postmodernist Approaches   *127*

Michel Foucault   *128*
The Life   *128*
The Philosophy   *131*
Decision-Making Tool   *132*
Suggested Media Application   *132*
Recommended Case Studies   *133*

Jean Baudrillard   *133*
The Life   *133*
The Philosophy   *135*

Decision-Making Tool   *137*

Suggested Media Application   *137*

Recommended Case Studies   *137*

Section III   Applications   141

Chapter 10   Decision Making   *145*

A Decision-Making Model   *147*

Using Philosophical Principles   *155*

Why Philosophy   *155*

Other Models   *155*

Real-Time Decision Making   *156*

Summary of Ethical Decision-Making Tools   *159*

Chapter 11   Ethical Issues and Case Studies in Journalism   *161*

Overview   *161*

Part I.   Some Major Ethical Issues   *162*

The Work of Journalists   *162*

News Values   *164*

Privacy   *165*

Public and Private Figures   *166*

Part II.   Instructional Case Study   *168*

Ethical Concerns Raised by the Case Study   *171*

Part III.   Other Ethical Concerns   *182*

Postmodern Ethical Concerns   *185*

Case Studies   *189*

Case Study #1. Supporting Professional Football

Case Study #2. Chopper Journalism

Case Study #3. A Glass Not So Transparent   192

Case Study #4. Conflict of Interest   193

Case Study #5. Stars Shine in Magazines   194

Chapter 12   Ethical Issues and Case Studies in Advertising and Public Relations   *197*

Advertising   *197*

Instructional Case Study   *200*

Appeals   *201*

Puffery   *204*

Sweepstakes   *207*

Tobacco Advertising   *209*

Alcoholic Beverage Advertising   *212*

Direct Mail Marketing *213*

Telemarketing *214*

Advertiser Influence on Media Content *215*

Applying Ethics to Advertising *217*

Public Relations *218*

Spin Control *218*

Fake News *221*

Loyalty and Truth *221*

Case Studies *222*

Case Study #6. Taken for a Ride? *222*

Case Study #7. Nike Takes a Hit *223*

Case Study #8. The 1997 Lemon Awards *224*

Case Study #9. Put on a Happy Face *226*

Chapter 13   **Ethical Issues and Case Studies in the Book, Recording, and Radio Industries**   *231*

Overview *231*

Instructional Case Study *231*

Book Publishing *232*

Economic Concerns *232*

Recording Industry *239*

Promotion Practices *241*

Radio *242*

Content *243*

An Observation *247*

Case Studies *248*

Case Study #10. The Romance Writer *248*

Case Study #11. Marv Takes a Loss *249*

Case Study #12. Jay Tells a Joke *250*

Case Study #13. Reading Can Be Instructive *252*

Chapter 14   **Ethical Issues and Case Studies in the Television-Entertainment and Film Industries**   *257*

Overview *257*

Television Entertainment *257*

Instructional Case Study *258*

Entertainment Content and Program Ratings *258*

Television Talk Shows *263*

Public Television *266*

The Film Industry *268*

Character and Content *269*

Political Involvement   *270*

Editing Techniques   *271*

Business Practices   *272*

Case Studies   *275*

Case Study #14. Offering Advice to Postmodern Teens   *275*

Case Study #15. Annie Sprinkle Goes to College   *276*

Case Study #16. Exploring South Park   *277*

Chapter 15   Ethical Issues and Case Studies in New Media Technology   *283*

Overview   *284*

Electronic Communication: The Internet   *284*

Instructional Case Study   *286*

Electronic Communication: Privacy   *286*

Electronic Communication: Sex on the Internet   *289*

Education and the Internet   *292*

Economic Issues   *294*

Other Concerns   *296*

Special Issues for Journalists   *298*

Ethical Considerations   *299*

What Lies Ahead?   *300*

Case Studies   *300*

Case Study #17. Online Therapy   *300*

Case Study #18. Touching a Nerve   *301*

Case Study #19. Is There a Problem with My Term Paper?   *302*

Case Study #20. An Unusual Confession   *304*

Chapter 16   Facing the Postmodern Maelstrom   *309*

A Call To Action   *309*

A Backward Look   *311*

A Look Ahead   *311*

Real-Time Case Studies   *312*

Case Study #1. Divulging Information   *312*

Case Study #2. Making the Call   *313*

Case Study #3. The Jumper   *314*

Case Study #4. The Profile   *315*

Glossary   *317*

Index   *321*

PREFACE

As any physicist can tell you, the second law of thermodynamics—sometimes called the entropy law—is not designed to comfort optimists. It means, in essence, that everything in the universe began with structure and value and is moving in the direction of random chaos and waste. It would appear, then, that recent social and political developments, particularly those indicating that our culture's moral standards have slumped, are natural and to be expected. It is only natural, too, to expect media—as an important part of the culture—to be on that same downward path. Star Trek's Scotty once told Captain Kirk, as the Enterprise was being pulled to certain destruction in the atmosphere of a remote planet, "I canna' change the laws of physics." But, shortly thereafter, Scotty did change the laws of physics by utilizing Spock's theoretical formula for restarting the ship's engines. Thus was tragedy averted.

It is my belief that those of us who write textbooks are much like Mr. Spock. Although we sometimes feel that the culture may be headed toward ultimate decline, there is no reason to accept it *right now,* or to accept it without a fight. Textbook authors are really trying to make their disciplines more ordered, more understandable, more accessible. We, like instructors, encourage our students to persevere, grow, and progress, even in the face of much evidence that the world around us may be going in the opposite direction. I wrote this text to comfort and support those individuals whose behavior is already ethical and to inspire others to set and achieve higher personal and professional moral standards.

A textbook can be many things. It can be assigned by an instructor and purchased by a student but never used or referred to in class. It can be used as a reference book or as a supplement to course lectures or class activities. It can determine how a course is structured, that is, in what order topics are covered and how much time is devoted to each. It may even replace the course instructor as the primary source of information. No doubt there are other uses.

The media ethics text you now hold in your hands has essentially three purposes: to inform, to entertain, and to inspire. You would most likely quickly agree with the informational and inspirational purposes, but you may be somewhat puzzled by the entertainment function of the book. A brief explanation of each of these purposes seems in order.

There is no question that a text—any text—should be informative; otherwise, why bother? A text should be filled with information useful to students and with information that broadens their horizons, expands their minds, and stimulates their imaginations. It is here that this text improves on others in the field. It does so chiefly by providing additional ethical theories that may be used in decision making and by viewing important issues in a contemporary, that is, postmodern, context. It is this postmodern context that makes this text an important one for the teaching of ethics.

Second, a text should be entertaining, but not in the traditional sense. An entertaining text is one that is clearly and crisply written. The people in this text should come alive and be seen as real people with real lives and real problems. Yet while struggling with their own lives, these individuals advanced powerful philosophical and ethical concepts. These are clearly presented, and their impact should be clearly understood.

Finally, a text should inspire. It is becoming increasingly difficult to inspire—or engage—some of today's students. As products of a postmodern culture—a culture dominated by media, moral relativism, and complex technology—today's students face an unusually large number of competing choices. How can education, to say nothing of a single course, successfully compete with the many social, political, and economic pressures and choices students have? After working the late shift at their jobs, or after a night of partying with friends, what can get students up the next morning and in their classroom seats for an early class? Will a textbook provide the motivation necessary to engage students? No, but motivated, enthusiastic, and creative instructors can use texts, together with a variety of teaching and active learning activities, to challenge students, to involve them, to give them a powerful reason to attend that early (or late, or midday) class. This approach is perhaps best summarized by a quotation attributed to Plutarch: "The mind is not a vessel to be filled, but a fire to be kindled."

This media ethics text is an outgrowth of more than thirty years of teaching, a dozen of them in a media ethics classroom at a large southeastern university. The course from which this text was developed has, quite naturally, changed over time. Nevertheless, its overall purposes remain the same: to inform, to entertain, to inspire. The students who have taken the course have consistently reported that it was a worthwhile learning experience for them. As noted earlier, a textbook can't do it all; however, it can provide a solid foundation on which a creative, energetic instructor can build. This text is meant to be used as raw material for kindling a fire in students.

No text is perfect, and this one doubtless has some shortcomings. One is that most of the philosophies presented are ones advanced by dead white males. Much of philosophy's canon is the product of eras in which men, particularly Western men, were in control. Women and minorities had few rights during these times and almost no opportunity to contribute to the established learning of their time. In their book *A Short History of Philosophy,* professors Robert C. Solomon and Kathleen M. Higgins note that although "recent research has uncovered a significant number of women throughout the history of philosophy, it is no easy matter to resurrect those who were buried, often unpublished and long ignored, and to distinguish their contribution from those of the men with whom they worked and who may have become known for their ideas" (p. 289). Solomon and Higgins advance Hypatia (AD 370–415) as an example. She is "far better known for her awful death (she was killed by a mob) than for her own (Neoplatonic) philosophy" (p. 289).

There are other missing perspectives here, too. No attention is given to Eastern philosophies, several of which have millions of followers and much to say about ethical behavior. No philosophies from Africa or South America have been included. These exclusions should not be interpreted as the advancement of any political or social agenda. I chose to take a traditional approach to ethical philosophies as a matter of practicality. A media ethics text, designed to fit a typical semester, cannot cover everything. I simply selected the philosophies that students in my classes seem to have appreciated knowing about and ones which they later reported to have been useful to them in solving ethical problems. It should be noted that my media ethics course, in fact, covers forty-four different philosophies, including three Eastern ones. While that many philosophies can be made to work in a classroom, a text cannot really accommodate that many without overwhelming the other material in the book.

I realize that some changes would be in order should this text go to a second edition. Suggestions are welcomed, both from instructors and students, regarding important perspectives that should be considered for future editions. Suggestions may be sent to me at the School of Mass Communications, CIS 1040, University of South Florida, Tampa, Florida 33620.

No author writes in a vacuum. A work is often the product of the sum total of the author's personal and professional experiences. I had the advantage of wonderful, supportive, moral parents. I had the opportunity to grow and develop both personally and professionally. In terms of this book, I had access to a variety of perspectives from many of my colleagues in the School of Mass Communications at the University of South Florida: Tim Counts, Jay Friedlander, Humphrey Regis, Scott Liu, Randy Miller, Gary Werner, and Rick Wilber, and Donna Dickerson, now at the University of Texas-Tyler. My thanks to all of these and to the hundreds of students with whom I have had contact. I have gained much from our interaction.

My special thanks to the gang at Houghton Mifflin, especially George Hoffman, Jennifer Wall, and Fred Burns. Their support and enthusiasm for the book made the writing of it a pleasure.

I also wish to thank the following reviewers for their helpful comments: K. Tim Wulfemeyer, San Diego State University; David Arant, University of Memphis; Michael Leslie, University of Florida; John Ginn, University of Kansas; Mike Cowling, University of Wisconsin-Oshkosh; Ken Waters, Pepperdine University; Karen Slattery, Marquette University; Kit Rushing, University of Tennessee at Chattanooga; Maria B. Marron, Southwest Texas State University; Oscar Patterson III, University of North Carolina at Pembroke; Chris W. Allen, University of Nebraska at Omaha; and Ronald Loneker, Jr., College of Saint Elizabeth.

LARRY LESLIE

MASS COMMUNICATION ETHICS

Introduction and
Historical Context

Peanuts reprinted by permission of United Features Syndicate, Inc.

▼ ▼ ▼

Americans have the richest, most technologically advanced society that has ever existed. We have a safe, abundant food supply. Improvements in health care have given us longer life spans than many had believed possible. We have much individual freedom. Yet we can't seem to solve the ethical and moral dilemmas that face us. Many of our problems have ethical and moral implications: crime, drugs, AIDS, corrupt or incompetent politicians, poor schools, the homeless, and the mentally ill. While these problems are national in scope, there are still a host of other problems that face each of us as individuals. Our material richness has not brought us moral and cultural comfort. Why haven't we made much progress in this area? One explanation is that solving ethical and moral problems is difficult because of the culture period in which we live: postmodern America.

Human civilization has experienced many culture periods. You don't have to be a student of history to be familiar with the Egyptian and Greek cultures. And, although you may not know exactly what happened during the Middle Ages or the Renaissance, you have at least heard these terms applied to specific historical periods. It is important that you have an acquaintance with history as you go through this text. Most of the philosophers presented in Section II of this book are grouped by historical culture period, and understanding them and the times in which they lived will help you grasp their ideas and realize their significance.

You should be aware that dealing with history is a slippery enterprise. While we have developed the ability to keep good records over the last two hundred years or so, for much of the time that humans have been on this planet, poor records exist—or none at all. Historians have been able to fill many of the gaps, but even they realize that some dates and events are approximate and others conjectural. Nevertheless, these approximations and conjectures have not been made lightly but have been based on the best historical evidence available.

Believing that we are in a relatively new culture period—the postmodern era—requires one to understand that it is the nature of culture to ebb and flow, and that the movement from one historical period with certain characteristics to another period with a different set of characteristics is both natural and more often gradual than abrupt. But the process is somewhat linear and fairly easy to follow.

At the risk of oversimplifying, a historical time line has been provided that should strengthen your grasp of history as a process. Additionally, the time line should help you place the philosophers discussed in Section II in their proper historical context. It should be noted, however, that not all personalities and accomplishments are detailed for each historical period, and, as mentioned earlier, some dates are approximate. Still, the time line provides an important frame of reference for some of the ideas presented in this book.

▼ ▼ ▼

Culture Period ■ Approximate Dates	General Description ■ Key Personalities
Egyptian 3100 B.C.–200 B.C.	Era of the Pharaohs; the Sphinx and the pyramids; agriculture influenced by Nile River; strong belief in an afterlife; Ramses II, Cleopatra, King Tutankhamen
Greek 1200 B.C.–320 B.C.	Era of development in literature, philosophy, and architecture; competing city-states Athens and Sparta; Persian and Peloponnesian wars; Socrates, Plato, Aristotle, Alexander the Great, Sophocles, Pythagoras
Roman 753 B.C.–A.D. 410	Empire extended over much of known world; politically and socially influential; important contributions to literature and art; Christ's birth A.D. c. 4; rise of Christianity, but declining secular morality; Nero, Caligula, and other Caesars, Horace, Ovid, Marcus Aurelius
Middle Ages A.D. 4000–A.D. 1300	Much political and social activity in Europe; increase in influence of popes; contributions to art, music, and literature; the Crusades; the Vikings, Charlemagne, Muhammad, St. Augustine, Dante
Renaissance–Reformation A.D. 1300–1650	Era of much political, social, intellectual, and religious activity; rise of the church and increased power of popes; significant contributions to art, music, and science, especially from the West (England): Chaucer, da Vinci, Michelangelo, Copernicus, Galileo, Henry VIII and the English kings, Martin Luther, John Calvin, El Greco, Rembrandt, Shakespeare
Enlightenment 1650–1850 *Note:* In America, the colonies continued to grow and develop following the establishment of the Virginia Charter in 1606 and the founding of the New England colonies around 1620. Declaration of Independence was signed in 1776.	An era of the awakening of the human spirit and the human mind; emphasis on reason; rise of science as an influence on life and thinking; major contributions in art, music, philosophy, religion; political and social turmoil in Europe; Louis XIV, Louis XVI and Marie Antoinette, Handel, Haydn, Mozart, Bach, Beethoven, Wordsworth, Byron, Keats, Emerson, Napoleon, Darwin, Newton
Modern age 1850–1945	The Industrial Revolution takes hold; steel developed; much political and social change in America (Civil War) and in Europe (World Wars I and II); significant contributions in art, music, literature, science; Pasteur, Einstein, Wright Brothers, Hugo, Marx, Freud, Picasso, Hitler, Stalin
Postmodern age 1945–Present *Note:* Many scholars set 1945, or the end of World War II, as the time of the transition to the postmodern era. This is probably true, especially in Europe, but your author fixes the date more precisely in the United States at about 1965. More discussion of this can be found in Chapter 1.	Rapid social and political change; life becomes more complex; much ambiguity and discontinuity in the culture; rise of influence of media; institutions of modern age (families, schools, churches) undergo profound change; rise of technology as a life influence; increasingly important global economy

This text will dip into the various historical culture periods and extract some key ethical philosophies that will prove helpful in making sound, appropriate, ethical decisions. Can ideas from the past be useful in solving contemporary problems? Of course. Most ethical problems relate to individuals and their behavior. Although individuals today are certainly different from individuals in, say, ancient Greece, both groups are still human and subject to the needs, desires, events, and pressures of their respective times. Ethical behavior is not time-bound, though the application of ethical principles to specific situations will necessarily vary from one historical period to another.

This first section will argue that we have gone beyond the *modern* period in our civilization into a complex culture period called the *postmodern* era. In the two chapters in this section, you will learn about postmodern culture, how it influences life and work, its relationship to the general field of ethics and ethical behavior, and how understanding it can assist you in making ethical decisions involving the media.

SUGGESTED READINGS

Anderson, Walter Truett, ed. *The Truth about the Truth* (New York: Putnam's, 1995).

Carter, Stephen L. *Integrity* (New York: Basic Books, 1996).

Eagleton, Terry. *The Illusions of Postmodernism* (Cambridge: Blackwell, 1996).

Halberstam, Joshua. *Everyday Ethics* (New York: Viking, 1993).

Howard, Philip K. *The Death of Common Sense* (New York: Random House, 1994).

Murchison, William. *Reclaiming Morality in America* (Nashville, TN: Thomas Nelson, 1994).

CHAPTER 1

Postmodern America

Postmodernism Defined

The term *postmodern* may be used to describe contemporary culture, a culture characterized by discontinuity and ambiguity in all aspects of life. *Postmodernism* is a little more difficult to define. The term has been stretched in all directions and applied to several different academic disciplines. The result is that there is no widespread agreement on its precise definition. Some scholars believe postmodernism "tries to avoid all encompassing definitions or truths."[1] Others suggest that "its adherents leave its definition deliberately vague."[2] This lack of agreement is not a major inconvenience, however, because there are several workable definitions and there is some agreement among scholars whose work forms the bulk of postmodern writing.

Charles Jencks's definition is a good place to begin. He defines postmodernism as a social condition, a cultural movement, and a worldview. In terms of culture, it suggests a "plurality of subcultures where no one ideology dominates for long."[3] James Carey, in observing the world of modern media, notes that "one encounters ceaseless and disorderly flows of new people and new things moving outward to new places along new routes."[4] The suffix *-ism* means action. Therefore, postmodernism is the application or action of the attitudes, practices, and conditions of the postmodern period.

An important characteristic of postmodernism is its rejection of modernism. *Modernism* is the term used to describe the historical culture period that preceded the present era. Some scholars say the modern period began as early as the mid-1400s with Gutenberg's invention of movable type. Most believe, however, that the modern period began in the mid to late 1800s. The modern period was characterized by an increase in the influence of reason, and particularly of science, as a way of gaining knowledge and of solving problems. Its institutions—schools, churches, families—were strong; and advances were made in the arts, literature, and technology, especially the technologies of mass production and communication.

Currently, postmodernists see modernist views of the world as inadequate, harmful, and costly. Modernism's approach to arriving at truth and solving problems has not worked, they say. Modernism has failed to come to grips with contemporary issues and remains content to spin reason and the scientific method as the best ways for gaining new knowledge. Our current culture is more complex than this worldview allows, postmodernists say. In short, postmodernism may be viewed as the intellectual, political, and social framework that characterizes the current environment in which we find ourselves, an environment that breaks sharply with some aspects of the past and presents a unique set of challenges for each individual.

A Backward Look

Philosophers and historians tell us that the ethical problems facing us today are not new. Moral dilemmas have always been with us, but we view them from our own historical context. Take, for example, the late 1800s in England. The Irish poet W. B. Yeats wrote,

> Things fall apart; the center cannot hold . . .
> The best lack all conviction, while the worst
> Are full of passionate intensity.[5]

The poem from which these lines were drawn expresses Yeats's sense that civilization is dissolving or at least completing a "cycle." In Yeats's complex symbolic philosophy, a new cycle will follow, but it will not necessarily be better than the one before. Yeats feels that "surely some revelation is at hand."[6]

Yeats's feelings were probably part of a general notion held by many writers and artists at the end of the nineteenth century. This end of the century—*fin de siècle*—brought significant cultural change. Some viewed the 1890s as "naughty," others preferred "decadence" to describe the general tenor of the times. But generally, "the phrase *fin de siècle* was applied to a wide range of trivial behavior, providing it was sufficiently perverse or paradoxical to be shocking."[7] However, the phrase also refers to more serious and consistent cultural attitudes of the time. One essential characteristic was that "all established forms of intellectual and moral and social certainty were vanishing."[8]

Historians could doubtless provide evidence of similar moral and social turbulence in the many centuries preceding the twentieth. The important point here is not so much what occurred but the fact that rapid moral and social change did occur, and with some regularity, prior to our present day. Thus, facing social and moral dilemmas is nothing new, but only new to us because we view them in our present-day context. It is interesting to note that many today believe, as they did at the end of the nineteenth century, that moral and social certainty are vanishing.

One theory suggests that things are still very much out of balance because of the unique historical context in which we find ourselves today. While it is true that each generation likely views itself as having a complex set of problems in a unique historical context, a strong argument can be made that this is precisely the problem with ethical behavior in present-day America. In other words, as a culture we appear to have gone beyond the modern age to the postmodern era and thus have encountered a set of complexities that we are ill-equipped to handle.

Postmodernism Explained

Some scholars believe that the postmodern era began in America in the 1960s. The sixties were years of rapid change. Openness was the key to successful participation in the lifestyle of the time. Everything was open: sex, drugs, politics, rebellion. Woodstock and the Vietnam War are often seen as artifacts of that decade but ones that reveal much about the prevalent philosophies of those years. The 1970s brought Watergate and the decline of politics as a force in American life. The decade of the eighties ushered in open, alternative lifestyles: gay and lesbian behavior, for example, was no longer widely condemned but was accepted by many as equal to the traditional heterosexual lifestyles.

This new openness in almost all aspects of life produced a number of changes. Chief among them was the view that institutions, especially the government, parents, and other "establishment" types, were not to be trusted. "Don't trust anyone over 30" was a common phrase in the sixties. Each person was urged to "do your own thing." This rebellion against the institutions of America and against authority led, some believe, to the current distrust of our social, political, religious, and educational institutions. The old ways of belief have broken down and nothing as yet has replaced them. The glue that once held us together has dissolved; no new cement has been applied, and so we are at a loss to find meaning in many of our current life activities.

While we are still reacting to many of the changes wrought in the sixties, new and more complex challenges have beset us. The political and social cultures changed rapidly in the 1980s and 1990s. Technology developed to such a degree than even the most electronically sophisticated could barely keep up. Those who were not computer literate were left behind, probably forever.

Information multiplied rapidly. There is now far more information available than can be reasonably conceptualized, much less scanned or read. Information overload often results in our simply giving up, in accepting or rejecting whatever comes to hand. We no longer take the time or make the effort to seek out information, to gather the facts.

Postmodern behavior has many characteristics. It is not possible to list all of them here. Nevertheless, a discussion of some of the most common aspects of postmodern behavior should serve to illustrate how it has influenced the way we see and do things. Piling change on top of change, with little time to digest what is already on our plates, is bound to present us with a complex, often confusing set of problems. In terms of the cultural environment, intellectual activity, and social norms, our times lack continuity, cohesion, and logical sequence.

For example, one characteristic of postmodern America is a renewed *emphasis on consumption*. Advertising seems to have blurred the line between what we need and what we want. We seem to "need" everything. We are encouraged to buy, buy, buy. We feel we must keep up with our neighbors and friends in terms of the material goods we accumulate. A bumper sticker popular during the early 1990s summarizes this notion perfectly: "He who dies with the most stuff wins." First the Yuppies and then members of Generation X began to select jobs they did not necessarily enjoy, but ones that paid well. After all, it takes lots of money to acquire "stuff."

2

Of concern to many in postmodern America is the *loss of common sense*. Common sense—the ability to observe the world, reason, and arrive at simple truths—appears to be significantly diluted in the postmodern era.

Item: A high school principal suspended a female honor student from school because she took a Midol tablet. The school had a policy prohibiting the use of drugs on school property, and the principal viewed Midol, a common over-the-counter product used to relieve menstrual distress, as a drug.

Comment: Common sense would tell most of us that there is a difference between Midol and illegal drugs. School drug policies are usually geared toward keeping marijuana, cocaine, heroin, and other illegal drugs off campus. Midol is legal and contains mostly acetaminophen, an aspirin substitute. It also contains caffeine, about as much as you would find in a cola drink. Is Midol a drug? Technically, it probably is, but is it the sort of drug the policy was developed to include? Would students take Midol to get high? Unlikely. Male students would probably refuse to even touch a tablet, much less swallow one. If one does not have menstrual distress, one would receive little or no benefit from taking the pill. Is there a common-sense solution to this problem? Did the principal take the common-sense approach to a solution? Only in postmodern America could the routine taking of an over-the-counter painkiller be turned into a major problem.

Item: Another school principal suspended a 10-year-old boy for bringing a weapon to school. The lad brought a 1-inch plastic gun to school from his G.I. Joe toy set.

Comment: Did the student bring a weapon to school or simply a toy? Did the principal make a common-sense decision in the case? It is certainly easier to take the toy and suspend the student, but why not reason the issue out? Perhaps the principal was afraid he would have to justify the decision to others. In postmodern America, one's common sense is so diluted that one often takes the action that requires the least amount of thinking or effort.

The dilution of common sense has also resulted in our ability to accept or, perhaps, ignore *cognitive dissonance*. The idea of cognitive dissonance was first advanced by Leon Festinger, and it is easily explained. As humans, we have a need to experience a consistent world. "If we detect inconsistencies in our beliefs, attitudes, or behavior, we suffer from a strong sense of uneasiness (cognitive dissonance) and this acts as a drive to change what we are doing so as to restore consistency."[9]

3

Life in postmodern America is filled with *inconsistencies*, yet few seem to even notice them, much less move toward any sort of attitude or behavior change. We have, essentially, learned either to accept cognitive dissonance as simply a characteristic of life or chosen to ignore the discomfort it is said to cause.

> **Item:** According to a poll of Americans under age 30, 40 percent said they learned something about the 1996 presidential campaign from late-night television comedians.

> *Comment:* This continues a trend that many find disturbing in American politics: a decrease in the interest in and understanding of the political process. We now trust media to bring us all we need to know about political candidates. As individuals, we no longer have the responsibility to inform ourselves. We let media, particularly television, do it. What facts, what kinds of information would late-night television comedians be able to convey that would be useful in making a decision about whom to support for president? Their approach to political candidates and issues is designed to generate laughs, not provide a rational basis for decision making. Yet many younger Americans are using these late-night comments to do precisely that. Isn't there something dissonant about this phenomenon? Has postmodern thinking so penetrated us that we no longer find this sort of behavior inconsistent with our responsibilities as citizens of a democracy?

> **Item:** The owner of a professional football team, when asked why the public should build a new stadium for use by his team when the city's public library services were being cut, responded, "The pride and presence of a professional football team is far more important than 30 libraries."

> *Comment:* Is there something inconsistent about the priorities we assign to various aspects of our lives? In postmodern America, there is. Hardly anyone registered surprise or complaint about the owner's comment. Do we feel sports activities are more important than educational services? Many do. There is much evidence across America that city services— including schools—are being stretched to the limit and asked to do more with less, while rich sports team owners bask in the glory and profit of new stadiums, funded at taxpayer expense.

4

Yet another characteristic of postmodern culture in America is the trend toward *victimhood*. It seems almost everyone can qualify as a victim these days. None of us is responsible for personal behavior. If one is a victim, one may unleash "an emotional and self-righteous response to any perceived slight."[10] One does not have to argue or reason but, rather, *feels* in response to an issue or problem. The result is that some members of a particular class, race, gender, or lifestyle group define themselves solely by their status as victims, thereby reducing "the complexity of social relationships to a single monotonic world view."[11]

Item: An unemployed 45-year-old woman was leaving a well-known department store in Southern California when she noticed several streams of water running across the sidewalk near the garden shop. As she attempted to step over the first stream, she fell and fractured her knee. She sued and was awarded $75,000. The store argued, unsuccessfully, that she could have detoured around the water and that her medical bills were inflated.

Comment: This case is very much like the famous McDonald's coffee case in which Stella Liebeck was awarded $640,000 for injuries she suffered when she placed a cup of hot McDonald's coffee between her legs, and while trying to get the top off, spilled it in her lap, seriously burning her groin area. A jury originally awarded her $3 million, but a judge reduced the amount to $640,000. Of course, the key issue in this case and in the one above is this: What responsibility do we have as individuals to accept the risks involved in our own behavior instead of looking around for an organization with "deep pockets" and suing that organization in court? The postmodern answer is that we bear no responsibility. Such "accidents" are not accidents at all, some say, but manifestations of negligence on the part of the business involved. In postmodern America we are not responsible for detouring around water, nor should we think twice about placing a cup of hot coffee between our legs. Litigation has become a "shortcut to innocence, meaning, and justification: If something has gone wrong, *someone must be at fault.* And it is not me."[12]

It is interesting to note that before the twentieth century, people accepted the risks of life; death, disease, and accident were familiar to most. However, over time, "people have come to expect more out of government, out of law, out of life." When they don't get it, they sue. The ethical question here is this: Are we rewarding the acceptance or the rejection of personal responsibility?[13] In postmodern America, the *failure to accept personal responsibility* is often most rewarding. Ask anyone who has won hundreds of thousands of dollars by suing a business or organization—forcing the business or organization to accept corporate responsibility for actions that many would say fall under the realm of personal responsibility.

Another important characteristic of postmodernism is that it has fostered a *renewed polarization of views.* Many conflicts have emerged: us versus them, men versus women, the haves versus the have-nots, blacks versus whites versus Hispanics, conservatives versus liberals, and on and on. Technology has given us a global culture, a new arena for testing a variety of belief systems. The problem is that we are not sure what our belief system is. Do we have one that everyone subscribes to, or is there one for each individual, more than 285 million in America alone?

Item: A philosophy professor whose work includes the study of feminism suggests that many mainstream women's magazines—*Redbook, Working Woman, Mademoiselle, Glamour,* and *Parenting,* among others—put out a subtly biased political message. They portray women as perpetual victims, Republicans as enemies, and big government as their friend. The professor goes on to say that the magazine editors are not radical feminists but are simply caught up in the victim culture. For example, *Cosmopolitan* informed women that "'A March of Dimes study names battering during pregnancy as the leading cause of birth defects and infant mortality.' But March of Dimes officials say they did no such study."[14]

Comment: The presentation of misinformation has always been a problem for societies. Nevertheless, we do bear the responsibility for negative outcomes, resulting from the exchange of such information, especially when it results in continued social conflict. Reporting the bogus March of Dimes study served no positive purpose. If anything, it may have exacerbated the continuing conflict between men and women over a variety of issues, this case emphasizing stereotypical, "battering" male behavior. Abuse does happen, but it did not happen as reported in *Cosmopolitan.* To report the fictional study as fact merely encourages the further polarization of the sexes. Adding Republicans and big government to the mix only widens the social and communication gaps. How can this sort of organized attack result in anything but resentment, especially if one is male and a member of any of the groups singled out for attention? In postmodern America, this polarization of views has become the norm rather than a problem that all should work on. One wonders whether the real purpose of what might be called "the polarizing effect" is to change male behavior or "to politicize sexual relations and create female solidarity as an end in itself."[15]

Clearly, postmodern America confronts important challenges. Can we restore continuity and consistency to life? How do we go about applying clear moral standards to discrete events? Can we learn to accept personal responsibility for our actions, thereby reversing the trend toward victimhood? Is it possible to reduce the social and communication gaps that separate us as individuals and as members of groups?

We can never go back to "the good old days," nor should we want to. The times in which we live are exciting, but we could be making so much more of them than we are. Postmodernism has frayed our lives at the edges. We have been besieged by a thousand tiny cuts. Taken individually, they hardly seem to matter. Taken collectively, they present a much more serious problem. Perhaps it is time for us to accept some personal responsibility for the state of things and begin to address some of these issues in our own lives and in our own corner of American society.

Will ethics solve all these problems? Probably not. But ethical behavior is a logical place to begin because it deals with the actions of the individual and with one's relationships to others in the society. Without a moral awakening, there can be little positive change in our social, intellectual, business, and political lives. Because American media are clearly influential in the lives of regular citizens, ethical behavior is even more important to those who plan media careers.

In the chapters that follow, you will find a number of ethical philosophies. You will also encounter some forthright discussions of many of the ethical issues facing media today. It is the purpose of this text to analyze the ethical issues and present case studies, particularly as they reflect postmodern thinking and practices, and to suggest ways to solve these dilemmas using ethical concepts drawn from well-known, established ethical philosophies.

QUESTIONS FOR DISCUSSION

1. *Modern* and *postmodern* are the two most recent historical culture periods. Think about the historical culture periods that occurred before the modern period, that is, before 1850. What were some of the important characteristics of those periods? Are any of those characteristics still a part of the current culture period?

2. What role does reason play in contemporary life? Are reason and common sense related? How?

3. Define accountability. How important is accountability in developing ethical behavior?

4. Look again at the definition of cognitive dissonance in this chapter. State this definition in your own words. What are some of the situations you have faced that have caused cognitive dissonance?

5. Is it important for media, and particularly those employed in media, to understand contemporary culture? Why?

ENDNOTES

1. Michael Fegan, "Postmodernism," http://atl46.atl.msu.edu/reh/ams/post.html, 7 November 1996.

2. Paul Hartman, "What Is Postmodernism?" http://olympus.athens.net/~hartman/essay/15.htm, 7 November 1996.

3. Charles Jencks, "The Post-Modern Agenda," in *The Post-Modern Reader*, ed. Charles Jencks (New York: St. Martin's Press, 1992), 11.

4. James W. Carey, "The Press, Public Opinion, and Public Discourse," in *Public Opinion and the Communication of Consent*, ed. Theodore L. Glasser and Charles T. Salmon (New York: Guilford, 1995), 397.

5. W. B. Yeats, "The Second Coming," in *The Norton Anthology of English Literature*, Vol. 2, ed. M. H. Abrams (New York: W. W. Norton, 1962), 1355.

6. Ibid.

7. Bernard Bergonzi, "Aspects of the *Fin de Siècle*," in *The Victorians*, ed. Arthur Pollard (New York: Peter Bedrick Books, 1987), 464.

8. Ibid., 464.

9. Melvin L. Defleur and Sandra Ball-Rokeach, *Theories of Mass Communication*, 5th ed. (New York: Longman, 1989), 277.

10. Charles J. Sykes, *A Nation of Victims* (New York: St. Martin's Press, 1992), 16.

11. Ibid., 18.

12. Ibid., 126.

13. Ibid., 125, 244.

14. Christina Hoff Sommers, "Convincing Women That They're Victims," *St. Petersburg Times*, 11 January 1997, 10A.

15. David Denby, *Great Books* (New York: Simon & Schuster, 1996), 386.

▼▼▼
CHAPTER 2

Ethics in America

Ethics is a hot topic in America. Pick up any newspaper or magazine or tune in any news program and you are sure to find an ethics story of some sort. Universities have rushed to set up ethics institutes; corporations have scheduled ethics workshops for their employees; federal, local, and state governments have established ethics commissions whose main task is to monitor the ethics of politicians and others in government service. Ethics courses have been added to educational curricula. Everywhere, it seems, there is a renewed interest in "doing the right thing."

Current Concerns

The last three decades of the twentieth century may come to be known to future generations as a period of ethical incongruities. In the face of a renewed emphasis on ethics, major political, economic, social, and religious scandals were revealed. The alleged exploits of Wall Streeters Ivan Boesky and Michael Milken (insider trading and junk bond scams), religious leaders Jim and Tammy Bakker (using church money for personal perks) and the Reverend Jimmy Swaggart (soliciting a prostitute), Marine Colonel Oliver North (questionable arms-for-hostages deal with Iran), baseball's Pete Rose (betting on games), House Speaker Newt Gingrich (shady book deals and speaking fees), and President Bill Clinton (affair with a White House intern and possible perjury), as well as a host of others, dominated the news. The presidential election campaigns of 1992 and 1996 were said to be two of the most misleading and misdirected campaigns in recent memory. Questions were raised regularly about the fund-raising practices and advertising campaigns of many candidates for public office.

Ethical problems were not limited to public figures or to those in powerful positions. They also touched many aspects of our own daily lives. Résumé fraud continued to be a problem for many employers. One survey reported a "stunning 80% of checked résumés included lies about applicants' job histories." More startling is the idea that "nobody expects job candidates to be totally candid . . . a little gilding of the lily is understandable—and acceptable."[1]

Early in 1997, residents of a poor Miami, Florida, neighborhood scooped up almost half a million dollars in cash and a quarter of a million dollars worth of food stamps when a Brinks armored truck flipped on an overpass and spilled its cargo. Area residents made off with most of the cash and stamps. Appeals by Brinks to return the money, with no questions asked, went virtually unheeded. Two weeks after the accident, only two people had come forward to turn in a total of $20.38.[2] Additional appeals were made, and within three weeks of the accident, almost $300 had been returned. When questioned, many area residents said they did not intend to return the money. "Finders keepers, losers weepers," many said.

Education had its share of ethical problems, too. A University of Virginia study found that when students talk to their mothers, "they lie about once in every two conversations" and that "they lie even more to strangers."[3] A 1993 survey of undergraduates at the Massachusetts Institute of Technology revealed that 83 percent cheated, from collaborating on homework answers, to plagiarism, to copying on exams.[4]

Plagiarism in scholarly writing continued generally unchallenged. At the time this chapter was being written, only one organization, the American Historical Association, had taken steps to improve the ethical behavior of its members; it discussed the possibility of disclosing the names of those who plagiarize or who are otherwise in serious violation of professional ethics.[5]

Another survey, this one conducted in connection with the 1996 presidential campaign, noted that 65 percent of Americans do not believe character is important in deciding whom to support for president.[6] If character is not an important quality in the president of the United States—the leader of the Western world—then for whom is it important?

There is much talk but little action when it comes to acting ethically. Why has all our talk resulted in so little behavioral change?

Ethics Defined

There are probably as many definitions of the term *ethics* as there are individuals asked to provide one. Nevertheless, most definitions are similar and none is all that complicated. The simplest and most straightforward definition is this one: *ethics are moral principles for living and making decisions*. There are, of course, any number of other good definitions. Some might say that ethics are the morals, beliefs, norms, and values that individuals and societies use to determine right from wrong. Others might say that ethics are the moral guidelines one uses in living and making decisions in a world of hard choices. A few might consider ethics to be a human mental construction that serves as a basis for understanding what is right and what is wrong. As a field of philosophical inquiry, ethics concerns itself with such concepts as good, right, wrong, duty, value, and responsibility, among others.

The word *ethics* comes from the Greek *ethos*, which means "character." As a practical matter, your ethical behavior is governed by the sort of person you are, as well as by the value or relative worth you assign to various activities or aspects of life. For example, one person might see value in pursuing wealth and position in life and might aspire to own many valuable material goods,

Ethical issues are not limited to media organizations. Many areas of life—from business to politics—face ethical problems. *Left: © CORBIS / James Marshall; right: © CORBIS / Marc Muench*

such as jewelry, real estate, and the like. Another person might value relationships the most, working to develop or enhance relationships with a spouse, children, friends, and significant others. Still others might value travel, personal time, or recreational activities.

There are no givens in terms of what a person may value. As individuals, we may assign to the various aspects of our lives whatever relative worth we deem appropriate. However, the freedom to assign worth to any one or more of a number of activities or aspects of life does not absolve us of the responsibility of pursuing these goals in an ethically appropriate fashion, especially since our actions will most certainly involve others. We must be careful in determining just what values will guide our actions.

Morality is closely related to ethics, and the terms are often used interchangeably. However, the word *morality* comes from the Latin *moralis*, meaning "customs and manners." In this respect, morality can involve issues that may go beyond the individual to a larger society. Society is often seen as the arbiter of proper behavior. One is encouraged to follow society's customs and manners, that is, society's view of the proper way of doing things. Because concepts like good and evil, right and wrong, and ethics and morality often have imprecise definitions, many people are comfortable with leaving the whole issue of ethical and moral behavior to others. However, "to the degree that we get our ethical bearings only from the society around us, we remain as vulnerable as the citizens of Nazi Germany to . . . ethical distortions. We, too, can be led to commit atrocities and call it 'good'."[7]

Americans have always valued the freedom to choose certain things for themselves; it seems only natural that no one should dictate specific behaviors. Nevertheless, wrestling with ethical issues is difficult for some and impossible for many. A word of warning: ethics should not be considered only in terms of the individual. One should not develop a private morality; it is dangerous to drift toward *moral relativism*, the notion that all ethical systems are equal and that we are free to choose our own regardless of how others might be affected. There are moral absolutes; not everything depends on the individual or the situation. The key to successful ethical decision making is developing a set of moral beliefs that serve not only the self but also the culture. Moral behavior is always important, regardless of what we value or what others value. Ethics, therefore, is applicable to all life situations and should not be discarded simply because there are differences in what individuals say or do in their lives. One must work through these differences—adjusting, modifying, improving, growing, both as an individual and as a member of society.

Many people are comfortable with a theory of behavior that is not an ethical theory at all but a legal one. *Moral legalism* is the notion that whatever is legal is ethical, and conversely, whatever is illegal is unethical. This legalistic approach is satisfactory to many. It may, in fact, be the "default" ethical philosophy in America—that is, the philosophy almost everyone follows in the absence of some other system that has been rationally developed and empirically applied.

For many people, however, moral legalism is barely workable. Its most significant flaw is that many human behaviors that are not illegal—lying to a friend, for example—are clearly unethical. Other individuals see little value in allowing the criminal justice system to determine right and wrong, beyond the necessities of law and civil order. We need more than a set of legal principles for living and making decisions; we need a set of moral principles, too.

Ethics in Journalism/Mass Communications Programs

Two studies, both published in 1996, give us some idea of the importance of the study of ethics to students in journalism and mass communications programs. A survey of 73 freestanding media ethics courses at universities across the country revealed that "classes are full. The number of courses, students, teachers, and material are all on the growth curve."[8] Another study noted that 44 percent of all the schools responding to its survey required students to take a journalism/mass communication ethics course.[9] Media organizations have told educators that they value students who can think critically, solve problems, and who have developed a keen sense of ethics.

However, there are reasons for studying ethics that go beyond what potential employers want or expect. Proper behavior is a necessity for growth and order. If it is one of the objectives of an education to promote the growth and development of the individual, then the place to start is with one's own behavior. Developing a sense of what is right and wrong, or appropriate and inappropriate, will promote order, not only in the life of the individual but also in the structure of society at large. Think, for example, of the order required to move traffic on roads and highways. Speed limits are set, proper directions are indicated, and numerous suggestions are made—seat belts, for example—so that travel by automobile will be reasonably safe and efficient. Without the "rules" of the road, travel would be chaotic. Order is required if we are ever going to get anywhere. The same could be said of ethical behavior. It sets "rules" for proper human activity and as a result promotes growth, development, and order in our lives.

It should be noted, however, that ethics is not a panacea for every problem one encounters in the world. Not every problem is an ethical one, and even when an ethical problem does present itself, we sometimes make the wrong ethical decision, or we make the right ethical decision and it results in unforeseen negative consequences. Nevertheless, we must realize that without a large number of individuals "doing the right thing," most of us would not be doing much at all except fighting for survival and trying to figure out an increasingly chaotic world. Things are bad enough with ethics; think how bad they might be without them.

"Rather than accept the way things are, the ethical person asks how things ought to be."[10] Ethics promotes not only a better individual but also a better society. Idealists might suggest that doing the right thing is a valuable end in itself, regardless of the degree to which it contributes to life or to the culture. Others see ethics as more practical, as a tool that can lead to positive personal and social outcomes.

The real test of ethics may be in "how we treat the stranger—whether we are able to recognize the humanity and dignity of the stranger. We are all prepared to acknowledge the dignity of those we think of as like ourselves and to treat them with respect. It is those we perceive as different that we are tempted to treat differently."[11]

Some Basics

Remember that ethics is just a small part of a much larger philosophical taxonomy; ethics is really a subarea of philosophy. There is much to be studied and learned in philosophy that does not deal with ethics at all. It might be useful to categorize philosophy into four main subject areas: metaphysics, epistemology, logic, and axiology.

Metaphysics is the study of the nature and functions of reality. *Epistemology* concerns the acquisition of knowledge and the knowing process. *Logic* studies the nature of reasoning and the rules for correct thinking. *Axiology* is the study of ethics and aesthetics—that is, the examination of what human values are and the ways in which they can be symbolized or expressed.

While this discussion is something of an oversimplification, it will serve our present purposes. Ethics is a part of axiology, and, with aesthetics, concerns what we value and why, as well as what we find pleasing and why. Implicit in these simple definitions is the notion that these are areas we need to consider as we go through life, making decisions and touching the lives of others.

QUESTIONS FOR DISCUSSION

1. Define ethics. Ask one or two of your friends or relatives for their definitions of ethics. How do their definitions compare with yours? With the ones offered in this chapter?
2. Why do you think so many prominent individuals in business, politics, and entertainment seem to have serious ethical problems?
3. Why is character an important part of any person's social and psychological being? In what ways is character reflected in an individual's actions?
4. Many people firmly believe that when it comes to money or other items, it's "finders keepers, losers weepers." Is this an ethical philosophy? Why?
5. Why do many media industries encourage journalism and mass communications programs to offer ethics courses?
6. Are there times when an ethical philosophy should be absolute? Are there times when an ethical philosophy should be relative? Provide examples of situations where each of these approaches might be appropriate.

ENDNOTES

1. "Résumé Fraud," *Manage*, August 1989, 21.
2. Robert Steinback, "Spilled Cash Puts Virtue to the Test," *Tampa Tribune*, 15 January 1997, Nation/World, 9.
3. "It's the Truth," *Tampa Tribune*, 16 August 1995, A5.
4. "83% of MIT Undergrads Are Cheaters," *Tampa Tribune*, 3 December 1993, A5.
5. Karen J. Winkler, "Historians and Ethics," *Chronicle of Higher Education*, 40 (44), 6 July 1994, A17–A18.
6. Jean Heller, "Character Not Issue for Voters," *St. Petersburg Times*, 9 October 1996, 5A.
7. Darrell J. Fasching, "Necessary Ethics," *Creative Loafing*, 6 (40), 6 January 1994, 7.
8. Clifford G. Christians and Edmund B. Lambeth, "The Status of Ethics Instruction in Communication Departments," *Communication Education*, 45 (July 1996), 241.
9. Betty Medsger, *Winds of Change*, The Freedom Forum (May 1996), 16.
10. Fasching, 10.
11. Ibid., 11.

Philosophical Foundations

© CORBIS / Roger Wood

▼ ▼ ▼

In the chapters ahead you will meet a number of philosophers and learn something about their lives and their ethical philosophies. Some philosophers may be familiar; others may not. Many of their ideas will be appealing, but some will strike you as unworkable for your own personal ethical philosophy.

These philosophies were chosen not because they always represent their historical periods (though many do) but because they are ones that emphasize important decision-making concepts and processes. For example, in Chapter 7, why was Arthur Schopenhauer selected over, say, Georg Hegel? Certainly Hegel was more widely known and respected than Schopenhauer during their time. However, I judged Hegel's dialectic method a bit too cumbersome for today's fast-paced media world. Individuals have some time to think about a decision but probably don't have enough time to set up the thesis-antithesis-synthesis structure that is required for a precise application of Hegel's ideas and method to problem situations. Schopenhauer's greedful will, on the other hand, is a concept readily grasped, comfortably held in the mind, and easily observed working in the real world.

It is not, however, always a matter of the simplicity of ideas. Some philosophies just seem to offer more in terms of their application to media situations. This text does not mean to suggest that the philosophies presented here are the only ones to be used, or perhaps even the best. They are simply tools you may use to assist you in making ethical decisions. As always, you are encouraged to explore the work of other philosophers and consider how their ideas might be useful to you.

To extend the tool analogy further, you could use several tools to remove a nail from a piece of wood. A pair of pliers, a hammer, or a crowbar could probably do the job. Is one better than the others? Perhaps, but not necessarily. Will all do the job? Probably. So it comes down to a matter of personal assessment of the situation. In much the same way, I have selected some philosophical tools that have proved useful in ethical decision making in a variety of personal and professional situations. It is up to you to examine the philosophies you have available and to select the one that seems to work for you in a given situation. If none of the ones provided meet your needs, you will need to search among the other philosophies for just the right one.

In order to provide you with a set of principles that you may use in ethical decision making, a decision-making tool is presented at the end of the discussion of each ethical philosophy. This tool—usually two or three statements—may be used to help you decide on and justify a course of action as you work your way through ethical problems. Too often, decisions are made with inadequate information about philosophical principles that may apply to a given situation. Look for the decision-making tools and use them as you make both personal and professional ethical decisions.

Many benefits are to be derived from the study of ethical philosophies. Some philosophies have proven themselves central to the human struggle with right and wrong. Also, studying philosophies introduces you "to certain frames of thought powerful enough to have lasted, with many variations" for hundreds of years.* Many of the philosophies presented in this text are straightforward. Admittedly, some are difficult; a few are somewhat obscure. Yet there is value in studying them all. One "falls"—particularly in ethics— by not "rising" to meet the intellectual challenge provided by some of the philosophies. That is, "you shrink by not stretching yourself . . . to [consider] work that lies outside your expectations."† You are supposed to be made a little uncomfortable by the variety and depth of ideas and by the various people who are part of your education. This is what learning is all about.

One word of caution: choose your decision-making tools carefully. You will want to develop or enhance your personal ethical philosophy in such a way that your actions and reactions in ethical situations are clear and consistent. A firm, clear, and consistent set of ethical principles is easier to apply and represents your best chance of successfully solving ethical dilemmas in the often confusing, inconsistent postmodern world.

SUGGESTED READINGS

Books

Christians, Clifford, and Traber, Michael, eds. *Communication Ethics and Universal Values* (Thousand Oaks, CA: Sage, 1997).

Constructing a Life Philosophy (San Diego: Greenhaven Press, 1993).

Eichhoefer, Gerald W., ed. *Enduring Issues in Philosophy* (San Diego: Greenhaven Press, 1995).

Gaarder, Jostein. *Sophie's World: A Novel about the History of Philosophy* (New York: Berkeley Books, 1994).

Hunt, Arnold D., Crotty, Robert B., and Crotty, Marie T. *Ethics of World Religions* (San Diego: Greenhaven Press, 1993).

Kieran, Matthew, ed. *Media Ethics* (New York: Routledge, 1998).

Merrill, John C. *Legacy of Wisdom* (Ames: Iowa State University Press, 1994).

Pearce, W. Barnett, and Littlejohn, Stephen W. *Moral Conflict: When Social Worlds Collide* (Thousand Oaks, CA: Sage, 1997).

Journals

Deigh, John, ed. *Ethics: An International Journal of Social, Political, and Legal Philosophy* (Chicago: University of Chicago Press).

Dillon, Michael, and Heelas, Paul, eds. *Cultural Values* (Malden, MA: Blackwell).

Yeager, D. M., ed. *Journal of Religious Ethics* (Washington, DC: Georgetown University and Scholars Press).

*David Denby, *Great Books* (New York: Simon & Schuster, 1996), 189.
† Ibid., 231.

▼▼▼
CHAPTER 3

The Greek View

In this chapter you will meet two influential philosophers from the ancient Greek civilization, a society that contributed much to Western culture. Both Plato and Aristotle are good representatives of their time. The Greeks contributed significantly to art, literature, and philosophy (see the time line).

Culture Period ▪ Approximate Dates	General Description ▪ Key Personalities
Greek 1200 B.C.–320 B.C. **Plato** (427 B.C.–347 B.C.) **Aristotle** (384 B.C.–322 B.C.)	Era of development in literature, philosophy, and architecture; competing city-states Athens and Sparta; Persian and Peloponnesian wars; Socrates, Plato, Aristotle, Alexander the Great, Sophocles, Pythagoras

The two men profiled here have well-known names, but their philosophies have been either poorly understood or vastly oversimplified. Nevertheless, their ethical philosophies provide concepts that may easily be applied to a variety of ethical dilemmas in media. The ethical philosophies of Plato and Aristotle may be said to be reasonable, even commonsensical, approaches to problems. These philosophies should be useful in combating the vagaries of a postmodern culture.

▼ Plato

The Life

Plato was probably born in 427 B.C., or perhaps a year or two earlier. We don't know much about his early life, but there is some evidence that his "real name was Aristocles, and that 'Plato' was a nickname (roughly 'the broad') derived either from the width of his shoulders, the result of his training for wrestling, . . . or from the size of his forehead."[1]

Ancient records are not in agreement "about the identity of his mother—or indeed of his father—[but] we do probably have enough information on

25

the sorts of aspects of Plato's life which are really relevant to an understanding of what he wrote."[2] Plato, coming from a well-to-do family, received a traditional education. He studied music and participated in gymnastics, becoming an accomplished wrestler and a passable poet/musician.

He was born during the early years of the Peloponnesian War between the Greek city-states of Athens and Sparta. The political and social atmosphere of the times was often tense and bitter, especially when Athens lost the war, yet Plato enjoyed the privileges that having a moderate degree of wealth provided. Together with his two brothers, Plato served in the military, probably the cavalry unit, which was likely engaged in major battles during 409 and 407 B.C.[3]

The most important part of Plato's early life, however, was his association with Socrates. This close relationship enabled Plato to develop his intellect and also guided him in terms of the personal choices he was to make. However, Socrates fell into disfavor with the ruling Athenian politicians when he refused to compromise his principles and play their political games. He was tried and convicted on a variety of trumped-up charges, and in 399 B.C. was executed by being forced to drink hemlock. Plato was shocked and grief-stricken by Socrates's death. He felt he had lost an important and decisive influence in his life. Disillusioned, Plato left Athens and traveled abroad for a dozen years or so, returning to Athens only occasionally. Although drawn to political life, "after the death of Socrates he made the radical decision to withdraw from public life and live for philosophy."[4]

Plato returned to Athens in 387 B.C., "purchased a house and garden, and established the Academy . . . [which] attracted and held, often for many years, some of the best minds in the Hellenic world."[5] The general purpose of the Academy was to educate and train potential statesmen and, Plato hoped, eventually to bring some stability, intelligence, and direction to public life. Except for two outside excursions, Plato remained teaching and writing at the Academy for the rest of his life. The establishment of the school was a major accomplishment. It "lived on for a continuous period of nine hundred years, a longer span of life than any other educational institution has yet known."[6]

Plato died in his early 80s in 347 B.C. "To the end of his life he was mentally alert and active and enjoyed the honor and respect conferred upon him by his circle of disciples."[7]

The Philosophy

Plato's philosophy was almost certainly a result of the overpowering influence of Socrates. Socrates awakened him to the one thing that is important: to care for your soul by leading the right life oriented toward eternal being."[8] It is not possible here to give a full account of all of Plato's views about ethics. Exploring all the connections between ethics and pleasure, moral responsibility, politics, society, and religion is a lifelong work. For the purposes of this part of the chapter, that is, using Plato's ethical philosophy to help make ethical decisions in the media workplace, it will be necessary to focus on only one small area of his writings: the early dialogues.

Plato wrote in *dialogues*—conversations—usually between Socrates and another individual or group of individuals. More than two dozen dialogues survive that can be "attributed with confidence to Plato,"[9] including his most famous, the *Republic.* The early dialogues are concerned with character and its development and provide the fundamental basis for Plato's ethical doctrines.

"One of the features of the Platonic dialogues which most immediately strikes the reader is the presence on virtually every page of a character called Socrates, and the apparent absence of the author, Plato. There is no character called Plato who participates in the conversations, and he is mentioned by name only twice."[10] Written for the most part in the fourth century B.C. but placed dramatically in the fifth century B.C., "the characters are real people of a previous generation."[11] The dialogues "are fictional, to the extent that the conversations they purport to record never in fact took place."[12]

Plato used a question-and-answer technique, later called the Socratic method, to raise key issues and concepts and submit them for philosophical examination. Plato took great care to create those conversations. He was content to give the spotlight to his good friend and mentor Socrates. "But we should not be fooled: behind all the dialogues, the controlling mind is Plato's."[13]

To understand Plato's philosophy, we must seek the answers to two questions: "How ought we to live," and, "How can we know how we ought to live?"[14] A good place to start searching for answers to these important questions is in the early dialogues: *Laches, Charmides, Euthyphro, Protagoras, Apology, Crito, Gorgias,* and *Lysis.* A close examination of the dialogues reveals five cardinal qualities that Plato considered important. These are *bravery, temperance, piety, wisdom,* and *justice.* Moving through the dialogues, we notice that each of these qualities is debated in turn among participants in the conversations.

Before examining these qualities individually, Plato allows his dialogue participants to discuss some basic concepts on which the qualities are based. Chief among these basic concepts are virtue and the good. *Virtue,* Plato wrote, consists of the correct knowledge of things and, as a result, can be taught. As the argument progresses, participants come to realize that virtue is a characteristic of each of the five cardinal qualities and that the practice of each of the qualities is highly desirable. Therefore, the five cardinal qualities become the five cardinal virtues.

In terms of *the good,* dialogue participants offer two possible meanings: "that which is useful to man" and "the pleasant, or that which gives pleasure."[15] After much discussion, this definition is offered: "the good is the end of action; whereas the pleasant is a mere means for the attainment of the good, not vice versa."[16] While this might appear to be a circular argument, it is Plato's method of trying to arrive at truth. Plato is careful never to present hard-and-fast definitions of the terms and concepts under consideration. The Socratic method provides a mechanism whereby ideas are examined for their worth, but the conclusions are left primarily to the individual.

Plato and his dialogue participants, however, do agree on one important thing about the good: "We are not to consult the unenlightened mass of humanity as to what is just or unjust, what is good and beautiful . . . the mass of humanity is incapable of deciding between the good and the bad."[17] Knowledge of the good rests with experts who have the wisdom (a combination of reason and experience) to provide insight. This, of course, means that the intellectual elites—that is, Plato and his circle of friends—were the ones in which the concept of the good resided.

Arguments and counterarguments abound in these early dialogues as Plato has Socrates and the others consider each of the five cardinal virtues. For example, bravery results from courage, which is nothing more than the knowledge of what is to be feared and what is not to be feared, enabling an individual to determine whether a given action is appropriate for him. Piety is correct behavior before God, assuming that a man's behavior toward other men is correct, as it must be before a relationship is begun with God.[18]

Obviously, there is much uncertainty here—and this is by design. It is the technique Plato uses to get you to work through these concepts and behaviors on your own. He provides the tools, but you must do the work. However, he is willing to offer advice along the way. For example, he has a long list of vices that he suggests one avoid: intellectual laziness, shameless arrogance, a lack of discipline or temperance in pleasure, injustice, cowardice, pettiness, and envy, among a host of others.

"The popular conception of Plato as an aloof unworldly scholar, spinning theories in his study remote from practical life, is singularly wide of the mark. On the contrary, he was a man of the world, an experienced soldier, widely traveled, with close contacts with many of the leading men of affairs" of his day.[19] "Plato's philosophical system and marvelous language make him one of the most gifted men who ever lived. Nothing was beyond the reach of his subtle, discriminating intellect."[20]

▶ DECISION-MAKING TOOL

Refrain from wrongdoing regardless of the consequences; set aside the views of society, acquire the knowledge necessary to make a good decision, then act in such a way that you are pleased and others are served by the action. The action must meet the tests of courage, moderation, respect, wisdom, and justice.

▶ SUGGESTED MEDIA APPLICATION ◀

Plato's ideas are not difficult to apply to the ethical problems one might face in the media world, but their application might not be popular. For one thing, Plato asks you to set aside the views of society. This will not be easy; media tend to do things because they feel "it's what the public wants." Plato was not in favor of allowing society to set the standards for behavior. You must rise above society and act in such a way that you are true not only to your own eth-

Plato and Aristotle are well known for their political and ethical philosophies. Their ideas have relevance for contemporary culture. *Detail showing Plato and Aristotle from* The School of Athens *by Raphael. Photo by CORBIS / Ted Spiegel.*

ical code of behavior but also to the needs (not necessarily the wants!) of others. It may not be easy to make a decision and then ask yourself whether the decision shows courage, moderation, respect, wisdom, and justice, but this is what Plato requires. The media fields of journalism and advertising could likely benefit from an application of Plato's ideas to their work.

RECOMMENDED CASE STUDIES
#9 (Chapter 12), #16 (Chapter 14), #19 (Chapter 15).

p. 226   p. 277   p. 302

▼ Aristotle

The Life

Hearing the name Aristotle conjures up visions of a kindly, bearded, wise old man, dressed in a toga-like garment and expounding on some philosophical point before an attentive group of young Greeks. This is the traditional view of the Greek philosophers, particularly Socrates, but Plato and

Aristotle fit the stereotype, too. Aristotle is often pictured in busts as "a stern and noble figure: a long face, a deep brow—and a luxuriant beard." However, an ancient biographer notes that Aristotle "had thin legs and small eyes; he wore fashionable clothes, and rings on his fingers—and he shaved."[21]

There is really no conflict here; no doubt one description of the man reflected his youthful years, the other description his later years. Whether he wore a beard or shaved regularly is, of course, of little philosophical importance. It does, however, illustrate an important point: we know little about him. "There are some known facts, some stable inferences, and many speculations based on what is known about the age rather than the man."[22]

We know with some certainty that Aristotle was born in Stagira in northern Greece near the Aegean Sea in 384 B.C. Nicomachus, his father, was a respected physician, serving the court of the king of Macedonia. Nothing much is known about his childhood and early youth. However, some of his writings are reflections on childhood experiences. For example, his writings reveal that Aristotle was particularly enthusiastic about "the rattle as a device for directing and releasing childhood energies." Although his writings make scant mention of a brother and a sister, we know that Aristotle's parents died when he was young and that he was raised by Proxenus, a relative.[23]

The young Aristotle enrolled in Plato's Academy at age 18 and remained there until Plato's death in 347 B.C. He was "a troublesome student who questioned Plato and openly disagreed with him."[24] Nevertheless, his years at the Academy were important ones, for they helped make Aristotle the man that he was: an indefatigable gatherer of information, a philosopher and a scientist.[25]

In 342 B.C., Aristotle was invited to tutor a young boy who would become Alexander the Great. In 335 B.C., he returned from Macedonia and founded his own school, the Lyceum, in Athens, where he taught for 12 years. The Lyceum "had a fine library, an extensive collection of maps, and a zoo in which Aristotle collected specimens of animal life."[26] Legend has it that Aristotle was sent specimens of rare organisms by Alexander as he journeyed on his military campaigns. Upon the death of Alexander in 323, Aristotle left Athens for Chalcis on the island of Euboea, where he died a year later, "from a stomach illness, it is said."[27]

During his life, Aristotle wrote extensively on a variety of subjects, including logic, physics, natural history, psychology, politics, ethics, and the arts. Enough material has survived to fill about 12 volumes. However, these are not books in the traditional sense. Aristotle's writings consist mostly of lecture notes that he used in teaching. It is not clear whether the notes were written before he made his teaching presentations or were recorded after the teaching sessions as summaries of what was discussed.[28] They do appear to have been "written in severe academic style."[29]

The Philosophy

Although Aristotle lived and worked more than 2,000 years ago, "his thought, like Plato's, is still a vital . . . part of Western culture."[30] He struggled with many of the same problems we face in contemporary society. For example, in Aristotle's day, "citizens had free time to enjoy the pursuits of leisure because they had slaves to take care of their estates and do menial work. It was also a society in which women occupied an inferior position."[31] On this issue, Aristotle disagreed with Plato, his teacher, who favored equality for women; "Aristotle accepted the more traditional view of his day concerning the inferiority of women."[32]

There are those who feel that Aristotle's philosophy is too ancient to be of much use in current times, that it would be better to deal with the ideas of someone who is more in touch with contemporary society. While it is true that much has happened since Aristotle's day, "he was sufficiently acquainted with the main outlines of the world in which we live to talk about it as if he were alive today."[33]

Aristotle's ethical theories can be found in three specific works: *Nicomachean Ethics,* thought to be a mature treatment of ethics; *Eudemian Ethics,* presumed to be his early ethical views; and *Magna Moralia,* which some scholars have termed a rambling summary of his ethical views.[34] When he died in 322 B.C., Aristotle "left a will, which gives us a valuable insight into his personal affairs and private moral opinions. . . . Many of the themes that he discussed with his students also play a prominent role in his will—the importance of friends and family and successful children, the social roles proper for a gentleman of property, generosity and dignity in the service of others, and the good judgment of trustworthy men."[35]

For Aristotle, the good is the object of all human striving. The good may consist of many things, but it most certainly contains virtue, "a state of character involving a capacity of choice consisting in a *mean* relative to us, which is determined by reason, that is, as the man of practical wisdom would determine it."[36] The mean Aristotle speaks of, popularly called the *Golden Mean,* is not an arithmetic mean but a "mean relative to the individual . . . a just-right point between excess and defect."[37]

This notion has its roots deep in the Greek tradition. The Greeks were famous for two brief, simple bits of philosophy, ideas designed to benefit both the individual and the society: *Know Thyself* and *Nothing in Excess.* So the "idea of the just-right as opposed to the too-much or too-little" seemed as reasonable an approach to life as it was to the craftsmanship skills of the day. For example, say an athlete is in training. If 10 pounds of food is too much for a person to eat and 2 pounds is too little, "it does not follow that the trainer will recommend six pounds." Aristotle compares the mean rather to "the idea of proportion in art . . . or harmony in music."[38] Extremes are therefore rejected in favor of a reasonable, just-right solution to an ethical problem. "Excess and deficiency alike destroy perfection, while the mean preserves it" (*Nicomachean Ethics,* II, 1106b9).

The selection of an appropriate solution depends on several other factors. One is that the individual does, in fact, have a choice in the matter; a second is that "there has been prior deliberation."[39] For Aristotle, deliberation means thinking. "Man is a rational animal, and he is at his best when he uses his reason in the best way. The correct and best use of reason is to know the truth."[40] The third factor is "what Aristotle calls *habituation*, that is, it is the result of the repeated doing of acts which have a similar or common quality"—in other words, deliberation.[41] Thus, "what is chosen is something in our power which is desired after deliberation" (*Nicomachean Ethics*, III, 1113a9). Therefore, "it is everywhere in moderated passions and actions that the *mean* is realized."[42]

Some scholars believe that Aristotle never meant always to exclude an extreme from being selected as a course of action. "On some particular occasion the appropriate action or feeling may be the 'extreme' . . . thus, the right state of character is that from which on each occasion the appropriate feeling and action results."[43]

It would be a mistake to believe that all Aristotle did was to concern himself exclusively with the mean as a guide for human ethical behavior. He studied and wrote extensively on issues such as anger, sensual pleasure, fear, social justice, money and wealth, respect, humor, social graces, and friends. He "created formal logic, specifically the systematic study of syllogistic reasoning."[44] He was also interested in politics, though he cautioned that one cannot depend on the law to solve ethical problems. He wrote, "the law . . . can never be anything but a leaden rule such as the stone masons . . . use; [ethical decisions] must be able to take the shape of the twists and turns of life."[45]

"Aristotle's works have been studied closely and continuously for many centuries, and not only in the West. They have an importance in the history of civilization which is not easy to exaggerate."[46]

▶ *DECISION-MAKING TOOL*

When faced with an ethical problem, avoid extremes by determining the mean, the just-right, and act by doing what is appropriate after considering all relevant factors.

▶ *SUGGESTED MEDIA APPLICATION* ◀

Aristotle's Golden Mean is perhaps the easiest ethical philosophy to apply to media situations. Aristotle can be made to fit almost any problem one might find in journalism, public relations, advertising, broadcasting, or film. One need only identify the extremes with regard to a problem, and then reject those extremes in favor of a just-right or moderate course of action between the two extremes.

For example, if you are a photojournalist, you might wonder whether it is ethical to snap a picture of the bloated body of a drowned child just as it is pulled from the water. Your editor will want a photo of some type to accompany the story of the incident. You won't have much time to make a decision here, but you can quickly identify the two extremes: snap the picture of the body just as it is pulled from the water or take no picture at all. It is your job to take a photo that adds to or illustrates the story the newspaper will run, so you will have to take a picture of something. Aristotle would advise you to avoid the extremes and perhaps take a picture of the body after it has been put on a stretcher and covered with a sheet. This does not in any way diminish the story, yet it honors the life of the child and respects the privacy of family members who survive. You have selected a just-right solution to your ethical dilemma.

RECOMMENDED CASE STUDIES

#2 (Chapter 11); #18 (Chapter 15).
p. 190   p. 301

QUESTIONS FOR DISCUSSION

1. Plato used dialogues, or conversations, as a way to arrive at truth. To what degree do we depend on conversations, or discussion, to help us determine truth in our postmodern culture? Is there any real value to Plato's method? Explain.

2. What is the difference between Plato's definitions of virtue and the good? What is the precise relationship between the two? What are the postmodern culture's definitions of these terms?

3. Why do you think Plato felt the unenlightened mass of humanity incapable of deciding between the good and the bad? How do we feel today about society's role in developing moral guidelines?

4. What is Aristotle's definition of the good? How does it differ from Plato's?

5. Aristotle valued deliberation as a way to proper ethical behavior. To what extent does the postmodern culture value deliberation as a means of determining what is right and wrong? Give examples.

ENDNOTES

1. C. J. Rowe, *Plato* (New York: St. Martin's Press, 1984), 14.

2. Ibid.

3. Constantin Ritter, *The Essence of Plato's Philosophy*, trans. Adam Alles (New York: Russell and Russell, 1968), 22.

4. Karl Jaspers, *Plato and Augustine*, trans. Ralph Manheim (New York: Harcourt, Brace, and World, 1962), 4.

5. Ronald B. Levinson, *In Defense of Plato* (Cambridge, MA: Harvard University Press, 1959), 43.

6. G. C. Field, *The Philosophy of Plato* (London: Oxford University Press, 1949), 8.

7. Ritter, 27.

8. Jaspers, 9.

9. Antony Flew, *A Dictionary of Philosophy* (New York: St. Martin's Press, 1984), 268.

10. Rowe, 1.

11. Ibid., 14.

12. Ibid., 1.

13. Ibid., 26 and 18.

14. Terence Irwin, *Plato's Ethics* (New York: Oxford University Press, 1995), 3.

15. Ritter, 42.

16. Ibid., 53.

17. Ibid., 48.

18. Ibid., 47.

19. Field, 10.

20. C. M. Bowra, *Classical Greece* (New York: Time Inc., 1965), 141.

21. Jonathan Barnes, "Life and Work," in *The Cambridge Companion to Aristotle*, ed. Jonathan Barnes (Cambridge: Cambridge University Press, 1995), 1.

22. Abraham Edel, *Aristotle and His Philosophy* (Chapel Hill: University of North Carolina Press, 1982), 16.

23. Ibid., 17.

24. Mortimer J. Adler, *Aristotle for Everybody* (New York: Macmillan, 1978), x.

25. Stephen R. L. Clark, "Ancient Philosophy," in *The Oxford History of Western Philosophy*, ed. Anthony Kenny (Oxford: Oxford University Press, 1994), 30.

26. Adler, x.

27. Edel, 26.

28. D. S. Hutchinson, "Ethics," in *The Cambridge Companion to Aristotle*, ed. Jonathan Barnes (Cambridge: Cambridge University Press, 1995), 197.

29. Diane Collinson, *Fifty Major Philosophers* (New York: Routledge, 1987), 22.

30. Ibid.

31. Adler, xi.

32. Ibid.

33. Ibid.

34. Edel, 253.

35. Hutchinson, 195–196.

36. Edel, 266.

37. Ibid., 270.

38. Ibid.

39. Ibid., 276.

40. Hutchinson, 205.

41. J. A. Smith, "Introduction," in *The Ethics of Aristotle,* ed. D. P. Chase (New York: Dutton, 1950), xvii.

42. R. A. Gauthier, "On the Nature of Aristotle's *Ethics*," in *Aristotle's Ethics: Issues and Interpretations,* ed. James J. Walsh and Henry L. Shapiro (Belmont, CA: Wadsworth, 1967), 14.

43. J. L. Ackrill, *Aristotle the Philosopher* (Oxford: Clarendon, 1981), 137.

44. Clark, 31.

45. Gauthier, 27.

46. Ackrill, 155.

▼▼▼

CHAPTER 4

Transition Figures

In this chapter you will meet three individuals whose philosophies were important in bridging the gap between ancient and modern times. Each was unique in his own special way, and each made an important contribution to philosophical thought.

Although the philosophies presented in this chapter come from the Middle Ages and early Renaissance, they can be useful in solving contemporary ethical dilemmas. Peter Abelard and St. Thomas Aquinas are clearly men of the Middle Ages and, specifically, men who reflect the religious thinking of their time (see the time line). Francis Bacon provides evidence that the Renaissance will bring major changes to the culture, particularly in science and philosophy. Bacon points the way toward some of the more progressive thinkers discussed in Chapter 5.

Culture Period ▪ Approximate Dates	General Description ▪ Key Personalities
Middle Ages A.D. 400–A.D. 1300 **Peter Abelard** (1079–1142) **Thomas Aquinas** (1225–1274)	Much political and social activity in Europe; increase in influence of popes; contributions to art, music, and literature; the crusades; the Vikings, Charlemagne, Muhammad, St. Augustine, Dante
Renaissance and Reformation A.D. 1300–A.D. 1650 **Francis Bacon** (1561–1626)	Era of much political, social, intellectual, and religious activity; rise of the church and increased power of popes; significant contributions to art, music, and science—especially from West (England): Chaucer, da Vinci, Michelangelo, Copernicus, Galileo, Henry VIII and the English kings, Martin Luther, John Calvin, El Greco, Rembrandt, Shakespeare

Two of the three philosophies in this chapter suggest *reason* as an important factor in the decision-making process. Although postmodernists reject reason as a means to truth, some ethicists see it, as Francis Bacon did, as a way to control unethical impulses. One could argue that contemporary media might be better off if they used reason, instead of appetite, in the doing of their work.

▼ Peter Abelard

The Life

Peter Abelard was born in Le Pallet, a tiny hamlet in Brittany in north-western France in 1079. He was the oldest son of Berengar and Lucia and therefore was heir to his father's land rights. Berengar was a knight and naturally wanted his oldest son to follow in his footsteps and pursue a military career, but he also believed that education was important. But it was Abelard's education that turned his life away from the military toward more scholarly pursuits. Education was closely tied to the church during the Middle Ages, so a life of learning also meant a religious life. Abelard traveled around France for a while, visiting schools and studying with some of the finest philosophical minds of the times.

In a time when learning meant little questioning of one's teachers, Abelard argued and criticized. He had strong opinions and he had no problem expressing them. He would publicly criticize someone if he disagreed with that person's views. One of his main concerns was that old scholars seemed to dwell on past experiences rather than moving ahead and developing new insights into theology and philosophy. His public criticism of some of the well-known teachers and religious figures often had negative results. He made many enemies, enemies who would eventually wreak their revenge.

Abelard spent some time at the school of William of Champeaux in Paris until the many confrontations he had with William motivated him to start his own school. Despite his conflicts with the religious and educational establishment, Abelard was apparently a dynamic, charismatic teacher. He had a strong, loyal following. His pupils would follow him from village to village just to hear his eloquent lectures. His influence as an inspirational teacher would shortly cause him some additional trouble.

One of the defining moments of Abelard's life was his romance with Heloise. Heloise was the niece of Canon Fulbert, a church official at Notre Dame. She was beautiful, smart, and young; she caught Abelard's eye immediately. In order to get closer to her, Abelard offered to be Heloise's private tutor if Fulbert would provide him lodging and meals at Fulbert's house. The deal was agreed to and Abelard moved in. It did not take very long for the 38-year-old man to fall madly in love with 17-year-old Heloise. Abelard writes, "Under the cloak of study we freely practiced love, and the secret retreats that the study of letters required were just what love wished."[1]

Fulbert was furious when he discovered the affair, especially after learning that Heloise was pregnant. He threw Abelard out of the house. Abelard, always the man of action, whisked Heloise to Paris, where they were secretly married. Once others became aware of this scandal, shame hovered over the

Fulbert household. His family had been disgraced, Fulbert felt, and strong action was required. He bribed one of Abelard's servants to unlatch the door one night, and "Abelard, taken unaware in his sleep by hired henchmen, was castrated."[2]

Abelard fled in shame to the monastery at St. Denis, and Heloise was sent to a convent. The philosopher and his love never saw one another again, although they did exchange letters from time to time. Abelard's ambitions now were not motivated by love but limited to the life of a monk. Although he worked at several monasteries during the years that followed, he was never really happy anywhere, nor was he warmly received anywhere. His longest tenure was at St. Glidas, where he was abbot for almost 10 years. But, as elsewhere, his desire to reform and his constant criticism made him no friends.

The enemies Abelard had made over the years now worked against him. Bernard, an old enemy, became pope and proceeded to have the church condemn Abelard for heresy. The church council, meeting at Sens in 1140, directed that his writings be burned and that he lead a life of perpetual silence. Abelard died less than 18 months later at age 63.[3]

The Philosophy

Abelard's thoughts and actions seem commonplace to twentieth-century thinking, but they were radical enough in the twelfth century to impede his religious career and threaten his physical well-being. Nevertheless, his years as a monk were productive ones for Abelard. He used the time to think and write. It is during these years that he developed most of his philosophical and ethical theories. He considered himself the only living philosopher of the time. Abelard's outlook was dominated by Christian morality and the moral philosophies of the Greco-Roman world. This makes him a key figure in bridging the gap between the philosophies of the ancient societies of Greece and Rome and some of the popular philosophies of the West.

One of Abelard's most popular books was *Yes and No,* a variety of arguments for and against some of the popular ideas of the time. His other major works included *Scito te ipsum* ("Know Thyself") and *Theologia,* his controversial book on God and the Trinity.

Abelard's ethical philosophy focuses around the notion of intention. Human actions do not make a man worse in the sight of God, because no human action, in itself, is either good or evil. *Intention determines the morality of an individual's actions.* Abelard wrote, "Indeed God alone, who considers not so much what is done as in what mind it may be done, truly considers the guilt in our intentions."[4] A person, he argued, is therefore accountable for the character of his or her life. Abelard offered the following example as illustration: "A poor woman lacks sufficient clothing to provide for her baby on a cold winter's night. And so she takes the infant to her breast and holds him so tightly throughout the bitter night that she unavoidably smothers him with her clasp of deepest love. Certainly, he argues, this woman incurs no guilt before God."[5]

▶ *DECISION-MAKING TOOL*

Actions can be considered good or evil, that is, ethical or unethical, depending solely on one's intentions.

▶ *SUGGESTED MEDIA APPLICATION* ◀

Abelard's ethical theory is easily applied to most ethical dilemmas in media. Whether you are in journalism, advertising, public relations, telecommunications, film, or other media area, all you need do is look within yourself and ask these questions: How am I inclined to solve this ethical dilemma? What are my intentions, my motivations? Does the proposed solution to my ethical dilemma speak to the highest, most honorable—and, therefore, good—human qualities? Or does it speak to that which is selfish, hurtful, or base?

The major disadvantage of Abelard's philosophy is that it is not concerned with the consequences of an action; its only concern is that the action is motivated by honorable intentions.

RECOMMENDED CASE STUDIES

#1 (Chapter 11); #6 (Chapter 12); #14 (Chapter 14).

p. 189   p. 222   p. 275

▼ St. Thomas Aquinas

The Life

Born in early 1225 in the castle of Roccasecca, near Naples, Italy, Thomas Aquinas was the seventh son of Count Landulf of the house of Aquino. His education began at age 5, and by age 14 he was attending the University of Naples, where he studied grammar, logic, rhetoric, arithmetic, geometry, music, and astronomy.[6] It was here that he was introduced to the work of Aristotle by Peter of Hibernia. The vibrant life of the city was probably important in the development of Aquinas's philosophy. His family hoped he would join the Benedictine order—an order of monks who have taken vows of chastity, poverty, and obedience and who stayed within the monastery until death. However, Aquinas preferred the Dominican religious order, a devout but somewhat less restrictive regimen. Aquinas became a Dominican friar in 1244.

To the secular twentieth-century observer, there may not seem a vast difference between becoming a monk and becoming a friar. Both lifestyles required obedience, celibacy, and devotion. However, in the thirteenth century there were clear differences between monks and friars. Monks generally served the middle class, and friars served the poor. Although monks were not rich, they had many of their needs met. Friars, on the other hand, were often reduced to begging just to meet basic needs.[7]

Aquinas's family, particularly his mother, was so enraged at his decision to become a friar that his brothers were sent to kidnap him as he journeyed from Naples to Paris. He was held captive in the family castle for more than a year. Never one to waste time, Aquinas studied Aristotle and copied some of the Greek philosopher's work on logic during his imprisonment. Certain events at the castle during his imprisonment helped Aquinas fashion his views on a variety of personal and religious issues. Take, for example, his decision to maintain chastity. That decision developed from the following incident:

> Either out of pity or out of cunning, his brothers one night sent a seductive wench to his cell to offer herself for his pleasure. Thomas leapt up, seized a brand from the fire, and drove her from the room. He fell into a sleep in which he dreamt that angels bound his loins in token of perpetual chastity. "From that time onwards," says his earliest biographer, "it was his custom always to avoid the sight or company of women—except in case of necessity or utility—as a man avoids snakes."[8]

When he was released in 1245, he continued his trip to Paris where, at the University of Paris and later at Cologne, he studied under Albertus Magnus (Albert the Great) who was impressed with Aquinas and offered to tutor him. Albert the Great was also a Dominican and an admirer of Aristotle, thus his tutoring reinforced some of Aquinas's views. During his time in Paris, some of his fellow students gave Aquinas the nickname "Dumb Ox," because he was heavyset, slow-moving, and quiet. It was Magnus, however, who predicted that "this dumb ox will fill the whole world with his bellowing."[9]

Aquinas was ordained to the priesthood in 1250 and received his theology degree in 1256. He spent much of the rest of his life traveling, teaching, and writing. His definitive work was *Summa Theologiae*. The section of this work devoted to moral philosophy is said to have been influenced by Aristotle's *Nicomachean Ethics*. Aquinas died in 1274, on his way to a General Council at Lyons. Fifty years would pass before his writings were regarded as sound. Pope John XXII declared Aquinas a saint in 1323.

The Philosophy

Aquinas's ethical ideology can best be described as a Christian view of ethics. His philosophy dealt with human ends and human actions. "One of Aquinas's gifts as a theologian was a guiding sense of how things in the universe fit together and worked as a whole."[10] His ideas on ethics reflect this notion. If properly applied, ethics can direct individuals toward appropriate behavior and the ultimate end. Like Aristotle, Aquinas identified the ultimate end with happiness. He believed happiness could not be equated with pleasure, riches, honor, or any worldly good but must rest in activity in accordance with virtue, especially intellectual virtue. Morally good action is conducive to man's attainment of the ultimate end, or final happiness.

Aquinas was convinced that all men naturally incline toward this final end. He found the main difficulty in moral life resulted from the selection and application of appropriate actions toward an end. Naturally, as a theologian, he believed that God's eternal law is the highest and ultimate standard for proper action. He amplified this reasoning by suggesting that there were certain general types of *goods* and *evils* for men. Some actions, he felt, were generally good because they tend to perfect man's being and powers and because they contribute to the public welfare. Among the good actions, Aquinas felt, were prudence, justice, temperance, and courage. Without these qualities, an individual has little chance of acting appropriately. These qualities guide the individual and are so important that Aquinas termed them the *cardinal*—or essential—*virtues*.

Other actions, however, may be viewed as evil if they are self-abusive, brutish, and selfish, or if they fail to promote the cardinal virtues. Aquinas believed that all people have a sufficient awareness of what is good and what is evil to enable them to live in a suitable manner.

▶ *DECISION-MAKING TOOL*

Ethical behavior stems from appropriate human action, action guided by the four cardinal virtues: prudence, justice, temperance, and courage.

▶ *SUGGESTED MEDIA APPLICATION* ◀

Aquinas's ideas are useful in media situations involving people, particularly people who might be less fortunate than others. This notion is not surprising, given Aquinas's life as a friar. Journalists, especially, should be prudent and have a sense of fairness in dealing with all types of people. It ill-behooves any media employee to approach a task or an ethical dilemma without the courage necessary to take a moral stand.

RECOMMENDED CASE STUDIES
#13 (Chapter 13); #20 (Chapter 15).

▼ Francis Bacon

The Life

On January 22, 1561, at York House, just outside London, Francis Bacon was born to Sir Nicholas and Anne Bacon. His father was employed by the British Royal Family; his mother was well educated and extremely religious.[11] Francis was intellectually gifted. He entered Trinity College at Cambridge when he was 13 and studied geometry, astronomy, arithmetic, music, science, and the philosophy of Aristotle. He began the study of law in 1579 and entered public life in 1584 when he was elected to Parliament.[12]

at age 23 (!)

Francis Bacon, an English philosopher and statesman, is considered one of the pioneers of modern scientific thought. *Left: CORBIS; right: Frontispiece of Bacon's book reproduced from the original by kind permission of the Folger Shakespeare Library.*

Bacon's friendship with Sir William Cecil, Queen Elizabeth I's secretary of state, enabled him to develop his political skills and also provided him access to the queen. Bacon communicated with Elizabeth on a variety of topics; however, he lost favor with her in 1593 when he became deeply involved in the internal politics of the court.[13] Nevertheless, he continued to polish his political skills and to climb the ladder of success in politics.

Bacon achieved some influence with James Stuart, Elizabeth's successor. He proposed measures to unite England and Scotland and offered recommendations for dealing with the Catholic population in England. For his accomplishments, he was knighted by James I in 1603. He held a variety of positions in England during his life, including attorney general, clerk of the Star Chamber, and even Lord Keeper of the Seal—the position his father had held. Bacon reached the top of his power and influence when he was appointed Lord Chancellor in 1618.

However, as history often shows, a quick rise to power is frequently followed by an equally quick fall from grace. Bacon was accused of, and confessed to, accepting bribes. He confessed that he was sorry for his deeds, but he was fined, exiled from Parliament and the courts, and imprisoned in the Tower of London. Although James I eventually pardoned him, Bacon never regained the political influence he had once enjoyed.

Bacon spent his final years writing on science, philosophy, and history. He died in London on April 9, 1626. Rumors circulated, however, that he did not die in 1626 "but escaped to Holland, that he was the real author of Shakespeare's plays, and that he was the unacknowledged son of Queen Elizabeth."[14] No convincing evidence has been offered to support these claims, yet they have attached themselves to the history of his life, giving it an air of mystery.

The Philosophy

Francis Bacon is regarded by scholars as a major philosopher, yet "he was not true to what he knew."[15] In other words, Bacon did not follow his own advice. He acknowledged that he had not fully used the talents he had been given and that he had squandered many opportunities to use these talents for the benefit of others. Nevertheless, he is considered a forerunner of enlightened scientific thought. Bacon clearly understood the power of knowledge. He felt mankind had an enormous capacity to learn and to apply what was learned toward the betterment of the human condition.

During the Renaissance, moral instruction often took one of two forms: "demonstrating the triumph of virtue over vice, or offering models of virtuous living for imitation."[16] Bacon himself believed the study of ethics involved not only the general study of ethical principles but also the detailed study of human nature which equips one to influence others.[17] Bacon argued that continually advancing the mind, through the search for knowledge and truth, would result in an individual becoming ethically enlightened.

For purposes of ethical decision making, we should focus on the six human powers Bacon felt each individual possesses: understanding, reason, imagination, memory, appetite, and will.[18] These powers enable individuals to acquire knowledge and to act appropriately. Understanding and reason are used to promote logical behavior, whereas ethical behavior involves appetite and will. Both imagination and memory are linked to the thinking process.

Appetite is the human power that causes emotional, non-reflective actions. It is involuntary, habitual, and immediate.[19] These sorts of actions take no thought of possible consequences. However, the will provides for reflective behavior. It encompasses the human ability to say yes or no prior to an action. Will is conscious behavior, and can call for a delay of action, resisting the quick decisions of appetite, until a logical—and ethical—course of action is determined. Bacon believed that each individual is subjected to both internal and external pressures, or passions. Ethics, for Bacon, are practical. Ethical behavior, guided by reason, should bring the passions under control. Yet, as his life clearly shows, Bacon himself fell victim to some of the passions of the world, particularly money, power, and influence.

Many historians agree that Bacon was a genius. He had magnificent ideas and an enthusiasm for truth. His charm endeared him to many. Still, "there was in Bacon's 'self' a deep and fatal flaw. He was a pleaser of men."[20]

▶ *DECISION-MAKING TOOL*

Apply the powers of reason, understanding, and will to control the appetites ~~that~~ life subjects each individual ~~to~~. Seek constantly for new knowledge and truth.

to which

▶ *SUGGESTED MEDIA APPLICATION* ◀

Bacon's ethical philosophy emphasizes self-control through the use of reason and can be used to solve many ethical dilemmas. It is most useful when you have a stake in the ethical problem, that is, in situations where you stand to be significantly affected by the outcome. Bacon's philosophy urges you to control the internal and external pressures that may push you toward a certain action. Substitute reason for passion and seek the truth. The truth is particularly important to journalists, advertisers, and people in public relations. In media fields devoted to entertainment, particularly film, the truth may be less important.

RECOMMENDED CASE STUDIES
#3 (Chapter 11); #8 (Chapter 12); #16 (Chapter 14).

p. 192   p. 224   p. 277

QUESTIONS FOR DISCUSSION

1. What events in the life of Peter Abelard might have inspired him to develop his ethical theory of intention?

2. How can you account for the continuing influence of Aristotle's ideas on the philosophers presented in this chapter?

3. Compare Abelard's ethical theory of intention and Aquinas's notion of the ultimate end in terms of religious influence.

4. In what ways can the philosophers presented in this chapter be considered transition figures between the Greek philosophers and many of the contemporary philosophies we subscribe to today?

5. Develop precise, ethically focused definitions for Aquinas's four cardinal virtues.

6. In what ways are Aquinas's cardinal virtues and Bacon's human powers similar? How are they different?

ENDNOTES

1. Claire Bloom and Claude Rains, *The Song of Songs/Heloise and Abelard*, phonodisc, Caedmon Records TC 1085, 1957.

2. Ibid.

3. Paul L. Williams, *The Moral Philosophy of Peter Abelard* (Lanham, MD: University Press of America, 1980), 171.

4. Ibid., 141.

5. Ibid., 140.

6. Anthony Kenny, *Aquinas* (New York: Hill & Wang, 1980), 1.

7. Ibid., 2.

8. Ibid., 3.

9. Ibid.

10. Steven Anthony Edwards, *Interior Acts* (New York: University Press of America, 1986), 1.

11. Anthony Quniton, *Francis Bacon* (New York: Hill & Wang, 1980), 1.

12. Catherine Drinker Bowen, *Francis Bacon* (Boston: Little, Brown, 1963), 46, 50.

13. R. W. Church, *Bacon* (New York: AMS Press, 1968), 35–36.

14. Loren Eiseley, *Francis Bacon and the Modern Dilemma* (Lincoln: University of Nebraska Press, 1962), 5.

15. Church, 2.

16. Lisa Jardine, *Francis Bacon* (Cambridge: Cambridge University Press, 1974), 159.

17. Ibid.

18. Ibid., 90.

19. Ibid., 93.

20. Church, 3.

▼▼▼

CHAPTER 5

Rebels

In this chapter you will meet four "rebels." Their philosophical and ethical views may make some people uncomfortable, but their work has been important in terms of its influence on both personal and political behavior. Machiavelli's reputation, of course, precedes him. Nevertheless, his pragmatic approach to politics (and ethics) is appealing to individuals who reject rigid ethical rules because they seem situationally unworkable. Hobbes is less well known, but his ideas contrast nicely with those of Machiavelli. Voltaire and Rousseau are confirmed rationalists, a view rejected by postmodernists who do not believe in reason as a means to the truth.

Culture Period ■ Approximate Dates	General Description ■ Key Personalities
Renaissance and Reformation A.D. 1300–A.D. 1650 **Niccolò Machiavelli** (1469–1527) **Thomas Hobbes** (1588– . . .)	Era of much political, social, intellectual, and religious activity; rise of the church and increased power of popes; significant contributions to art, music, and science—especially from West (England): Chaucer, da Vinci, Michelangelo, Copernicus, Galileo, Henry VIII and the English kings, Martin Luther, John Calvin, El Greco, Rembrandt, Shakespeare
Enlightenment A.D. 1650–A.D. 1850 **Thomas Hobbes** (. . . 1679) **François Marie Voltaire** (1694–1778) **Jean Jacques Rousseau** (1712–1778)	The awakening of the human spirit and mind; emphasis on reason; rise of science as an influence on life and thinking; major contributions in art, music, philosophy, religion; political and social turmoil in Europe; Louis XIV, Louis XVI and Marie Antoinette, Handel, Haydn, Mozart, Bach, Beethoven, Wordsworth, Byron, Keats, Emerson, Napoleon, Darwin, Newton

Note: In America, the colonies continued to grow and develop following the establishment of the Virginia Charter in 1606 and the founding of the New England colonies around 1620. Declaration of Independence was signed in 1776.

Machiavelli is squarely in the Renaissance and Reformation historical culture period (see the time line). Hobbes was born in this period but made much of his political and philosophical contributions fairly late in the period. Voltaire and Rousseau, on the other hand, clearly belong to the Enlightenment. These powerful thinkers provide convincing evidence that one culture period often overlaps another.

▼ Niccolò Machiavelli

The Life

No one much likes Machiavelli. His political philosophy may be widely practiced, but his morals are suspect. The philosopher Edmund Burke and the political activists Karl Marx and Frederick Engles find themselves in agreement about Machiavelli's influence: "the evils of Machiavellianism constitute one of the most dangerous threats to the moral basis of political life."[1] What lies behind this sinister reputation? Who was Machiavelli, and how did he come to hold what many would describe as extreme views?

Niccolò Machiavelli was born in Florence, Italy, on May 3, 1469. Little is known about his childhood, except that he began his study of Latin at age 7, and by age 8 had advanced to the study of grammar and arithmetic.[2] His family had a history of civic and political involvement. His father was a lawyer, and though his family was neither rich nor highly aristocratic, it was connected with some of Florence's most exalted circles.[3]

The Renaissance was in full swing during his childhood years, and Niccolò grew up with an appreciation for knowledge, art, and literature. He liked reading histories and was able to compose a Latin composition at age 12. Because his family was well connected, he came into contact with much of what passed for the progressive culture of the time in Florence. Niccolò was acquainted with many important figures, including Savonarola, the Borgias, the Medici, and several popes.

Not much is known about Machiavelli's adolescence or his early adult years, though there is some evidence that he may have been in the service of a Florentine banker from 1487 to 1495. He came to power in politics in 1498 when he became second chancellor of the Florentine republic at age 29. This was almost certainly a purely political appointment because Niccolò had no previous administrative experience, yet was appointed to a position that required some administrative expertise.

His work as second chancellor required him to deal with correspondence relating to the administration of Florence's territories. He was also responsible for serving with a committee charged with administering Florence's foreign and diplomatic affairs. As secretary to the committee's ambassadors,

Niccolò Machiavelli's ideas are often misunderstood. His political ideas—from which an ethical philosophy may be derived—can be found in *The Prince. CORBIS–BETTMAN*

Niccolò traveled a great deal and had the opportunity to see the workings of government close up.[4]

His experiences required Machiavelli to learn political processes and practices early. As he became more active in government affairs, he soon came to realize that, in terms of political effectiveness, procrastination was folly, appearing irresolute was dangerous, and that bold, rapid action was best.[5] His political writings clearly reflect this view. His most famous work is probably *The Prince*, a short book by modern standards, yet a work that attempts to provide individuals who are destined to come to power with a set of political principles designed to enable them to effectively grasp and use power and authority.

When the Florentine republic ended in 1512 and the Medici were restored to power, "Machiavelli was arrested, imprisoned and tortured, and then released and allowed to live in retirement in the country."[6] He began to write, dreaming of the day he might be called once again to political service. It was not to be, however, and he died in 1527.

The Philosophy

Although Machiavelli died more than 470 years ago, his name is still synonymous with "cunning, duplicity, and the exercise of bad faith in political affairs."[7] We are probably doing Machiavelli a disservice by only looking at the negative aspects of his philosophy. There is much more to it than one sees at first glance. In Chapter 15 of *The Prince,* for example, Machiavelli expresses his concern about how one ought and ought not to live. He provides a list of virtues and vices of which, he feels, we should all be aware. Among his virtues are mercy, faith, integrity, and humanity. These are obviously desirable qualities, but Machiavelli also recognizes that "human conditions . . . do not always permit [the application of these qualities] . . . because men are not all good."[8]

It should be noted that "terrorism, murder, cruelty, treachery, and military aggression to achieve political ends were . . . no more common in Renaissance times than today, nor was Machiavelli the first to advocate them. . . . Moreover, it would be a mistake to think that either Machiavelli personally was immoral, as has so often been suggested in the misapplication of the word 'machiavellian,' or that in his analysis of politics he ignored ethical ideals."[9] However, Machiavelli does make a distinction between the ideals and values governing private life and those governing public life.

Machiavelli believed that politics require certain kinds of actions from a leader in much the same way that Christian moral values require certain kinds of action from a spiritual man. Thus, there is often a difference between one's public and one's private lives, one's public and one's private ethics.[10]

Although Machiavelli effectively separated his personal and public views of ethics, and although he was primarily concerned with political behavior, it will suit our purposes here if we examine some of his key ideas and then synthesize them so that they can be used to solve ethical problems. We will not make the fine distinctions that Machiavelli made with regard to private morals and public morals, nor will we think only in terms of how principles and actions ultimately affect government and political power. Rather, we will see how to apply some of Machiavelli's ideas in a media ethics context.

Machiavelli's philosophy is complicated. It is not, however, time-bound. Let's examine four aspects of Machiavelli's philosophy and then synthesize them into a decision-making tool.

Virtu   Machiavelli writes that "the new prince must exhibit *virtu*." The word has Latin origins in *virtus,* meaning courage or valor. In Machiavelli's view, it may also mean ability, force, boldness, efficiency, action, bravery, energy, vitality, wisdom, power, strength, and prudence, among other qualities. But please note, "among the English words which this list should *not* [emphasis added] include is virtuous, meaning morally good, since Machiavelli ordinarily did not mean any Christian, or even classical sense of moral goodness."[11] The most important aspects of virtu involve "the ability to under-stand, accept, and adapt to change dynamically and avoid stagnation."[12]

The Un-Golden Rule   The Golden Rule is a well-known Christian maxim for living: Do unto others as you would have them do unto you. This is based on two passages of scripture, Matthew 7:12 and Luke 6:31. Machiavelli's take on this notion has been called the *Un-Golden Rule.* Simply stated it is: Do unto others as they would do unto you.[13] A quick reading might fail to differentiate between the two statements, but a more thorough examination reveals that significant differences do exist in the two approaches to human behavior. "The two rules resemble each other in urging reciprocated conduct: the scriptural one basing itself on wished-for conduct in others, Niccolò's on effective truth about others."[14] For Machiavelli, the scriptural directive is unrealistic in the real world. It won't work; it imagines men as they ought to be, not as they are. He prefers to deal with men as they are. "The harm men would do to you lays the moral basis for the harm you must do to them."[15] Essentially, Machiavelli is advocating a philosophy of doing things to others *before* they do things to you.

Appearances   One of the issues often discussed about contemporary culture is whether we have advanced—or declined—to the point where image is more important than substance in our society. Certainly there is some relevance with regard to some products and services regularly offered to the American people. Machiavelli had some ideas about this. He believed that "most men are so simple-minded, and above all so prone to self-deception, that they usually take things at face-value in a wholly uncritical way."[16] Machiavelli believed in keeping up appearances, in "avoiding the hatred of the people while at the same time keeping them in awe." This is not all that difficult to do for the skillful politician because "everybody sees what you appear to be, but few perceive what you are. Thus there is no reason to suppose that your sins will find you out."[17]

The Fox and the Lion   Machiavelli believed that one would do well to choose to be like the fox and the lion: a vicious lion and a sly fox. This results in being both feared and respected. You should be ready to substitute cunning and force for the ideals of decency, when necessary.[18] Take, for example, the practice of cruelty. Cruelty, which certainly has an element of evil intent, should be temporary, "used only when necessitated by the common good, and then done with dispatch, directed toward the common good and ceased." In this way, "it is permissible to say good of evil if that evil is but seeming evil and converts to a true good."[19]

This is an excellent example of Machiavelli's means-and-ends philosophy. For him, the result or end of an action or a behavior is paramount, and one need not be concerned about how one arrived at that result. In other words, one can do bad to ultimately achieve good. Machiavelli's view is a classic example of the notion that *the end justifies the means.* Placed in our current context, one would be allowed to be unethical if some ultimate good would result, and, for Machiavelli, that good was often the common good as it might be defined by a ruler or other person in authority.

Synthesis

There is little doubt that Machiavelli was the ultimate pragmatist. For him, it was practical, reasonable, and even ethical to twist the qualities of good behavior to fit political ends. For Machiavelli, virtue means moral flexibility. His "relative values provide a foundation for situational ethics, which, in turn, approve all actions, regardless of their immorality."[20] One can be kind, if necessary; one can be cunning or savage, if necessary; one should keep up appearances; and one should always be ready to act on the Un-Golden Rule.

There is little question that Machiavelli's ethics were thin, pale shadows of a real ethical system. There is nothing moderate about his pragmatic or situational approach to ethical problems and issues. To modern sensibilities, Machiavelli's approach is offensive; to postmodern sensibilities, it doesn't seem quite so harsh. About the only saving grace of his flexible ethical system is his belief that after one has acted—in perhaps a cunning or savage manner—ethics take over and, as he notes in Chapter 8 of *The Prince*, "afterward one does not persist."[21]

▶ **DECISION-MAKING TOOL** ◀

Understand, accept, and adapt to change; avoid stagnation; examine a problem situationally, and flex the ethical absolutes only to the degree necessary to gain the desired ends.

▶ *SUGGESTED MEDIA APPLICATION* ◀

Great care must be taken in applying Machiavelli to media ethical dilemmas. You should not be seduced by his means-and-end philosophy. For example, as a journalist, you should not automatically designate the getting of a story as the good, thereby enabling you to do anything to get it. Advertisers should avoid producing misleading ads on the grounds that the end—the selling of the product—justifies any sort of ad.

The proper application of Machiavelli's ideas requires you to realize that there are essentially two worlds: the public and the private. To function in the public world, you must first understand the difference between the two worlds, then adapt to the public world by bending or flexing the principles governing your private world. This flexing should be neither automatic nor permanent; it should only occur when necessary and to the extent necessary to achieve a worthy goal.

This approach is pragmatic and real-world based. Unless you are comfortable accepting the responsibility for the consequences of this relative approach to ethics, you should probably avoid using Machiavelli's ideas in your professional media life, though you can undoubtedly see the philosophy at work in the lives of others.

RECOMMENDED CASE STUDIES
#6 (Chapter 12); #14 (Chapter 14).
p. 222   p. 275

▼ Thomas Hobbes

The Life

Thomas Hobbes was one of the most colorful and eccentric people of his time. He knew or was acquainted with, among others, Charles II, Galileo, Descartes, and Bacon.[22] Yet he began life in poor circumstances. He was born April 5, 1588, in the parish of Westport, northwest of Malmesbury, Wiltshire, England. Upon hearing the news that England was under attack by the Spanish Armada, his mother went into premature labor, thus Hobbes entered the world a little bit before his time. Some have said much the same regarding his philosophical views.[23]

Hobbes's father was a poor clergyman in the town of Malmesbury and likely "spent more time in the Westport alehouse than he did in his church."[24] He wasn't much of a role model for young Thomas, deserting his family following a brawl in the churchyard and dying in obscurity in London sometime later. Nevertheless, Thomas was given the opportunity to get an education by his wealthy uncle, who financed his study at Magdalen Hall and later at Oxford University.[25]

Hobbes profited from his study and, in addition to English, could speak and read Latin, Greek, French, and Italian. But he was particularly interested in geometry. It impressed him as a method for reaching sound conclusions. He was recommended in 1608 to William Lord Cavendish, Earl of Devonshire. Most of Hobbes's life was spent in "the employment of either of the Earls of Devonshire, or their neighbors or cousins, the Earls of Newcastle. He acted as secretary, tutor, financial agent, and general adviser."[26] This work proved to be the catalyst in the formation of Hobbes's philosophy. It gave him access to the political and philosophical views of the ruling class and afforded him the opportunity to travel. He made three trips to Europe with his various employers.[27]

Hobbes enjoyed having a good time. He was strongly influenced by the strict behavior expected of young college students, but he was equally impressed by drink, gaming, and other vices that were prevalent during the time. He developed "the detoxifying habit of vomiting after an evening of heavy drinking."[28] But he drank little after his sixtieth birthday and preferred fish to red meat.

Hobbes lived 91 years, a long time, considering that the average life expectancy in seventeenth-century England was about 40 years. This extraordinary longevity "may have been the result of a self-imposed regimen that

was centuries ahead of its time. . . . [He] exercised strenuously to induce per-
spiration [and] sang songs aloud as a way of expanding the lungs."[29] Yet during the last 20 or so years of his life, he suffered from the shaking palsy, probably Parkinson's disease. His trembling was so pronounced that he was
forced to dictate his writings to a secretary.[30] Hobbes died on December 4,
1679, after having been seriously ill for several months. The inscription that
appears on his tombstone was probably written by Hobbes himself:

> He was a virtuous man, and for his reputation for learning he was well known at
> home and abroad.[31]

The Philosophy

Although he was concerned with the problem of "natural right—the existence or non-existence of common ethical standards by which men should
live their lives"[32]—there is no mistaking the fact that Hobbes's ethical philosophy is based on moral relativism. A moral relativist is one who believes
that there are no universally true or valid standards of judgment and moral
behavior.[33]

Hobbes thought of himself as "applying scientific and mathematical
method to the study of man, and as achieving success in that study compa-
rable to the successes of Galileo in physics and Harvey in psychology."[34] He
may have had a somewhat inflated view of his accomplishments, given the
notion that scientific principles and scientific methods may not be all that
useful in studying man's behavior as an individual or his behavior in society.
Hobbes's approach certainly appeals to modern sensibilities. The modernist
tradition holds that the scientific method is applicable to almost all aspects of
life and that data gathered through the proper application of the scientific
method can—and should—be used as a foundation for making life decisions.
In terms of contemporary culture, the postmodern view is that the scientific
method is not the only method, and probably not even a good method, for
getting information on which actions may be based.

At the very least, Hobbes probably felt that men should be bound by certain moral rules and that their actions should contribute to an ordered society. Yet Hobbes believed that virtues require a secure environment in which
to function. In other words, there must be some unifying structure that makes
doing right possible and desirable. To Hobbes's mind, this structure was
most certainly the state.

Hobbes's desire for stability in politics is understandable. The times in
which he lived—the early and middle years of the seventeenth century—were
turbulent. For example, civil war broke out in England in 1642, and Charles I
was executed seven years later. These unsettled times probably led Hobbes to
his political and moral theories—particularly his desire for a strong state,
whose purpose would be to protect the people and promote peace.

Thus, Hobbes's moral system was grounded in the science of human nature and built on the foundation of a strong state where survival was assured

and men had the opportunity to concern themselves with moral behavior.[35] In order to synthesize a decision-making tool from Hobbes's philosophy, it will be necessary to consider some of his basic ideas.

Hobbes considered the following to be axiomatic:

1. There is no clear, objective truth about the external world.
2. "People take to be 'good' what is in their own interest."[36]
3. People can "do more than act from reasons of self-interest."[37]
4. The route to proper behavior lies through politics, that is, ethics taken independently of politics yields only the "grimmest version of skeptical relativism."[38]

These ideas are clearly evident in Chapter 6 of _Leviathan_, Hobbes's major work:

> But whatsoever is the object of any man's appetite or desire, that is it which he for his part calleth _good:_ and the object of his hate and aversion _evil_. . . . For these words of good, evil, . . . are ever used with relation to the person that useth them: there being nothing simply and absolutely so; nor any common rule of good and evil to be taken from the nature of the objects themselves; but from the person of man, where there is no commonwealth; or, in a commonwealth, from the person that representeth it; or from an arbitrator or judge, whom men disagreeing shall by consent set up.[39]

Given these unalterable principles, Hobbes can now consider a moral system.

Most moral systems are based on general principles or rules detailing how people ought and ought not to behave. Hobbes felt, as many philosophers have, that _ought implies can,_ that a person "ought to perform an act only if he is capable of performing it."[40] Further, Hobbes determined that these _ought-principles_ were essentially the laws of nature, which he defined as rational self-preservation.[41]

From such an approach to proper behavior, Hobbes would generate the following ethical principles:

1. Seek peace in a world of vulnerability and conflict.
2. Promote justice and strive for mutual accommodation.
3. Fulfill your obligations.[42]

One can certainly see echoes of other philosophies in these statements. For example, seeking peace in a troubled world was most assuredly a key aspect of the philosophy of Confucius. Aristotle's Golden Mean bears a strong resemblance to Hobbes's notion of promoting justice and working for mutual accommodation.

► DECISION-MAKING TOOL

Rise above self-interest; promote justice and strive for mutual accommodation; fulfill your obligations.

▶ *SUGGESTED MEDIA APPLICATION* ◀

Some care must be taken in applying Hobbes's ideas to media situations. Media have always been fiercely independent in America and have always opposed any government control over their work. How, then, does one use Hobbes's ideas, given the fact that Hobbes believed in a strong state or governing authority? It all depends on how one interprets what Hobbes meant about the influence of the state on moral concerns. It could be argued that Hobbes was not so much concerned with the state's supervision or control of a moral system as he was with the state's creation of the proper environment, or proper atmosphere, if you will, where moral concerns could be considered.

In America, we have a strong First Amendment that creates an environment conducive to the media's work. Media employees do not fear for their lives in the routine performance of their jobs. Their main concern is not the preservation of their lives but the performance of their duties, or as Hobbes might have put it—the fulfilling of their obligations—as members of the media. We need not, therefore, be much concerned about the influence of politics in the application of Hobbes's moral theory. Our political system has created an atmosphere where we, as media employees, can—and should—rise above self-interest and concern ourselves with how individuals ought to conduct themselves. Eliminating selfish motivations from our actions will help us deal fairly with others as we go about doing our jobs.

RECOMMENDED CASE STUDIES
#1 (Chapter 11); #8 (Chapter 12); #19 (Chapter 15).

p.189   p.224   p.302

▼ François Marie Arouet Voltaire

The Life

François Marie Arouet was born November 21, 1694, in Paris. Years later he adopted the name Voltaire and it is by this name that he is primarily known as an important French writer and philosopher. Almost no information exists about his early life. We do know that his mother had a difficult time with his birth and that she died when he was quite young. According to his baptismal record, he "often tried to pass as nine months older that he actually was, perhaps out of perversity, perhaps out of sheer love for deception."[43]

Nevertheless, Voltaire was not a strong baby. Later in life, he described his birth with characteristic wit. "I was born dead," he said. Actually, he was apparently so weak that he could not be baptized at church, so the baptism was conducted at home.[44] His health was to be a lifelong concern. "Voltaire was a histrionic hypochondriac, and he liked to appear as moribund as possible in order to lend color to his constant complaints of physical suffering."[45]

He was the son of a notary and apparently did not get on well with his father, who was methodical and businesslike and who thought his son would never amount to much. Voltaire received a classic education at the college Louis-le-Grand run by the Jesuits. At the age of 12 he was considered a brilliant student with a mind of his own. This independence of thought would serve him well throughout his life.

As a young man in Paris, he began moving in aristocratic circles and soon became known as a brilliant and sarcastic wit. Here is a short list of some of the witty statements attributed to Voltaire.

- "Marriage is the only adventure open to the cowardly.
- I have never made but one prayer to God, a very short one: 'O Lord, make my enemies ridiculous.' And God granted it.
- The art of government consists in taking as much money as possible from one class of citizens to give it to the other.
- All the reasoning of men is not worth one sentiment of women."[46]

Voltaire became one of the key figures in the Enlightenment, the Age of Reason that emerged in eighteenth-century France. Man's imagination was unleashed and great advances were made in art, music, philosophy, science, and politics. These advances were made possible through man's development both as a scientist and as an individual who could think for himself. The more primitive ideas and practices of the Renaissance and medieval times were abandoned as science began to reveal the marvelous possibilities of the world.

Voltaire regularly produced important writings, many of which involved him in lawsuits or resulted in the displeasure of those in high places. Voltaire championed free speech, a free press, and civil liberties. During his 11-month stay in the Bastille, where he had been imprisoned for writing a particularly biting piece about a French regent, Voltaire wrote his first tragedy, *Oedipe,* marking the beginning of a series of plays that would dominate the stage for the rest of the eighteenth century. Voltaire was detained in the Bastille a second time after a quarrel with a member of an important French family. This time he stayed only two weeks, promising to leave France if he were released. He moved to England, where he quickly learned the language, met powerful men, and studied English science, society, and philosophy.

Voltaire returned to France in 1728 and spent the next four years writing. His chief work was *English or Philosophical Letters,* which was an indirect attack on the political and religious institutions of France. This work, of course, brought him into conflict with the authorities, and he was forced to leave Paris once again. Later he traveled to Versailles and served two years in the Prussian court. He spent the last 20 years of his life in Ferney and continued to produce poems and novels.

"For over sixty years, he knew everybody who was anybody . . . wrote on a great range of subjects and in almost every kind of form . . . [including] twenty thousand letters" and numerous plays, poems, and novels.[47] His works have been translated into many languages and distributed the world over. In short, his work, like his life, was complex and massive.

Voltaire died in Paris on May 30, 1778. The church, reeling from his constant criticism, was determined that he should not be buried in consecrated ground. But his friends prevailed, and his body was "smuggled out of Paris to escape the indignities prepared for it."[48] When Voltaire died, those who suffered persecution because of their beliefs lost an eloquent and powerful defender.

Johann Wolfgang von Goethe, a German poet, writer, and scientist who was highly regarded throughout Europe, was once asked what words he would use to describe Voltaire. Goethe responded: "Profundity, genius, intuition, greatness, spontaneity, talent, merit, nobility, imagination, wit, understanding, feeling, sensibility, taste, good taste, rightness, propriety, tone, good tone, courtliness, variety, abundance, wealth, fecundity, warmth, magic, charm, grace, urbanity, facility, vivacity, fineness, brilliance, boldness, sparkle, mordancy, delicacy, ingenuity, style, versification, harmony, purity, correctness, elegance, perfection. Then, taking a deep breath, he added, to leave the reader in no doubt about his feelings, that Voltaire was the greatest writer of all time."[49]

The Philosophy

Although Voltaire was greatly influenced by Newton and others, he was his own man when it came to developing both an ethical and a political philosophy. It is his ethical philosophy that concerns us here. Voltaire was critical of abstract, all-inclusive systems of thought, whether from theology or philosophy.[50] Voltaire was not an enemy of religion or any other institution, but he was against the superstition and fanaticism that were prevalent in his day. Many of the ideas he attacked were basic and cherished beliefs of the time.[51]

Voltaire was a *deist*. Deists feel that belief in God is clearly reasonable to the human mind and that interference from religious institutions merely clouded important issues. In the Enlightenment, deism was taken to mean "God's leaving the Universe to its own lawful devices, without any particular interventions, once the process of creation had been completed."[52] Voltaire was strongly critical of the clergy and was not convinced that either government or religion was very much concerned with improving the human condition. He favored positive action; he felt neither the state nor religion was providing it.[53]

In terms of ethics, Voltaire considered himself a "sensible man—*un homme sensible*—in the sense in which this term was generally used in the 18th century."[54] In Voltaire's mind, man's feelings and natural impulses were basically good, regardless of the errors one might commit. Voltaire acknowledged that all men tend to be controlled by their passions, but he felt that a balance could be achieved between the inclinations of the heart and the dictates of the mind. This balance could be accomplished, he believed, through reason, though he acknowledged that one ought not place too much confidence in reason.[55] We note first, then, that Voltaire favored using reason to balance and govern the passions.

Let us turn now to Voltaire's own words to expand this ethical philosophy. In *A Treatise on Metaphysics* (1736), he wrote these words: "Virtue and vice, moral good and evil, are . . . whatever is useful or harmful to society. Good actions are nothing other than actions from which we all benefit."[56] In his *Letter to Frederick the Great,* Voltaire wrote: "All societies, then, will not have the same laws, but no society will be without laws. Therefore, the good of the greatest number is the immutable law of virtue."[57] The notion of acting for the greater good of society is a common ethical concept and one that would be popularized later by John Stuart Mill.

▶ *DECISION-MAKING TOOL*

Use reason to balance the passions; act for the greater good of society.

▶ *SUGGESTED MEDIA APPLICATION* ◀

Voltaire's philosophy can be readily applied to most media ethical dilemmas. You simply have to look at both the intellectual and emotional sides of an issue and determine a course of action that meets the needs of society. You have to set aside personal feelings and reactions to the ethical problem and analyze it carefully. Your solution should serve others, not self. Journalists and public relations practitioners may find Voltaire's balance between the emotions and the intellect particularly helpful.

RECOMMENDED CASE STUDIES

#6 (Chapter 12); #13 (Chapter 13); #15 (Chapter 14); #18 (Chapter 15).

p. 222   p. 252   p. 276   p. 301

▼ Jean Jacques Rousseau

The Life

Jean Jacques Rousseau was born to Isaac and Suzanne Rousseau on June 28, 1712, in Geneva, Switzerland. He was welcomed by François, a brother born 10 years earlier. Suzanne died a few days after Jean Jacques was born, having caught a fever and, at age 40, never having recovered fully from the childbirth experience. "I was born nearly dead," Jean Jacques—echoing Voltaire—wrote years later. "They had little hope of saving me, but a sister of my father's, a wise and good woman, took such good care of me that she saved my life."[58] The aunt's name was Theodora and she did indeed take good care of the youngster.

Theodora's care was made necessary because Isaac, the father, was described as footloose and irresponsible.[59] Isaac's frequent absences from the home may have been partly the result of his work, as he journeyed abroad to ply his watchmaker's trade. Isaac gave his children only his intermittent attention, and then his interactions with them often drove him to tears, especially when thoughts or conversation turned to poor Suzanne.[60]

When he was 12, Jean Jacques was sent to a pastor named Lambercier to receive a formal education, where he endured frequent spankings at the hands of the pastor's sister. This sort of discipline did little to advance his education. Reflecting on the experience in later years, Rousseau felt that such treatment of children really shapes a child's personality. He noted "this child's punishment . . . disposed of my tastes, my desires, my passions, myself for the rest of my life."[61] Rousseau, as a result, became somewhat comfortable in the role of the passive male.

His education into pleasure came at the hands of Madame Warens, wife of the Baronne de Warens, in whose home young Jean Jacques spent some time. Madame Warens was young, imaginative, and attractive, and she succeeded in converting Jean Jacques from the Calvinist religion of his fathers to Roman Catholicism. Though he was never a devout religious convert, Jean Jacques was much more devoted to Madame Warens's sexual instruction. She was 12 years older than Jean Jacques. After four years of cozy intimacy, she invited the young Rousseau into her bed. However appealing this might have been, it left Jean Jacques with a number of doubts and fears. For one thing, he knew that Madame Warens, or "Maman" as he called her, had intimate relationships with others. Nevertheless, he quickly found himself "a reluctant partner in a *menage a trois.*"[62]

Rousseau was to have a variety of work experiences, including being a footman, a student, a steward, a private tutor, an interpreter, and the secretary to the French ambassador.[63] In 1742, he found himself in Paris, where he began a new career. He made some important connections and met a number of prominent people, including Voltaire. He took a mistress, one Thérèse Levasseur, and had five children in rapid succession, all of whom he abandoned in foundling homes, thus adding another burden to a conscience already troubled by guilt and shame as a result of his experiences with Madame Warens.

In 1750, Rousseau entered an essay contest at the Academy at Dijon. He responded to this question: *Has the reestablishment of the arts and sciences contributed to the purification or the corruption of morals?* As he was walking to see a friend one day, he thought about the question and was so enchanted by it that he sat down under a tree to ponder the question more deeply. Recalling the experience later, he wrote, "If I had even been able to write a quarter of what I saw and felt under that tree, with what clarity I would have shown all the contradictions of the social system . . . with what simplicity I would have demonstrated that man is naturally good and that it is by his institutions alone that men become evil."[64] Rousseau won the essay prize with an effectively written piece—*A Discourse on the Sciences and the Arts*—that took the negative side of the proposition, that is, that the arts and sciences contributed to the corruption of morals. But it was as much his boldness in taking an unpopular view as it was his prose that won him the prize.[65]

For the next 10 years, Rousseau worked hard and was remarkably productive. He gained widespread recognition as difficult, embattled, and somewhat subversive, an accurate representation of him in many ways but one he grew to resent as the years passed. He produced his two masterpieces, *Emile* and the *Social Contract*, in 1762.

As he matured, Rousseau became interested in deism, a popular philosophy among the thinkers of the time. He did not consider himself an orthodox believer, yet deism interested him. The philosophy holds that "a beneficent god had created the world with its laws and then withdrawn from it to leave virtuous men to discover its moral rules and live according to its dictates."[66]

In late December 1764, Voltaire exposed Rousseau as a man who had abandoned his children by Thérèse Lavasseur. Rousseau suffered from the continuing criticism of religious authorities as well as the disapproval of many of his neighbors, some of whom threw rocks at his house.[67] After a short time in England with the philosopher David Hume, with whom he also had a falling out, he returned to France, completed work on his *Dictionary of Music*, and married Thérèse Lavasseur.

In May 1778, Rousseau moved with Lavasseur to Ermenonville, not far from central Paris, where he died on July 2, after a brief illness.[68] In the years since his death, his reputation has grown steadily. There is little doubt that he was an important presence during the years of the French Revolution. Since his death, Rousseau has become one of the great figures of Western civilization.

The Philosophy

Rousseau, it must be remembered, was first and foremost a political theorist, and he is often judged in the light of his political philosophy. "One of the most quoted remarks in the whole of political philosophy is the sentence with which Rousseau opens Chapter 1 of the *Social Contract*: 'Man is born free and everywhere he is in chains'."[69] The chains to which he refers are those of a legitimate government, a government elected by the people but turned insensitive to their needs in the use of its power. Yet there is a foundation of morality in much of his work. For example, *Discours sur l'inegalite* has as its theme, one critic notes, "man is good and becomes evil by embracing society."[70]

Morality, for Rousseau, was a matter of proper conduct. This conduct is guided by the principles that one holds to be important to self and others.[71] Rousseau recognized what he termed the morality of the times, that is, the standards of conduct generally expected, but he also recognized *true morality*, which he described "as serving one's country, obliging friends, relieving the unhappy; sometimes in terms of obedience to the promptings of conscience; and sometimes in terms of behaving in ways suitable to the condition and circumstances of man."[72] It is especially interesting that Rousseau would give some thought to morality and ethical behavior as a function of one's conscience, since his apparently bothered him for most of his life. He did, after all, give up his five children to foundling homes and did engage in sexual dalliances with Madame Warens.

Unfortunately, Rousseau never deals with the issue of conscience to any great extent anywhere in his writings, although there is evidence that he considered it to be very important in man's spiritual and moral makeup.[73] Rousseau gave a loose definition of conscience in the Vicar's creed: "There is in the depths of souls . . . an innate principle of justice and virtue according to which, in spite of our own maxims, we judge our actions and those of others as good or bad. It is to this principle that I give the name conscience."[74]

Conscience is accompanied not by feelings but by *reason*. For Rousseau, developing ethical insight, that is, combining conscience and reason, was not enough. One needed an awareness of and sensitivity to another's state of mind. Rousseau called this *compassion*.[75] The combining of conscience, compassion, and reason, then, results in action that promotes "the good order which makes for harmony between the good proper to each individual, each individual's good acts, and the promoting of good for others."[76]

▶ DECISION-MAKING TOOL

Use conscience, compassion, and reason to make ethical decisions that promote harmony among all involved.

▶ SUGGESTED MEDIA APPLICATION ◀

In the rough-and-tumble world of media—particularly in the highly competitive arena of journalism—it is sometimes easy to forget that almost everything one does involves human beings. Rousseau would have us deal with others carefully. We should try to understand them and then respect them for the individuals they are. We should check our consciences to determine our own motivations and to examine possible actions for their potential to be good or bad. We should then act in a way that promotes accord among all involved.

RECOMMENDED CASE STUDIES

#7 (Chapter 12); #11 (Chapter 13).

p. 223   p. 249

QUESTIONS FOR DISCUSSION

1. Machiavelli seems to prefer flexible ethical principles. This flexibility enables him to meet his objectives. This "end justifies the means" philosophy is much discussed. If one is willing to bend ethical principles when neces-

sary, why have them at all? Is there a difference between having ethical principles that can be bent, flexed, or ignored on demand and having no principles at all?

2. Is Machiavelli's Un-Golden Rule a valid ethical approach to life and work situations? Explain your reasoning.

3. Do you agree with Hobbes's notion that moral behavior can only be expected or required of individuals who are provided the proper unifying structure, that is, a strong government? Why or why not?

4. How is Hobbes's view of the individual, ethical behavior, and the state different from Machiavelli's?

5. What qualities are possessed by Voltaire's sensible man—*un homme sensible?* Can one be such a person in postmodern America? Explain.

6. What contradictions can you find when Rousseau's philosophy is applied to his life?

7. It might be said that Voltaire and Rousseau were anti-government and that Machiavelli and Hobbes were pro-government. Can you account for this difference in opinion? (*Hint:* What was the political situation in France during the Voltaire and Rousseau years?) To what degree should government be involved in ethics?

ENDNOTES

1. Quentin Skinner, *Machiavelli* (New York: Hill & Wang), 1.

2. Silvia Ruffo-Fiore, *Niccolò Machiavelli* (Boston: Twayne, 1982), 2.

3. Skinner, 4.

4. Ibid., 6.

5. Ibid., 8.

6. Diane Collinson, *Fifty Major Philosophers* (London and New York: Routledge, 1987), 42.

7. Skinner, 1.

8. Ruffo-Fiore, 45.

9. Ibid.

10. Ibid., 45–46.

11. Ibid., 37.

12. Ibid., 38.

13. Sebastian de Grazia, *Machiavelli in Hell* (Princeton, NJ: Princeton University Press, 1989), 299.

14. Ibid.

15. Ibid., 300.

16. Skinner, 44

17. Ibid., 41 and 44.

18. Ibid., 40.

19. de Grazia, 317.

20. Rita Slaught Gould, Machiavelli's *Il principe:* The Moral Conscience of Mankind, unpublished doctoral dissertation, University of South Florida, December 1990, I.

21. de Grazia, 316.

22. Arnold A. Rogow, *Thomas Hobbes* (New York: Norton, 1986), 9.

23. Ibid., 17.

24. Richard Tuck, *Hobbes* (Oxford: Oxford University Press, 1989), 1–2.

25. Tom Sorell, ed., *The Cambridge Companion to Hobbes* (Cambridge: Cambridge University Press, 1996), 15.

26. Tuck, 4.

27. Ibid.

28. Rogow, 10.

29. Ibid.

30. Sorell, 36.

31. Ibid., 37 and 38.

32. Tuck, 51.

33. David Boonin-Vail, *Thomas Hobbes and the Science of Moral Virtue* (Cambridge: Cambridge University Press, 1994), 59.

34. J. Kemp, *Ethical Naturalism: Hobbes and Hume* (London: Macmillan, 1970), 27.

35. Gregory S. Kavka, *Hobbesian Moral and Political Theory* (Princeton, NJ: Princeton University Press, 1986), 289–290.

36. Tuck, 55.

37. Boonin-Vail, 64.

38. Tuck, 64.

39. Thomas Hobbes, *Leviathan,* ed. by Edwin Curley (Indianapolis, IN: Hackett, 1994), pp. 28–29.

40. Kavka, 310.

41. Ibid.

42. Ibid.

43. A. Owen Aldridge, *Voltaire and the Century of Light* (Princeton, NJ: Princeton University Press, 1975), 3.

44. Ibid., 6.

45. Ibid., 3.

46. Peter Gay, *Age of Enlightenment* (New York: Time-Life Books, 1966), 58.

47. Theodore Besterman, *Voltaire* (New York: Harcourt, Brace, and World, 1969), 13.

48. Ibid., 527.

49. Ibid., 528.

50. R. S. Ridgway, *Voltaire and Sensibility* (Montreal and London: McGill-Queen's University Press, 1973).

51. Ibid., 17.

52. Antony Flew, *A Dictionary of Philosophy* (New York: St. Martin's, 1979), 87.

53. Ibid., 371.

54. Ridgway, 21.

55. Ridgway, 58.

56. *Voltaire: Selections,* ed. by Paul Edwards (New York: Macmillan, 1989).

57. Ibid., 210.

58. Frances Winwar, *Jean-Jacques Rousseau* (New York: Random House, 1961), 6.

59. Donald A. Cress, ed. and trans., *On the Social Contract,* by Jean-Jacques Rousseau (Indianapolis, IN: Hackett, 1987), 3.

60. Ibid.

61. E. S. Burt, "Developments in Character: Reading and Interpretation," in *Jean-Jacques Rousseau,* ed. Harold Bloom (New York: Chelsea House, 1988), 246.

62. Cress, 4.

63. Maurice Cranston, *The Nobel Savage: Jean-Jacques Rousseau 1754–1762* (Chicago: University of Chicago Press, 1991), 3.

64. Cress, 4–5.

65. Ibid., 5.

66. Ibid., 6.

67. N. J. H. Dent, *A Rousseau Dictionary* (Cambridge: Blackwell, 1992), 13.

68. Ibid., 14–15.

69. Collinson, 86.

70. Ernst Cassirer, *The Question of Jean-Jacques Rousseau,* ed. Peter Gay (New Haven, CT: Yale University Press, 1989), 6.

71. Dent, 162.

72. Ibid., 164.

73. Ibid., 60.

74. *Emile,* IV, 289.

75. Dent, 52.

76. Ibid., 61.

CHAPTER 6

Traditionalists

This chapter presents the philosophy of three individuals whose views have come to be accepted as traditional philosophical principles. Kant and Mill are somewhat better known than Spinoza, but all have useful ethical theories.

Culture Period ▪ Approximate Dates	General Description ▪ Key Personalities

Enlightenment   A.D. 1650–A.D. 1850
 	
   Benedict Spinoza   (1632–1677)
   Immanuel Kant   (1724–1804)
   John Stuart Mill   (1806 . . .)
 	
Note: In America, the colonies continued to grow and develop following the establishment of the Virginia Charter in 1606 and the founding of the New England colonies around 1620. Declaration of Independence was signed in 1776.
	The awakening of the human spirit and mind; emphasis on reason; rise of science as an influence on life and thinking; major contributions in art, music, philosophy, religion; political and social turmoil in Europe; Louis XIV, Louis XVI and Marie Antoinette, Handel, Haydn, Mozart, Bach, Beethoven, Wordsworth, Byron, Keats, Emerson, Napoleon, Darwin, Newton

Modern age A.D. 1850–A.D. 1945 **John Stuart Mill** (. . . 1873)	Industrial Revolution takes hold; steel developed; much political and social change in America (Civil War) and in Europe (World Wars I and II); significant contributions in art, music, literature, science; Pasteur, Einstein, Wright Brothers, Hugo, Marx, Freud, Picasso, Hitler, Stalin

Spinoza and Kant hold views that are clearly in step with the thinking of the Enlightenment period. Although Mill was born during the Enlightenment, many of his ideas were based on some of the popular notions of the time in England, a country struggling with the Industrial Revolution and moving into the modern period (see the time line).

Kant's categorical imperative suggests an individual act in such a way that the action would be appropriate as universal law—that is, acceptable behavior for all. This view requires one to consider others—the larger context of society—before acting. Postmodern culture stresses individuality; Kant looks beyond the individual to an action's implications for the culture and society at large.

Mill, too, suggests that individuality might have to be sacrificed if a greater good is to be served. Spinoza advocates the use of reason to solve problems. While all three philosophers appear to be out of step with postmodern thinking, they do provide useful and important ways by which ethical decision making can regain a place of importance in our culture.

▼ Benedict Spinoza

The Life

During the sixteenth century, to escape persecution, a group of Spanish and Portuguese Jews fled the Iberian Peninsula and settled in Amsterdam, Holland. Once in Holland they quickly established themselves as successful merchants and businessmen. Into this colony, about a century later, on November 24, 1632, Baruch de Spinoza was born. Baruch, which means "blessed" in Hebrew, was hailed by many as the next great Jewish scholar and rabbi.[1] Michael, his father, was a fairly well-to-do merchant and was highly respected by the local Jewish community.[2]

Baruch was a serious youth, preferring to spend time studying in the synagogue rather than helping in his father's business. However, in his study of the Talmud, the writings of rabbis, he discovered that he had more questions than the holy texts could answer. Nevertheless, it came as quite a surprise to his family, and to the whole Jewish community, when young Baruch announced his decision to leave his studies at the synagogue and pursue the study of Latin. Baruch hoped that the study of this language would be "a gateway to the intellectual world of his day."[3] The local Jewish community disapproved, of course, but anxiously watched to see what he would do next.

Baruch began studies under Franciscus Van den Ende, a well-known scholar of the time and a man with a wide variety of interests. He was a physician and something of a freethinker. Van den Ende's large library gave Spinoza the opportunity to read the works of some of the best thinkers of the day, especially those concerned with the new scientific speculation of the seventeenth century.[4]

Baruch's home life had been in turmoil for some time. His mother, sister, and half-brother had died, his other sister Rebecca had been given charge of the Spinoza household, and his father had just taken a third wife (Baruch's mother, Deborah, was his father's second wife). These unsettling events hampered Baruch somewhat in the pursuit of his studies, so when his father died, he moved in with Van den Ende and found that "life in the home of his Dutch master proved to be much more appealing."[5]

One of the things Spinoza found attractive about his new home was Van den Ende's daughter, Clara-Maria. There is some question as to how serious the relationship was, as Clara-Maria was only about 12 years old when Spinoza completed his studies with her father. Nevertheless, before Spinoza could fully consider the nature of his feelings for her and their possible future together, the fickle Clara-Maria lost interest in him when another student offered her a pearl necklace. This incident "definitely settled the issue for him in favor of the life of reason."[6]

During his studies, Spinoza read widely. He was apparently acquainted with the philosophies of Socrates, Plato, and Aristotle, as well as other ancient philosophers. But he particularly liked Descartes. Often called the father of modern philosophy, René Descartes, who was both a philosopher and a mathematician, believed that the key to knowledge of the universe lay in human reason, not in religious faith. This notion was gaining increased attention, primarily due to the accomplishments of Copernicus, Galileo, and Newton. Man was becoming much more aware of his physical world and how it operated. The work of these scientists was beginning to influence everyone, including young Spinoza.

As he delved deeply into Descartes's philosophy, Spinoza realized that the religious creed of his fathers was unable to answer all the questions he had. For example, Spinoza acknowledged that God is a body, but that the angels are "mere phantoms," and that there is no proof that the soul is immortal. Naturally, the Jewish community was shocked and outraged at these beliefs. The community tried for a while to get Spinoza to reaffirm his faith and to reject the heretical views of the scientific world. They reportedly offered him an annuity (perhaps 1,000 florins) if he would return to the fold. Spinoza refused, and on July 27, 1656, at the age of 24, he was excommunicated.

Spinoza did not seem particularly upset at being expelled from the Jewish fellowship. He knew his views were not popular among members of the Jewish community and he had not really expected them to accept those views. He changed his name from Baruch to Benedict (its Latin equivalent), took a room with friends, and set out to make a living.[7]

To support himself, Spinoza became a grinder of optical lenses. This vocation provided him with a modest living and allowed him time to study and write on a variety of subjects.[8] "The years that followed were quiet but fruitful ones. Spinoza worked at his trade by day and at his books in the evening, coming down occasionally for a pipe of tobacco smoked in the peace of the evening with his host and hostess."[9]

By all accounts, Spinoza's life was a simple one. He was not extravagant; he did not want much beyond what was required for his basic needs. Later "when offered a new gown by a distinguished guest who was surprised at the worn and rumpled one the philosopher was wearing, Spinoza replied that a man was none the better for wearing fine clothes."[10]

In 1673 he was offered the chair in philosophy at the University of Heidelberg, but declined the post for several reasons. One was that he was in poor health. He had inherited a tendency toward tuberculosis, a condition made worse by the glass dust he breathed while grinding lenses. Spinoza never married, preferring the life of a solitary thinker. He "stood head and shoulders above the men of his own day, seeing as no one else did the far-reaching implications of the new science of Copernicus, Galileo, and Newton, and the new philosophy of Descartes."[11]

"One Sunday afternoon in February, 1677, when the family with whom he lived was at church, Spinoza quietly passed away."[12] Only his physician was at his bedside. At his burial, many distinguished men stood in a steady winter rain to pay their respects. "He was in his own time condemned unreservedly as an atheist and enemy of religion. Yet by later critics his thought has been taken to be so fundamentally religious in spirit that he is described as 'God-intoxicated'."[13] Although his work shocked the orthodox and brought him much criticism during his life, history has treated Spinoza well. Many years after his death, a statue was erected in his honor at The Hague, capital of the Netherlands, and today he ranks among "the most influential men in the history of modern philosophy."[14]

The Philosophy

One of the central concepts on which this textbook is based is that an individual's philosophy and his or her life are not separate and unrelated but, rather, are parts of one larger whole. Sometimes the connection between a life and a philosophy is apparent, and sometimes the connection is not so obvious. However, "Spinoza's case is one of those in which the underlying principles of his philosophy are as apparent in the life he lived as in the pages of his great treatise on *Ethics*."[15]

Spinoza's *Ethics* is not an easy book to read and understand. For one thing, it is written in Latin and a reader must depend on an accurate translation. To complicate matters further, the book resembles a geometry text, with propositions, axioms, and proofs set out in detail. Many of these propositions, or theorems, as they are often called, are difficult to follow. Nevertheless, for our purposes here, this is not much of a problem. We are looking only for aspects of his ethical philosophy that will be useful in helping to make ethical decisions in the media workplace. For that, we need not go much beyond the basics of Spinoza's philosophy, and these basics are not difficult to grasp.

The key to Spinoza's ethical philosophy begins with an understanding of three fundamental aspects of life and nature. First, Spinoza has confidence "in the ability of reason, and reason alone, to supply us with accurate and dependable knowledge." Second, Spinoza firmly believes that "the universe itself is governed by rational law, that by the proper use of reason we comprehend an eternal, rational order in the nature of things." Finally, he is convinced "that reason is the one acceptable guide to living."[16]

Although he provides definitions for some basic ethical terms and concepts, Spinoza warns us that many of these "must be recognized as purely relative terms . . . [describing] our reaction to life, not to the enduring nature of things . . . it is our reaction that determines the quality of our experience."[17] Nevertheless, Spinoza gives us some useful definitions that will be important in developing our decision-making tool.

Good, Spinoza says, is "that which we certainly know to be useful to us."[18] We must be careful, however, in how we interpret the word *useful*. Spinoza does not consider the word to mean practical or helpful. *Useful*, to Spinoza, means the degree to which something approaches an ideal. So *good* must be an idea or action that stands up well when compared to the ideal of that idea or action. The ideal becomes the standard and our actions are *good*, that is, *useful*, to the degree that they meet this standard.

Evil, on the other hand, is "that which we certainly know hinders us from possessing anything that is good."[19] In other words, anything that makes it difficult for us to rise to the ideal, to work toward the standard, is evil. Take, for example, *honesty*. If we set the ideal for honesty as "always and completely living and telling the truth," then particular actions may be judged against that standard. If we tell a white lie, we are engaging in behavior that falls short of the standard and would, therefore, not be considered good, but such action might be considered a better *good* than a malicious lie, which would fall considerably short of the standard. Furthermore, if someone encouraged us to tell that white lie, or any other lie, that individual's actions would be deemed evil. Remember that Spinoza stipulates that these (and other) terms are relative, and they must be fully defined and realized in the mind and experience of the individual.

How does one go about doing all this thinking, this setting of the ideal? "Method, for Spinoza, consists in understanding the true idea, [the ideal] . . . and the only way to understand it is to have it and think about it."[20] Spinoza further cautions us to eliminate passion and emotion from the thinking process. "Most of us are in bondage to our passions and emotions," he says. Emotion is a confused idea, Spinoza believes. It derives from "a lack of clear understanding of the situation which confronts us. We feel strongly because we understand dimly."[21]

Spinoza advises us to develop our own code of morality, memorize it, and apply it in day-to-day situations.[22] Be ready to respond to this question: *Why did you do what you did?* Having adequate reasons for an action is of prime importance. It is clear, therefore, that Spinoza believes that "men who are governed by reason . . . will desire for themselves nothing which they do not also desire for the rest of mankind, and, consequently, are just, faithful, and honorable in their conduct."[23]

Spinoza took 12 years to complete the *Ethics*, finishing it in 1675. In looking back at the work, Spinoza remarked, "I do not claim to have found the best philosophy. But I know this—that I think it the true one." Yet Spinoza made no effort to publish the work, probably because of the uproar some of his previous work had created. "When he died, in 1677, the *Ethics* was still carefully locked in his writing desk."[24] However, several months later, some friends arranged for its publication. Spinoza never saw the *Ethics* in print nor did he know of its impact on philosophical thought.

▶ DECISION-MAKING TOOL

Use reason to determine the proper course of action. First, determine the *good*—that is, the ideal or standard against which the action may be judged. Then set aside emotion, think through the problem, and reach a just, faithful, and honorable conclusion. Be prepared to provide a rational answer to the question, "Why did you do what you did?"

▶ SUGGESTED MEDIA APPLICATION ◀

Spinoza's ethical theory, like some of the others you have studied, relies heavily on reason in making ethical decisions. You must use reason to develop your own personal moral code. This includes determining the good, or the ideal or standard against which you must judge any given action. You must avoid emotional responses and think through a problem. Above all, you should be able to provide a reasonable justification for your action.

All areas of media can make use of Spinoza's philosophy. One thinks first of journalism as an activity that needs an intellectual more than an emotional approach to its work. Television news, for example, often follows the "if it bleeds, it leads" philosophy. This sort of news programming may be seen as emotional in several respects: it is certainly designed to grab the viewer's emotions (and thus attention), and news editors who select this sort of story may be swayed more by its emotional than intellectual appeal.

RECOMMENDED CASE STUDIES

#11 (Chapter 13); #17 (Chapter 15).

p. 249   p. 300

▼ Immanuel Kant

The Life

Imagine never traveling more than 40 miles away from your hometown. In contemporary society, most people have journeyed at least that far from home before they are a year old. Historians agree that Immanuel Kant rarely left his hometown of Konigsberg, East Prussia, and that on the rare occasions when he did leave, he was never more than a few miles away.

Kant was born on April 22, 1724, to Johann Georg Kant, a harness maker, and his wife, Anna Regina, the daughter of a saddler. He was the fourth child in a family that would eventually have nine children; only five would survive childhood. Kant himself was a sickly, fragile child. The new arrival was given the biblical name Immanuel, which in the Hebrew means "God with us."

Immanuel Kant was a teacher, philosopher, and scholar. He produced most of his influential work late in life. *CORBIS–BETTMAN*

Kant had an older sister, two younger sisters, and a brother. He grew up in an environment of hard work and honesty.[25] His mother died when he was 13, but Kant well understood her contribution to his life. "I shall never forget my mother," he once said, "for she implanted and nurtured the first seed of the good in me."[26]

The Kant household was a strict one emphasizing the highest human qualities. Religion was an essential part of their everyday life. Recalling it years later, Kant observed that there was a joy, serenity, and inner peace there that was undisturbed by quarrels and anger, no matter what happened within or without.[27]

When he was eight years old, Kant was sent to the state secondary school where Pastor Franz Schultz, a family friend, was principal. He remained there for eight years studying Latin, theology, and a smattering of Greek and Hebrew. Although conditions at the school were severe, young Kant seemed to enjoy his studies. There were no vacations for the pupils, classes began at 7 A.M. (students were to be in their places by 6 A.M.), and the first half-hour of each day was devoted to prayer. Classes ended at 4 P.M. On Wednesday and Saturday, students had the opportunity to take elective classes in math, music, French, or Polish. Kant's poor health "hindered him in his studies, but quick-wittedness, good memory, and sheer diligence" helped him reach the head of his class; "he graduated second from the top."[28]

In the fall of 1740, Kant entered the University of Konigsberg, but records do not indicate his field of study. "Konigsberg was one of the most undistinguished of German universities," and its professors were likewise generally undistinguished men.[29] Nevertheless, the university was composed of four schools: theology, medicine, law, and philosophy. Philosophy was not highly respected as an area of study, so young Kant may have begun in medicine or theology. His interest turned to physics when he became acquainted with the work of Newton, but he lacked the background to advance very far in this field.

During his time at the university, Kant supported himself by tutoring. His father was not a rich man and had difficulty helping him financially. Kant often borrowed shoes and clothes from some of his more well-to-do classmates. He may have added to his income by winning at billiards and cards. He was apparently skilled at both.

Kant left the university in 1747 without completing requirements for his degree. He didn't go very far, however. He found employment as a tutor in three small, remote Prussian villages. Unwilling to waste time, Kant used his absence from the university to begin work on several manuscripts on a variety of scientific issues, particularly astronomy.

Finally, in April 1755, Kant submitted his dissertation to the university; it was "twelve calligraphically written pages, in Latin." It was never defended, but was accepted as admission to his final exams, which Kant took four weeks later. He passed, but was asked to submit a second dissertation before being awarded the *magister,* or doctor of philosophy, and being fully admitted to the academic fellowship. He prepared a second dissertation and defended its ideas in public, thereafter obtaining "the post of adjunct assistant professor, or member of the faculty whose salary was not paid by the state but by his students."[30] Thus began the 41-year teaching career of Immanuel Kant. It would be another 14 years before he would become a full professor.

To most outside observers, Kant's life was apparently trouble-free, perhaps even somewhat monotonous. However, his inner life, the life of the mind, was anything but monotonous. His thought "roamed continents, pushed beyond the confines of the earth, strove to the fartherest reaches of the universe . . . delved deeply into the human soul."[31] Kant was essentially a man who "felt all the influences of the eighteenth century. . . . He was an omnivorous reader, with all-round interests and an insatiable appetite for facts."[32] However, it would be a mistake to say that he was a recluse. He was educated, sociable, and possessed good manners.[33] He was something of a figure in Konigsberg society. He lived his life in a precise, crisp fashion. This precision did not go unnoticed. "The citizens of Konigsberg, so we are always told, used to set their clocks by him as he passed their windows on his daily walk."[34] He never married nor held public office. He devoted his life to philosophy, to his students, and to the university.

During his years at the university, Kant carried a heavy teaching load. A typical teaching day might run thus: 8–9 A.M., logic; 9–10, mechanics; 10–11, theoretical physics; 11–12, metaphysics. After the midday meal, 2–3, physical geography, and 3–4, mechanics. It was an exhausting schedule. He had little time or energy left for writing, but he was making a decent enough living to pay his bills and hire a servant.[35]

Although he remarked at one time, "Every day I sit behind the anvil of my lectern and hammer my way through my lectures that are very much alike," Kant nevertheless became an excellent teacher. He used notes but did not use a text and "regurgitate or systematize material; he used it to incite controversy." His lectures became dialogues. He required students to participate, to explain "the heart of the matter" under discussion.[36] His lectures were well attended and he quickly became a distinguished man at the university. "He disliked it when his pupils took notes. It disturbed him when he noticed that important points were neglected and unimportant ones carefully written down." He constantly urged his students to think for themselves, to inquire, and to stand on their own feet.[37]

Years passed. His publications were scattered; long periods would pass with nothing being published, then something would suddenly appear. Although his health was never good, he adopted a strict program of personal discipline, which helped him meet all his commitments. He arose at a quarter to five. Between five and six he drank tea, smoked a pipe of tobacco, and planned his day. He then devoted an hour to preparing his lectures for the day. He had classes until noon, then he had lunch. He often invited three or four friends to eat with him, and sometimes a student or two. There were more lectures in the afternoon, followed by dinner and his regular walk. He read until ten o'clock and then went to bed.[38]

In November 1801, Kant retired from the university at full salary. During his retirement, he "rarely left his house and received no visitors. Very few were given leave to call upon him."[39] Soon, his health began to fail. It wasn't long before he "could not walk without a supporting hand. Someone had to be in attendance at all times. . . . Now and then Kant sat down at his desk. He traced broken sentences in a shaky hand." By December 1803, he was unable to read, was almost deaf, and had stopped eating. "He no longer recognized his sister."[40]

On February 12, 1804, with only a friend at his bedside, Kant died. Although he had made arrangements for his burial years before (he wanted to be buried on the third day after his death in an ordinary cemetery with only a few friends present), such was not to be. He was laid out for 16 days so that the city could pay its respects. "A great host of people 'of the highest and lowest condition' streamed in to see . . . many came back two and even three times."[41] Twenty-four students carried him to his grave, followed by thousands of mourners. Kant was buried in the professors' crypt in the north wall of the cathedral at Konigsberg.

Immanuel Kant "did not seek fame, he did not gain power; neither in living, nor loving, did he encounter turbulence . . . but very early there developed in him one life interest which extinguished everything else: philosophy. To this interest he yielded his whole being. For him, life was work; in work he found joy and meaning. Kant's life is an example of fusion of word and deed, of instruction and action."[42]

The Philosophy

If Kant had died before 1781, he might have been nothing more than just another little known eighteenth-century German professor.[43] But in that year he published his *Critique of Pure Reason,* a work that would significantly influence Western philosophical thought. Kant highly valued intellectual and moral integrity, and he lived a life that exhibited both.[44] The direction of Kant's philosophical interests are contained in the following passage from the *Critique:* "Two things fill the mind with ever new and increasing admiration and awe . . . the starry heavens above and the moral law within" (5:161).

As was the case for many of the philosophers of his day, Kant was troubled by the thinking that arose in the new science, the science of Galileo, Newton, and Descartes, among others. "They viewed the universe as an enormous machine governed inexorably by precise physical laws that can be discovered by observation and experiment and that ultimately are mathematical in nature."[45] Kant had no desire to oppose this new science, but was troubled by the worldview it suggested. Under such a system, freedom and responsibility disappear (the world operating only under deterministic physical laws), and once freedom and responsibility disappear, so does morality. Therefore, Kant set about developing a system of morality that would enable one to function in a world that was becoming increasingly impersonal.

Kant's ethical system is based on what he called the *categorical imperative.* Even those who are not students of philosophy have likely become acquainted with this principle. It is simply stated: "Act as if the maxim of your action were to become through your will a universal law of nature" (*Groundwork of the Metaphysics of Morals,* 4:421/89). Through the years this principle has yielded to many paraphrases, most of them accurately capturing the key idea. However, before rushing to apply this principle, one should understand the thinking on which it is based. Having such an understanding will help in correctly applying the principle.

Begin with some fundamental assumptions. Kant believed, first and foremost, that humans have the *ability to reason.* Second, he held that we are *moral agents*—that is, we are able to act on our own thinking. This power Kant called *pure practical reason.*[46] Kant stressed that morality cannot be grounded in a system emphasizing "what is pleasurable and what is painful . . . its principle must come from pure reason within instead."[47]

Before acting on the categorical imperative, one needs to consider other factors in the thinking, or reasoning, process that precedes an action. First, "what moral reason commands must always be within our power to do so."[48] This is the well-known *ought-implies-can* concept. We ought not to be required to do something that is not within our power to do. Next, we are charged to consider *prudence*, which Kant defines as "taking care of our own interests." We must do this to survive, to lead a quality life, but these interests are based in personal wisdom, and not in an uncontrolled pursuit of pleasure. We are further urged to consider our basic moral obligations to others. We have a duty to promote virtue and good health in others, and to respect their dignity. Only when we have reasoned through these issues can we then think about acting.

Let's consider an example, a maxim offered by Kant himself:

m: "Whenever I believe myself short of money, I will borrow money and promise to pay it back, though I know I will never, in fact, repay it."[49]

We should note that a *maxim* "is a personal or subjective plan of action . . . it is general . . . like a private rule."[50] To test a maxim for moral permissibility, ask: "How would things stand if my maxim became a universal law?" For the example here, Kant's answer is that "promising" would be impossible "since no one would believe that he was promised anything, but would laugh at all utterances of this kind as empty shams."[51]

Consider a second example:

m: "Always be a parasite, living off of someone else."

This maxim fails to meet the test of logic, because if generalized, all people would live like parasites, "then off of whom would they live?"[52] Some people could be parasites, but not all. This maxim fails other tests, too. It fails to treat others with dignity; it uses people as a *means* and not an *end*. Kant cautions us that there is a distinct difference between people and things. *Things* are only relatively good, and have no unique, absolute, or intrinsic worth. *People*, on the other hand, are unique, worthy individuals, having been created by God. The maxim also fails the test of prudence. Although it might enable us to survive, the maxim does not promote a quality life. Kant's goal was to find a set of maxims, or moral absolutes, that would result in "a completely irrefutable system of ethics . . . and obeying the rules of this system would be what is moral."[53]

Immanuel Kant provided convincing proof that the "life and work of a philosopher cannot be unraveled into separate strands."[54]

▶ *DECISION-MAKING TOOL*

Considering your responsibility to self and others, act only on those principles that you would have generalized to all. Ask these questions: "What is the rule authorizing this action I am about to take?" "Can it become a universal law for all people to follow?"

▶ *SUGGESTED MEDIA APPLICATION* ◀

Kant's categorical imperative is easy to recall and easy to use in solving ethical dilemmas. However, you should be extremely careful in the application of Kant's ideas. Do not take his ideas lightly. It is very easy to say that you are taking such-and-such an action as a solution to an ethical problem and that you wouldn't mind if everyone acted in a similar fashion. But Kant was essentially a *consequentialist*. That is, he believed that actions have consequences and that if you undertake an action, you should be willing to have others undertake the same action and that you must accept the same consequences. For example, if you are a public relations practitioner and you twist the truth to benefit your client, the implications are larger than simply allowing other practitioners to do the same. You should place yourself on the receiving end of the information, that is, imagine yourself as the individual who is being given a half-truth. Do you approve of others failing to disclose the complete truth to you? Do you like others telling you the whole truth? Essentially, then, if you decide to use Kant's categorical imperative to solve ethical problems, you must give considerable thought to all sides of the issue and apply the principle not just from one point of view but from all points of view.

The categorical imperative can be applied to other media, too. For example, if you are a journalist and are in hot pursuit of a story to the extent that you are infringing on an individual's privacy, you must be willing to have a journalist pursue you with the same vigor and with the same pressure on your privacy. If you are not willing to be the object of your actions, you should not apply Kant's principle.

RECOMMENDED CASE STUDIES

#5 (Chapter 11); #10 (Chapter 13).

▼ John Stuart Mill

The Life

There have been few more miserable childhoods than that of John Stuart Mill. "The story is a strange one; and were it not so well substantiated, doubts as to its accuracy would be legitimate." Understanding why and how Mill suffered through what might be called a mutilated childhood requires that we give some attention to his parents.[55]

James Mill, John Stuart's father, was an intelligent, well-educated man. The elder Mill worked as a tutor and studied for a while at the university before embarking on a literary career in London. He soon met and married Harriet Burrow, whose mother ran an asylum for lunatics in London. They settled in Pentonville, a London suburb. Harriet was 10 years younger than James, and "though loving, kind, and practical, was totally lacking in brains."[56] She soon found that James was not perfect either. She thought him "too absorbed in his philosophical and literary pursuits properly to discharge the duties of domestic life."[57] James, for his part, did not hide the contempt he held for his wife; she was not his intellectual equal and apparently had difficulty carrying on an intelligent conversation, particularly on topics of interest to James.[58]

John Stuart was born into this unhappy family on May 20, 1806, and his nightmare childhood began almost immediately. "From infancy, he was subjected to a carefully prepared and rigorous curriculum, every detail of which was predetermined, and the goal as carefully defined." Before he was old enough to object, his father forced him to suppress all feeling and emotion and to feed only his intellect.[59] In his *Autobiography*, Mill tells us that he was able to read at the age of two; by age three, he had begun a study of Greek; by the time he was seven, he had read much of the ancient Greek and Roman literature; at age eight he knew the first six *Dialogues* of Plato.

As if that weren't enough, he was also required, by his tenth birthday, to master English history and literature, as well as philosophy. His father was still not satisfied with his effort and so assigned him additional work.[60] Students in today's elementary and secondary schools (and most colleges and universities) would be horrified were they to be given such a program of study. At a time when many feel that little is expected of today's student, it seems incredible that Mill could survive such rigorous training. But he survived—and took on more. Before he was 13, he had tackled differential calculus, geometry, algebra, logic, and Latin. Yet the elder Mill was not done. He forced his son to begin instructing the younger Mill children, some of whom were barely out of diapers. He was not allowed to have friends his own age. Strangely enough, John Stuart was not terribly unhappy during these years. He was a strong boy and was totally obedient to his father. A trip to France at age 15 brought him a little relief, but even there he added zoology, chemistry, botany, and metaphysics to his study curriculum. He did, however, have time to enjoy the warmth of French life, particularly music and dancing.[61]

He customarily took long walks with his father during which the elder Mill reviewed the day's lessons and introduced new material. John Stuart was expected to reproduce the substance of these discussions in manuscript form the next day. Dinner for John and the other children was often delayed because one mistake was made in their lessons.[62] Later, Mill wrote of these experiences: "Most boys or youths who have had much knowledge drilled into them, have their mental capacities not strengthened. . . . They are crammed with mere facts, and with the opinions or phrases of other people, and these are accepted as a substitute for the power to form opinions of their own. . . . Mine, however, was not an education of cram. My father never permitted anything which I learnt to degenerate into a mere exercise of memory" (*Autobiography*, 21–22).

Mill's outlook on life changed when he discovered utilitarianism—a philosophy first outlined by Jeremy Bentham. Like his father, young Mill joined the Utilitarian Society and began to vigorously promote the concept of the greatest good for the greatest number.

Mill was now on the verge of having this rather disciplined intellectual life disrupted. Two events signaled major change. In 1826, he began to doubt the strength of his beliefs.[63] His trust in the power of reason and in his sense of accomplishment wavered, and he fell into deep depression. Throughout his life thus far, he had always emphasized reason and the power of the mind to accumulate, process, and use information. But now he was reaching a point where he was perhaps thinking too much. He worried about all sorts of things over which neither he nor anyone else had any control. For example, he was quite concerned about "the possible exhaustibility of musical combinations."[64] He was depressed, exhausted, and devoid of emotion, and he had no one he could turn to for advice. Seen from a contemporary perspective, it appears that Mill was having a nervous breakdown.

Gradually, his condition improved. He read the poetry of William Wordsworth, and his outlook brightened. Once, he burst into tears as "he was reading a pathetic French story." This sudden gush of emotion revived his spirits somewhat.[65]

The second major event to change Mill profoundly was his relationship with a woman, a woman who was married to someone else. He became acquainted with Harriet Taylor in 1830. She was, at that time, the wife of a London merchant. She thought Mill intellectually superior and socially more adept than her husband. In turn, he was stunned by her beauty and quick wit. They were drawn to each other, and their friendship blossomed.[66] The Taylors were soon separated and Mill began spending more and more time with Harriet. Meanwhile, James, his father, expressed disapproval of his son's dalliance with another man's wife. Mill readily admitted that his relationship with Mrs. Taylor was likely to be misunderstood, but he was emphatic that their connection was based solely on affection and the confidential nature of their private conversations.[67] John Taylor died in 1849. Mill and Harriet, close friends for twenty-one years, were married two years later. The marriage was to last only seven years—Harriet died in 1858. Nevertheless, the couple was happy. Mill firmly believed that his wife was brilliant and that if she had been given the chance, "would have become eminent among the rulers of mankind."[68]

Mill busied himself by pushing hard for political, economic, and social reform in England. He became friends with the author Thomas Carlyle and continued to follow the philosophy of Jeremy Bentham. He wrote a series of essays on some fundamental issues, including justice, utility, liberty, and religious belief. He served for a time in Parliament before retiring to Avignon in 1868, where he continued to write and publish.

John Stuart Mill died of a fever on May 8, 1873. Ironically, "three days before his death he had taken one of those extremely long and arduous country walks which—like his father—he so much enjoyed."[69]

The Philosophy

Most philosophers are inclined, even anxious, to develop and promote their own ethical theories. This was not the case with John Stuart Mill. He did not originate a theory but promoted an existing philosophy—*utilitarianism.* But "Mill was also much more than a philosopher. He was a radical reformer in political and social life," and his work had practical implications.[70]

By the age of 15, Mill was well acquainted with utilitarianism. It was his father's ethical system and also the ethical system of his father's friend, Jeremy Bentham. Even at this early stage in his life, Mill thought that the greatest happiness principle represented the dawn of a new era of thought.[71] It is easy to see why utilitarianism became one of nineteenth-century England's most popular ethical philosophies. People were attracted to the simplicity of its message: that pleasure and happiness are what everyone desires and has the right to obtain.[72] Yet, as he grew older, Mill developed his own insights into the theory, fitting it to his own moral beliefs.

Mill's version of utilitarianism differed somewhat from Bentham's. Bentham considered all pleasures equal. Mill did not. Mill firmly believed that "it requires a moral sense to determine what pleasures are high and what are low."[73] Moral behavior must come from within each individual. We must seek higher pleasures than those of mere sensation.[74]

Mill gives us an example. "Few human creatures would consent to be changed into any of the lower animals, for a promise of the fullest allowance of the beast's pleasures; no intelligent human being would consent to be a fool, no instructed person would be an ignoramus, no person of feeling or conscience would be selfish or base, even though they should be persuaded that the fool, the dunce, or the rascal is better satisfied with his lot than they are with theirs." In other words, "they would not resign what they possess . . . for the most complete satisfaction." Mill draws this distinction even more sharply. "It is," he says, "better to be a human being dissatisfied than a pig satisfied."[75]

The point Mill is making is that "human happiness is not an open concept in the sense that it consists of pleasures completely unspecified."[76] Human happiness has particular qualities: well-being, independence, freedom, excitement, security, justice, individual rights, and dignity, among others. We are required to make a rational decision about what constitutes happiness. We should not submit ourselves to totally hedonistic desires; however, understanding what gives us pleasure and happiness is important as we submit issues for rational examination.

Utilitarians are generally thought to apportion themselves into two camps: *act utilitarians* and *rule utilitarians.* "The act utilitarian judges each and every individual act by the greatest happiness principle," whereas the rule utilitarian "judges the particular action by the moral rule which it falls under and he judges the moral worth of the rule by the greatest happiness principle."[77] This distinction can be important, but it is not necessarily crucial for using utilitarianism to solve an ethical problem. Mill's modification of the original Bentham idea yields yet another variation: *philosophical utilitarianism,* the belief that "the good, or well-being, of individuals is the only ethical good."[78]

Mill did a lot of thinking about how to apply Bentham's basic ideas properly. "His influence on his generation was enormous and if advocates of democracy, political economists, sociologists, and moralists of today, see farther than their fathers, it is because they stand on the shoulders of John Stuart Mill."[79]

► *DECISION-MAKING TOOL*   utilitarianism

Act by following the moral rule that will bring about the greatest good, or happiness, for the greatest number.

► *SUGGESTED MEDIA APPLICATION* ◄

Mill's utilitarianism, like Kant's categorical imperative, is easily recalled and easily applied. However, you should not apply utilitarianism to an ethical problem unless you are confident you have sure and certain knowledge about what would be best for the greatest number of people. At the very least, you should have a firm grasp of what good is and how it might be served by your solution. Too, what evidence do you have that this action would promote the good for the greater number of people? Do journalists do their jobs for the greater good, or for the financial good of the few who own stock in their newspapers or radio or television stations? Do advertisers disseminate product information designed to promote the greater good, or just their own interests? Seen as a larger question, to what degree do we sacrifice our personal and institutional goals for the benefit of the larger number of people? This tool must be carefully applied with a view toward the possible consequences.

RECOMMENDED CASE STUDIES

#2 (Chapter 11); #14 (Chapter 14).
p. 190   p. 275

QUESTIONS FOR DISCUSSION

1. In what ways are the underlying principles of Spinoza's philosophy evident in his life?

2. Why does Spinoza suggest that one eliminate emotion in making ethical decisions?

3. Reason plays an important part in the philosophies of both Spinoza and Kant. Explain how each uses reason as a foundation for ethical decision making.

4. Is there a conflict between Kant's categorical imperative and the philosophical notion that *ought implies can?* Explain.

5. What aspects of the life of John Stuart Mill might have led him to embrace wholeheartedly utilitarianism?

6. What is the difference between act and rule utilitarianism? Which seems more practical in a postmodern culture?

ENDNOTES

1. R. H. M. Elwes, trans., *Ethics* by Benedict de Spinoza (Buffalo, NY: Prometheus Books, 1989), v.

2. Robert F. Davidson, *Philosophies Men Live By* (New York: Dryden Press, 1952), 139.

3. Ibid.

4. Ibid.

5. Edwin Curely, ed. and trans., *A Spinoza Reader: The Ethics and Other Works by Benedict de Spinoza* (Princeton, NJ: Princeton University Press, 1994), x; Davidson, 140.

6. Davidson, 140.

7. Ibid., 141.

8. Elwes, v.

9. Davidson, 141.

10. Ibid., 142.

11. Ibid.

12. Ibid., 148.

13. Ibid., 138.

14. Ibid., 148.

15. Ibid., 139.

16. Ibid., 159.

17. Ibid., 160.

18. Thomas Carson Mark, *Spinoza's Theory of Truth* (New York: Columbia University Press, 1972), 101.

19. Ibid., 102.

20. Ibid., 40.

21. Davidson, 161.

22. Ibid., 162.

23. Ibid.

24. Ibid., 145.

25. Arsenij Gulyga, *Immanuel Kant, His Life and Thought*, trans. Marijan Despalatovia (Boston: Birkhauser, 1987), 9.

26. Ernst Cassirer, *Kant's Life and Thought*, trans. James Haden (New Haven, CT: Yale University Press, 1981), 13.

27. A. D. Lindsay, *Kant* (Westport, CT: Greenwood Press, 1970), 2.

28. Gulyga, 10.

29. Lindsay, 3.

30. Gulyga, 23.

31. Ibid., ix–x.

32. Lindsay, 6.

33. Gulyga, x.

34. Anthony Kenny, "Descartes to Kant," in *The Oxford History of Western Philosophy*, ed. Anthony Kenny (Oxford: Oxford University Press, 1994), 166.

35. Gulyga, 24.

36. Ibid., 79.

37. Lindsay, 7 and 8.

38. Ibid., 9.

39. Gulyga, 254.

40. Ibid., 255 and 256.

41. Cassirer, 414.

42. Gulyga, ix–x.

43. Roger J. Sullivan, *Immanuel Kant's Moral Theory* (New York: Cambridge University Press, 1989), 1.

44. Ibid., 2.

45. Ibid., 11.

46. Ibid., 78.

47. Paul Guyer, "Introduction," in *The Cambridge Companion to Kant*, ed. Paul Guyer (Cambridge: Cambridge University Press, 1992), 11.

48. Sullivan, 66.

49. Bruce Aune, *Kant's Theory of Morals* (Princeton, NJ: Princeton University Press, 1979), 53.

50. J. B. Schneewind, "Autonomy, Obligation, and Virtue: An Overview of Kant's Moral Philosophy," *The Cambridge Companion to Kant*, ed. Paul Guyer (Cambridge: Cambridge University Press, 1992), 318–319.

51. Aune, 53.

52. Jacques P. Thiroux, *Ethics: Theory and Practice* (Encino, CA: Glencoe, 1980), 60.

53. Ibid.

54. Gulyga, ix.

55. Samuel Parkes Cadman, *Charles Darwin and Other English Thinkers* (Freeport: NY: Books for Libraries Press, 1971), 95 and 102.

56. Josephine Kamm, *John Stuart Mill in Love* (London: Gordon & Cremonesi, 1977), 12.

57. Cadman, 94.

58. Kamm, 12.

59. Cadman, 94 and 95.

60. Ibid., 96.

61. Ibid., 97 and 100.

62. Kamm, 14.

63. Cadman, 101.

64. Cadman, 102.

65. Karl Britton, *John Stuart Mill* (New York: Dover, 1969), 19.

66. Ibid., 24.

67. Ibid., 25.

68. Ibid.

69. Ibid., 44.

70. Ibid., 8–9.

71. Ibid., 45.

72. Samuel Enoch Stumpf, *Philosophy: History and Problems* (New York: McGraw-Hill, 1989), 362.

73. Cadman, 111.

74. Ethel C. Albert, Theodore C. Denise, and Sheldon P. Peterfreund, *Great Traditions in Ethics* (New York: Van Nostrand, 1975), 231 and 235.

75. Ibid., 236 and 237.

76. Fred R. Berger, *Happiness, Justice, and Freedom* (Berkeley: University of California Press, 1984), 39.

77. H. Gene Blocker, *Ethics, An Introduction* (New York: Haven, 1986), 283.

78. John Skorupski, *John Stuart Mill* (New York: Routledge, 1989), 16.

79. Cadman, 139.

▼▼▼

CHAPTER 7

The Continental Connection

In this chapter you will meet two men who had unusual and precise ways of thinking and whose work is highly respected by philosophers today. One, Schopenhauer, felt that ethical behavior ought not be prescriptive and that there is not much we can do to change our basic nature, which, he believed, is controlled by the will. Yet he also believed that individuals are nevertheless responsible for their actions. Schopenhauer's ideas regarding balance, experience, and respect for others provide us with a useful ethical decision-making tool. Durkheim, the other, believed that individual control of one's behavior was possible and that society should set behavioral norms. All action, then, should be taken with a view toward how it is suggested by and how it ultimately benefits the social structure.

Culture Period ▪ Approximate Dates	General Description ▪ Key Personalities
Enlightenment A.D. 1650–A.D. 1850	The awakening of the human spirit and mind; emphasis on reason; rise of science as an influence on life and thinking; major contributions in art, music, philosophy, religion; political and social turmoil in Europe; Louis XIV, Louis XVI and Marie Antoinette, Handel, Haydn, Mozart, Bach, Beethoven, Wordsworth, Byron, Keats, Emerson, Napoleon, Darwin, Newton
Arthur Schopenhauer (1788 . . .)	
Note: In America, the colonies continued to grow and develop following the establishment of the Virginia Charter in 1606 and the founding of the New England colonies around 1620. Declaration of Independence was signed in 1776.	
Modern age A.D. 1850–A.D. 1945	Industrial Revolution takes hold; steel developed; much political and social change in America (Civil War) and in Europe (World Wars I and II); significant contributions in art, music, literature, science; Pasteur, Einstein, Wright Brothers, Hugo, Marx, Freud, Picasso, Hitler, Stalin
Emile Durkheim (1858–1917)	
Arthur Schopenhauer (. . . 1860)	

Although Schopenhauer was born during the Enlightenment and Durkheim was born after the period presumably ended (see the time line),

87

they are as much transitional philosophers as they are representatives of any particular culture period. Durkheim's philosophy, for example, is closer to Voltaire's than it is to the highly individualistic philosophers of the modern period. Schopenhauer, on the other hand, tends to be individualistic but doesn't believe that the individual has much power. In addition to providing you with two useful decision-making tools, these two philosophers will help ease you into the modern period.

▼ Arthur Schopenhauer

The Life

Heinrich Schopenhauer, a successful Danzig merchant, loved to travel. One of his journeys around Europe took him to England. He discovered that he greatly admired the English lifestyle and wanted his first child to be of English nationality. When his pregnant wife, Johanna, was close to her due date, he took her to England to await the birth of what he hoped would be a son. He waited. The days grew dark and gloomy as the English winter fog settled in. Still, he waited. The child was not necessarily beyond its due date, but it was beyond Heinrich's patience to wait any longer. He dragged his highly pregnant wife back to Danzig where, on February 22, 1788, Arthur was born.[1]

Like some of the other philosophers in this text, Arthur was not born into a happy family. Heinrich, his father, was an enlightened man and a successful merchant.[2] Johanna, his mother, was from an influential family. Heinrich was passionate and exacting, but Johanna was brittle, socially oriented, and devoid of true feeling.[3] Although they shared some of the same interests, this may not have been a very good match. Nevertheless, both parents welcomed Arthur to the family.

At the age of five, the Schopenhauers were forced to flee Danzig when Prussian troops invaded. They settled in Hamburg. Once his education got underway, there was some disagreement as to its direction. Heinrich thought his son should be trained in commerce, and, as we say today, "follow in his father's footsteps." Too, the elder Schopenhauer did not have much respect for traditional schooling.[4] Arthur was not convinced that he wanted a career in commerce, but he accepted his father's plan for his life. At age nine, Arthur was placed with a French tutor and acquired a thorough knowledge of the language during his two years of study. He was briefly enrolled in a school in Wimbledon, England, but it was operated by a clergyman, and Arthur chafed under the strict, devout lifestyle expected of the pupils.[5]

By age 16, Arthur was already troubled by much of what he had seen of the world. For example, in his travels with his parents, young Arthur was particularly struck by the squalid living conditions of the poor. This gave him something of a bleak outlook on life, an outlook that was further worsened by the sudden death of his father.[6]

Arthur Schopenhauer was a precise thinker. He felt worldly influences tend to corrupt the individual and that extra effort is required to combat these influences. *CORBIS–BETTMAN*

The elder Schopenhauer was found one day in a canal, having fallen (or jumped) from the upper level of a grain storage warehouse. Some thought the death a suicide; Heinrich was growing progressively deaf and becoming increasingly irritable.[7] The family did not publicly acknowledge that it could have been suicide. Johanna's official notice of her husband's death called it an "unfortunate accident." Arthur referred to it as "a sudden accidental and bloody death."[8] It was clear, however, that Heinrich would have had no apparent reason to visit the building from which he had fallen.

Regardless of the circumstances, his father's death profoundly affected young Arthur. He had been fairly close to his father even though the two had disagreed more than a few times about the nature of Arthur's education and career. Nevertheless, out of respect for his father, he continued to work for two more years in the family business in Hamburg.[9]

By 1807, he felt his obligation to his father had been discharged. He resigned from the business, enrolled in a school in Gotha, and began to study Greek and Latin. He didn't last long at Gotha; he antagonized one of the masters and transferred to Weimar, living and studying with Franz Passow, a classical philologist of some note. This was a convenient arrangement, for his mother had moved to the same town a short time before, and he was able to visit her. His education under Passow progressed nicely, but his relationship with his mother grew more troublesome. They quarreled about almost everything.[10]

When Arthur became 21, he received his share of his father's estate. Now financially independent, he entered the University of Gottingen as a medical student, but turned to philosophy in his second year. He was especially interested in Plato and Kant. Arthur was to make few friends at the university. He quarreled with his professors, feeling that he already had the answers to most philosophical questions. Having already made up his mind, he was not open to the ideas and solutions of his instructors, a position that gained him the reputation of being overbearing and arrogant.[11]

His university education ended in 1813, when the war in Europe began to spread. Schopenhauer hated military action of any kind; he liked France, but cared little for Napoleon. He disliked Prussia for having invaded his hometown of Danzig years earlier. He fled to a small town south of Weimar and worked on his doctoral thesis. The finished thesis, *On the Fourfold Root of the Principle of Sufficient Reason,* was submitted to the University of Jena, and Schopenhauer received his doctorate. The thesis was published in book form, but did not attract much public notice. By 1814, he was in Dresden, busy on his chief work, *The World as Will and Idea.*

In 1820, Schopenhauer became a lecturer in philosophy at the University of Berlin. Also on the faculty at the time was Georg Hegel, who was at the height of his popularity. Schopenhauer opposed Hegel's ideas, which he considered obscure and ambivalent, particularly with regard to the role of reason and religion in philosophy.[12] In an attempt to counteract Hegel's influence, Schopenhauer scheduled his lectures at the same time as those of Hegel. It was a popularity contest he was destined to lose. More than two hundred students swarmed into Hegel's lectures; only five signed on with Schopenhauer.[13] His course collapsed for lack of attendance, and he withdrew into himself, becoming increasingly bitter about Hegel and the way his own philosophical ideas were being ignored. He stayed on at the university for two more years hoping to draw attention to his ideas, but he failed. His career as a university teacher was at an end. He was not troubled financially; he still had his share of his father's estate and could live comfortably for the rest of his life.[14]

Schopenhauer valued the qualities of character and temperament but acknowledged that he himself did not possess these qualities to any great degree. For example, he disliked women, yet sought them out for brief affairs from time to time. He never married, but thought about it some. Shortly after his resignation from the University of Berlin, Schopenhauer was sued by a seamstress. Schopenhauer hated to be disturbed. Apparently, the woman in question had irritated him by talking loudly outside his room. He lost his temper and shoved her down the stairs. She sued. The fall injured her arm (she alleged), preventing her from earning a living.[15] In her complaint, the woman charged that Schopenhauer had "torn her cap, kicked and beaten her, and left on her person the marks of his violence."[16] Schopenhauer, acting as his own lawyer, admitted that he had called her an offensive name, but that otherwise he was only defending "his rights as a lodger."[17] The court took more than a year to render its verdict: Schopenhauer was ordered to pay most of the court costs and to provide the woman with a regular stipend.[18] This decision angered Schopenhauer, but he complied. Little wonder years later when the old woman died that Schopenhauer inscribed these words on her death certificate: "The old woman dies, the burden departs."[19]

Schopenhauer always lived alone, but he was not opposed to conversation with sympathetic companions. He was apparently an entertaining and animated talker. He was well dressed, and his rooms were simple, neat, and clean.[20] He kept a statue of Buddha on a stand in the corner and a bust of Kant on his writing desk. He enjoyed good food and good wines, traveled some, and read widely. There is considerable evidence that he took his reading seriously. The Schopenhauer archive in Frankfurt reveals that "it was his custom to make marginal notes, often extensive, in the same language as the book he was reading. These notes . . . are sometimes written with such vehemence that the pencil has almost pierced the paper."[21] He could do this for almost any book he was reading, as he was fluent in Latin, Greek, French, English, German, Italian, and Spanish.

His daily routine showed Kant's influence on his life. His schedule was similar to Kant's but tailored to meet his own particular needs. He would get up early, take a cold bath, and drink a cup of coffee. He would write until noon, play the flute for 30 minutes, then dress in a tailcoat and white tie and go out to lunch. After lunch, he read until four o'clock, followed by a two-hour walk and a visit to the theater or to a concert. He ate a light, cold supper and was in bed by ten o'clock.[22]

By 1860, Schopenhauer began to tire easily, and he suffered shortness of breath, curtailing his walks to some extent. On the evening of September 18, he complained to a friend that his heart wasn't beating properly.[23] On September 21, "he had risen as usual, and sat down to breakfast. A few minutes after the maid had left, his doctor entered and found him lying back dead in the corner of the sofa, his countenance calm, as if his end had been swift and painless."[24] A simple service and burial followed shortly thereafter. His flat, granite tombstone bears only two words: Arthur Schopenhauer.

The Philosophy

For most of his life, Arthur Schopenhauer was a difficult man. He argued with his parents, his teachers, his university colleagues, his neighbors, and with the courts. By middle age, he had become a cynical, bitter, old curmudgeon—the great pessimist, he was called.[25] Nevertheless, he was extremely well educated, a profound thinker, and a clear, concise writer. An important philosopher, his work includes substantial contributions to a theory of knowledge, metaphysics, aesthetics, and ethics.[26] His ethical theory is one of the most difficult in this text. It requires an open mind, one that can grasp original, sometimes startling, ideas and follow the development of those ideas through precise philosophical reasoning.

Schopenhauer's ethical theory has as its fundamental base three concepts: the will, character, and pleasure (or happiness). The most important of these is the *will*. He provides a useful definition of the concept in *On the Freedom of the Human Will:* the will is "all desiring, striving, wishing, demanding, longing, hoping, loving, rejoicing, jubilation . . . all abhorring, fleeing, fearing, being angry, hating, mourning, suffering pains—in short all emotions and passions."[27] Essentially, the will is the unique controlling force inside each individual. *Character*, too, is individual, though differences among persons may be very subtle, and it underlies the regularities in our behavior. Character is dependent on the particular quality of the will and the degree to which we can control our responses to the world.[28]

Schopenhauer believes that the will is not free and that, for the most part, character cannot be changed. What are we to do, then, in terms of modifying our behavior to conform to some sort of ethical standard? If everything is determined for us, what control have we over anything we think or do? Here is where Schopenhauer begins to draw some razor-sharp philosophical distinctions. He feels that because the will is not free, ethics "cannot be conceived as a prescriptive discipline . . . that is, as a plan or map of what one 'ought' to do."[29] Nevertheless, he continues, people are responsible for their actions.

On the issue of *pleasure, or happiness*—the terms are often used interchangeably by Schopenhauer—we have a clear philosophical position. Pleasure is actually a negative concept. As Schopenhauer says, "Pleasure is only the negation of pain, and that pain is the positive element in life."[30] This does not mean that pain is positive in the sense of being good or desirable, but positive in the sense of being the typical state of things; pleasure, because it occurs rarely, is the atypical state of things, and therefore negative.

Obviously, these concepts present difficulties for someone trying to develop a useful ethical theory. However, Schopenhauer himself shows us how it may be done. Morality, he says, follows from three other concepts: experience, balance, and respect for others.

Take *experience* first. We are required to use experience to help us make decisions.[31] Second, we should seek *balance* in all we do. Schopenhauer was an admirer of Aristotle's philosophy, so it is little wonder that he feels balance—something similar to Aristotle's Golden Mean—is an important aspect of moral behavior. The will may lead us to extremes; after all, it is composed mostly of our passions and emotions. How easy it is to let those control us! How difficult it is to control, or balance, the will! Difficult, but necessary, Schopenhauer argues.

The third moral quality is *respect for others*. Although Schopenhauer did not possess this quality in his own life, he clearly recognized its importance in the world. Respecting others includes not doing them harm, helping where possible, and tolerating views and practices different from one's own. Remember that others, too, are only following their respective wills. In striving to use experience, develop balance, and respect others, Schopenhauer believes we will come face-to-face with the three fundamental incentives of human action: *egoism, malice,* and *compassion.* We must rise above our self-interest, eschew malice, and show compassion. This, for him, is the fundamental basis for ethics.[32]

Even if one intellectually grasps these concepts and sees how they interact to promote ethical behavior, it might not be perfectly clear how it all works in the real world. Schopenhauer understands this, so he gives us an example. He calls it the fable of the porcupines: It seems that on a cold day, several porcupines decided to huddle together for warmth. They got too close and began to prick each other with their quills. They dispersed but became cold, and so moved together again, seeking warmth. They got too close, pricked each other, and dispersed again. After repeated attempts, the porcupines came together but not too close. They were close enough to provide some warmth but not close enough to get pricked by each other.[33]

In this fable three fundamental concepts are at work: experience, balance, and respect for others. The porcupines used their *experience* in huddling to *balance* their actions, and as a result of their *respect for others (and for themselves),* were able to *suffer less (promote happiness).* Schopenhauer feels that using this ethical philosophy enables us to deal with reality, even though the will often pushes or pulls us in undesirable directions.

▶ DECISION-MAKING TOOL

Think carefully about any action you may be inclined to take. Acknowledge the influence of the will but use experience to achieve a balance and act with compassion so that you respect yourself and others.

▶ SUGGESTED MEDIA APPLICATION ◀

Schopenhauer's philosophy can be used by people in any of the media, but may be particularly useful to journalists. Gathering and reporting the news often requires one to intrude upon the life of another. Schopenhauer would urge journalists to resist the will—the passion and emotion generated by a desire to "get the story"—and strike a balance between doing their job and respecting those who are involved in the story. Remember the porcupines: avoid injuring others. Use your experience to determine alternate ways of approaching a task.

RECOMMENDED CASE STUDIES

#4 (Chapter 11); #10 (Chapter 13); #20 (Chapter 15).

p. 193   p. 248   p. 304

▼ Émile Durkheim

The Life

In the small town of Epinal, nestled in the scenic foothills of northeastern France, Melanie Durkheim gave birth to a child who was to become one of France's most engaging teachers and a founder of modern sociology. Young Émile arrived on April 15, 1858. Moise, his father, was chief rabbi of his synagogue and served as spiritual adviser to members of the Jewish faith in the surrounding province. The family had a modest income. Conditions might have been worse, but Melanie ran an embroidery shop and earned a little extra money.[34]

The family was happy, close-knit, and Orthodox Jewish. It was expected that Émile would follow tradition and become a rabbi. When many of the children in the town were outside playing their games, young Émile was often inside studying. He apparently was considering no other occupation than that of a Jewish rabbi until he came under the influence of one of his teachers, a woman of the Catholic faith. As a result of her interaction with him, "the young Durkheim had some kind of mystical experience, the details of which are unknown, and he emerged from it an agnostic, a position he was to retain for the rest of his life."[35]

It was obvious to Émile that he was not suited for the rabbinate. He was academically inclined, however, and he expressed an interest in becoming a teacher. Although he was now leaning toward a secular career, the early religious experiences had apparently led to his interest in proper human behavior.[36]

Émile advanced rapidly through the elementary and secondary schools in his hometown, winning prizes for superior achievement. Having made the decision to pursue an academic career, he went to Paris, hoping to gain admission to the famous Paris academy, Ecole Normale Superieure. Graduates from this prestigious institution could usually find productive, lifetime jobs. It was in Paris, however, that he experienced his first real disappointment. He failed to be admitted to the school on his first try. His second attempt at admission also failed, so he elected to undertake study at a preparatory school. On his third try, at age 21, he passed the required tests and was admitted. His classmates were men who would later become distinguished scholars in archaeology, anthropology, philosophy, logic, and various other fields.[37]

A second disappointment soon followed. Durkheim did not like the course of study he was required to follow. He disliked Greek and Latin, long staples of a classic education, and he was irritated by the inflexible structure of the classes and by the assignments he was required to complete. However, his teachers tolerated his complaints, remembering as they did a well-known French educational principle: "One of the surest signs of future greatness in a student is his rebellion against his teachers."[38] Nevertheless, he managed to survive the rigors of the school and even enjoy it from time to time. Unlike Schopenhauer, Durkheim was not a solitary man. He joined his classmates and other French citizens in the many festivals and holiday celebrations that swept the streets of Paris.

Upon graduation, Durkheim began his career and for five years taught philosophy at three area schools near Paris. Philosophy was not an unusual course offering in French secondary schools. By the time students were ready to graduate, they had a firm grounding in the humanities, especially logic, ethics, and metaphysics. Durkheim enjoyed teaching, and had no trouble communicating philosophical ideas to 17-year-olds.[39]

After a travel break to Paris and Germany, Durkheim was told that a special course had been created for him at the University of Bordeaux; he joined the faculty there, anxious to try out some of the new teaching techniques he had observed in his travels. His years at Bordeaux were productive ones. He published three of his four major works while on the faculty there, and he continued to develop and offer new courses, each with a sociological twist.

Little is known about his family life. He married Louise Dreyfus, and they had two children, Marie and Andre. The marriage was a happy one. Louise apparently served as his editor, proofreading his manuscripts and answering his correspondence. This gave him more time to devote to his books and articles.[40]

After 15 years at Bordeaux, Durkheim was called to the University of Paris as a substitute for a professor who had been elected to public office. It was here that his courses would begin to emphasize ethics. He continued to be a brilliant teacher. His lectures were well planned, clear, and to the point. He was both eloquent and profound. In an essay one of his students compared him to Aristotle, Descartes, Spinoza, and Kant.[41] Fine company indeed!

The last years of his life, however, differed from the quiet, earlier ones. Durkheim became caught up, as did all of Europe, in the turbulence of World War I. The war had a profound effect on him, principally because he saw so many of his students lose their lives in battle. Among these was his son, Andre, who died in a Bulgarian hospital in 1915.

Life lost much of its joy thereafter, and Durkheim's energy sagged. He did not express his grief outwardly but held his feelings in. Friends were cautioned not to speak of the boy in Durkheim's presence. Before long, the strain was too much for him. In December 1916 he collapsed after speaking passionately at one of his seemingly endless committee meetings and died less than a year later on November 15, 1917.[42]

Émile Durkheim was only 59 years old when he died, yet he "had produced a large body of scholarly work and founded one of the most coherent sociological perspectives of the nineteenth century."[43] His contribution might have been greater, but some of his papers were destroyed during the Nazi occupation of France in World War II. Marie Durkheim, his daughter, forgot her father's papers as she evacuated to the south of France to escape the Nazis. All his papers had been stored in one room of her house and were apparently thrown out as garbage when new residents moved in.[44] When

Marie remembered that she had left them and made inquiries, the papers were nowhere to be found.

Durkheim is buried in the famous Montparnesse Cemetery in Paris. In the late 1980s, his gravesite was in disarray. The headstone was crumbling and the chain surrounding the site had collapsed. The grave showed no evidence of being cared for. This was in marked contrast to "the freshly-cut flowers on Jean-Paul Sartre's grave and the graves of other famous persons in Montparnesse."[45]

The Philosophy

The most common word in Durkheim's writings is *society*. It is also the most difficult to pin down with a precise meaning.[46] Although he did not devote one work specifically to the subject, Durkheim's body of work was concerned with ethics.[47] Because of his interest in society and because of the degree to which society figures into all his work, including his ethical theory, Durkheim may be thought of as a *social* rather than a *pure* philosopher.[48]

Durkheim's ethical thinking can be easily divided into two periods: his early ethical theory work (1885–1893) and his mature ethical theory work (1893–1917).[49] His early work is characterized by his belief that ethics involve the application of scientific knowledge. Sometimes called *scientific naturalism,* this view reflected his belief that the scientific method could be applied to his "social" field and to ethics particularly. It took several years of writing, discussion, and investigation before Durkheim gave up the notion that ethics could be scientific.[50]

As his thought matured, Durkheim refocused his ethical theory. He still firmly believed that the morality of the people derives principally from those practicing it, that is, from society. Further, "If morality is a product of society, then judgments of ethical right and wrong are justifiable only in the context of the society within which they are made."[51] Therefore, at any given time, the moral principles considered absolute by individuals are really reflections of what society considers to be absolute.[52] In short, Durkheim believes that society and morality—or ethics, if you prefer—are inextricably intertwined.

As Durkheim moved into his mature ethical period, he toyed for a while with the notion that right and wrong were related to normal and abnormal behavior in a society, but this perspective faded as he refined his ideas. He was somewhat concerned that his theory would not draw much attention; some people felt that morality is and should be a matter left entirely to the individual. Durkheim agreed that individuals have a right to determine their own moral principles, but that right does "not exempt them from the morality of society."[53] Society is the larger context in which individuals must function and therefore becomes critical in defining ethical behavior. This approach to ethics might accurately be called *cultural ethical relativism.* In other words, ethics are relative to, that is, dependent on, standards set by society. As society changes, so do ethics.

Durkheim felt that the moral agenda of his age was replacing the old religious morality with its secular equivalent.[54] Of course, the question arising from this approach is whether a secular notion of morality can motivate people to proper behavior with the same force as religion did in past ages. Seen another way, the question becomes this: Does society have as much or more power than religion to motivate ethical behavior? Critics disagree on the answer to this question. Some say Durkheim is on the right track and that society does indeed have the strength to motivate proper behavior; others feel that leaving proper behavior in the hands of society, a group of disorganized, diverse, semiliterate individuals, is asking for trouble.

Durkheim, however, believes that if society is wrong about some ethical issue or situation, it is possible, even desirable, to try to modify its stance. Ethical standards should always be sensitive to needed changes.[55] "Collective rules and values are always or usually right because society is a higher, richer, and presumably more intelligent psychic reality than any single individual."[56] Nevertheless, we can, and should, intervene to change society when necessary.

It might be useful at this point to distinguish between moral facts and moral ideals. A *moral fact* is "a type of statement that contains a prescription or directive as to specific actions that we must perform. . . . They are statements that imply obligation, duty, and sanction."[57] *Moral ideals* "refers to a body of standards that a society sets for its members. These standards are embodied in the institutions, traditions, and precepts of the society, and they constitute what society wishes to transmit to its young."[58] Thus, moral ideals are derived from moral facts; these ideals are not abstract concepts but concrete realities.

Reason is an important part of this process because it must be used in determining and understanding the facts and truths that guide behavior in the natural world. Thus, being moral is not limited to simply taking an action; the morality of an action must ultimately be judged on the degree to which the action benefits society and the degree to which we have a reason for our conduct.[59]

▶ *DECISION-MAKING TOOL*

Determine the moral ideal or moral fact that governs a planned action. Explain how society benefits from the action. That is, how does the proposed action contribute to and reflect the existing social and moral fabric of life?

▶ *SUGGESTED MEDIA APPLICATION* ◀

Durkheim's philosophy is applicable to all media. Journalists, advertisers, public relations practitioners, and others can use Durkheim to solve a variety of ethical problems. In considering possible solutions to an ethical dilemma, you should first determine the moral fact or moral idea, that is, the standard or rule, that supports a proposed solution. You can then consider how the proposed solution benefits society. Durkheim would recommend rejecting a solution if the benefit to society is not clear; however, if society benefits from the proposed solution, it may be accepted. Journalists, particularly, often view their work as having benefits to society. Durkheim's philosophy would work well in a public relations setting where practitioners, on behalf of their clients, might have to communicate negative information to the public. Advertising, too, conveys information and should therefore be society-sensitive.

RECOMMENDED CASE STUDIES

#3 (Chapter 11); #16 (Chapter 14).

p. 192   p. 277

QUESTIONS FOR DISCUSSION

1. Look again at Schopenhauer's definition of the will. If the will is the controlling force inside each individual, how can one's character be changed?

2. Explain why Schopenhauer sees pleasure as a negative concept.

3. What are Schopenhauer's definitions of the philosophical terms *right* and *wrong?*

4. Early in life, Durkheim felt that ethics were merely the result of the application to life of scientific knowledge. Is there a connection between ethics and science? Explain.

5. Later in life, Durkheim believed that society, not science, should provide the context for ethical decision making. What role does an individual play in a culture whose ethics are society-based?

6. What is the difference between Durkheim's moral facts and his moral ideals?

ENDNOTES

1. Rudiger Safranski, *Schopenhauer and the Wild Years of Philosophy,* trans. Ewald Osers (Cambridge, MA: Harvard University Press, 1990), 7.

2. Patrick Gardiner, *Schopenhauer* (Baltimore: Penguin, 1963), 11.

3. Bryan Magee, *The Philosophy of Schopenhauer* (New York: Oxford Books, 1983), 10.

4. Gardiner, 11.

5. Ibid., 12.

6. Ibid.

7. W. Wallace, *Life of Arthur Schopenhauer* (London: Walter Scott, 1970), 47.

8. Safranski, 55.

9. Gardiner, 12–13.

10. Ibid., 13.

11. Ibid., 13–14.

12. Ibid., 18.

13. Safranski, 252.

14. Magee, 20.

15. Gardiner, 18.

16. Wallace, 152.

17. Ibid.

18. Gardiner, 18.

19. Ibid.

20. Ibid., 21.

21. Magee, 9

22. Ibid., 24.

23. Wallace, 212.

24. Ibid.

25. John E. Atwell, *Schopenhauer, the Human Character* (Philadelphia: Temple University Press, 1990), 3.

26. Ibid., 4.

27. Julian Young, *Willing and Unwilling: A Study in the Philosophy of Arthur Schopenhauer* (Dardrecht: Martinus Nijhoff, 1987), 51.

28. Ibid., 52.

29. Atwell, 7.

30. Arthur Schopenhauer, *Counsels and Maxims,* trans. T. Bailey Saunders (New York: Macmillan, 1899), 3.

31. Ibid., 25.

32. Schopenhauer, *On the Basis of Morality,* 167.

33. Schopenhauer, *Counsels and Maxims,* 35.

34. Ken Morrison, *Marx, Durkheim, Weber* (Thousand Oaks, CA: Sage, 1995), 120.

35. Robert Bierstedt, *Émile Durkheim* (New York: Dell, 1966), 19.

36. Ibid., 21.

37. Ibid., 21–22.

38. Ibid., 22.

39. Ibid., 26.

40. Ibid., 30.

41. Ibid., 29, 31.

42. Henri Peyre, "Durkheim: The Man, His Time, and His Intellectual Background," in *Émile Durkheim,* ed. Kurt H. Wolff (Columbus: Ohio State University Press, 1960), 17.

43. Morrison, 120.

44. Stjepan G. Mestrovic, *Émile Durkheim and the Reformation of Sociology* (Totowa, NJ: Rowman and Littlefield, 1988), 19–20.

45. Ibid., 23.

46. Robert N. Bellah, ed., *On Morality and Society by Émile Durkheim* (Chicago: University of Chicago Press, 1973), x.

47. Ernest Wallwork, *Durkheim, Morality and Milieu* (Cambridge, MA: Harvard University Press, 1972), 159.

48. Ibid., 1.

49. Ibid., 159, 166.

50. Robert T. Hall, *Émile Durkheim, Ethics and the Sociology of Morals* (Westport, CT: Greenwood Press, 1987), 177.

51. Ibid., 183.

52. Ibid.

53. Ibid., 184.

54. Ibid., 190.

55. Ibid., 191.

56. Wallwork, 176.

57. Barry Chazan, *Contemporary Approaches to Moral Education* (New York: Teachers College Press, 1985), 13.

58. Ibid., 14.

59. Ibid., 17, 20.

CHAPTER 8

Modern Influences

The four philosophies presented in this chapter were influential ones in a world advancing technologically and socially into the twentieth century. Sartre, Rand, and Kohlberg are all firmly grounded in the modern culture period (see the time line). In many ways, they reflect the complex thinking of the time, particularly the struggle to find meaning and the individual's proper role in a rapidly changing world. The fourth philosophy—the Judeo-Christian tradition—was developed many centuries ago but is included here because of its continued and strengthened influence in the modern period. Many people turned to religion for help in adjusting to the complexities of modern life. The Judeo-Christian tradition is not time-bound and could just as easily have been placed in some other historical period.

Culture Period ▪ Approximate Dates	General Description ▪ Key Personalities

Modern Age   A.D. 1850–A.D. 1945
 	
  Jean-Paul Sartre   (1905 . . .)
  Ayn Rand   (1905 . . .)
  Lawrence Kohlberg   (1927 . . .)
	Industrial Revolution takes hold; steel developed; much political and social change in America (Civil War) and in Europe (World Wars I and II); significant contributions in art, music, literature, science; Pasteur, Einstein, Wright Brothers, Hugo, Marx, Freud, Picasso, Hitler, Stalin

Postmodern Age   A.D. 1945–Present
 	
  Jean-Paul Sartre   (. . . 1980)
  Ayn Rand   (. . . 1982)
  Lawrence Kohlberg   (. . . 1987)
	Rapid social and political change; life becomes more complex; much ambiguity and discontinuity in the culture; rise of influence of media; institutions of modern age (families, schools, churches) undergo profound change; rise of technology as a life influence; increasingly important global economy

Note: Many scholars set 1945—or the end of World War II—as the time we began the transition to the postmodern era. This is probably true, especially in Europe, but your author fixes the date more precisely in America at about 1965. More discussion of this can be found in Chapter 1.	

Jean-Paul Sartre's existentialism is essentially a theory of modern man's dilemma. It is rarely viewed as an ethical theory, yet because it involves humans and their actions, it does have ethical implications. Sartre himself acknowledged the importance of ethics and even planned a full-length-book treatment of the topic, but never got around to it. Ayn Rand is also not in the mainstream of modern ethical thought. Her work as a novelist enabled her to advance a political and social theory she called objectivism. Embedded in that philosophy are components addressing right and wrong behavior.

On the other hand, one could argue that most elements of the Judeo-Christian tradition and Lawrence Kohlberg's philosophy *are* about proper behavior. The Judeo-Christian tradition is concerned particularly with behavior as it relates to God and to one's relationships with others. Kohlberg's ideas relate to the growth and development of an individual's ethical decision-making capabilities.

These philosophies will serve to broaden your view of political, social, and ethical issues and provide you with additional tools that may prove useful in decision making.

▼ Jean-Paul Sartre

The Life

Although it might seem so, there is no law that requires philosophers to have unhappy childhoods. Yet as we have seen, many of them did. The childhood experiences of Jean-Paul Sartre were different from, but no less unhappy than, the experiences of some other philosophers. Sartre's early life had an almost unreal quality, and it has provided psychologists with much material for analysis and interpretation.

One writer, with whom Sartre had several lengthy conversations, noted that although Sartre was born a boy, he was pampered and petted as one might a daughter. He wore his hair in long, golden curls; other children called him a sissy.[1] Jean-Baptiste Sartre, his father, was already dying when Jean-Paul was born on June 21, 1905, in Paris. The elder Sartre, a marine officer, managed to live for two more years, but he never had the opportunity to interact much with his son. Jean-Paul's mother, Anne-Marie Schweitzer, spent much of her time nursing her husband, but as Jean-Paul later recalled, such devotion only served to exhaust her with worry and sleepless nights.[2]

After the death of Jean-Baptiste, young Sartre and his mother moved in with Charles and Louise Schweitzer, Anne-Marie's parents. His grandfather became the dominant male force in his life. Charles considered himself the supreme authority in all matters, a God-figure.[3] He was a professor of German who expected his students to treat him like a deity. He considered both Anne-Marie and Jean-Paul his children, even though Anne-Marie was an adult who had been married and had borne a child. Of course, Jean-Paul was Charles's

Jean-Paul Sartre and Simone de Beauvoir were French café intellectuals. Many of their ideas were developed in conversations with each other and with friends. © *Bruno Barbey / MAGNUM*

grandson, not his son, but these were distinctions Charles did not care to recognize. He promptly assigned the two to the same bedroom and began treating them as brother and sister. Although they did not sleep in the same bed, Anne-Marie and Jean-Paul began to lose their mother-son identity and develop a sister-brother one. On more than a few occasions they were required to undress in front of each other, as young siblings might have to do from time to time. The situation proved to be both confusing and uncomfortable.

Charles took responsibility for young Sartre's education. Always a harsh man, Charles was strict and demanding, yet he continually flattered the youngster, telling him that he was smarter and better than other children and that great things were in store for him. Petted by one hand and disciplined by the other, young Jean-Paul hardly knew what he was supposed to do or be. Charles took the time to teach him history, art, and literature. It was all bewildering at first; Jean-Paul was surrounded by books, but all he could do was stare at them, for he did not yet know how to read. Nevertheless, he developed a love for books. One day, he smuggled a book to his room, where he pretended to read it, turning the pages and scanning the lines with his eyes as he had seen Charles do. He recited a story from memory to his mother and grandmother; when he had finished, he told them he knew the story because he had read the book. "But my darling . . . you don't know how," his mother quipped. When Charles was told about the incident, he patted Jean-Paul on the head and said, "Very good. My boy will be a great thinker, no doubt about it."[4]

No more important words were ever spoken to Jean-Paul. As far as he was concerned, his life was set, his success assured. All he need do was let it play out. By the time he was three, Jean-Paul had reached several conclusions: his grandfather was a poor substitute for his real father; his mother was his sister; and his mission in life was predetermined.[5]

Often pictured as a good, gentle, and mature child who was perfectly happy, he was, in fact, quite the opposite.[6] In a sense, he faked much of his childhood in order to please the adults who controlled him. "My grandfather didn't give a damn if I had comrades as long as I was brilliant," he wrote. When his mother took him to the park, the other children refused to play with young Jean-Paul. He was an outsider, and he understood why: he was superior to them. So he just went home.[7]

Soon Jean-Paul began to grow weary of his home life. As far as Jean-Paul was concerned, his grandfather was a fool and everything about his life was uncomfortable. He stole some of his grandfather's books and sold them, not so much for the money as for the opportunity it provided him to assert himself.[8]

Finally, at age 10, Jean-Paul was allowed to go to school. He enrolled as a day pupil at a local school and promptly failed his first test. His teacher noted that he "never gives the right answer on the first try. Must learn to think more."[9] This performance displeased his grandfather, of course, but Jean-Paul remained in school, determined to survive in an atmosphere where he was not pampered.

More trouble was to come. His mother remarried in 1917. Suddenly, she was not his sister anymore but his mother again, and he had a new (step)father, Joseph Mancy. He resented his mother's marriage and disliked everything about his stepfather. The relationship between Jean-Paul and his mother soured. For the most part, he remained an outsider at school, doing poorly in his studies. He did not know how to relate properly to others, so he made up stories, told lies, and, as a result, "was considered a phony, a good-for-nothing," yet he persevered.[10]

His life took a turn for the better in 1924, when, at age 19, he was accepted at the Ecole Normale Superieure (ENS) and began to study philosophy. Living conditions at the school were not the best, but he accepted the physical and intellectual challenges and was a successful student, scoring a first on his final exam. Upon his graduation, he, like Durkheim, took a position teaching secondary school philosophy.

Something else of importance happened to Jean-Paul during his student years at ENS. He met Simone de Beauvoir, also a student. Although they never married, the two "became life partners, sharing the same preoccupations and interests."[11] Also a teacher of philosophy, Simone was a good intellectual match for Jean-Paul. She had come in second on the exam, although some instructors had rated her first and Jean-Paul second. Their relationship was to last 51 years.

In the 1950s, Sartre involved himself in all the major political and social controversies of the decade. Politically, he was radically left-wing, and although he cooperated with the Communist party, he never joined. He criticized Soviet intervention in Hungary and Czechoslovakia. Simone de Beauvoir was always by his side. A social man, Sartre enjoyed whiskey, jazz, and women. Beauvoir appeared to be totally devoted to Sartre, but he was not all that devoted to her. According to one observer, "in the annals of literature, there are few worse cases of a man exploiting a woman."[12]

Sartre continued to expand his elite circle of friends; they often met in cafés for deep philosophical and political discussions. Both Sartre and Beauvoir were prolific writers. Sartre's major work, *Being and Nothingness*, was published in 1943. It ran to 722 pages and was somewhat obscure, though it was widely read and admired.[13] He spent much of the 1950s explaining and refining his philosophy of existentialism.

In 1964, Sartre was awarded the Nobel Prize for Literature, but he refused it, saying that it was not fair to the reader of his works to add the weight of such extraneous influences to the power of the writer's words. Sartre continued to write, publish, and speak out—as before. However, the world was changing, and so was France. He spent much of his time in the 1960s revising and explaining his work. He edited *Les Temps Modernes,* a monthly that promoted socialist and existential views.

As Sartre entered the 1970s, his productivity slackened. He began to have health problems, although his mind remained alert and active. One critic described Sartre as "an increasingly pathetic figure . . . prematurely aged, virtually blind, often drunk, worried about money, uncertain about his views."[14] He apparently spent considerable time traveling between his various mistresses' homes, including Beauvoir's. One of his particular favorites was Arlette, with whom he had become involved when she was only 17 years old. Sartre claimed that he had secretly "adopted" her. At his death, she inherited everything, including his literary property; Beauvoir was left with nothing.

On March 20, 1980, Sartre was taken to a hospital where he was diagnosed as having pulmonary edema, a symptom of heart failure described as fluid in the lungs, often caused by the inefficient pumping action of the heart. He died at 9 P.M. on April 15, 1980, with only Arlette present. On the next day, every paper in France, whether of right or left political persuasion, devoted several pages to his life and work. Testimonies flowed in from all over the world.

His funeral, on April 19, was like his life, something of a wild affair. The funeral procession began at the hospital, moved through the streets of Paris, passed all of his favorite places, and ended at the Montparnasse Cemetery. The crowd was unexpectedly large; more than 50,000 people attended. There were tears, screams, and fights. One man "fell into the open grave onto the coffin."[15] This outpouring of grief and passion was convincing evidence that Sartre was still a symbol of intellectual power. Simone de Beauvoir was at the gravesite, but was reportedly so full of whiskey and tranquilizers that she had to be propped up in a chair, "where she sat, stupefied, for ten minutes while the crowd seethed around her."[16]

Sartre was cremated on April 23 and his ashes buried at the Montparnasse Cemetery on the same day. Beauvoir was too ill to attend this ceremony. She was to recover, after a while, and continue with her life. She died on April 15, 1986, six years to the day after Sartre's death, and was buried next to Sartre in the Montparnasse Cemetery.

The Philosophy

During his years as a teacher in the French school system, Sartre was dedicated to teaching his students *individual responsibility.* He required students to get on their feet in the classroom and deliver an oral report—a startling new method in an academic world where the lecture reigned supreme. Even in those early days he was something of a revolutionary. He did not discipline his students; he did not take attendance; he gave no exams; he assigned no grades. He discouraged competition among class members and was opposed to note taking and memorization.[17] It was clear that *freedom* and *individual responsibility* were important to Sartre; they form the basic foundation of *existentialism.*

It should be noted that Soren Kierkegaard (1813–1855) is considered the father of existentialism. The philosophy was also part of the work of Martin Heidegger (1889–1976) and others. However, Sartre is given credit for popularizing it, and the philosophy came to be more closely associated with him and his circle than with any of the other philosophers. Some scholars believe that many of Sartre's ideas were given him by de Beauvoir, though there appears to be no way to verify this.

Existentialism was popular in France and other parts of Europe in the 1950s, but was slow in coming to the United States. When it did arrive, in the 1960s, the philosophy was popular only on college campuses, and there primarily in departments of philosophy or literature where Sartre's work was read and discussed. College theater departments often staged his plays. That this philosophy did not generate much excitement in America is not surprising. Existentialism was more than a little obscure (as we shall see shortly). Most Americans were busy with their lives and were not all that interested in discussing abstract philosophical concepts. It was, however, an attractive philosophy to many of America's young who were searching for meaning in the turbulent 1960s.

Generally, existentialism is a philosophy "opposed to rationalist and empiricist doctrines that assume that the universe is a determined, ordered system intelligible to the contemplative observer who can discover the natural laws that govern all beings and the role of reason as the power guiding hu-

translate

man activity."[18] This simply means that no person has a predetermined place or function, that the world is not an ordered system, that reason is not necessarily an adequate means for determining facts about the world, and that, as a result, each of us must accept the responsibility of making choices.[19] Existentialism, therefore, holds that *what* an individual is is a function of the choices one makes. At no time or place can individuals plead that what they are has been shaped by any factor other than themselves.[20]

At the conclusion of *Being and Nothingness*, Sartre wrote that he wished to develop an entire work on morality. Although bits of ethical theory are scattered here and there in his works, Sartre never did publish a major work on morality or ethics. He did keep notebooks in which he recorded many of his ideas relating to ethics, but these are not complete and were not published until after his death.[21] The notebooks contain phrases, sentences, and paragraphs of various lengths on ethical issues and concepts. However, the material is, at times, loose, rambling, disjointed, and unorganized, and therefore may not be an accurate reflection of his views.

Because existentialism is somewhat ambiguous and because Sartre did not often write to be easily understood, a casual look at the Sartre material might give the reader the wrong impression of his ethical philosophy. For example, the phrase *everything is permitted* is often advanced as a capsule summary of existentialist ethics. The philosophy is obviously more complicated than that. Nevertheless, given the notion that the world is determined by a multitude of individuals making a multitude of individual choices, it follows that any number of things, perhaps even everything, could be permitted. Sartre would not disagree with this, but he would not support the idea that everything is permitted *from an ethical point of view.*

Sartre holds that there exists no uniform set of ethical or moral standards that govern human behavior. "In order to perform even a single action with moral relevance, there must be a choice. Before the choice is made it is neither the case that anything is permitted, ethically, nor that it is not permitted: the category of the ethical is simply not yet constituted."[22] It is, therefore, the responsibility of the individual to make choices. In doing so, each person establishes an ethics for him- or herself, but not for others. Our particular situations are so unique that our moral codes must, of necessity, apply to us alone. This might be called *radical individualism* or *radical subjectivism*. Sartre notes that truly moral beings are true to their own moral codes, codes developed according to their individual natures.[23]

Sartre recognizes that while individuality, choice, flexibility, and the like have their place, there is a point beyond which we should not go. For example, it is simply wrong to play with the lives of others without their consent, or to try to make another individual one's slave, or to waste one's wealth while others starve.[24] Moral truths are created by free human action, but these truths must be balanced by human reason or intuition. Following the same line of thinking, it becomes obvious that cruelty for its own sake is wrong, that we ought to value pleasure over pain and health over sickness.

How would Sartrean ethics work in a real situation? It might be helpful to consider Sartre's most famous example of a moral dilemma: a young student "must choose between fighting for France against the Nazis and staying at home to care for his aged mother." According to Sartre, traditional moral systems "are incapable of determining what the young man should do."[25] The proper ethical choice here is a personal choice. That is, regardless of *what* the young man chooses to do, he would be right because his free choice would constitute the right. This is radical individualism at work.

Sartre's solution may not be all that satisfying for several reasons. First, he does not explain why *this* situation is a genuine moral dilemma. It may not be much of a moral dilemma, since both courses of action could be considered good. It is certainly good to fight for one's country, and it is likewise good to care for those you love. What is it about this situation that qualifies it as a moral dilemma? Second, although no ethical truths exist *prior to* a choice, they most certainly exist *after,* since the act of choosing constitutes the truth. What, then, is the ethical truth that this decision establishes?

At the time of his death, Sartre was apparently refining his views on ethics, although there is no evidence that any radical change was pending.[26] Some of Sartre's revised ideas may be gleaned from his tape-recorded interviews and from his conversations with some of those close to him. While interesting, this is flimsy evidence on which to suggest that a radical change was occurring in Sartre's thinking. It is clear, however, that in his later years, Sartre seems to have developed a renewed respect for human needs, values, and goals, especially as they relate to other humans.

It might be helpful at this point to consider another of Sartre's moral dilemmas. This one can be called "The Case of the Lying Husband." A young couple lives in a puritanical society. The wife has cancer. Her husband alone knows that she has only a year to live. It has been the practice of this couple to be completely truthful with each other in every aspect of their lives together. However, if the husband tells his wife the truth about her condition, he risks ruining what is left of his wife's life. But not telling her violates their moral practice of always being truthful with each other. The husband, therefore, must answer the following question: "Should I tell her the truth, namely, that she is ill with leukemia and will die in a year's time?"[27]

What choices does the husband have? He may lie to her about the situation, feeling that it is important not to reduce his wife to despair and knowing that giving her the bad news would do just that. However, since she is sick, she will surely realize that she is seriously ill and may despair anyway, unless her husband lies to her, thereby avoiding despair. If he tells her the truth, she will almost certainly despair, but not telling her can be seen as robbing her of information she needs to exercise control over her own life. What action treats her as another free human being, and what action treats her as an object?

Sartre supports a lie in this instance. He concludes that, as life unfolds, one is often required to adopt a new course of action. The husband is free to make a choice; he chooses to lie to his wife. He abandons the historical action of the past (always telling the truth) and replaces it with an ethical action in the present (saving his wife from despair).

The arguments in this case seem to turn in circles. No clearly superior moral action is suggested by the facts of the case. The husband is free to act, but neither of his choices is without possible negative consequences. This, Sartre would say, is modern man's dilemma, and the essence of existentialism. Man is *condemned to freedom,* and, in the absence of a standard set of prescriptive ethical rules, any action establishes the rules for conduct, and one must therefore take total and unconditional responsibility for one's actions.

▶ **DECISION-MAKING TOOL**   *Popularized existentialism (see top of p. 107)*

Get a clear and accurate picture of a situation by examining the choices of action available. Select an option for which you can provide a justification and for which you accept total responsibility.

▶ *SUGGESTED MEDIA APPLICATION* ◀

It would be a mistake to suggest that Sartre's philosophy allows media, and/or individuals, to do anything they wish. While it is true that much is permitted if one is willing to accept total responsibility for an action, it is also true that much care must be taken in determining the action. Human reason, intuition, and a concern for others must all play a part. Within this context, individuals must determine their own definitions of good and evil, develop a set of moral principles, and consistently apply them. This philosophy can be used in all media situations—from journalism to public relations—to assist one in reaching an appropriate solution to an ethical problem.

RECOMMENDED CASE STUDIES

#5 (Chapter 11); #18 (Chapter 15).
    p. 194   *p. 301*

▼ Ayn Rand

The Life

Her first glimpse of America did not match the ideal she had constructed in her mind, chiefly from watching old American movies. She had expected a bright and shining city—an example of the prosperous West, a place where dreams could come true. Bitterly disappointed because the fog obscured what she was sure was a grand and glorious city, Alissa returned to her cabin to await the inspection of her passport by immigration officials.

Her relatives met her a short time later, and Alissa was soon standing on the pier at the Hudson River. She could now see New York's beautiful skyline.

The skyscrapers were magnificent in the gently falling snow. "This is truly a new beginning for me," she thought. "A new beginning calls for a new name." She selected Ayn as her new first name, replacing Alissa. Ayn (rhymes with *mine*) was the name of a Finnish writer whose works she had never read, but whose name she liked.[28] Gazing at the tall buildings, Ayn Rosenbaum took stock of her situation. She had a new name, fifty dollars in her pocket, her typewriter, and several stories outlined in her head. Yes, she thought, America would provide her the opportunity to become what she had long wanted to become—a writer.[29]

Before her arrival in America, Alissa Rosenbaum had a rather unremarkable life. She was born February 2, 1905, in St. Petersburg, Russia, to Fronz and Anna Rosenbaum. Her family occupied a large, comfortable apartment over her father's chemist shop. The family was Jewish, but religion was not an important part of the home. She respected her father, but received little affection from him. She and her mother argued almost constantly. Able to read and write before she was six years old, Alissa showed a particular interest in mathematics. But by age nine, she had decided that writing would be her life's work. The family was not rich but was able to provide her with a private school education.[30]

When Alissa was 12, Czar Nicholas was overthrown by the Bolsheviks, who formed a new government based on communist principles. This meant that all private property now belonged to the state. Her father's business was taken, and the family had to live on savings.

She finished her regular schooling and entered the University of Petrograd (later Leningrad), where she majored in history. She read widely, including the works of Aristotle, Plato, and Nietzsche.[31] Upon graduation in 1924, she took a job as a guide in a historical museum. During these years many things captured her attention, but two most of all. She detested the Russian communist system of government, its leaders, and the way individuals were treated in her country.[32] And she developed an intense interest in America, primarily through American movies. She envisioned the United States as a free, joyous, purposeful, active place. She often let her imagination conjure up stories of life in America.

She was excited, naturally, when the Portnoys, relatives living in Chicago, invited her to come for a visit. She applied for a passport, not really thinking that it would be granted. It was, and she made plans to leave home. She had mixed feelings about leaving; she would miss her family and beautiful St. Petersburg, but she knew that in America she would find opportunities that would never be available to her in Russia. In February 1926, she boarded the *De Grasse* for the eight-day trip across the Atlantic. She never saw her family again. Now here she was in New York; she had a new name; she was on her way to Chicago. Her new life had begun.

Although Ayn liked America, she disliked Chicago; her main complaint seemed to be that it wasn't New York. She was uncomfortable with the affectionate, religious Portnoys. Still, she never really gave much thought to returning home. She was more interested in going to Hollywood to seek work as a writer. Arrangements were made to provide her with permanent papers so she could stay in America. A letter of introduction to the Hollywood movie maker Cecil B. DeMille was also provided, and she made plans to head west. But she felt she needed a new last name. Rosenbaum just didn't seem to be the kind of name that suggested Hollywood success. She wanted her new last name to begin with "R" since that was the beginning of her real last name. As she was thinking about it one day, her eyes fell on her typewriter. It was a Remington-Rand. Remington didn't seem musical enough for her, but Rand was perfect! In the late summer of 1926, Ayn Rand left Chicago for Hollywood.

Upon her arrival in Hollywood, she registered at the Hollywood Studio Club and set out to present her letter of introduction to DeMille. Some critics dispute the details of her first few meetings with DeMille, but they apparently did meet, for she was offered, and accepted, a job as an extra in the De-Mille production of *King of Kings*, the 1926 version of the life of Jesus. The job paid $7.50 per day.[33]

During her second week on the set, it happened! She saw him! He was Charles Francis (Frank) O'Connor, an Ohio native who was also an extra in the DeMille production. They spoke to each other on and off over the next several days, as casual acquaintances might. But for Rand, the acquaintance was more than casual. Later, recalling those days, she said, "It *was* love at first sight. I was always on the lookout for my kind of face . . . but here was my ideal face." In one of their chance meetings one day, O'Connor said, "Let's go out." They walked, talked, and had dinner. Thus began a relationship of 50 years.[34]

Rand was given a job as a junior scriptwriter a short time later, a job that paid $25 a week. But DeMille closed his studio within a year and Rand was out of work. She took whatever jobs she could find, just to scrape by. "There was one month . . . when she lived on thirty cents a day. In the morning, she ate a chocolate bar in her room, with hot water from the bathroom; during the day, she ate a can of cold spaghetti or beans."[35] She was careful to work as far away from her room as possible, so that Frank, who was often in the neighborhood, would not see her performing menial labor.

Although Frank, too, was on an uncertain income, the two decided to get married, and on April 15, 1929, they became husband and wife. Shortly after her marriage, Rand found work in the wardrobe department of the R.K.O. studios. She began as a filing clerk at $20 per week and, in a year, rose to department head at $45 a week. She was able to pay their bills, and she had time to write. She became a naturalized American citizen in 1931.

Her first major success was *The Fountainhead*, published in 1943. It was a bestseller. Her writing attracted the attention of Nathaniel Branden and Barbara Weidman, two UCLA students. After weeks of letters and phone calls, the three met and discovered they shared many of the same ideas and philosophies. They became Rand's personal disciples.

The close working relationship between Nathaniel and Ayn was not without its problems. By this time, Nathaniel had married Barbara, but he found himself attracted to Rand. Rand was also attracted to him, so the two apparently approached their respective spouses about the possibility of their having an affair—without destroying their marriages. Feeling they had little choice, Frank and Barbara agreed. It was a most uncomfortable arrangement for all involved, but the affair took an especially heavy toll on Rand. She was working on a new novel, but the pressure of the affair and the guilt she felt at what she was doing to Frank sent her into a deep depression. She couldn't write. Her work was stalled, and her personal life was a mess. Rand did the only thing she could do; she ended the affair with Nathaniel.[36] Slowly her depression lifted, and she was able to finish _Atlas Shrugged_, her second great novel, in 1957.

Rand moved to New York and, for the rest of her life, wrote essays, delivered speeches, sat for interviews, and generally worked to spread her philosophy called _objectivism._ She served as a visiting lecturer at many universities, among them Columbia, Princeton, Yale, Wisconsin, Johns Hopkins, Syracuse, Harvard, and MIT. She was never really accepted by the academic community, but her ideas were intriguing to both students and faculty.[37] Rand was not a favorite with members of the press, either. One writer (John Kobler, _Saturday Evening Post,_ November 1961) "found her almost completely devoid of grace, with a personality as compelling as a sledgehammer, slow to smile, on guard against laughter, intolerant of humor. . . . [She] had an opinion on every subject and was not afraid to speak her mind."[38]

Rand established the Objectivist Institute and circulated a regular newsletter. Having broken with Nathaniel Branden, Rand began grooming Leonard Peikoff (Barbara Branden's cousin) as her heir apparent. Peikoff was given control over her literary and intellectual property after her death.[39]

Rand became ill in December 1981. When her condition worsened, early in 1982, she was hospitalized with cardiopulmonary problems. She went home in March but lived only a few days. Frank had died in 1979. On the morning of March 6, 1982, the attending nurse phoned Leonard Peikoff and told him to hurry over, but he "arrived moments too late. Ayn Rand was dead."[40] More than 800 admirers passed through the funeral home on Madison Avenue where her body lay in state. Many stood outside in the cold waiting to pay their respects. A private burial followed in Valhalla, New York.

Ayn Rand had difficulty dealing with people and had trouble changing her views or listening closely to the views of others. She could inspire or frustrate, engage or enrage. "While primarily a novelist, Ayn Rand constructed a philosophic system, which . . . is integrated, coherent, and compelling. . . . [She was] one of the most intriguing and dynamic figures in twentieth-century thought."[41]

The Philosophy

Ayn Rand took great pride in calling herself the only modern _rationalist._ She claimed that her thinking followed in a direct line from that of Aristotle, the father of reason. Consequently, Rand had little respect for modern philosophers. She especially disliked Immanuel Kant's philosophy.[42] Kant claimed that an action performed out of duty was a moral action. Rand held just the opposite view. Her philosophy of objectivism is a philosophy of self-interest. Man ought to live for himself, Rand said, not for others.

Rand always felt John Galt's speech in *Atlas Shrugged* contained all the themes and theories of objectivism. The speech took two years to write and runs to 35,000 words. "Galt's message to the American people was a call for each man to earn his keep, take responsibility for his own but for no one else's life, and be a rationalist, an individualist, a producer."[43] In an postscript to *Atlas Shrugged*, Rand wrote, "My philosophy, in essence, is the concept of man as a heroic being, with his own happiness as the moral purpose of his life, with productive achievement as his noblest activity, and reason as his only absolute." This is the core of objectivism.

Both Galt, in *Atlas Shrugged*, and Howard Roark, in *The Fountainhead*, are fictional representations of objectivism. Roark is devoted to his work and rejects custom and public opinion. Galt is a rationalist who earns his own keep and takes responsibility only for himself. They are Rand's heroic men who embody the virtues she thought all men should strive for.

Philosophically, objectivism is based on several premises. First, universal concepts or ideas have an objective reality. Second, man's mind is capable of perceiving and interpreting these concepts and ideas through the senses. Third, man uses his reason to integrate his perceptions and act on them. Objectivism can be applied to ethics in a fairly straightforward manner. According to Rand, morality, or ethics, is "a code of values to guide man's choices and actions."[44] Such a code is "necessary for human survival, well-being, and happiness."[45] Ethics, then, is rational self-interest.

This is a startling contrast to the philosophies already presented in this book. Most philosophers have developed systems of thought that require, as a part of an individual's life, some attention to the needs of others. Sartre probably comes closest to Rand's view, but even he felt that an individual has some responsibility to others. Mill's utilitarianism—doing what is best for the greatest number of people—is obviously a philosophy that could, at times, require self-sacrifice. Rand views this emphasis on others with utter contempt.

To explain further, let's take another example. As noted earlier, Rand was no fan of Kant's philosophy, especially his ideas about the morality of actions motivated by duty. Rand "condemns the notion of duty as one of 'the most destructive anti-concepts in the history of moral philosophy'." . . . Duty, for Rand, means "the moral necessity to perform certain actions for no reason other than obedience to some higher authority without regard to any personal goal, motive, desire, or interest."[46] Rand would substitute standard-based ethics for duty-based ethics.

A standard may be defined as a principle used to guide one's actions. We need standards because they enable us to determine whether our actions are conducive to our goals. One does not obey or disobey a standard, but rather one "adopts and follows a standard, in a given context, for a given purpose."[47]

You follow a standard if, in your judgment, doing so will help you achieve your goal. Whereas rules demand obedience and threaten punishment if not followed, a standard does neither.

Is this a selfish philosophy? "When broadcaster Mike Wallace asked her if hers were a philosophy of selfishness, she answered vigorously: 'Selfish? Most certainly. Every man has a right to exist for himself and not to sacrifice himself for others'."[48] Man is by nature a selfish being, Rand proclaimed, yet she acknowledged that selfishness had a negative connotation.

Rand's philosophical system can be summarized in four statements: "Her metaphysics is objective reality; her epistemology is reason; her ethics is self-interest; and her politics is radical capitalism."[49] Ayn Rand's life can be characterized as a struggle against conformity and the status quo. She worked to develop a system of philosophical thought that she felt would provide a sound, productive future for America. Her contribution was both unique and lasting.

▶ *DECISION-MAKING TOOL*

Examine the reality of a situation in as objective a manner as possible. Determine the standards to be followed and the goals to be met by a decision. Submit these observations to a reasoning process yielding a solution that meets your needs as an individual.

use p. 113

▶ *SUGGESTED MEDIA APPLICATION* ◀

Rand's ethical philosophy is based on two concepts: reason and self-interest. Reason may usually be applied to most ethical dilemmas. According to Rand, effective use of reason in a situation requires you to determine the reality (or realities) that bear on the problem, then determine the standard(s) that will guide a problem solution, always keeping in mind that you need not take an action that is against self-interest. It is this self-interest concept that may cause you difficulty. Many of the philosophers presented in this text concern themselves with doing what is best for others. Rand does not object to this action if such action is also best for you, but you are under no obligation to subordinate your individualism to the needs of others, unless you *choose* to do so.

This self-interest aspect of Rand's philosophy may be somewhat difficult to use in media situations, especially in view of the media's oft-stated goal of providing news, information, and entertainment (for others) at great expense and effort to themselves. Those who are highly critical of media could argue that the media really operate according to Rand's philosophy, that is, they do things out of self-interest rather than a concern for others. Nevertheless, Rand was a dedicated capitalist; she would have no objection to media generating a profit from their work as long as the profit did not come at the expense of the rights of all those involved. When confronted with an ethical problem, workers in media must be skillful, both in doing their jobs and at the same time pursuing their goals.

RECOMMENDED CASE STUDIES

#5 (Chapter 11); #17 (Chapter 15).

p. 194   p. 300

▼ Lawrence Kohlberg

The Life[50]

By most accounts, Lawrence Kohlberg was, in many ways, the stereo-typical college professor. He was slightly rumpled in appearance, yet he had a likable, engaging personality. He made friends easily and was always willing to talk with those who held views opposite to his. Students flocked to his courses, and many sought him as their dissertation adviser.

Born to Alfred and Charlotte Kohlberg, Lawrence was tutored in prestigious college preparatory schools. His father was a wealthy businessman and could afford to provide his son with this sort of quality education. It was expected that Lawrence would continue his education after high school, but he chose instead to join the merchant marines and travel the world.

Following his tour of duty, Lawrence enrolled at the University of Chicago where a student did not necessarily have to attend class and could get credit for a course by passing the final exam. He got his B.A. in one year and later earned his Ph.D. at Chicago. He taught at Yale for a while and formed the Child Psychology Training Program, an important early part of the field of developmental psychology. He challenged the notion that morality was a function of the socialization process. He felt that the individual, not the group, was the important focus in moral decision making. In 1968, Kohlberg joined Harvard's Graduate School of Education and established the Center for Moral Development and Education.

Kohlberg's life changed dramatically in December 1973. He contracted a disease on a trip to Central America that weakened his health and drained his energy. For the next 13 years of his life, he was always dizzy and nauseated. On some days he was not able to get out of bed. He experienced periods of severe pain and depression. Yet despite his declining health, he was able to work and write. One of his major accomplishments during this time was *Essays in Moral Development*.

"Lawrence Kohlberg, born in Bronxville, New York on October 25, 1927, was reported missing on January 17, 1987." His body was found later in a marshy area near Boston's Logan Airport. Apparently, he committed suicide by drowning himself. At a memorial service sometime later, the 59-year-old Kohlberg was remembered by family, friends, and students as a rare man of considerable talent. Many claimed that "he was the most influential person in their intellectual development."

The Philosophy

Lawrence Kohlberg's work crossed three academic disciplines: philosophy, psychology, and education. It was based on theories and ideas formulated by John Dewey, whose work in moral education Kohlberg found helpful, and by Jean Piaget, whose work in human growth and development was highly influential. He sought to develop a comprehensive system of moral development and provide a model for moral education.[51] His approach was simple: create a climate in which students can experience and practice moral decision making. Challenge them to use their own thinking and to consider the thinking of others in their growth process. Although Kohlberg developed his theories primarily for application to classroom situations, his ideas have broad implications and may be effectively applied in every day, real-world situations.

Although Kohlberg's theory is often referred to as a theory of moral development, it is, in fact, really a theory of the development of moral judgment.[52] Morality is usually thought of as involving good or bad character or proper or improper behavior. For Kohlberg, "Morality is most powerfully explained in terms of the logical processes through which one conceives and resolves moral conflicts."[53] This sort of activity obviously requires the use of an individual's capacity to reason, but Kohlberg's approach is unique because of his theory of the stages of moral judgment.[54]

The theory is based on four assumptions:

1. "Morality develops in stages.
2. Everyone passes through the same stages of moral development.
3. Moral reasoning is related to behavior.
4. Discussion is needed for moral growth."[55]

Kohlberg developed a framework of six universal stages of moral development. He grouped these stages into three levels, with two stages per level. This taxonomy can be summarized as follows:

Preconventional Level

Stage 1: Avoid punishment
Stage 2: Self-benefit

Conventional Level

Stage 3: Acceptance by others
Stage 4: Maintain social order

Postconventional Level

Stage 5: Contract fulfillment
Stage 6: Ethical principle[56]

At the *preconventional level,* a moral problem is approached from the perspective of self-interest. An individual operating at this level is not concerned with right and wrong but only with the rewards (or punishment) resulting from his or her action. Young children who have not yet developed the rational capacity to distinguish right from wrong are at this level. Individuals of all ages may find themselves at this level if they have not sufficiently developed the ability to reason and/or are not concerned about morality.

At the *conventional level,* a moral problem is approached from a member-of-society perspective. An individual operating at this level takes into consideration the norms or expectations of the group or society within which the person functions. Society expects certain things, and an individual at this level wishes to follow society's guidelines. Individuals also wish to avoid punishment, but they also want to be good members of society.

The *postconventional level* is the most mature level of moral decision making. Here a moral problem is approached from a prior-to-society perspective. An individual looks beyond the norms and laws of society and determines the principles that form the basis of any good society. For example, if two individuals enter into a contract that, in effect, consigns one of them to slavery at the hands of the other, the contract might constitute a legal document but would not constitute a moral one. In other words, what is permitted by law might not be permitted ethically if one follows a higher principle—the principle in this case being that one human being should not have control over another human being. If laws violate a principle, one acts on the principle. Principles typically have two important characteristics: they recognize the equality of human rights, and they respect the dignity of individuals as human beings.[57]

Moving from one level to the next requires a linear progression of sorts that begins with *logical reasoning* leading to *mature moral judgment* resulting in *mature moral action.* Not everyone is capable of reaching the postconventional level, or even the conventional level. Moving from one level to another is based, in large part, on one's ability to reason logically. This requires a certain level of intelligence and the ability to analyze, classify, infer, think abstractly, and think concretely. By some accounts, 70 percent of all Americans "operate on the conventional level, at the upper end of stage three and the lower end of stage four."[58] The overall pattern of an individual's responses to moral dilemmas determines at which stage an individual is functioning. An individual may move among the stages at different times and as a result of various ethical or unethical, mature or immature actions, but one cannot be assigned to a stage on the basis of a response to a single dilemma alone.

No discussion of Kohlberg would be complete without consideration of his classic moral problem, the Heinz dilemma.

> In Europe, a woman was near death from a special kind of cancer. There was one drug that the doctors thought might save her. It was a form of radium that a druggist in the same town had recently discovered. The drug was expensive to make, but the druggist was charging ten times what the drug cost him to make. He paid $200 for the radium and charged $2,000 for a small dose of the drug. The sick woman's husband, Heinz, went to everyone he knew to borrow the money, but he could only get together about $1,000, which is half of what it cost. He told the druggist that his wife was dying, and asked him to sell the drug cheaper or let

him pay later. But the druggist said, "No, I discovered the drug and I'm going to make money from it." So Heinz gets desperate and considers breaking into the man's store to steal the drug for his wife.[59]

This scenario is followed by a number of questions designed to explore the ethical implications of the situation. "Should Heinz steal the drug?" "If Heinz doesn't love his wife, should he steal the drug for her?" "Suppose the person who is dying is not his wife, but a stranger. Should Heinz steal the drug for a stranger?" "It is against the law for Heinz to steal. Does that make it morally wrong?" Each of these and the other questions relating to the case are followed by "Why or why not?" This, of course, is part of the Kohlberg approach. It encourages discussion and an exchange of ideas. Individuals must think about and justify their responses. This process, Kohlberg believes, is crucial to moral education and development.

At the risk of oversimplifying, one can easily see how certain responses seem to indicate a particular level or stage of moral development. For example, a solution suggesting that "Heinz should not break in the store and steal the drug because he might get caught and put in jail" indicates a response at the preconventional level. A solution suggesting that "Heinz should not break in the store and steal the drug because breaking-and-entering and stealing are against the law" indicates a response at the conventional level. A postconventional response would be "It is acceptable for Heinz to break in and steal the drug because human life is more important than property."

Obviously, some of Kohlberg's ideas are controversial, but he was bold and enthusiastic about promoting his theory. His focus on justice and on autonomous decision making, especially the notion that one ought to act on principle above all, was very much a philosophy for his time.

▶ DECISION-MAKING TOOL

Before attempting to find a solution to an ethical dilemma, determine on which moral level you are presently functioning. As you approach a new ethical problem, make a decision that is backed by logical reasoning and sound moral judgment, always moving toward the more mature postconventional level of decision making.

▶ SUGGESTED MEDIA APPLICATION ◀

Kohlberg's ethical theory is surprisingly easy to apply to media situations. You need only familiarize yourself with his three levels of moral development. A proposed solution to an ethical problem can then be evaluated to see on which level you are operating. Naturally, Kohlberg would urge decision makers to strive for the postconventional level where decisions are made as a matter of ethical principle, but sinking below the conventional level (acceptance by others, maintain social order) ought to be avoided.

RECOMMENDED CASE STUDIES
#6 (Chapter 12); #17 (Chapter 15).

p. 222   p. 300

▼ Judeo-Christian Tradition

The Rationale

Religion is an important part of life for many people. Religious beliefs are often closely held and usually form the basis for life decisions, including ethical ones. Contemporary America is a diverse nation, and many different religions are practiced. It is not possible to examine or even mention all of these. Although only two religious schools of thought are discussed here, this does not mean that other religions are unimportant or that their principles are unworthy of study. The two religions singled out for attention are those judged to have the most followers in contemporary American culture: the Christian Way, represented by the Catholic and Protestant faiths, and the Jewish Tradition, Judaism.

Not everyone in America believes in a supreme being. Many who do believe do not worship regularly. Nevertheless, there is no denying that religion is and always has been an important part of American life. A quick glance at American history reveals that religion played an extremely important role in the establishment of the colonies, particularly in New England. "The first American colonists came seeking religious freedom."[60] The Pilgrims wanted more religious freedom than was afforded them by the Church of England. The political, economic, and social order established by the Pilgrims at Plymouth, Massachusetts, in the winter of 1620 was clearly based on religious principles. The Mayflower Compact—signed in November 1620 before they came ashore—clearly indicates their purpose: "Having undertaken for the glory of God, and the advancement of the Christian faith . . . a voyage to plant the first colony in the northern parts of Virginia, do . . . combine ourselves together into a civil body politic, for our better ordering and preservation and furtherance of the ends aforesaid." The Pilgrims intended to land in Virginia, but poor navigation pushed them northward, and they landed at Cape Cod. They came to be known as *Puritans,* reflecting their desire to *purify* certain aspects of religious practice.

The influence of religion in the establishment of America is further evidenced in the literature and schools of the time. Early American writers included, among others, William Bradford, Edward Taylor, Cotton Mather, and Jonathan Edwards, famous for his sermon "Sinners in the Hands of an Angry God." Schools were established for the purpose of acquainting the young with the Scriptures.[61] Many of the textbooks used for instructional purposes contained proverbs and Bible stories. These were intended to develop and promote proper moral conduct among the students. "It was the Sunday School movement which first promoted the idea of public education."

Church groups would establish schools "to teach . . . children on Sunday when they weren't working."[62]

However, by the beginning of the nineteenth century, religious schools were replaced by schools operated and funded by the government, shifting the educational emphasis from religious to secular. Nevertheless, moral instruction was still very much a part of the curriculum, particularly principles that stressed capitalism and democratic values.[63]

To omit religious philosophies from an ethics text would be to deny the very foundations of our country. Religion has been an integral part of the fabric of American life for more than three centuries. The Christian and Jewish traditions are presented here as faiths containing principles that can be useful in making ethical decisions. Other faiths may contain similar principles, and students desiring different viewpoints are encouraged to seek information about other religions and search for additional useful ethical tools.

The Jewish Tradition

"The Jewish religious tradition stems from the Torah, the first five books of the Bible, in which are to be found a large number of rules and commandments."[64] When the Torah is combined with the Talmud, the more extensive encyclopedic compilation of the oral interpretation of Jewish law, the foundation is formed for deriving Jewish ethics. This religious tradition, like most others, is highly complex. Much depends on interpretive judgments made by Jewish rabbis. The Torah, however, remains "the primary source of truth for the Jewish community."[65] Being Jewish means having a relationship with God, being a part of the local ethnic community, and accepting the historical and religious traditions of the faith. The development of a system of Jewish ethics, therefore, "should take place in the context of the search for 'integrity,' the integration of past, present, and future into a coherent whole."[66]

Some Jewish scholars believe that Jewish ethics involve not only *halahka* ("The established consensus as to the correct interpretation of Jewish law") "but also *intuitive* moral responses arising from [a] . . . relationship with God." In other words, "conscience and/or moral intuition functions both alongside halahka and, to some extent, within it." Moral behavior, then, "emerges from a coalescence of divine and human energies."[67]

There are, of course, both traditional and contemporary views of Jewish ethics. But two issues appear to be common to most interpretations of Jewish law and tradition: (1) "the respective roles of God and Israel in defining moral norms, and (2) the respective power of self and community to determine the scope of moral responsibility."[68] What this means is that no single standard of ethical behavior can be established beyond what is, by consensus, contained in Jewish law. To this must be added the various interpretations of rabbis working with individual Jewish communities. The law, the community, and the individual all bear the responsibility of generating a code of moral behavior. This code will be specialized and will necessarily vary somewhat from community to community, from individual to individual. Those who are looking to Judaism for a set of rules that can be copied on a piece of paper, shoved in the pocket, and later extracted and used to solve ethical dilemmas will be disappointed. Jewish ethics are complex, tied to Jewish law and tradition, and dependent on rabbinical and community interpretation.

The Christian Way

"Christianity . . . is the name given to a vast clearinghouse of religious ideas."[69] Contemporary Christianity is rooted in the Hebrew heritage. It accepts the Old Testament laws and traditions and adds the New Testament teachings of Jesus, popularized by the apostle Paul. Jesus who came to earth and died on the cross for man's sins is the central focus of Christianity, but God is "the author and creator of all."[70] The Bible is seen as the supreme authority, yet it too requires interpretation. The essence of Christianity is often said to be contained in a verse of scripture from the New Testament Gospel of John: "For God so loved the world that he gave his only son that whoever believes in Him should not perish but have eternal life" (Revised Standard Version, 3:16).

Christian ethics involves more than asking, "What would Jesus do?" The answer to that question, of course, does not yield much useful information. The fact is that no one knows precisely what Jesus would do in any given situation. One may assert what Jesus would do based on one's knowledge of His teachings (found in the scriptures), but such judgments as might be made on this basis are subject to human error. The clergy are often of some help in interpreting and applying the ethical principles found in the Bible. One could always rely on the Ten Commandments, found in the Old Testament book of Exodus (20:1–17). These principles can be written on paper, pocketed, and consulted from time to time when ethical problems arise. But, of course, the Ten Commandments do not cover all the problems that arise in contemporary life.

There is always the question of what constitutes Christian ethics. "The ethics of the Bible? The moral standards of Christendom? The ethics of the New Testament? The ethical insights of Jesus?"[71] Some scholars have tried to extract a single principle on which one may depend and which may be used in any ethical dilemma. Joseph Fletcher's Christian Situation Ethics is a good example of this approach. Fletcher suggests that the key principle is *love*, but not just any kind of love. Fletcher believes that it is unconditional love, or *agape*, that should rule our behavior. This is the most God-like kind of love possible, for God unconditionally loves each and every individual, no matter how good or bad. For Fletcher, "the only valid ethical test is what God's love demands in each particular situation."[72]

Of course, there are other views. Both Catholics and Protestants have their own religious traditions and interpretations on which they base ethical principles. There is, however, much common moral ground, although the reasons for their positions on specific issues may vary. Nevertheless, all Christian religions believe that an individual's relationship to God is of primary importance. Bible study and prayer help one find God's way.

▶ *DECISION-MAKING TOOL*

Remembering that an individual's primary responsibility is to serve and be faithful to God, resolve an ethical dilemma by acting in accordance with the principles set forth by the Jewish or Christian religious tradition.

▶ *SUGGESTED MEDIA APPLICATION* ◀

Although some would argue that media are immoral (based on their journalistic practices and their entertainment content), the best one can probably say about media is that they are *amoral*. Media are capitalistic and secular. Given this environment, you, as a media employee, may have some difficulty in applying the principles of the Judeo-Christian tradition to media ethical dilemmas. A religious philosophy that emphasizes others, eschews the accumulation of wealth, and advocates adherence to a specific set of behavioral rules, including one's allegiance to God above all else, will be hard to apply in today's media environment. Some individuals have found that making it known that they follow strict religious principles and/or declining a particularly troublesome assignment are ways of avoiding thorny problems. This is not always possible, or even always desirable. Some other individuals have discovered that they would be happier in a non-media work environment and have left the media field. But many have developed skills to make this philosophy work.

RECOMMENDED CASE STUDIES
#15 (Chapter 14); #20 (Chapter 15).

p. 276   p. 304

QUESTIONS FOR DISCUSSION

1. Sartre believed that an individual was free to make choices and that these choices essentially constituted that individual's ethical system. How free are we to make moral choices in contemporary culture? Can you name several moral choices that are made for us?

2. Human reason and intuition play a part in applying Sartre's ethics. How can this approach be useful in a postmodern culture that essentially rejects reason as a means of discerning truth? What is the difference between reason and intuition?

3. To what degree does reason play a part in Rand's philosophy of objectivism?

4. How would postmodern culture view Rand's notion that man ought to live for himself, not for others?

5. Why do you think Rand's ideas were so popular in the mid-1900s?

6. Kohlberg felt that very few people advance to the postconventional level of moral decision making. Do you agree? Explain.

7. Can you account for the continued influence of Judeo-Christian ideas in our culture? Can Judeo-Christian ideas be attributed to one individual or to many? Explain.

8. Are Judeo-Christian ethical principles absolute or relative in terms of human behavior?

ENDNOTES

1. John Gerassi, *Jean-Paul Sartre, Hated Conscience of His Century* (Chicago: University of Chicago Press, 1989), 41.

2. Ibid., 42.

3. Arne Naess, *Four Modern Philosophers* (Chicago: University of Chicago Press, 1965), 265.

4. Gerassi, 46.

5. Ibid., 41.

6. Ibid., 48.

7. Ibid., 52.

8. Ibid.

9. Ibid., 54.

10. Ibid., 59.

11. Naess, 266.

12. P. Johnson, *Intellectuals* (London: Weidenfeld and Nicholson, 1988), 235–236.

13. Naess, 271.

14. Johnson, 250.

15. Annie Cohen-Solal, *Sartre, a Life,* trans. Anna Canogni (New York: Pantheon, 1987), 523.

16. Kate Fullbrook and Edward Fullbrook, *Simone de Beauvoir and Jean-Paul Sartre* (New York: Basic Books, 1994), 182.

17. Cohen-Solal, 83–84.

18. Anthony Flew, *A Dictionary of Philosophy* (New York: St. Martin's Press, 1979), 115.

19. Ibid., 116.

20. Ethel C. Albert, Theodore C. Denise, and Sheldon P. Peterfreund, *Great Traditions in Ethics* (New York: Van Nostrand, 1975), 352.

21. Jean-Paul Sartre, *Notebooks for an Ethics,* trans. David Pellauer (Chicago: University of Chicago Press, 1992).

22. Naess, 346.

23. H. Gene Blocker, *Ethics, an Introduction* (New York: Haven, 1986), 233 and 237.

24. David Detmer, *Freedom as Value: A Critique of the Ethical Theory of Jean-Paul Sartre* (LaSalle, IL: Open Court, 1988), 208.

25. Ibid., 213.

26. Thomas C. Anderson, *Sartre's Two Ethics* (LaSalle, IL: Open Court, 1993), 169.

27. Ronald Aronson and Adrian van den Hoven, *Sartre Alive* (Detroit: Wayne State University Press, 1991), 65–66.

28. Barbara Branden, *The Passion of Ayn Rand* (New York: Doubleday, 1986), 63.

29. Ibid.

30. James T. Baker, *Ayn Rand* (Boston: Twayne, 1987), 1.

31. Ibid., 3.

32. Ibid., 4.

33. Branden, 77.

34. Ibid., 79 and 83.

35. Ibid., 91.

36. Ibid., 272–273.

37. Baker, 18, 19, 20.

38. Ibid., 19 and 21.

39. Ibid., 352 and 357.

40. Ibid., 403.

41. George H. Smith, *Atheism, Ayn Rand, and Other Heresies* (Buffalo, NY: Prometheus Books, 1991), 193.

42. Baker, 18.

43. Ibid., 94.

44. Ayn Rand, *The Virtue of Selfishness* (New York: New American Library, 1961), 13.

45. Smith, 202.

46. Ibid., 215.

47. Ibid., 216 and 217.

48. Baker, 97–98.

49. Ibid., 96.

50. Little biographical information exists on Lawrence Kohlberg. The life profile that follows contains information taken from an article by James Rest, Clark Power, and Mary Brabeck that appeared in the May 1988 issue of *American Psychologist* (43, 5): 399–400.

51. Richard H. Hersh, John P. Miller, and Glen D. Fielding, *Models of Moral Education: An Appraisal* (New York: Longman, 1980), 119.

52. Ibid.

53. Ibid., 120.

54. Ibid.

55. Beverly A. Mattox, *Getting It Together* (San Diego: Pennant Press, 1975), 20–21.

56. Ibid., 22.

57. Lawrence Kohlberg, "Moral Stages and Moralization: The Cognitive-Developmental Approach," in *Moral Development and Behavior: Theory, Research, and Social Issues,* ed. Thomas Lickona (New York: Holt, Rinehart, & Winston, 1976), 34–35.

58. Mattox, 22.

59. Hersh, Miller, and Fielding, 122.

60. Larry C. Jensen and Richard S. Knight, *Moral Education: Historical Perspectives* (Washington, DC: University Press of America, 1981), 73.

61. Ibid.

62. Ibid., 77.

63. Ibid., 86.

64. Clive Lawton, "Judaism," in *Ethical Issues in Six Religious Traditions,* ed. Peggy Morgan and Clive Lawton (Edinburgh: Edinburgh University Press, 1996), 135.

65. Louis E. Newman, "Covenantal Responsibility in a Modern Context," *Journal of Religious Ethics* 25 (1997): 191.

66. Ibid., 188.

67. Ibid., 196–197 and 201.

68. Ibid., 204.

69. Geddes MacGregor, "Ethical Consequences of the Christian Way," in *World Religions and Global Ethics,* ed. S. Cromwell Crawford (New York: Paragon House, 1989), 188.

70. Ibid., 193.

71. Georgia Harkness, *Christian Ethics* (Nashville, TN: Abingdon Press, 1968), 14.

72. Joseph F. Fletcher, *Situation Ethics: The New Morality* (Philadelphia: Westminster Press, 1966), 55, 79.

▼▼▼

CHAPTER 9

Postmodernist Approaches

There are several contemporary philosophers whose work might be labeled postmodern. The two profiled in this chapter have ideas that provide an interesting contrast to the ideas of other philosophers in this text. Unlike many of those other philosophical ideas, postmodern philosophy is a work-in-progress, with many additions and revisions still to come. We are, after all, living in the postmodern period (see the time line), and new cultural ideas and practices may lie just ahead.

Culture Period ▪ Approximate Dates	General Description ▪ Key Personalities
Modern Age A.D. 1850–A.D. 1945 **Michel Foucault** (1926 . . .) **Jean Baudrillard** (1929–)	Industrial Revolution takes hold; steel developed; much political and social change in America (Civil War) and in Europe (World Wars I and II); significant contributions in art, music, literature, science; Pasteur, Einstein, Wright Brothers, Hugo, Marx, Freud, Picasso, Hitler, Stalin
Postmodern Age A.D. 1945–Present **Michel Foucault** (. . . 1984) *Note:* Many scholars set 1945—or the end of World War II—as the time we began the transition to the postmodern era. This is probably true, especially in Europe, but your author fixes the date more precisely in America at about 1965. More discussion of this can be found in Chapter 1.	Rapid social and political change; life becomes more complex; much ambiguity and discontinuity in the culture; rise of influence of media; institutions of modern age (families, schools, churches) undergo profound change; rise of technology as a life influence; increasingly important global economy

Both Foucault and Baudrillard were born in the modern period; however, their philosophical outlooks are clearly postmodern. Both subscribe to the notion that modernity failed to solve most of society's problems. The reaction to this failure, together with the rejection of science and reason as dominant truth paradigms, has led us to the postmodern era, a culture period characterized by a discontinuity and ambiguity in all phases of life.

127

▼ Michel Foucault

The Life

Teacher, thinker, writer, activist. These words are often used to describe philosophers. Most of the philosophers already discussed qualify for all these labels. It should come as no surprise that many philosophers in contemporary—postmodern—society can also be described in this same way. In fact, the four descriptors nicely summarize the life of Michel Foucault.

In the French town of Poitiers, Paul-Michel Foucault was <u>born</u> to Paul and Anne Foucault on <u>October 15, 1926.</u> He was welcomed by an older sister, Francine, and by a nurse, a cook, and a chauffeur. The elder Foucault was a wealthy surgeon and a highly respected medical school professor of anatomy, and Paul-Michel's mother was the daughter of a surgeon and medical school professor. The family was not overwhelmingly rich, but enough money was available to provide a lifestyle that was clearly more luxurious than that of most other French families.

Since he was the firstborn son, the newest member of the Foucault household was given the name Paul, a name shared with both his father and grandfather. It was almost a family requirement that he be named Paul. Madame Foucault was not terribly fond of this tradition, so she added a hyphen and the name Michel. As time passed and he grew, young Paul-Michel would drop the first part of his hyphenated first name and use only Michel.[1]

Michel's early years were not particularly remarkable. He received an adequate education. He was a reasonably good student, in language and history, but found math difficult. Although his father wanted him to become a doctor, Michel was more interested in history. His father groused about this a bit, but his mother took his side, and little more was said about his intellectual interests, especially after the Foucaults' second son (and third child), Denys, indicated that he would like to become a doctor.

Michel completed his early educational experiences and enrolled in the Academe de Poitiers with a view toward entering the famous Ecole Normale Superieure (ENS), where only the best of the best were trained for important roles in French cultural and political life. But at the Academe, he was an unhappy student. He had few friends, did not mix well, and spent most of his time studying alone. When he took the ENS admission exam in July 1945, he did not qualify for admission. Determined to try again, he moved to Paris for further preparatory study. But life in Paris after World War II was difficult. Real problems, including food shortages, faced everyone. Nevertheless, he survived and was admitted to the ENS in 1946.

One might have expected that his successful admission to the most important of French schools would brighten his spirits and change his outlook somewhat. It did not. He was still a loner; he argued constantly with everyone, and almost everyone hated him. In 1948 Michel attempted suicide, slicing his chest with a razor. This was the first of several attempts at suicide dur-

Postmodern thinker Michel Foucault was a historian, a social reformer, and a popular teacher. He was concerned with power and legitimization. *UPI / CORBIS—BETTMAN*

ing his school years. His father was naturally alarmed at his son's action and requested that he be evaluated by the school's doctor. The doctor complied and served up this diagnosis: young Michel's "troubles resulted from an extreme difficulty in explaining and accepting his homosexuality."[2]

It should be noted that during this time, the 1940s, homosexuality was not an acceptable alternative lifestyle as it is in some quarters of today's society. For the most part, homosexuals kept their lifestyle secret, because revealing their sexual preferences would likely bring them nothing but shame. Many homosexuals, Michel among them, felt repressed and guilty that their actions and desires had to be secret.[3] Nevertheless, Michel was a hard worker. He read constantly, took copious notes, and carefully organized his boxes of note cards.

He developed an interest in psychology at the ENS and was licensed in 1949. He joined the Communist party in 1950 and began his teaching career as an assistant lecturer at the University of Lille in 1952. By 1955, Foucault was tired and needed a change of scene. He left his teaching position at Lille and traveled to Sweden, Poland, and Germany. He taught at several universities during this time, but primarily he used this time to think. He returned to Paris in 1960. The primary benefit of this journey, it appears, was that it turned him against communism. He had apparently seen what the communists were up to, particularly in Poland.

Foucault joined the philosophy department of the University of Clermont-Ferrand in 1960, traveling between Paris and Clermont each week. Foucault was now a changed man. He was happy and relaxed and seemed to interact well with others. He was a stylish dresser. "He wore a black corduroy suit, white turtleneck sweaters, and a green loden cape" at his once-a-week class at Clermont.[4] He was a striking figure in front of the class and possessed an animated teaching style. He moved rapidly back and forth in front of the room, talking nonstop. He would occasionally pause to consult notes or to pose a question. He liked to challenge his students with difficult questions, but most were too afraid to respond, so Foucault usually ended up answering his own question, and answering it at some length. However, his students liked and admired him. They gathered to talk with him after class and often had a social drink with him. During his last year at Clermont, Foucault was rewarded with a round of applause at the end of every lecture.[5]

Foucault taught later in Tunisia and at the University of Vincennes, before settling in at the College de France in 1970. During this time, he involved himself, like Jean-Paul Sartre, in many of the social, political, and academic issues of the time. He was especially interested in prison reform and in overhauling the French legal system. Although he did not subscribe to any of Sartre's views, he worked with Sartre on several occasions, one of them in June 1979 when the two led a group who spoke for the rights of the Vietnamese boat people. Foucault, Sartre, and others, including the actors Yves Montand and Simone Signoret, demanded that more of these refugees be allowed to enter France. In 1980, Foucault was one of the throng of 50,000 mourners who followed Sartre's coffin to the Montparnasse Cemetery.

Foucault visited America in the early 1980s, speaking at Berkeley, New York University, UCLA, and the University of Vermont. He liked America, particularly New York and San Francisco. He felt homosexuals in these two cities were treated more civilly than elsewhere. Foucault took to the American gay subculture quickly. He had been part of both the gay and drug subcultures in Paris for some time, admitting in the late 1970s to having tried LSD, cocaine, and opium. He reportedly grew marijuana plants on his apartment balcony.[6] Foucault actually gave some thought to moving to the United States permanently, but his health began to fail, and any notion he had of moving was abandoned.

On June 2, 1984, Foucault collapsed in his apartment and was taken to a local hospital. He had complained of a particularly virulent strain of the flu for sometime. He was frequently tired, had coughing fits, and suffered from severe migraine headaches. Some friends say he did not know he had AIDS; others say he knew, but "did not want to know."[7] When he died on June 25, *1984* the official death notice did not mention AIDS as the cause of death. Foucault was buried in a little cemetery near Vandeuve on June 29 with only family and a few friends present. At his request, there was no religious service.[8]

At the time of his death, Foucault's "books, essays, and interviews had been translated into 16 languages . . . [he may have been] the single most famous intellectual in the world."[9] Like Sartre, he was considered something of a national treasure by the French. Also like Sartre, newspapers gave considerable space to summaries of his life and work.

The Philosophy

Foucault's best known work is probably *Madness and Civilization: A History of Insanity in the Age of Reason,* published in 1961. This is the sort of work one might expect from a historian; it shows how madness was silenced and tucked away out of sight and away from daily experience. *Discipline and Punish: The Birth of the Prison* (1975) is critical of the penal system's surveillance and control methods. Later, his three-volume *The History of Sexuality* (1976–1984) discussed power-knowledge relationships and stirred considerable interest.

Some scholars note that Foucault's work can be apportioned neatly along two dimensions: his early work as a philosophical historian and his later work as a philosopher offering "theories of knowledge, power, and the self."[10] It is from this second dimension that we shall derive his ethical system.

Foucault would most likely have opposed an effort to organize his ideas into an ethical system. He felt ethics were important, but thought that a "system" of ethics was inappropriate inasmuch as any such system would establish "universal standards of behavior that legislate conformity and normalization . . . in accordance with a least common denominator."[11] Foucault claimed that there should be no universally applicable rules of ethics. An individual's ethics should result from personal reflection.

Nevertheless, Foucault can be of help in solving ethical dilemmas. Postmodern solutions to problems are not always the best ones, but such solutions should be available alongside more traditional ones. Focusing on some of Foucault's ideas about power and the self and placing these ideas in a mass communications context should prove both interesting and helpful.

For Foucault, a sense of identity is a necessary prelude to ethical action. One develops this identity through *self-formation.* This process calls for an individual to examine "that part of himself that will form" a moral practice, "define his position relative to the precept he will follow, and decide on a certain mode of being that will serve as his moral goal."[12] In other words, an individual must formulate moral practices and precepts and internalize them.[13] Ethics then become more than a set of rules one follows; ethics become "a lifestyle, a way of thinking and living."[14]

Along with the development of the self, one needs also to consider the notion of *power.* This is fundamental to an understanding of the world and equally fundamental to the practice of moral conduct. According to Foucault, all human interactions are ultimately concerned with power, sometimes in complex, obscure ways. Power "organizes the resources of modern societies under the pretense of attending to the care of the species and the health of the individual."[15] Further, those who hold and exercise power reach their goals by making sure other human beings do the work but have no say in matters that concern them.[16] In other words, power enables those who possess it to use it to control others while pretending to work on behalf of those others. Foucault felt that exposing the inner workings of power would, at least for a time, render that power temporarily less effective and less dangerous.[17] Power can be neither totally eliminated nor consistently limited, but it can be neutralized to some extent for a short period of time in a local context.

It should also be noted that Foucault believed that power exists everywhere, not just in the hands of large, impersonal businesses or institutions.[18] In a 1977 interview, Foucault said: "When I think of the mechanics of power, I think of its capillary form of existence, of the extent to which power seeps into the very grain of individuals, reaches right into their bodies, permeates their gestures, their posture, what they say, how they learn to live and work with other people." Foucault acknowledges that power has something of a negative reputation; nevertheless, as he wrote in *Discipline and Punish*, "Power produces; it produces reality; it produces domains of objects and rituals of truth."

If we understand the importance of the self and the influence of power, how are we to use this knowledge in determining what constitutes proper ethical conduct? One begins with a fundamental basis of truth. Foucault believed that there exists "a set of truth obligations: discovering the truth, being enlightened by the truth, telling the truth."[19] This is essentially an individual's ethical work: to develop moral conduct that satisfies the obligations of truth and that is an integral part of the self; to understand the power relationships inherent in all life situations; to expect movement or adaptation from the created self in order to survive and satisfy the demands of practical existence.

Foucault's contributions to ethics "involved neither the articulation of a new moral theory nor the advocacy of an alternative" to the techniques of power. He preferred to "investigate the conditions under which particular subjects are found and to expose the hidden power interests that are served by each type of subject."[20]

▶ *DECISION-MAKING TOOL*

Recalling the set of truth obligations, examine an ethical problem and determine a desired course of action. Ask two questions: "Is the proposed solution a reflection of my personal ethical standards?" "What power relationships influence the solution?" If you are comfortable with the answers to each of these questions, implement the desired action.

▶ *SUGGESTED MEDIA APPLICATION* ◀

Although somewhat abstract and often difficult to understand—there is always the problem of an accurate translation from the French—Foucault's ideas appear to have some implications for mass communications, particularly in terms of power relationships. American media are widely acknowledged to be extremely powerful, though industry executives would probably deny it. The power certainly exists in terms of economics, and many would argue that in terms of ideas and cultural practices, media are indeed powerful.

The June 3, 1996, issue of *The Nation* contained an article by Mark Crispin Miller that clearly demonstrated that media industries wield considerable economic power. The article included a foldout section showing the octopus-like connections (power relationships) among American media and four giant corporations: General Electric, Time Warner, Disney/Cap Cities, and Westinghouse. The influence of these four companies goes beyond media to businesses such as insurance, fuel, aircraft engines, mutual funds, plastics, and medical services, among others. There is almost no aspect of American life that these four companies fail to touch. These complex business and power relationships are unknown to most media consumers. If they were known, it is unclear how many consumers would care.

Nevertheless, if one is sensitive to Foucault's notion of power, one might be a bit more critical of what American media are doing to the culture. Foucault called it *subjectivation,* the process by which we are "gradually transformed into subjects" invested with little power and many limitations. For all media's trumpeting of the diversity of information and entertainment available, the subjects—that is American consumers of media—really have little choice about many media practices. For example, if consumers object to the way television network newscasts frame every conflict between Caucasians and African-Americans in terms of race, or frame every story about family problems in terms of gender conflict, or even something as straightforward as concentrating too heavily on crime news, they have no way to make their voices heard. The argument that they could tune out and let the ratings inspire change is a red herring. When it comes to news, a ratings slump usually brings cosmetic (set, hairstyle, anchor), not substantive, content changes. Much research data indicate that the media are quite good at *setting the agenda* for what Americans talk and are concerned about. The question Foucault might have asked is this one: Whose agenda is being set, and what power relationships are involved in the setting?

RECOMMENDED CASE STUDIES
#4 (Chapter 11); #12 (Chapter 13).

▼ Jean Baudrillard

The Life

When asked to discuss his background in a 1991 interview, Jean Baudrillard replied, "No background." This is just the sort of response one might expect from him. Growing up, he had none of the advantages that some other French philosophers had: certainly not the advantages of Foucault, born three years earlier, and probably not the advantages Sartre had. In order not to highlight the obvious differences between his early life and the early lives of many of his contemporaries, Baudrillard chose to deflect the question.

Actually, not much is known about his early life. He was born in the northeastern French city of Reims in 1929. His grandparents were peasants, but his parents were civil servants, trying to work their way to a higher socioeconomic level. As a youngster, he was a reasonably good student and graduated from secondary school in about 1947. He then "went to Paris for a year's intensive study at the Lycee Henri IV, in preparation for a university education."[21] He lasted only two months. He left, hating the school, the Paris culture, everything. However, he soon returned to Paris, convinced that if he wanted to make a living, he needed a university education.

Like so many others before him, Baudrillard began teaching at the conclusion of his work at the Lycee Henri IV. But his teaching career fell short of the success achieved by others. Baudrillard taught German in the French secondary school system. By comparison, Foucault was already well on his way to becoming Chair of Philosophy at the University of Clermont-Ferrand. Baudrillard took the entrance exams for ENS, but was not successful in gaining admission. Nevertheless, even after he defended his thesis at the University of Paris in 1966, he had difficulty getting a high-profile job in the French university system. He took a teaching assistant position at a branch campus (Nanterre) in 1968, and eventually became an assistant professor.

His slow progress through the university teaching ranks was probably a good thing. He was not overly fond of teaching and did both himself and his students a favor by retiring early.[22] Still, he spent almost two decades (1968–1987) teaching. Like most of the other French philosophers, he continued to write and to speak out on social and political issues. His writings were even slower in coming to America than were Sartre's. Baudrillard's early work was not translated into English nor did he play a significant part in French culture until postmodernism emerged as a cultural philosophy in the 1980s.[23]

Baudrillard was always an outsider of sorts, even after his work brought him considerable attention in the 1980s. He regularly contributed to a variety of French magazines and journals. He lived "in central Paris, in a quarter alive with restaurants, cinemas, small shops."[24] Interviewers described him as likable and witty. One noted: "He was rather like a union boss, thickset, and indeed rolled his own."[25] This last phrase, of course, refers to his habit of rolling his own cigarettes. Another interviewer reported him "rumpled, unpretentious, and curiously placid."[26] His Left Bank apartment was rather plain and well used. However, one interviewer was struck by the "fifty televisions, set side by side and one atop the other, [that] line one wall."[27] Although not a lover of contemporary culture, Baudrillard apparently feels the need to observe it.

Baudrillard traveled a great deal. He visited America several times in the late 1980s and two books resulted from his travel experiences: *America* and *Cool Memories*. He was both fascinated and repulsed by American culture. He was particularly disturbed by the way America had become a consumer culture, interested primarily in commodities. Yet he found the culture vibrant and alive: "the latest fast-food outlet, the most banal suburb, the blandest of giant American cars, or the most insignificant cartoon-strip majorette is more at the center of the world than any of the cultural manifestations of old Europe. . . . This is the land of 'just as it is.' "[28]

The Philosophy

Although dismissed by some scholars, Jean Baudrillard is considered by others "to be an insightful thinker of uncommon originality whose work is invaluable in beginning to comprehend the impact of new communications forms on society."[29] Whatever his critical reception, it is clear that, like Voltaire, Baudrillard can deliver a powerful message in a witty line or two. Here is a sampling:[30]

> All situations are inspired by an object, a fragment, a present obsession, never by an idea. (1)

> The whole art of politics today is to whip up popular indifference. (16)

> The compact disc. It doesn't wear out, even if you use it. Terrifying. It's as though you'd never used it. . . . If things don't get old anymore, then that's because it's you who are dead. (32–33)

> . . . in front of a pile of rubbish by the side of the road, a sign which reads: "This is not a dump." (53)

> Radicality is an end-of-career privilege. (63)

> Since the media always make you out to say the opposite of what you say, you should have the courage always to say the opposite of what you think. (56–57)

> Communicate? Communicate? Only doors communicate. (80)

Baudrillard is often regarded as the high priest of postmodernism. In a 1991 interview he was asked whether he accepted this role. He replied, "This reference to priesthood is out of place. . . . [B]efore one can talk about anyone being a high priest, one should ask whether postmodernism, the postmodern, has a meaning. It doesn't as far as I'm concerned. It's an expression, a word people use but which explains nothing. . . . [A]n empty term has been chosen to designate what is really empty."[31] Nevertheless, Baudrillard has spent a lot of time writing and talking about contemporary culture. His observations describe many of the conditions others say are characteristic of the postmodern era. So whether or not he considers himself a contributor to postmodernism, others certainly think his insights important in attempting to determine the broad outlines and specific characteristics of our present historical cultural period.

Baudrillard believes that, in large part, human needs form as a result of the media's influence, which reinforces our desire for the accumulation of goods.[32] Baudrillard makes this powerful argument: "Consumption is the virtual totality of all objects and messages presently constituted in a more or less coherent discourse. . . . [Yet] in their supreme egoism, everyone feels unique even as they conform and are manipulated by the media and the culture industry."[33]

Going a step farther, Baudrillard suggests "that the great cornucopia of consumer goods in advanced industrial societies constitutes a coded system by which material things shape the very needs they fulfill. . . . There are no limits to consumption but also the boundless urge to consume fails to bring satisfaction."[34] The result is a *hyperreal world* where "contemporary, postmodern existence is dominated by the circulation of fictions and signs that have no referent, origin, or meaning."[35]

Baudrillard sees the United States as the ultimate postmodern culture. America, he charges, is gripped by a *must exit* logic. The poor, the aged, and the infirm are shoved out of sight because they can interfere with the wealth and efficiency of the culture. Although he might appear to be a supporter of minority and special-interest-group causes, Baudrillard is anything but politically correct. For example, he believes that some hallmarks of postmodern culture—consumerism, concern with appearances, desire, insatiability—are feminine in nature. Thus, "femininity holds a purely negative function: it seduces the masculine world of power, differentiation, and ideas. It does not contribute anything positive to human culture."[36] This notion will likely win him no friends among the women of the world.

In short, Baudrillard believes we live in "a social world of circulating fictions in which nothing is real, true, or grounded in any sort of . . . permanence." His advice is to "adopt a form of passive resistance to . . . an invasive and manipulative culture." He says we must "conquer the world and seduce it through an indifference that is at least equal to the world's."[37]

Being indifferent to ethical behavior would be a postmodern response to problems, but not the response that this text is promoting. Our emphasis has always been on active participation in ethical issues, particularly through the use of basic ethical philosophies and human reasoning. So we are going to take Baudrillard's work a step farther by deriving a useful ethical principle from his philosophical theories, asserting in the process that action is preferable to indifference, even in a postmodern society.

The only aspect of Baudrillard's philosophy that we must modify to derive an ethical theory is his notion of indifference as a response to contemporary culture. Since we want to promote ethical behavior in all aspects of life, we must set aside Baudrillard's indifference suggestion. This action is not particularly damaging to his other ideas. In fact, his statement about indifference was preceded by a statement suggesting "passive resistance" as a course of action. Without getting into an argument over semantics, it seems clear that Baudrillard did not mean indifference in the purest sense of the term but that we ought, passively or mildly, to resist the negative aspects of contemporary culture. Resistance would require some effort on our part; indifference would not. Baudrillard himself shows that he is as much a consumer of the culture as he is a critic of it. Remember the 50 television sets in his apartment? This does not suggest indifference to the culture. For our present purposes, then, we may conclude that Baudrillard favors resisting the intrusive and manipulative nature of the culture, though not rejecting it entirely.

▶ *DECISION-MAKING TOOL*

Examine possible responses to an ethical dilemma and select the one that is least manipulative and intrusive, the one that most closely represents true reality.

▶ *SUGGESTED MEDIA APPLICATION* ◀

Baudrillard believes that media, in all the various forms—and here we add advertising and public relations activities to the well-known news and entertainment industries—are highly intrusive and significantly manipulative. As a result, we have become a consumer-oriented people who find little meaning in anything except consuming—that is, fulfilling the needs we are told we have by the media and by other segments of postmodern society. In other words, media shape reality, and that reality is often a false one, certainly one that is devoid of meaning and context.

Simulation, Baudrillard's term for this phenomenon, is the substitution of the false for the real; it is dangerous because we cannot not tell the real from the unreal. His classic example involves a scenario where a man pretends to rob a bank using a fake pistol. The pretend robber is the only one who knows it is a fake pistol and that he is only pretending; the police who confront him are using real guns and real bullets; they think he is serious about committing the crime. To everyone but the robber, this is real. But the pretend robber has substituted the false for the real, and events will play themselves out as if everything were real, with possible tragic consequences.[38]

It should now be fairly obvious what our ethical approach to media problems should be. We should resist the intrusive and manipulative nature of media and society and attempt to produce work that is meaningful, work that mirrors a truer reality. As Baudrillard suggests, "The only weapon of power . . . is to re-inject realness and referentiality everywhere."[39]

RECOMMENDED CASE STUDIES

#9 (Chapter 12); #12 (Chapter 13).

QUESTIONS FOR DISCUSSION

1. Explain Foucault's concept of the influence of power in contemporary life and its impact on ethical behavior.

2. What are the three obligations Foucault says we owe to the truth?

3. What are the characteristics of Baudrillard's hyperreal world?

4. Can you find examples in advertising, public relations, and journalism that support Baudrillard's notion that nothing in contemporary society is real, true, or grounded in permanence? Are there examples that refute his view?

5. Baudrillard feels that action should be undertaken after one has determined the true reality of a situation. How does one go about determining true reality in a postmodern culture?

ENDNOTES

1. Didier Eribon, *Michel Foucault,* trans. Betsy Wing (Cambridge, MA: Harvard University Press, 1991), 4.

2. Ibid., 26.

3. Ibid., 27.

4. Ibid., 138.

5. Ibid., 141.

6. Ibid., 315.

7. Ibid., 325.

8. Ibid., 330.

9. James Miller, *The Passion of Michel Foucault* (New York: Simon & Schuster, 1993), 13.

10. Gary Gutting, "Introduction, Michel Foucault: A User's Manual," in *The Cambridge Companion to Foucault,* ed. Gary Gutting (Cambridge: Cambridge University Press, 1994), 2.

11. James W. Bernauer and Michael Mahon, "The Ethics of Michel Foucault," in *The Cambridge Companion to Foucault,* ed. Gary Gutting (Cambridge: Cambridge University Press, 1994), 153.

12. Ibid., 143.

13. Ibid., 144.

14. Ibid., 154.

15. David Conway, "Michel Foucault," in *The Encyclopedia of Philosophy,* ed. Donald M. Borchert (New York: Simon & Schuster, 1996), 201.

16. Ibid.

17. Ibid., 202.

18. Annette Lawson, "Michel Foucault," in *The Annual Obituary 1984,* ed. Margot Levy (Chicago: St. James Press, 1984), 309.

19. Michel Foucault, *Ethics: Subjectivity and Truth,* ed. Paul Rabinow (New York: New York Press, 1997), 177–178.

20. Conway, 201.

21. *Current Biography Yearbook 1993,* ed. Judith Graham (New York: H. W. Wilson, 1993), 32.

22. Mike Gane, "Introduction," in *Baudrillard Live: Selected Interviews;* ed. Mike Gane (New York: Routledge, 1993), 2.

23. Ibid.

24. Ibid., 11.

25. Ibid.

26. *Current Biography,* 35.

27. Gane, 11.

28. *Current Biography,* 34.

29. Ibid., 32.

30. Jean Baudrillard, *Cool Memories II: 1987–1990,* trans. Chris Turner (Durham: Duke University Press, 1996). All quotes followed by page number.

31. Gane, 21–22.

32. *Current Biography,* 32.

33. Stjepan G. Mestrovic, *Durkheim and Postmodern Culture* (New York: Aldine de Gruyter, 1992), 49.

34. *Current Biography,* 33.

35. Mestrovic, 140.

36. Ibid., 45.

37. Ibid., 35.

38. Jean Baudrillard, *Simulations,* trans. Paul Foss, Paul Patton, and Philip Beitchman (New York: Semiotext, 1983), 38.

39. Ibid., 42.

Applications

▼ ▼ ▼

Applying philosophical concepts to everyday life is often difficult. In ethics, applying what you know to life's ethical problems is extremely important. Because ethics deals with issues of right and wrong, that is, appropriate and inappropriate behavior, your decisions may have far-reaching implications for yourself and for others. This section provides you the opportunity to see ethical principles applied to media.

You have a number of decision-making tools at hand. You may wish to review these from time to time as you work your way through the chapters in this section. You also have the decision-making model presented in Chapter 10. If you add a little common sense and some clear thinking, you should be able to solve most of the ethical issues that will confront you, both in your personal life and in your media work life.

The examples presented in the chapters just ahead illustrate how to go about analyzing and solving an ethical dilemma. It is not possible to cover all the potential problems that you might encounter, but you should be able to use the analytical skills you have developed and the skills you see at work in the chapters in this section to raise important issues, ask probing questions, and reach satisfactory, that is, ethical solutions, to situations that go beyond this text's examples.

Here is an important suggestion: Do not be reluctant to use the philosophies you learned in Section II. These philosophies are more than theoretical concepts. They are practical. Take Kant's categorical imperative, for example. Kant developed the concept with the idea that it would be used. Of course he understood that the concept would be discussed in philosophy classes and perhaps in other academic settings, but he felt strongly that the concept should be applied to life and that life would be the better for it. In Kant's view, acting only on those principles that you would have others act on leads to a better world.

Remember, too, that you must resist the postmodern tendency toward fuzzy thinking. Postmodern culture fails to recognize inconsistency. It rejects reason as a means toward problem resolution. Common sense has all but disappeared. In order to make the best possible ethical decisions, you must use reason, develop some common sense, and recognize inconsistencies. Casting off the trappings of postmodern culture gives you the best chance to make a good ethical decision. Of course you still have to live in the postmodern culture, but you need not let the culture dictate the way you make moral judgments. You must make these on your own and accept the responsibility that comes with such decision making.

With a little practice, you can become a practical, confident ethical decision maker. You will likely face a number of interesting challenges in your work in media. Not all will relate to ethics, but when an ethical problem presents itself, remember that you are well prepared to solve it.

SUGGESTED READINGS

Books

Berger, Arthur Asa. *Manufacturing Desire; Media, Popular Culture, and Everyday Life* (Somerset, NJ: Transaction, 1995).

Dennis, Everette E., and Pease, Edward C. *Children and the Media* (Somerset, NJ: Transaction, 1996).

Dyson, Kenneth, ed. *Culture First! Promoting Standards in the New Media Age* (Herndon, VA: Cassell Academic, 1996).

Ewen, Stuart. *All Consuming Images* (New York: Basic Books, 1988).

Jensen, J. Vernon. *Ethical Issues in the Communication Process* (Mahwah, NJ: Lawrence Erlbaum Associates, 1997).

Perkinson, Henry. *Getting Better: Television and Moral Progress* (Somerset, NJ: Transaction, 1995).

Video

"Ethical Considerations in Journalism," #JT149, 23 minutes (New York: Insight Media, 1989).

"The Glitter: Sex, Drugs, and the Media," #JT407, 23 minutes (New York: Insight Media, 1995).

"Why Ads Work: The Power of Self-Deception," #JT470, 21 minutes (New York: Insight Media, 1995).

Journal

Black, Jay, and Barney, Ralph, eds. *Journal of Mass Media Ethics* (Mahwah, NJ: Lawrence Erlbaum Associates, quarterly).

CHAPTER **10**

Decision Making

Now what? We have a number of ethical decision-making tools at hand and have established that the postmodern world "is characterized by a continual change of perspectives, with no underlying common frame of reference."[1] Not only is a frame of reference lacking, but the diversity of interpretations of modern culture is coupled with a loss of belief that one can determine truths or even get a grasp on reality.[2] How can we make ethical decisions given such conditions?

Is it possible even to recognize a proper ethical course, much less follow it, given the pressures exerted by postmodern culture? The answer, of course, is yes. It is still possible to consider ethical problems seriously and to reach satisfactory solutions. Being able to resolve ethical issues is of utmost importance to you as an individual, but is even more important when you consider your role as a worker in the powerful and influential media industries. Media audiences will often take behavioral cues from what they see, hear, or read. As a participant in what might be called the *great communications conversation*—the interaction between media audiences and those who provide media content—you must carefully consider each action for its ethical implications.

One of the keys to successful ethical decision making is being able to resist postmodern tendencies and engage in a rational, systematic examination of an ethical problem and its possible solutions. This sort of activity will be difficult because postmodern thinking has essentially rejected the *reasoned* approach to the framing and solving of problems. Reason doesn't count for much in the postmodern era, principally because individuals have moved away from the absolutes, the rules, the structures that reason often produces.

Reason, or rational thinking, is essentially a product of the Enlightenment, which began in the eighteenth century. The movement was grounded in the notion that all the world's diverse peoples could be made to see things the same way—the rational way. It held that "linear progress, absolute truths, and rational planning of ideal social orders"[3] was possible—indeed, desirable—if society was to grow and develop to its full potential. The German philosopher Immanuel Kant, summing up the convictions and ambitions of some of the more radical scholars and intellectuals of the time, wrote that

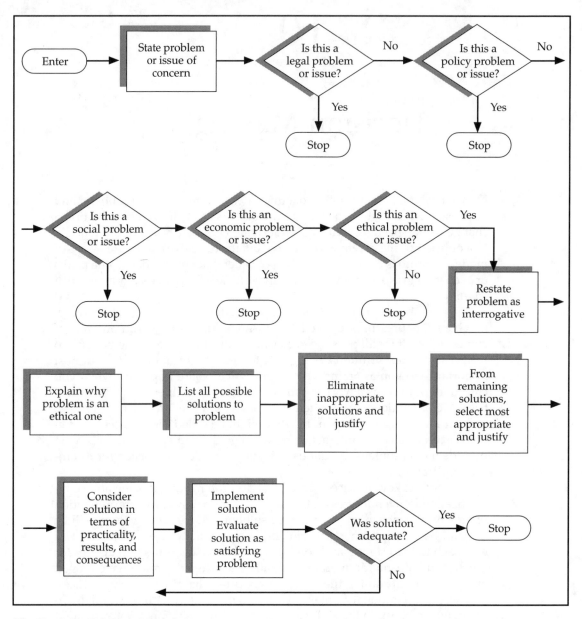

The Decision-Making Model

man's immaturity was not caused by a "lack of intelligence, but lack of determination and courage to use that intelligence. . . . Dare to know! Have the courage to use your own intelligence!"[4] Understanding man, his nature, and the natural world was to be accomplished primarily through science.

Although you cannot turn back the clock and return to the "good old days," you can and should reestablish the ability to use a human's most powerful organ—the brain—in coping with the many challenges of life. Not all these challenges will be ones involving ethics, but many are. The task may not be all that difficult once you agree that it is necessary, that some truths can indeed be determined, that reality is not always slippery, and that applying reason to many situations yields useful and proper results.

Let us retrieve reason—or rational thinking—from the scrap heap of modernism and drag it—perhaps kicking and screaming—into the postmodern era, reasserting its influence as a mechanism for ethical decision making.

The filmmaker Spike Lee gained rapid fame in the early 1990s with his film *Do the Right Thing.* While doing the right thing is a legitimate ethical goal, if one focuses only on that phrase, the *doing* becomes paramount in the mind. How can one do something, that is, take some sort of action, until one knows what that action is. *Doing* must be preceded by *thinking,* particularly determining *what* should be done and *why* and *how* it should be done. The thinking required to reach the end result of doing the right thing must take place within the individual. It will result from a number of individual factors, including environment, intelligence, judgment, courage, and vision, among others. To change Spike Lee's wording just a little, one ought to "Be the Right Thing." Being precedes doing, and being requires thinking.

A Decision-Making Model

In order to assist you in the decision-making process, a model has been developed in the form of a flowchart. Computer programmers use flowcharts "to tell a computer what to do and in what sequence."[5] Applied to ethical decision making, it is simply a pictorial plan showing what you want to do and in what order. The purpose of using a flowchart is to improve the ethical decision-making process by making it both systematic and rational. The model can be useful to you as you work through an ethical problem, but can also be useful to others in understanding how and why you reached a particular decision.

Let's take the model one step at a time. Look at Figure 10.1. You begin the process by entering the model and stating the problem or issue that concerns you. You may express this problem orally or you may simply fix it as a statement in your head, but the problem you are dealing with must be clear and precise. Once you have the problem or issue clearly in mind, you may move on.

To illustrate how the model works, let's introduce a problem and work through the model to a resolution. Consider the following situation:

Early one morning, a man enters a bank in a suburban community. He steps up to one of the tellers, pulls a gun, and demands money. He is about to leave when he spots a police car, cruising by on routine patrol. In the meantime, one of the tellers has tripped a silent alarm. The man hesitates and becomes agitated when

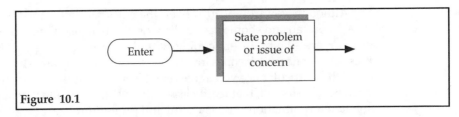

Figure 10.1

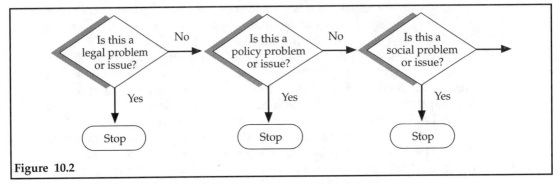

Figure 10.2

he sees the police car stop down the street, turn around, and return to the bank parking lot. It is joined moments later by three other law enforcement vehicles. Seeing there is no escape, the man corrals the four people in the bank (three employees and one customer) into a corner, indicating to them that they will not be harmed if he is able to leave without being apprehended.

You are a member of a two-person television news team. You were only a few blocks away from where the incident occurred, and your news director has ordered you to the scene to cover the story. When you arrive, you discover that cellular phone communications have been set up with the robber and that he has indicated that he will hold the four people in the bank until he is able to speak to a reporter.

As the standoff continues, police and FBI negotiators come up with a plan: disguise two sheriff's deputies as a reporter and a cameraman. The FBI wants to borrow your camera and have you teach a deputy how to operate it. Your reporter colleague is asked to surrender her reporter's notebook so that the deputy who poses as "on-camera talent" will look authentic. They plan to enter the bank and then overpower the robber. The FBI agent looks at you and says, "That's our plan. Will you help?"

In Figure 10.1, note that the first step is to state the problem or issue of concern. The problem here appears to be one involving the use of media personnel and media hardware (the camera) to assist in the apprehension of a bank robber who is holding hostages. Helping out seems to be the natural thing to do, yet you will be engaging in deception if you participate in this charade. Too, you will essentially become part of the story and may not be able to report on it objectively.

Figure 10.2 shows that the next step in the model involves your first decision. Is this a legal problem or issue? In other words, are there laws, legal opinions, court decisions, or the like that provide the solution to your problem? If your answer is *yes*, you should exit the model because a solution to your problem has been found in the law. In our example, you must decide whether there are any laws governing both the FBI's request and your response. While there are laws that prohibit an individual from interfering with a police officer, there is no law that says you must assist an officer by turning over your possessions to him or her. You are probably free to assist if you choose to do so, but you will not likely be violating the law if you refuse. Your answer to the first question in Figure 10.2 would, then, be *no*. Right away you are presented with two more questions in the next two flowchart elements. Is this a policy problem or issue and is this a social problem or issue?

Think about the policy concern first. It is possible that your television station has a policy of never participating in a news event. Perhaps the station management feels that any participation in a story you are sent to cover will result in a loss of perspective and a resulting loss of credibility among your viewers. They might, therefore, make it station policy that you are to observe and report only, not participate. Or perhaps your station has a policy against being deceptive. Management may feel that it is not appropriate for reporters to disguise their identities or to assist in any sort of deception in the performance of their duties. On the other hand, management may have indicated that you are to cooperate 100 percent with law enforcement officials. If they need something, you should assist them in any way possible. If a policy covering these sorts of activities exists at the station for which you work, you should answer yes and exit the model. Your course of action here would be to follow station policy.

Let's assume that your station has no policy covering these sorts of requests by law enforcement officials. This means that you are essentially on your own. Therefore, your answer to the second question in Figure 10.2 is *no*. You should next consider the social issue.

A social issue may be defined as a problem that occurs with some regularity in society and one that in all probability is controversial. A good example of a social issue is the use of vulgar language in public places. You will not likely be arrested if you use the F-word or other obscene language in a restaurant, for example, unless you create a significant disturbance or shout these words at the top of your lungs. If you speak in a normal voice and are overheard at the next table, the diners there may complain to the management and you may be approached to tone down your language. But unless you are causing a major disruption, you will most likely be able to get away with all sorts of unsavory language if you deliver it at a normal conversational level. Nevertheless, it would appear that the use of vulgar language in a public place, especially where you may be overheard, is a social problem that society tolerates.

Returning to our decision model, you must ask yourself whether the problem you are now facing is a social problem. Although it could be argued that every problem in America is a social one, the problem in front of you does not seem to deal with any obvious social issue. Your answer, therefore, is *no* and you move on.

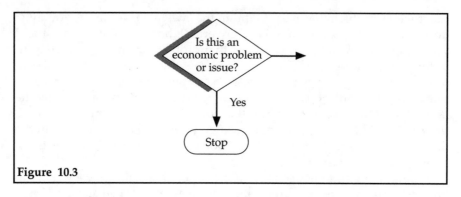

Figure 10.3

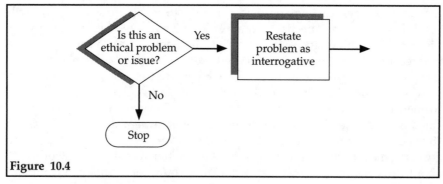

Figure 10.4

Figure 10.3 presents one more question that should be handled in much the same way as you handled the others. Is the problem an economic one? *No,* although a bank is being robbed. That does not necessarily make this problem economic in terms of its impact on you, though it may have some economic implications for your station's ratings, depending on how you cover the story. But the connection to economics is tenuous at best.

It should be noted that once a problem is identified as being a legal, social, or economic one, you should exit the decision-making model and seek additional input or expertise in an attempt to address the problem. You don't leave the problem hanging; it should be solved, but not necessarily by using ethical principles and processes. Suppose, for example, that you do not feel that your salary is adequate. There is probably no legal or social reason why your salary can't be higher, but there may be an economic one. You should probably discuss this situation with your supervisor or station management. This problem does not necessarily have to involve ethics, although under certain circumstances it may.

The final question in our series of decision points asks whether this problem involves an ethical issue. Having eliminated the other options, you may safely conclude that you likely have an ethical problem here. Figure 10.4 asks you to restate the problem as an interrogative. Putting the problem in question form enables you to focus the problem and eventually to provide an-

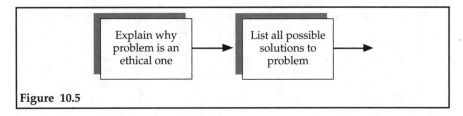

Figure 10.5

swers that will lead to a satisfactory resolution. Let's put our problem with the FBI and the bank robber in question form: Should I turn over my camera to the FBI so that it can be used to apprehend the bank robber? Or should I assist the FBI in deceiving the bank robber so that he may be apprehended? Either question will enable you to continue with the model. But let's go forward with the first question.

Figure 10.5 presents two extremely important steps in the decision-making model. You are first asked to explain *why* this is an ethical problem. Too often, individuals think that almost every problem they have is an ethical one. Some problems are ethical ones; others are not. In order to make sure that you do indeed have an ethical problem here, you should be prepared to explain why it is such.

One of the most common responses to this flowchart element is the following: "This is an ethical problem because it deals with issues of right and wrong behavior." You could use any one of a number of pairs of words to describe the issue choices. *Right* and *wrong* are used above, but you could just as well substitute *appropriate/inappropriate, desirable/undesirable,* or *positive/negative.* In some cases, one of the polar choices might involve extremes—a *good/evil* choice instead of a *right/wrong* choice. The good/evil choice does not work well for the present example. Regardless of whether or not you decide to assist law enforcement, your decision could not be viewed as evil, if one defines evil as malicious intent, wickedness, corruption, or moral bankruptcy. Since our example involves issues of right and wrong behavior, you can be confident that you have an ethical problem, and you can move on through the model toward a workable solution.

The second element of Figure 10.5 asks you to list all possible solutions to the problem. This is an extremely important step in the process because your eventual response to the problem will likely be contained somewhere in the list of solutions you create. You should list all possible solutions, even those that seem obvious or extreme. Here is a list of possible solutions to our FBI-bank robber problem:

1. Agree to assist law enforcement; turn over camera and notebook; coach deputy on camera operation.
2. Decline to assist law enforcement.
3. Call your station's news director for advice.
4. Agree to assist, but stipulate that you operate the camera and accompany the reporter-deputy.

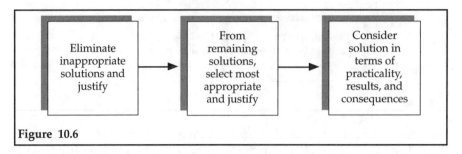

Figure 10.6

5. Propose an alternate plan: tell the robber that he is going on television "live," and send in your team, plus two deputies (deputies could pose as sound and light men, additional reporters, or other technicians).
6. Suggest that law enforcement do exactly as the robber requested and send in the reporter.

There may be other possible solutions to the problem, but for present purposes this list should be sufficient.

Figure 10.6 requires you to examine your solutions list and eliminate inappropriate responses, justifying your action. From the list of possible solutions, you should eliminate solution possibilities 4 and 5, for several reasons. First, these two options merely complicate the situation by placing additional individuals in harm's way. Also, these options are your suggestions and you are not a trained law enforcement officer; moreover, you are involving yourself in the story, not reporting it.

You should also eliminate solution 6 on essentially the same grounds. You are encouraging law enforcement to meet the robber's demands. This is something you are neither trained nor qualified to suggest. You are telling law enforcement officials how to do their job. This is neither your role nor your purpose in being on the scene.

Option 3 looks attractive but should also be eliminated. Most field reporters are expected to know and do their job without having to call for advice. Management expects you to exercise your careful judgment in the field and not always be running to them for guidance. Besides, management is not on the scene and may not fully understand the situation as it is playing out. If you lack confidence in your own judgment, you should probably not be reporting from the field at all, on this or any other story.

Then there is the possibility that if you call, you will be exchanging one ethical problem for another. Suppose you call and your news director gives you advice that conflicts with your own personal set of ethical values. Do you follow the news director's advice or follow your own conscience? You have exchanged one problem for another. The problem of assisting law enforcement has been replaced by the problem of whether you ought to follow your supervisor's advice. And what if the news director goes beyond advising and orders you to undertake a particular action in this case. The situation is suddenly extremely complicated and may have developed into a no-win situation for you. You must reject option 4 as inappropriate in this case. This leaves you with two possible solutions, 1 and 2.

The next element in Figure 10.6 asks you to examine the remaining solutions, select the most appropriate one, and justify. At this point, it is probably becoming clear to you that some ethical problems have more than one reasonable solution. A solution will often depend on the ethical principle or philosophy to which you subscribe. You have had the opportunity to study many different ethical perspectives and to develop or refine your own set of ethical values. However, for purposes of our example, let's assume you selected solution 2 as the most appropriate solution to the problem. Your justification might rest on the notion that it is inappropriate, that is, unethical, for reporters to involve themselves in stories they have been assigned to cover. Involving yourself in this story might raise questions in the minds of your viewers about other stories you have (or will) report on and make them wonder how much you get involved with all your stories. A journalist with poor credibility is almost no journalist at all. If a journalist's job is important—and many say that a well-informed public is a critical component of a democracy—then you must take steps to maintain a high level of performance and do your job so that the emphasis is on the elements your audience needs to know about a situation and not on how you participated in the story.

In short, you feel that by assisting law enforcement, you would be compromising your credibility and integrity as a journalist and that the focus of the story would necessarily change from what happened to what you did. This, to you, seems unethical.

You might cite Kohlberg's philosophy as supporting your decision. Specifically, you could argue that Kohlberg's notion that the most mature ethical decisions come from acting on an ethical principle provides the rationale for your decision not to assist law enforcement in this instance. Kohlberg's decision-making tool requires you use logical reasoning and sound moral judgment. You have used the tool effectively; you have gone beyond the laws and customs of society and have reasoned a solution based on an important ethical principle.

Other decision-making tools could also have been used. Mill's utilitarian approach would call for you to decline to assist law enforcement officials in this case on the grounds that, by refusing, you would be promoting the greatest good for the greatest number of people. By helping, you might be serving the few people involved as hostages, but in doing so you might damage your credibility as a reporter for the thousands of people who watch your news reports each day and believe what you say. You would not want to cause your viewers to ask: "If reporters can lie and be deceptive when it suits their purposes, how do I know they are not lying and being deceptive in everything they do?" The needs of the larger audience would, according to utilitarianism, outweigh the needs of the smaller group.

The final element in Figure 10.6 asks you to consider the solution in terms of its practicality, results, and consequences. In responding to this element,

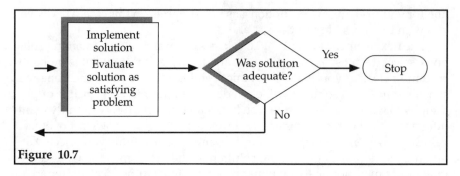

Figure 10.7

you will necessarily become something of a *consequentialist*, an individual who considers the possible consequences of an action as an important factor in making an ethical decision. *Nonconsequentialists* believe that one need not consider the consequences of an action as part of an ethical decision-making process. The final element in Figure 10.6 actually forces you to become a consequentialist by asking you to consider the possible consequences of your proposed solution. However, it is not necessarily wrong to eliminate this element if you consider yourself a nonconsequentialist.

Well, is the solution practical? What sorts of actions might result from your solution? Can you foresee any positive or negative consequences—for anyone—as a result of your solution? These questions, of course, have any number of answers, but they are certainly ones you'll want to consider at this point in the decision-making process.

Figure 10.7 directs you to implement the solution and evaluate it as solving the problem. If you selected solution 2 and declined to assist law enforcement, then your ethical problem is essentially solved. Remember that you posed the problem as a question (see Figure 10.4): Should I turn over my camera to the FBI so that it may be used to apprehend the bank robber? If you decline to assist, then your question has been answered. No, you should not surrender your camera. You should move immediately to the next element in Figure 10.7 and begin to assess whether your solution was adequate. While your solution may satisfy the problem—that is, answer the ethical question you posed for yourself—it might not be adequate. In other words, it might not be strong enough to remove the ethical problem from consideration. If you find that you are still not satisfied that your solution is sufficient, you may wish to reenter the model and continue work on the problem. If you are comfortable with your solution and feel that it is adequate to the situation, exit the model.

As you can see, making ethical decisions is not always easy. There are many things to consider. There may be more than one solution to a problem. Some aspects of ethical decision making are *absolutes*, principles or concepts that are strong, firm, unchangeable. Other aspects are *relative* or flexible, variable. Your solution to our example problem might depend on whether you consider reporter noninvolvement in a story an absolute or relative principle.

Using Philosophical Principles

In working through our sample ethical problem, you may have felt a little overwhelmed, being asked to make decisions and justify those decisions with little help or knowledge of some of the ethical principles that can be used to guide decisions. Unless you have studied philosophy before, you may have been relying primarily on your first reaction in making the decisions the model called for. Sometimes your first reaction is appropriate; sometimes it is not.

Some scholars believe that "people who study ethics for the first time are often disappointed to find that neither the ancient nor modern philosophers can give them principles that will solve everyday dilemmas."[6] Others believe that philosophical principles can be helpful. For many people, having some knowledge of philosophical, ethical principles is useful in helping to reach a satisfactory solution to an ethical problem. Chapters 3 through 9 of this text provided you with many decision-making tools. When you reach the model decision elements in Figure 10.6, for example, you could use some of the tools to help you eliminate inappropriate solutions and select the most appropriate one. The decision-making tools are summarized for your convenience at the end of this chapter.

Why Philosophy

"If my initial reaction to the problem was the right one, why do I need all these philosophies," you might ask. The quick answer is that not all problems are easily solved by an application of one's first impression or gut reaction. Many problems are complex and resist quick solution. The problem might be such that you don't have a first impression of what should be done, or even if you do, it might not be the most appropriate action to take. Reacting quickly and without careful thought can be seen as a postmodern phenomenon. Remember we are trying to move away from postmodern thinking when we are confronted with an ethical problem and work toward a more rational solution to a problem.

Other Models

A number of texts have provided models for the analysis of ethical problems. Regardless of the model, there is widespread belief that students need direct guidance in the decision-making process.[7]

Bivins has developed an Ethics Worksheet for Case Studies—a series of 13 steps—that will lead students "to extract the most relevant information common to all cases in as succinct a way possible while maintaining the integrity of the ethical decision-making process."[8] Black, Steele, and Barney, in cooperation with the Society of Professional Journalists, have developed a series of questions for resolving an ethical dilemma.[9] This model consists of ten questions that will lead to an ethical solution. There are other models, of course, but all models share some common elements and all appear to borrow freely from others.[10]

The whole point of providing models is to get you away from making knee-jerk decisions. The model offered earlier in this chapter is neither better nor worse than others. It does, however, have the advantage of being in a visual, process-oriented format, although you might reach the same solution to a problem if you used the Bivins's model or the Black-Steele-Barney model.

Real-Time Decision Making

Well, you might say, those decision-making models are all well and good, but what if I don't have time to work my way through a flowchart or to answer a set of questions? Especially in crisis situations, I may be asked for a quick decision. What if I don't have the time to do all the things this text is asking me to do?

This, of course, is a legitimate concern. In addressing the issue of what might be called *real-time problem solving,* we need to keep in mind one abiding principle: having limited time to make an ethical decision does not absolve you of the responsibility of arriving at an ethical course of action. In other words, you cannot use lack of time as justification for making the wrong decision or not making a decision at all. Almost everything in contemporary culture is time-sensitive in one way or another. You may be given just a few hours to prepare a written or oral report for your boss; you may have 24 hours in which to decide whether to accept a new job; a proposal of marriage will often require an answer within 60 (or fewer) seconds.

In some cases, you may have 10, 20, 30 minutes or more to make an ethical decision. Given this amount of time, you would almost certainly have time to work your way through any decision-making model. But it is also true that in some cases you may have only two or three minutes in which to make a decision. What then?

You can still use the decision-making model presented in this chapter. You will have to use it efficiently. How can this be accomplished? Let's take a simple analogy. Learning to make ethical decisions is much like learning to drive a car. As a beginning driver, you settle yourself behind the wheel and carefully buckle the seat belt. You take time to adjust the seat and the rearview and outside mirrors. Next, you slip the key into the ignition and start the vehicle. You may pause a moment and gaze at the various dashboard gauges and indicators to make sure the vehicle is operating properly. You depress the clutch and shift into reverse, ready to back out of the parking space. You place your arm over the back of the front seat and turn your head to look out the back window. You then release the clutch to just the precise friction point, and the car starts to move. You gently guide the vehicle from the parking space, turning the wheel to the right or left, as needed. For a beginning driver, one unaccustomed to the *start-up process,* these activities may take four or five minutes. However, once you become an accomplished driver, the process will likely take fewer than 30 seconds. Why the difference? Experience and practice.

In much the same way, as a beginning ethical decision maker, you may take much longer to reach a decision than you will once you become an experienced decision maker. You will not eliminate any of the procedures, but you will become more efficient in the doing of them. With practice and experience, you'll be able to use the model efficiently enough to reach workable, ethical decisions in a short time. In other words, you'll be able to deal with problems in real time.

As we've noted, not every ethical problem you have will require a quick decision, but some will. Over time, you'll be able to use any model quickly. But like the beginning driver, you must concentrate on every task at the early stage of your development. As you become more experienced, you'll find that each task is more rapidly and efficiently handled than it was when you first began.

After you have used the decision-making model to solve the issues presented in the case studies in Chapters 11 through 15 of this text, try your hand at using the model under time constraints. Four real-time case studies have been provided at the end of Chapter 16. Try to use the decision-making model and reach an ethical solution in the short time indicated in each of the four case studies. You may find that you can make good ethical decisions in a relatively short time. Or you may find that you need some additional experience before you are able to use the model quickly and efficiently. Knowing how you handle the model under time pressure is an important thing to know about yourself.

QUESTIONS FOR DISCUSSION

1. What are the advantages and disadvantages of using decision-making models to help you arrive at a solution to an ethical problem?

2. At what point in any decision-making process should you consider formal ethical philosophies, like those presented in Section II of this text, for example, to aid you in solving an ethical problem?

3. Suppose you and a fellow student reach fundamentally different solutions to an ethical dilemma, but each of you has a strong supporting philosophy to back up your individual stands. How would you resolve such a situation?

4. What role, if any, should your first reaction, your gut instinct, play in the ethical decision-making process?

5. Do you agree that *being* the right thing is a necessary prerequisite for *doing* the right thing? Explain your thinking.

ENDNOTES

1. Steinar Kvale, "Themes of Postmodernity," in *The Truth about the Truth,* ed. Walter Truett Anderson (New York: Putnam's, 1995), 21.

2. Ibid., 19.

3. David Harvey, *The Condition of Postmodernity: An Enquiry into the Origins of Cultural Change* (Cambridge: Blackwell, 1989), 27.

4. Peter Gay, *Age of Enlightenment* (New York: Time-Life Books, 1966), 11.

5. Mario V. Farina, *Flowcharting* (Englewood Cliffs, NJ: Prentice Hall, 1970), 1.

6. C. June Martin, "The Case of the Lost Ethic: Making Moral Decisions," *Journalism Educator* 43(1), Spring 1988, 14; Philip Meyer, *Ethical Journalism* (New York: Longman, 1987), viii.

7. Thomas H. Bivins, "A Worksheet for Ethics Instruction and Exercises in Reason," *Journalism Educator* 48(2), Summer 1993, 7–8.

8. Ibid., 9.

9. Jay Black, Bob Steele, and Ralph Barney, *Doing Ethics in Journalism,* 3rd ed. (Needham Heights, MA: Allyn & Bacon, 1999), 30–31.

10. Ibid., 9.

	Summary of Ethical Decision-Making Tools
PLATO	Refrain from wrongdoing regardless of the consequences. Set aside the views of society, acquire the knowledge necessary to make a good decision, then act in such a way that you are pleased and others are served by the action. The action must meet the tests of courage, moderation, respect, wisdom, and justice.
ARISTOTLE	When faced with an ethical problem, avoid extremes by determining the mean, the just-right, and act by doing what is appropriate after considering all relevant factors.
ABELARD	Actions can be considered good or evil, that is, ethical or unethical, depending solely on one's intentions.
AQUINAS	Ethical behavior stems from appropriate human action, action guided by the four cardinal virtues: prudence, justice, temperance, and courage.
BACON	Apply the powers of reason, understanding, and will to control the appetites that life subjects each individual to. Seek constantly for new knowledge and truth.
MACHIAVELLI	Understand, accept, and adapt to change; avoid stagnation; examine a problem situationally and flex the ethical absolutes only to the degree necessary to gain the desired ends.
HOBBES	Rise above self-interest; promote justice and strive for mutual accommodation; fulfill your obligations.
VOLTAIRE	Use reason to balance the passions; act for the greater good of society.
ROUSSEAU	Use conscience, compassion, and reason to make ethical decisions that promote harmony among all those involved.
SPINOZA	Use reason to determine the proper course of action. First, determine the good, that is, the ideal or standard against which the action may be judged. Then set aside emotion; think through the problem and reach a just, faithful, and honorable conclusion. Be prepared to provide a rational answer to the question, Why did you do what you did?
KANT	Considering your responsibility to self and others, act only on those principles that you would have generalized to all. Ask these questions: What is the rule authorizing this act I am about to perform? Can it become a universal law for all human beings to follow?

Summary of Ethical Decision-Making Tools *(continued)*

MILL	Act by following the moral rule that will bring about the greatest good (or happiness) for the greatest number.
SHOPENHAUER	Think carefully about any action you may be inclined to take. Acknowledge the influence of the will, but use experience to achieve a balance and act with compassion so that you respect yourself and others.
DURKHEIM	Determine the moral ideal or moral fact that governs a planned action. Explain how society benefits from the action, that is, how does the proposed action contribute to and reflect the existing social and moral fabric of life?
SARTRE	Get a clear and accurate picture of a situation by examining the choices of action available. Select an option for which you can provide a justification and for which you accept total responsibility.
RAND	Examine the reality of a situation in as objective a manner as possible. Determine the standards to be followed and the goals to be met by a decision. Submit these observations to a reasoning process yielding a solution that meets your needs as an individual.
KOHLBERG	Before attempting to find a solution to an ethical dilemma, determine on which moral level you are presently functioning. As you approach a new ethical problem, make a decision that is backed by logical reasoning and sound moral judgment, always moving toward the more mature postconventional level of decision making.
CHRISTIAN	Remembering that an individual's primary responsibility is to serve and be faithful to God, resolve an ethical dilemma by acting in accordance with the principles set forth by the Jewish or Christian religious traditions.
FOUCAULT	Recalling the set of truth obligations, examine an ethical problem and determine a desired course of action. Ask two questions: Is the proposed solution a reflection of my personal ethical standards? What power relationships influenced the solution? If you are comfortable with the answers to each of these questions, implement the desired action.
BAUDRILLARD	Examine possible responses to an ethical dilemma and select the one that is least manipulative and intrusive, the one that most closely represents true reality.

CHAPTER 11

Ethical Issues and Case Studies in Journalism

Overview

In this chapter and the ones that follow, we will examine the different media in some detail. An instructional case study will appear in each chapter. We will present and discuss important ethical issues specific to a given medium, referring to the instructional example to illustrate the main points. At the conclusion of each chapter, several real-world case studies will be presented. You are encouraged to use your ethical problem-solving skills to address the issues in each case study.

In this chapter our concern is with the ethical issues faced by journalists. The term *journalist* is used in its broadest sense; it refers to those whose job it is to gather, prepare, and report the news. This includes individuals who work for magazines and newspapers, commonly called the *print media*; it includes those who work for radio or television stations or for cable news organizations. These are commonly called the *electronic media*. It also includes those who provide the pictures that often accompany news reports—photojournalists, videographers, photographers, and the like.

Obviously, there is much variation in the way journalists do their jobs. We do not wish to minimize the differences inherent in the various aspects of their job responsibilities. However, many ethical problems are common to all who work at gathering, preparing, and reporting the news. At times we may need to focus on an ethical issue specific to only one type of job. Otherwise, our discussion will have broad application to all those who call themselves journalists.

The instructional case study for this chapter is a lengthy one, but it is important because it illustrates many of the ethical concerns journalists and others have about reporting the news. In order to present a wealth of material in the most efficient fashion, this chapter has been divided into three parts. Part I presents some of the major issues that raise ethical concerns in journalism. Part II presents the instructional case study, and, drawing from the information in Part I, offers an ethical analysis of the problems presented by the case study. Part III introduces other ethical issues of importance to journalists.

▼ Part I. Some Major Ethical Issues

The Work of Journalists

Journalists consider themselves an important part of contemporary society. Most subscribe to the belief that a well-informed population is of primary importance to the effective functioning of a democracy and to the growth and development of the individuals who support that democracy. Americans need news and other sorts of information to make intelligent decisions about their own lives and about the individuals selected to run their government. The responsibility to provide this news and information invests journalists with considerable power and influence and, for some, great financial rewards. Television network anchors are paid millions of dollars to report the news. Those who gather the news and write the reports that are fed to the audience by the anchor are less well paid but still receive handsome salaries for their work. Even local television news anchors are paid well. In major television markets, it is not uncommon to pay a top-rated anchor several hundred thousand dollars a year in salary. What does an individual's salary have to do with the news or with ethical issues? Quite a bit, as we shall shortly see.

One of the most interesting debates about the nature of a journalist's job concerns whether the job qualifies as a trade or a profession. This is more than a matter of semantics. If the job is considered a trade, it would have characteristics somewhat different from those of a profession. When one thinks of a trade, one often conjures up images of plumbing or house painting, jobs that provide a service but for which an extended formal education is not required. Many who perform these sorts of services learned their skills "on the job." To be sure, it may have taken several weeks, but much of the work becomes routine. For example, the skills a painter develops can be applied routinely in any number of different situations: painting a house, painting a garage, painting an office building, or whatever. These skills can be learned in a relatively short period of time. The same could be said of those whose trade is plumbing, auto body work, or any one of a number of other necessary services. Tradespeople play a vital role in keeping the country up and running. Without them, our lives would be considerably more chaotic than they are.

By contrast, a profession may be defined as a job that requires considerable formal educational training. Professionals in all areas usually hold one or more college degrees. Their work has some routine, but it often requires them to exercise considerable judgment and to hold themselves to extremely high standards of performance and behavior.

So the question becomes this: Is journalism a trade or a profession? Some say that a journalist's skills are roughly akin to those learned by any tradesperson. Gathering facts and writing a story using those facts are skills that can be taught in a few weeks. Use of cameras and the other technical equipment of the electronic media can also be learned in a few weeks, often through on the job training. College degrees, while required by some media outlets, are

Diana, Princess of Wales, felt that the paparazzi never left her alone. She especially resented their intrusion into her family life. © *Ian Waldie / Reuters*

not really needed for this sort of "routine" job, many say. Others suggest that journalists are indeed professionals. They must be trained to think logically, to derive meaning from the facts they gather, to work ethically, to promote truth, to understand political ideologies, and to be persuasive. These sorts of activities, it is often argued, require significant formal training and represent work that is far beyond the routine of the trades. Journalism is an activity of the mind as much or more than of the hands, and this elevates it to the status of a profession, the argument goes.

Journalism professor John Merrill makes a convincing case for journalism as a trade. He says that journalism lacks many of the traits that distinguish a profession: (1) there are no rules for admission to the job, "no minimum entrance requirements" to become a journalist; (2) "no exclusive body of knowledge" that comprises the field; (3) "no mechanism for getting rid of unqualified or unethical practitioners"; and (4) no governing body that oversees the work of those in the field.[1] Merrill further notes that some feel that journalism would be enhanced if it were to become a profession. It would become "more efficient, more responsible, more skillful, and more accurate."[2]

While this may be true, Merrill continues, it would result in journalism being something of a closed profession. This would be disadvantageous in an open society such as America's. Placing controls on journalism would have more negative than positive consequences, Merrill feels. The profession needs to be as open as the society in which it operates.

Regardless of whether journalism is a trade or a profession, the need to act ethically in the performance of the work is of primary importance.

News Values

Among the many judgments made by journalists is this one: What is news? In other words, in the face of all the events and activities in the world on a given day, what qualifies as worthy of being reported? There is neither time enough nor space to report everything. Some things must be omitted from a television or cable newscast and some things must be left out of a newspaper or magazine. This sort of judgment is exercised regularly—and often without much debate—at all news media outlets. How does one approach this task in an ethical fashion?

First, it is important to consider the issue of news values—the basic, intrinsic characteristics of a news story. Most introductory textbooks on reporting discuss news values in a preliminary section or chapter. An attempt is made to give a definition of news, but most conclude that there are many definitions of news. For example, Harris, Leiter, and Johnson admit that news is "constantly changing directions and expanding" and that much depends on the "persons who select it for print." "To some extent," they conclude, "the newspaper reporter has to depend upon intuition in recognizing news."[3] Is this an ethically reliable practice? Intuition often results from broad, practical experience and an "instinctive" feeling about something. Is this a "gut reaction," and, if so, shouldn't we replace intuition with *reason,* as many of the philosophers presented in this text have suggested?

What are these news values, anyway? Brooks, Kennedy, Moen, and Ranly provide a workable list.

1. *Audience.* Will this directly affect the lives of this newspaper's audience?
2. *Impact.* How many people are affected?
3. *Proximity.* How near to the audience is the event?
4. *Timeliness.* Is it important today? Will it be old tomorrow?
5. *Prominence.* Are well-known individuals involved?
6. *Unusualness.* Is it different from (beyond) the normal, the usual, the routine?
7. *Conflict.* Are oppositional forces (social, political, economic, environmental, etc.) at work?[4]

Of course, there is no widespread agreement about how many of these values must be met before a situation qualifies as a news story and thus gains status by being printed or broadcast. Harris, Leiter, and Johnson suggest that a good story is one that hits on one or more of the news values. What is the proper ethical stance here? Since the list of news values is entirely arbitrary, is it ethical to suggest how many of them must be met? Is it ethical to even have such a list of values? Would we be on more solid ground if we were to develop some other way of judging the ethics of news story selection?

Privacy

Here is another important issue: *privacy*. Privacy may be defined as the right to be let alone, to have one's personal affairs and property protected from unwanted examination by the government, the media, or other individuals. Privacy began as a legal concept in 1890 with the publication of a scholarly article in a law journal. The American right to privacy, as it operates today, rests with the courts in the form of four principles:

1. *Intrusion.* Americans have the right to be free from unwanted intrusion in their lives. For example, intrusion might result from the theft of an individual's private papers, or from a reporter trespassing on one's property in order to get a story. Using long-distance photo lenses to snap pictures or using covert listening devices to overhear private conversations are also forms of intrusion.

2. *False light.* There are several ways in which an individual may be placed in a false light. They all involve taking a factual situation and changing it in some way so that it suggests something other than what it actually is. For example, if a photographer snapped a photo of you on a public beach, one where dozens of others were present, and the photo appeared as part of a story about how people are enjoying the nice weather at the beach, that would not likely be deemed an invasion of privacy. However, if the photo were used as part of a story on individuals who have deserted their families, you could charge the publisher (and perhaps the photographer) with invasion of privacy by having placed you in a false light. In other words, using your photo with the desertion story implies that you are one of those who have deserted his or her family. If untrue, you would have grounds for an invasion of privacy suit.

3. *Private, embarrassing facts.* It is an invasion of an individual's privacy to reveal private facts about the person, facts that could cause embarrassment or loss of reputation or standing in the community. For example, a story on common medical problems might run in a local newspaper, and you might be identified as a person who has a bedwetting problem, even though you are 22 years old. Unless you gave the writer permission to use this information, you have grounds to charge the newspaper and the writer with a violation of your privacy; they have revealed a private fact about you that caused you considerable embarrassment at work and in your neighborhood.

4. *Appropriation.* If your name, picture, or other likeness of you is used for commercial purposes without your permission, you may charge the user with invasion of privacy due to appropriation. Consider the example where you were photographed walking on a beach. If the photo were used in a print or video commercial designed to sell a sunscreen product, you could charge that your likeness had been "appropriated" for commercial purposes without your consent.

As these privacy principles have developed through the years, the precise definitions and applications have blurred somewhat. Significant case law exists on these issues, and not all of it is consistent. Nevertheless, most Americans feel they have a right to privacy and a right to the protections offered by the four privacy principles. In postmodern America, the right to privacy has diminished significantly, largely because of an increasing level of technological sophistication. For example, the Internet and computer technology have enabled government, media, and business, as well as private individuals, to gather detailed information about the private lives of almost anyone. A complete discussion of the issues and implications of this sort of activity is provided in Chapter 15.

Public and Private Figures

There are two important distinctions with regard to privacy. First, as privacy issues have made their way through the various courts, a difference has been noted between individuals who are private figures and those who are public figures or public officials. A *private figure* is someone who does not work in the national or international public arena, an individual who does not invite broad attention by the nature of his or her work. Most Americans are private figures. But some individuals, particularly those who hold high-profile political positions or who make their living in show business or sports, are often designated *public figures.* Public figures and public officials may expect to have their privacy reduced somewhat. Given the fact that many depend on—and some even appeal to—the public for support, they may not be entitled to privacy to the degree that private individuals are. You and I are private figures, but basketball great Michael Jordan retired from the Chicago Bulls, actors Leonardo DiCaprio, Demi Moore, and Mel Gibson, and baseball sluggers Mark McGwire and Sammy Sosa are public figures.

This is not to suggest that public figures have no privacy rights at all, but merely to point out that when one leads a public life, one must expect to be closely watched and photographed. The public wants information about individuals who hold public office, individuals who star in movies and appear on television, and individuals who are major sports figures. In the case of those who hold elected political office, one could certainly argue that much detailed information about those individuals is needed in order to judge their worth as public servants.

A second important privacy distinction involves the issue of *the public's right to know*—the battle cry of journalists for many years. They have used it to their advantage, often as justification for being allowed access to information they might not otherwise get. This practice has sometimes resulted in the American people getting important and needed information. At other times, the information may not have been vital to the proper functioning of a democracy, but it may have resulted in a good story.

It should be noted, however, that this phrase does not appear in any American constitutional document. It does not appear in the Declaration of Independence or the Constitution. The First Amendment to the Constitution, among other things, directs Congress to make no law abridging freedom of the press. But this does not address the issue of the *rights* of the public to certain kinds of information. The media critic and communications professor Neil Postman notes that the phrase, the public's right to know, was part of a short, popular piece of poetry in the seventeenth century.

> From public schools shall general
> knowledge flow,
> For 'tis the people's sacred
> right to know.[5]

Thus, the early use of the phrase applied not to media but to education—that is, an individual had a right to a public school education. Media personnel have essentially stolen the phrase from its original context and used it to facilitate their own work. Nevertheless, the phrase has made its way into the national consciousness, and most people now expect the media to go places they cannot, see things they cannot, get information they cannot, and report their findings.

Care must be taken not to interpret the phrase too broadly. There are, in fact, many things an individual needs to know to function effectively in a democracy. Media provide much of this information. However, a *right* to know is not the same as a *want* to know. Human beings are curious creatures. Some may want information to satisfy a morbid curiosity or simply to be "in the know" regarding private facts about other people. They may want a certain type of information, but that does not necessarily mean they have a right to it. For example, after hearing numerous loud, heated arguments from your next-door neighbors, you may want to know whether they are in the process of getting a divorce. You have no legal right to this information. Your neighbors may share this information with you, but there is no inherent right in your having it simply because you want it. Some media, most notably the *tabloids*, those half-size newspapers that publish stories of a sensationalistic nature, are very good at peeking under beds, peering in windows, and poking around in the personal affairs of all sorts of individuals. Their rallying cry, in justifying their existence, is that their readers want this sort of information. Want it or not, the public may not be entitled to it.

▼ Part II. Instructional Case Study

The soft, white clouds had thickened somewhat as the day wore on, but they could not keep the late afternoon sunlight from spilling over the rural English countryside. The sleek, black hearse moved slowly toward the gates of the country estate at Althorp. The roof and windshield of the car were almost completely covered with flowers, thrown by mourners who lined the motorcade route. The hearse eased gently through the gates, turned slightly to the right and disappeared. It was the last glimpse the world would have of the coffin containing the body of Diana, Princess of Wales. Although the funeral had been a public affair in England's Westminster Abbey, the burial service was attended only by family.

When Diana was killed in a grinding automobile crash in the early morning of Sunday, August 31, 1997, in Paris, no one could have predicted the effect her death would have, not only on her native England but also on the world. At the time of her death at age 36, she was, without doubt, the most photographed woman in the world. She had graced the cover of *People* magazine a record 44 times, more than any other person. She possessed youth, beauty, charm, wealth, and influence. Her funeral on Saturday, September 6, 1997, brought England and much of the rest of the world to a standstill. Millions poured into London to leave flowers, letters, poems, candles, and mementos in front of her Kensington Palace residence, Buckingham Palace (home of the royal family), and St. James Palace, home of her former husband and future king of England, Prince Charles. Tens of thousands lined the funeral procession route through the most historic part of the city. Television devoted dozens of hours to coverage of Diana during the week-long period between her death and funeral. Newspapers trumpeted the death on their front pages, then followed with page after page of analysis and detail inside.

It was said that perhaps 2 billion people worldwide viewed the funeral, carried live almost everywhere in the world where the technology to receive satellite broadcasts made it possible. Why did the death of this former member of the British Royal Family generate so much interest among the people and so much coverage by the media? What ethical issues were involved?

Diana Frances Spencer burst onto the international scene on July 29, 1981, when, at age 20, she married Prince Charles, the future king of England and a man 12 years her senior. The wedding was carried on live television and was the most talked-about international event for several days. The audience for that broadcast was modest by current standards. In 1981 there were fewer electronic media outlets available to carry the broadcast than there are today. Nevertheless, it was a majestic event.

Diana was the daughter of the Earl of Spencer. Although not royalty, her family was titled, indicating that her forefathers were from aristocratic British stock—that is, men of noble birth, wealthy landowners, members of the English Parliament. Diana herself was pictured as a shy, sincere, proper young lady who, though not highly educated, had been trained as a preschool teacher. She had a special way with children. Prince Charles probably noticed this; the press certainly did. She was photographed regularly with a young child in her arms or a group of children at her feet. She was a fresh face, and the media loved her. It was also noted that Charles was in his 30s and not married. He had yet to produce an heir to the English throne. The couple was greeted warmly by the media when the engagement was announced, and there followed a lavish wedding. The English people approved of the marriage and had high hopes for this new royal couple.

In its early years, the marriage produced two sons: William and Harry. William, as the firstborn, would inherit the throne from his father. All seemed well, yet the seeds of discord had been sown, and trouble was just ahead. Mostly unaware that there were problems in the marriage, the media kept close watch on the couple. Their comings and goings were regularly chronicled, as were the growth and development of William and Harry, "the heir and the spare," as they were frequently called.

It became clear a year or so after the birth of Harry that all was not well with the couple. British newspapers, including the famous tabloids, reported that Diana was dissatisfied with her life, that other members of the royal family were cold and aloof, and that Charles was not a warm and affectionate husband. When reports surfaced that Charles had been seeing his longtime friend Camilla Parker-Bowles, and that the relationship was not entirely platonic, Diana became depressed, developed an eating disorder (bulimia), had her own brief extramarital affair, and reportedly considered suicide. The couple continued to live together, though it was obvious to all, including the media, that they were growing apart. The two soon separated and were finally divorced in 1996. At that time, the words "Her Royal Highness" were removed from Diana's title, though she was allowed to keep the title "Princess of Wales." A generous financial settlement was provided (about $22 million), and Diana was granted liberal visitation rights with her two sons.

It was after the divorce that Diana became something of a media star. She was young, charming, beautiful, and rich. Many felt that she had not been well treated by the British Royal Family, and almost everyone wished her much happiness and success. Although she had always been interested in charitable causes, her support for these efforts now took on new significance. She was photographed embracing an AIDS patient, shaking a leper's hand, and cradling children whose limbs had been damaged by land mines. She was a tireless worker for these and other worthy causes. She was pictured as a sincere, caring person, a person who had not found true love in her life but who had the capacity to give love to others.

In addition to promoting various charitable causes, Diana began to live the life of a beautiful, wealthy, single woman. She was seen in the company of several rich, attractive men. Freelance photographers, called paparazzi, shadowed her constantly. The tabloid press was hungry for news about her and her love life. A candid photo of her in a compromising position or with a new boyfriend could mean thousands of dollars, or more, to the lucky photographer. The paparazzi became bolder, chasing her from place to place, jumping in front of her as she walked through an airport, even placing a hidden camera in a gym to catch a shot of her working out. These pictures were sold, primarily to the tabloids, but many were picked up by the mainstream media after they had first been run in the tabloid press.

For her part, Diana felt she provided photographers with ample opportunity to photograph her. She did not object to them snapping pictures of her when she attended the latest fund-raising event for one of her favorite charities, or when she made other public appearances. There were other "photo calls," too. What she objected to was the almost total invasion of privacy in all aspects of her life. She was unable to take a trip with her two sons without the paparazzi stalking her, trying to get that unusual shot. She had no private time. She often approached the photographers and asked them to give her and her sons some privacy. Some agreed; others continued to dog her every step.

This complex situation was to have tragic consequences in the late summer of 1997. In early August, the paparazzi had used long-distance lenses to photograph Diana in the company of a new friend, Dodi Fayed, son of Mohammed Fayed, owner of England's famous Harrod's department store. Dodi had something of a playboy reputation, but Diana seemed happy, and many felt she might finally have found "Mr. Right." Tabloids ran pictures of Diana relaxing aboard Dodi's yacht and of Diana and Dodi embraced in a kiss. Rumors were that the two planned to marry. This would be news indeed!

And so it was that on the night of August 30, Diana and Dodi returned to Paris from the southern coast of France where they had been vacationing. They first tried to have dinner at a trendy Paris restaurant, but the paparazzi made it impossible. They intruded into the event, and the couple fled to the Ritz Hotel, an establishment owned by Dodi's father. There, of course, they could eat in peace. They dined privately, and shortly after midnight, dispatching a decoy vehicle from the front of the hotel, left the hotel by a rear door in order to escape the paparazzi. They were headed toward Dodi's Paris apartment. Apparently the paparazzi discovered that the couple had left the hotel and gave chase on motorcycles.

Exactly what happened in the next few minutes is not perfectly clear. But this much is clear. The Mercedes, carrying Diana, Dodi, a bodyguard, and the driver, slammed into a concrete support in a Paris tunnel near the Seine River. Trying to escape the paparazzi, the car was reportedly traveling at a high rate of speed. Some reports said 60 miles per hour; others said more than 100 miles per hour. Whatever the speed, the results were obvious enough. The car was totally destroyed. Dodi and the driver, Henri Paul, whose blood alcohol level was found to be three times the legal limit in France, were killed immediately. Diana and the bodyguard, Trevor Rees-Jones, were seriously injured.

There were conflicting reports about what happened next. Some observers said the paparazzi were busy snapping pictures of the crash and the victims and that they made no attempt to help the injured. Others said they shoved those who were trying to help out of the way so pictures could be taken. Some said the paparazzi were not close to the accident when it happened, and that they conducted themselves appropriately at the crash scene. A Frenchman who was driving a car just ahead of the Mercedes said he saw, in his rearview mirror, a motorcycle cut in front of the Mercedes and a flash, presumably the flash of a camera. The observer felt this was the cause of the accident. French police arrested the paparazzi who were on the scene and confiscated their cameras and cellular phones as part of the investigation.

Diana was apparently alive, but in very critical condition when the medical teams arrived. They transported her and the bodyguard to a nearby hospital. Doctors worked feverishly for two hours trying to repair the damage to her chest and heart, but they were not successful. She was pronounced dead at 4 A.M. Paris time on Sunday, August 31, 1997. The bodyguard, the only one wearing a seat belt, survived.

Ethical Concerns Raised by the Case Study

When a public figure meets a tragic death, there is often much sadness among those who knew the person or followed the person's life and career. In Diana's case, the tragedy was particularly difficult to absorb for many people. Diana was young, charming, graceful, beautiful, and very involved in humanitarian projects. Following the accident, one of the first questions asked by the media—and probably by many outside the media—was: Who is to blame for this accident, for the deaths of three individuals? In our struggle to find meaning in life and in death, it is sometimes helpful if we are able to assign blame. Establishing this causal link (*X* is to blame for *Y* happening) usually enables us to cope, but rarely to understand. Nevertheless, much newspaper space and airtime were devoted to discussions of who should shoulder the blame for this unfortunate accident.

In considering this case study, it will be necessary to set aside some of the issues about the accident that concerned many. Since this is a text in media ethics, it will be our task to examine media behavior surrounding the incident. We will not argue whether it was right or wrong for the driver of the car to have been drinking, though common sense would suggest that driving drunk is foolish. Neither will we argue that the car's occupants should have had their seat belts fastened (only one did). In focusing on the media performance relating to the incident, three issues bear detailed examination.

Celebrity   The historian Daniel Boorstin once described celebrities as people who become famous for being famous. However the term is defined, there is little question that we love our celebrities. Film and television stars, sports figures, and others who live the lifestyle of the rich and famous are individuals whose lives are intensely interesting to many Americans. Psychologists may be able to tell us why this is so; perhaps many of us have lives that are routine and unexciting. We can spice things up a bit by living vicariously through the lives of celebrities. They have the money, power, and influence we wish we had. They do things we wish we could. Russell Baker of the *New York Times* notes that we have an almost insatiable appetite for celebrities. "Americans now consume celebrities like potato chips," he says.[6]

But celebrity is not a one-way street. While we want the media to bring us information about celebrities, the celebrities themselves are often just as demanding of the media. Among those who spoke publicly about the death of Princess Diana were Tom Cruise and Michael J. Fox. Cruise called the Cable News Network (CNN) in the hours following the reporting of Diana's accident. He told a nationwide audience that he, too, had been chased through that same Paris tunnel by paparazzi. Fox was quick to condemn the photographers, yet is "notorious for calling news executives constantly in an effort to get publicity."[7] Diana, too, was known to have used the media to her advantage time and again. Should she have been annoyed, then, by their continued attention?

Two questions arise. Was Diana a celebrity? Do celebrities have a right to some privacy? The answer to both questions is yes. It is abundantly clear that Diana was an individual in whom many people were interested. It matters little how she got to be a celebrity; the fact is that she qualified as "rich and famous," and many people worldwide wanted to know what she was up to. On the other hand, there is nothing in the law or in any ethical code that suggests she should have given up all her privacy because she was a celebrity and a public figure, nor should she have given up all her privacy simply because the public "wanted" to know about her.

The Code of Ethics of the National Press Photographers Association does not address issues of privacy and intrusion directly. It does stress taking "into consideration our highest duties as members of society," and lifting "the level of human ideals and achievement higher than we found it." The code further suggests that photographers use "common sense and good judgment." If there were members of the National Press Photographers Association among the paparazzi who chased Diana into that Paris tunnel, they most certainly violated the association's code of ethics in their relentless pursuit of a photo.

Is Diana entitled to have a private dinner with a male friend? The answer is yes. In fact, we may not have much of a news story here, especially if we emphasize the *need* to know instead of the *want* to know. Recall the list of news values introduced earlier. The story fails on several of the seven news values, meeting only one or two of them. The dinner will not directly affect the lives of a newspaper's readers (fails on the *audience* value). It will not affect a large number of people (fails on the *impact* value). Certainly most of the audience for a photo of the two is nowhere near the event (fails on the *proximity* value). Is having dinner with a male friend unusual, beyond the normal? No, but it is unusual for a member (or former member) of the British Royal Family to date (and consider marriage) to someone outside the normal British circle of influence. Fayed was an Egyptian and, some said, something of a playboy. However, attractive young women often align themselves with wealthy, international personalities. For example, Jacqueline Kennedy, President John Kennedy's widow, married the Greek magnate Aristotle Onassis. It is therefore debatable whether this story qualifies on the *unusualness* value. Is there conflict of some sort here? Perhaps, but it revolves around the same issue as the unusualness value. We can see a possible conflict between what Diana might have wanted to do and the behavior expected of her by the royals. Let's assume that the story qualifies on the *conflict* value. So we have a situation qualifying on two of the seven stated news values: *prominence* and *conflict*. Is that enough? Some journalists would say yes; others would say no.

From a logical point of view, one would have to admit that a news story has to "hit" on more than one or two values. If we define a news story as one that meets only one or two values, we could justify almost every event in the world as a news story, because there is usually something about a single event that would theoretically qualify it as a news story. For example, a fender-bender traffic accident on an interstate highway running through a large city might back up traffic for an hour or two. Are people affected? Yes. Large numbers of people? Perhaps. If there were no injuries, would this accident make the evening television news? Doubtful, unless it was an extremely slow news day. Would it be a front-page story in tomorrow's city newspaper? Doubtful. Does the accident meet the conflict value? Perhaps. The conflicting paths of the two autos came together to cause the accident. But is this conflict the sort that makes it suitable enough to qualify the event as a news story? Probably not.

In thinking of Diana, would the fact that she was a celebrity, and therefore a prominent person, be sufficient for photographers to follow her and watch her every move? Is it ethical to pursue an individual and significantly invade that individual's privacy for no other reason than that the person is well known? These questions have no simple, easy answers, but the ethical philosophy of Rousseau may provide some help. Rousseau felt that an ethical course of action results from the use of conscience, compassion, and reason, and that ethical decisions are those that promote harmony among all those involved. Did the photographers show compassion? Were they acting in such a way as to promote harmony for all involved, or merely in a way that served their self-interest? Hobbes notes that one should rise above self-interest and strive for mutual accommodation. Did the photographers follow Hobbes's philosophy? The issue of celebrity, then, raises serious ethical concerns about privacy and about how to qualify a news story in terms of its news value.

Tabloids and the Paparazzi   Tabloid journalism has been around for a long time. In the late 1800s and early 1900s, William Randolph Hearst, publisher of the *New York Journal,* and Joseph Pulitzer, publisher of the *New York World,* engaged in an intense battle to increase their respective paper's circulation. Although these papers were not tabloid in size, their content was similar to the content of tabloids today as each seized every opportunity to capture more and more of the reading audience by printing stories of an increasingly sensationalistic nature. This type of activity was termed *yellow journalism.*

Today many tabloids, both in England and America, regularly seek out the most sensational stories they can find and splash them on their front pages with bold, often suggestive, headlines. For example, just a week before Diana's death, an American tabloid headline screamed, "Di Goes Sex-Mad, 'I Can't Get Enough.' " The paper was in the racks at the time of the accident but was pulled by its distributor when Diana's death was confirmed.

It should be noted that some *mainstream* newspapers—newspapers taking a less sensationalistic, more traditional approach to reporting the news—also appear in tabloid, or half-size format. The *Chicago Sun-Times* is a good example. It is tabloid in format, but traditional in content. Nevertheless, the term *tabloid* has come to mean those sensationalistic newspapers that feast on scandal, sex, and celebrities. In America, *The Inquirer* and *The Globe* are two well-known tabloids; in England, the *News of the World* and the *Sunday Mirror* are two of the more popular tabloids. The term *tabloid* may also be applied to syndicated television programs such as *Inside Edition* or *Hard Copy*. These often appear to be news programs in that they feature anchors on what appears to be a news set, but they are in fact programs filled with celebrity gossip, exposés, and other sorts of entertainment features. They are the electronic media equivalent of the print media tabloids.

Tabloids almost always defend their work by saying that they are only meeting the public's voracious appetite for celebrity news. If the public didn't want it, the public wouldn't buy the papers. Since these papers sell out regularly, they argue, a needed service is being provided. The tabloids muddy the waters further by proclaiming that they do not directly hire the freelance photographers, the paparazzi, who chase celebrities. Tabloids do, however, purchase photos from them, often through independent photo agencies. This, the tabloids argue, does not make them in any way responsible for what the paparazzi do in getting the photos.

The logic of this argument is fuzzy at best. It resembles the classic "chicken-and-egg" quandary: Which came first, the chicken or the egg? Which comes first, the paparazzi or the tabloids? Do the paparazzi chase celebrities because they know the tabloids will purchase their photos, or do the tabloids merely purchase the photos because the paparazzi chase celebrities? No one wants to take responsibility for this sort of journalistic activity.

Mark Saunders and Glenn Harvey, two members of the paparazzi, provide an important perspective on this issue. In 1996, Saunders and Harvey published a book titled *Dicing with Di.* The book details their pursuit of Diana and their attempts to get pictures of her and her family. Some of their activities included hiding out in trees, bushes, and phone booths, or pretending to be window cleaners. Saunders argues that there is really nothing wrong with this. He says, "Diana had no right to expect privacy when the public had such an appetite for pictures of her."[8] This public-driven rationale for bad behavior simply does not wash with most ethicists. Those who work in media need to hold themselves to a higher standard. The "market standard" might suffice in some life or business situations, but we must raise the bar of expectations when it comes to media behavior. Diana apparently considered leaving England but felt she could not because of her sons. When the lives of human beings are involved, media must be very careful indeed. Columnist Russell Baker notes that although being a celebrity photographer is "a shameful way to make a living," the practice will probably continue because "invading the privacy of the rich and famous pays too well to be abandoned simply because the work is crude and coarse."[9] The British tabloid *Sunday Mirror* reportedly paid $400,000 for that grainy photo of Diana kissing Dodi.

One could well argue that, regardless of the official findings of the French police, the paparazzi and the tabloids, and to some extent the public, share responsibility for the accident. It is true that "the paparazzi . . . pursued the couple like a jackal its prey,"[10] but "tabloids love to chop the famous down to size [and] the rest of us follow the story."[11]

There are other ways in which the media can invade an individual's privacy. Not everyone who works in the "celebrity business" is a photographer. For example, just prior to Diana's funeral, some journalists requested the Royal National Institution for Deaf People, a British charity, to provide professional lip readers to note the royal family's private conversations during the funeral. The charity rejected the request as inappropriate and an invasion of privacy.

As might be expected, the events surrounding Diana's death and funeral resulted in calls for new laws protecting the privacy of celebrities, or, at the very least, new operating guidelines for the media. Actually, American laws already exist to rein in the paparazzi. In 1973, the U.S. Court of Appeals ruled that photographer Ron Galella had violated the privacy of Jacqueline Kennedy Onassis, former wife of slain President John F. Kennedy. The court barred Galella from further harassment and required him to stay 25 feet away from Mrs. Onassis. Celebrities may seek relief in American courts for excessive intrusion into their lives, but few have pursued this option.

In the wake of Diana's death, the tabloids at first seemed interested in modifying their behavior. Several papers reported they would refrain from zealous and intrusive coverage of Diana's sons, William and Harry. They made no such pledge with regard to other celebrities. Almost immediately, however, the tabloids raised another interesting issue. "Where is our Queen?" asked the *Sun*. The *Mirror* weighed in with "Your People Are Suffering. Speak to Us Ma'am." It was apparently the opinion of many British subjects, and a view subsequently picked up by both the tabloids and the mainstream press, that the queen and the royal family were not showing appropriate grief at Diana's death. The royals had ensconced themselves in Scotland's Balmoral castle and were making no public appearances or public statements.

As might have been predicted, public opinion became focused on the royal family, and the tabloids took the lead in demanding a public outpouring of grief from the royals. Yielding to media-enhanced public pressure, Queen Elizabeth went on live television to express her regret at Diana's passing, and other members of the royal family visited several of the memorial sites and talked briefly with mourners. One columnist noted that "the public's surrender of its sensibilities and concerns to mass media was never more evident. . . . It was embarrassing."[12] Were the tabloids merely responding to what they heard from the British people, or were they just trying to stir things up? There is little evidence on which to base an answer, but any sort of manipulation of public opinion by the tabloids—in cooperation with the mainstream press— cannot in any way be considered appropriate, ethical behavior.

In the weeks that followed the Diana tragedy, Britain's Press Complaints Commission, a self-regulatory body of both broadsheet and tabloid newspaper editors, proposed a new set of guidelines aimed at restricting the paparazzi. Among other things, the guidelines speak to issues of harassment and taunting, stalking and hounding, as well as protecting children and respecting personal privacy.

Aristotle's ethical philosophy would probably be a good one for both the tabloids and the paparazzi to follow: When faced with an ethical problem, determine the mean, the just-right, and act by doing what is fitting in the full complexity of the situation, with a sensitive rational view of all relevant factors. Had such a philosophy been a part of the lives of those who take celebrity photos and those who work for the tabloids, Diana likely would be alive today, and the public might be much less dependent on the media to tell them what to think and feel.

However, suppose the paparazzi were given a chance to defend themselves on these pages. Could they argue that they were perfectly ethical in performing their duties? Indeed they could. They might suggest that they were simply following the ethical philosophy of Ayn Rand. Rand's philosophy would require them to determine the goals to be met by a decision, and engage in a reasoning process yielding a solution that meets their needs as individuals. They could argue that their goal was to get a fresh picture of Diana and Dodi and to sell that picture. They have a right to make a living and would reason that the only way to get the desired picture is to get as close to the couple as possible, take lots of photos, and hope that one or more of them will sell. Their needs would almost certainly be met by this sort of action. The paparazzi could then assert that they are off the "ethical hook," so to speak, that they cannot be accused of unethical behavior.

Not so fast, an ethicist would say. In responding to the paparazzi's argument, one could begin by pointing out that most ethical philosophies cannot be so literally applied. While the philosophies are often stated in precise language, it is the broad sense of the philosophy and not the individual words that contain its value. It is most assuredly true that Rand believed that an individual should pursue one's own goals, and that the pursuit of those goals was an ethical activity. However, she did not believe that in the pursuit of one's goals one was entitled to run roughshod over the rights of other individuals. As Rand notes, "A moral code is a set of abstract principles; to practice it, an individual must translate it into the appropriate concretes."[13] "The mere fact that a man desires something does not constitute proof that the object of his desire is *good*." Moreover, "any alleged 'right' of one man which necessitates the violation of the rights of another, is not and cannot be a right."[14] Rand is suggesting, of course, that philosophical concepts must be carefully reasoned and just as carefully applied to real situations.

The paparazzi are on even more of a slippery slope than they realize if the reports from some of the crash scene observers are true. Observers reported the paparazzi did not call for help (an observation supported by an examination of cellular phone records), but instead may have opened the car's doors and positioned some of its occupants to get a better photo. One observer said he saw someone with a video camera at the scene. If only one or two of these observations turn out to be true, the paparazzi's claim to having acted in an ethically appropriate fashion may be dismissed.

In the weeks following the Diana incident, photographers demonstrated that they could make their importance felt. Many engaged in protests, objecting to the continuing criticism they were receiving about their work. In late September 1997, 80 photographers laid down their cameras and refused to photograph two high-level French government officials as they left a conference at the French presidential palace. The photographers stood, arms folded, along the walkway from the palace but refused to take any pictures. Also in late September, photographers attending the premiere of George Clooney's new movie *The Peacemaker* refused to take pictures of him as he attended the event. Clooney had been a critic of the paparazzi's harassment of celebrities, delivering a stinging rebuke to them in the hours following Diana's death.

One other point is worth making here. In most cases, an ethical philosophy of some sort can be found to justify almost any action. The selection of a philosophy to assist in the solution of an ethical problem is, therefore, often a personal choice, but it should be backed by a sound reasoning process. Murder, rape, and the like cannot be successfully defended by any ethical philosophy unless such philosophy is twisted to make it fit. A truly ethical person will avoid twisting a philosophy to meet his or her individual needs. Philosophies work best when they are a good fit—when they apply to a given situation in a logical, moral, straightforward manner.

Mainstream Media Coverage   Unlike the American poet E. A. Robinson's Miniver Cheevy—who was born too late—the Canadian communication theorist Marshall McLuhan was born too early—about 30 years too early. McLuhan's ideas about media were trendy in the 1960s when they were first advanced. There was some passing interest in his ideas, but he was never much accepted as a scholar whose insights about media explained the things we wanted to know during those years. Most communications theory books give his ideas a couple of paragraphs, perhaps a page. Many scholars consider his approaches to media superficial at best. Nevertheless, McLuhan now appears to have been ahead of his time. His ideas about what rapid technological advances would do to media and to media audiences now seem prophetic, especially when examined in light of media performance after the death of Princess Diana.

Particularly applicable to our instructional case study is McLuhan's notion of a *global village*. McLuhan felt that "time has ceased, 'space' has vanished. . . . Ours is a world of allatonceness."[15] This state of affairs is the direct result of instantaneous, electronic media communication. All the peoples of the world are tied together by media technology. Space and time barriers have disappeared, and language and other cultural differences become insignificant in a world linked by media. This was the case with the media coverage of Diana's funeral. An estimated worldwide audience of 2 billion saw the same pictures and commentary: London, Toronto, Atlanta, Hong Kong, and Sarajevo, among many other cities. No one had to wait for a report of the events surrounding Diana's funeral. Everyone was there—simultaneously—thanks to sophisticated electronic technology. McLuhan suggested that this sort of experience was bound to change what people thought, felt, and did. Certainly in Diana's case, media were able to cultivate feelings of sadness and loss among the viewers, as well as the notion that Diana was a great humanitarian.

This latter notion held for almost a week, until the death of another prominent woman on the world scene. Mother Teresa of Calcutta, India, died on Friday, September 5, 1997, less than a week after Diana and only one day before Diana's funeral. Media were now presented with something of a problem. Mother Teresa, a Catholic nun who founded the Missionaries of Charity in Calcutta and satellite missions elsewhere in the world, was a genuine humanitarian. She was never rich, never had a flagrant lifestyle, yet she devoted most of her 87 years to helping the poor, the sick, and the disabled. Diana's good works, substantial though they may have been, paled beside the lifelong contribution of Mother Teresa. Yet for almost a week, the media had been praising Diana as if she were the ultimate humanitarian model.

The news of Mother Teresa's death was also flashed to the global village, but nothing much was made of it until after Diana's funeral. It was then that the media turned their attention to Mother Teresa. Many of the news organizations that covered Diana's funeral indicated they would go to Calcutta to cover the funeral of the Nobel Prize–winning nun. *Newsweek* Senior Editor Jonathan Alter observed that if Mother Teresa had "died in a different news cycle than Diana, Teresa would have received respectful coverage, but nothing close to what she got. . . . Mother Teresa's legacy also got a cosmic boost from the shame felt at hyping an adulterous princess over a living saint."[16]

Other Issues   How well did the media cover the Diana story? The answer to that question depends on the medium. Newspaper coverage was, for the most part, detailed and accurate, without being overwhelming. Several pages were typically given over to coverage of the death and related issues, but newspapers continued to report other news. Newspaper coverage often featured a mix of British and American reports on the death, public response, and funeral preparations. Some papers connected the story to local people. For example, a woman in Tampa, Florida, had purchased several of Diana's gowns at a charity auction. It seemed natural, therefore, for the two Tampa Bay newspapers (*Tampa Tribune* and *St. Petersburg Times*) to provide a feature story on a local person who had some connection to Diana.

Electronic media news coverage of Diana's death and its aftermath was more controversial than newspaper coverage. Initially, the electronic media (television and cable) handled the news reasonably well. Information was slow to come from the accident site. The electronic media simply reported the information they had and refrained from speculation. Some of what they reported was untrue. For example, one report noted that Diana was injured but that she had been seen walking around outside the car talking to medical personnel. We now know that her condition was so critical that she was not able to move around and may not have ever been conscious. Nevertheless, the electronic media merely reported what observers had told them, and media cannot be faulted for reporting breaking stories with such information as they have, albeit later discovered to be untrue. When Diana's death was confirmed, the electronic media reported it in a straightforward, respectful manner, often taking news feeds from the British Broadcasting Corporation.

But in the days following Diana's death, the electronic media may have gone overboard in their coverage. Some of what they did was appropriate; some things were ethically questionable; and some clearly bore the mark of a "postmodern" approach to news reporting. For two consecutive nights, almost nothing but Diana news appeared on the evening network television and cable news programs.

As the day of the funeral neared, coverage diminished somewhat, but still often consumed two-thirds to three-fourths of the 30-minute nightly network newscasts. The all-news cable channels appeared to be obsessed with the story. They ran little else. Hour after hour of discussion was presented. Every news clip of Diana was found and played over and over. We saw her getting out of cars at charity events; we saw her greeting her sons; we saw her with the sick and dying; we saw her running through airports; we saw her dancing; we saw her walking down the aisle on her wedding day; we saw her riding in carriages; we saw her waving from the Royal Palace balcony. We may have seen every single piece of Diana videotape the news organizations possessed. It certainly seemed that way. Not so bad, you might say. It would be interesting to see these sorts of things. Yes, perhaps once or twice. But why present this information over and over again, hour after hour, day after day?

While the repetitious Diana coverage may not be considered an ethical problem—some say this sort of thing is unavoidable given the time-cycle nature of news—some aspects of the coverage did raise ethical issues. MSNBC, an all-news/talk cable service, frequently used a question-and-answer program format featuring several "experts" of one sort or another. These experts were commonly British historians, members of the British or American media, or individuals who had some sort of connection, either past or present, to the royal family. The news anchor would introduce four or five of these individuals and begin by asking one of them a question about some event or issue surrounding the accident. The question would lead to comments and observations by other members of the panel.

At first blush, this seems to be a useful approach, but it fell short of being useful in practice. Guests were apparently expected to speak in *sound bites,* brief sentences or phrases suitable for excerpting. Almost without exception, guests were neither allowed to present an idea completely nor provide any context or background for what was being said. They were almost always interrupted by the anchor in mid-sentence or mid-thought. The anchor often chimed in with his or her views of the situation. Members of the viewing audience were frequently invited to call in and participate in the discussion, yet were not allowed any real input into the proceedings. Some guests and most callers got to say little or nothing, since discussion was often cut off with a "sorry, but we have to take a break" comment.

This sort of "news" activity raises some important ethical questions. What is the main purpose of this sort of program and this sort of approach? It certainly is not designed to provide information. Nor does it stimulate thoughtful discussion. Conveying information and provoking discussion take time. Participants must be allowed to make their points fully and to provide some rationale for their views. Others must be given time and opportunity to respond. One might ask, with Abelard, what were MSNBC's intentions? If intentions were simply to keep things stirred up, to keep the discussion rolling and nonspecific, to keep viewers tuning in, to provide a stimulating vehicle for commercial announcements, then they were probably successful. Would Aristotle consider this a "just-right" approach? It might be just right for purposes of commercial viability, but not for the larger purpose of informing the public. Would Mill say this approach promotes the greatest good for the greatest number?

This, of course, highlights an issue that has long had ethical implications: the economic needs of the medium versus the information needs of the public. A brief look at the history of journalism, particularly broadcast journalism, shows that for a while in media's history, news was considered so important a part of a medium's work that it was provided to the public regardless of the cost. Broadcast news was, in its early days, a *loss leader.* It did not make much, if any, money for the medium, but it was a necessary and needed part of the service the medium provided. Times changed, of course, and now news is a big money maker for the broadcast and cable industries.

Thus, the question for a medium becomes, "What is the most important element in our work: making money for ourselves or providing high-quality news and information to the public?" "Both," might come the clever response. Unfortunately, experience reveals that these two options are mutually exclusive. You can't do both. Hobbes would urge media outlets to rise above their self-interest and fulfill their obligations. Mill would urge media to engage in the sorts of activities that would bring the greatest good (important news and information) to the greatest number (the audience), not the greatest good (profit) to a few (stockholders and employees).

It is acknowledged that this sort of people-first philosophy will not be popular with some. Your author might be accused of being anticapitalistic. But the broadcast media should be reminded that the Communications Act of 1934 charges them with meeting the public interest, convenience, and necessity. They are not charged with using the public airwaves to make large profits for a few private individuals, yet this is primarily what they do. The great CBS newsman Edward R. Murrow made this important point in a speech to the Radio Television News Directors Association in October 1958. Murrow said, "If . . . news is to be regarded as a commodity, only acceptable when saleable, then I don't care what you call it—I say it isn't news."[17]

At the beginning of this chapter, some reference was made to the large salaries that network anchors, particularly, command. To support those large salaries and to provide the worldwide reach required of news organizations these days, electronic media outlets often feel that they must maximize the income from their news programs. While no one would wish to prevent them from making money to support the gathering and reporting of news, it is curious that many organizations have making money, not providing news and information, as the driving force in their work. This is a *means-and-end* issue. What is the *end*, or the ultimate goal, of the activity? What *means*, or techniques, do we use to get there?

Given the recent performance of the broadcast media, at least, the end is making money (and lots of it) and the means is presenting their particular version of the news. This is ethically questionable; if the airwaves belong to the public, shouldn't serving the public be the end of any sort of activity using those airwaves? Why not use entertainment programming to generate additional revenue and provide news and information in a pure, more meaningful way? The reality is that most broadcasters consider the Communications Act of 1934 passé and are not much troubled by what it means to serve the public interest.

The situation is somewhat different for newspapers and magazines. These media do not use the public airwaves and are not directed by a law like the Communications Act to serve the public in any specified way. While essentially the same battle between news space and advertising space exists, the conflict does not seem as pronounced, given the declining influence of newspapers in the last dozen years or so. In any case, newspapers and magazines are not using public property (the air) to do their work as broadcasters are. These distinctions exist among media (and there may be further distinctions between broadcast and cable news outlets). All media would do well to ask themselves the question Ed Murrow asked in 1958: "Do we merely stay in our comfortable nests, concluding that the obligation of these instruments has been discharged when we work at the job of informing the public. . . or do we believe that the preservation of the Republic is a seven-day-a-week job, demanding more awareness, better skills, and more perseverance than we have yet contemplated?"[18]

Before moving on to other important ethical issues in journalism, we need to examine one other aspect of our instructional case study. Because there is a five-hour time difference between England and America, coverage of Diana's funeral began here on most electronic media news services in the early hours of Saturday, September 6, 1997. For example, NBC began its coverage shortly before 4 A.M. Eastern Time, but cable services began an hour or two earlier. In any case, when the funeral cortege left Diana's Kensington Palace home at 9 A.M. British time and moved toward Westminster Abbey, cameras were rolling and newspersons were ready with detailed commentary. Cameras captured the cortege as it moved along its three-mile route, but nothing of significance happened until the procession passed St. James's Palace, where Diana's two sons, William and Harry, together with her brother, Earl Spencer, her ex-husband Prince Charles, and Charles's father Prince Philip, joined the procession, walking just behind Diana's coffin for the rest of the trip to Westminster. Once at the Abbey, the coffin was carried in, and the service began.

It must be admitted that the coverage of the funeral was compelling. The camera work was excellent, and commentary was kept to a minimum, especially on the BBC and on cable or network services carrying the BBC feed. Some of the networks, notably NBC, chose to take their own feed, and a commentator often overwhelmed the effect of the music by providing details about one thing or another. Nevertheless, interruptions were kept to a minimum in most cases. When left alone, the funeral coverage was an excellent example of how media can provide an audience with a look at events it would not ordinarily see. Without commentary, audiences were on their own to react to what they saw. Still, when the service had concluded and Diana was on her way to her family home for burial, most commentators could not resist passing judgment on some key aspects of the service, particularly the eulogy of Earl Spencer, Diana's brother. Spencer had lashed out at the media for their role in Diana's death, noting that she was a good person who was hunted down by those (media) "at the other end of the moral spectrum." Nevertheless, on balance, coverage of the funeral did not appear to raise any serious ethical issues. In retrospect, it seems clear that television and cable news are at their best when they function as the proverbial "fly on the wall," seeing all that happens but not involved in what happens. This sort of approach to news frequently ensures that few ethical problems will arise.

▼ Part III. Other Ethical Concerns

There are several other important ethical issues not directly related to the instructional case study that need examining. All of the following have ethical implications and may be encountered in some form as journalists go about their jobs.

- Conflict of interest
- Checkbook journalism
- Staged news events
- Hidden cameras and deception
- Manipulation (alteration) of photographs

A *conflict of interest* may occur when media employees engage in any outside activity that might influence the way they do their jobs. This could include using your newspaper column or radio or television program to promote, without proper payment, a business in which you have a financial or other interest. It could also include failing to write or follow up a news story because you have some connection to one or more of the individuals involved. Conflict of interest also results from the acceptance of an expense-paid trip to some desirable location, called a *junket*, when the sponsoring organization is in some way related to one's work.

Checkbook journalism refers to the practice of paying for interviews with newsmakers. The newsmakers are often controversial, and money requested often runs to tens of thousands of dollars. Some news organizations are willing to pay significant amounts of money for the privilege of getting an exclusive interview with an important person in the news. Other organizations feel that this practice violates an important news tenet: news is a *good* in itself and, as such, it must not be treated as a commodity to be purchased but as important information that, by its virtual existence, rises above economic interests to meet the demands of a democracy. Paying money for information is an ethically questionable practice.

Although time has shown that a *staged news event* is almost always exposed for the deception it is, some news organizations still engage in this unethical practice. Most notable is the *Dateline NBC* incident. On November 12, 1992, the *Dateline NBC* program aired a segment titled "Waiting to Explode." The story concerned alleged fire hazards in old General Motors (GM) pickup trucks. These trucks apparently had gas tanks on the sides of the vehicle where they would be particularly vulnerable to a crash. The climactic moment of the segment ran just under 60 seconds and showed an auto crashing into the side of a GM pickup. The truck exploded in flames. GM executives were suspicious of claims made by the broadcast and hired detectives to investigate the incident. The detectives determined that NBC had attached small rocket engines underneath the truck so that when struck by another vehicle, the tanks would rupture and the spilled gas would ignite. At first NBC denied that the incident had been fixed, then admitted that it had "dramatized" the point. Such behavior, while not widespread, is clearly unethical. NBC apologized to all involved, thus avoiding a threatened GM lawsuit.

Individuals have been taking surreptitious pictures probably for as long as cameras have been in existence. It is not unusual for a friend or family member to sneak up on a person and snap a picture. Such behavior is generally harmless. However, when media organizations take pictures or shoot videotape from hidden locations, the result may not be harmless, especially if those pictures are printed or broadcast. At the very least, there are privacy or other legal issues to consider. Using *hidden cameras and deception* in the gathering of news is ethically questionable. For media organizations caught in this practice, it can be expensive. Consider the case of *ABC* v. *Food Lion*.

In 1992 ABC's *Prime Time Live* program charged that the Food Lion grocery chain was selling rotten meat and rat-gnawed cheese. ABC producers passed themselves off as employees and used hidden cameras to tape the store's food-handling practices. Videotape showed store employees washing spoiled meat in bleach, packaging the meat, and placing it out for sale. Food Lion sued the network, but not for libel, that is, it did not allege that the story was untrue. Instead the company charged fraud (lying on job applications) and trespassing. A jury awarded Food Lion $5.5 million in punitive damages. When questioned after the verdict was entered, members of the jury said they did not object to the principle of undercover, investigative news reporting, but did object to media organizations using dishonest means to get a story. Members of the jury agreed that they were essentially sending the media a message: do your job, but do it honorably. Agreeing with ABC that the $5.5 million figure was excessive, a judge later reduced the cash judgment to $315,000. As this chapter was being written, Food Lion asked a federal appeals court to reinstate the $5.5 million damage award against ABC News.

Could ABC have argued, philosophically, that its action was appropriate? Abelard's philosophy supports ABC's action. ABC's intentions were good—the network was trying to expose practices that had potentially harmful effects on the public. On the other hand, Plato would not have supported ABC's actions. Plato charges us with refraining from wrongdoing regardless of the consequences. It was wrong for ABC producers to pose as store employees and wrong of them to hide a camera. Food Lion, however, has no ethical ground on which it can stand.

One other important issue relating to pictures or photographs needs comment. Is it unethical to engage in the *manipulation (or alteration) of photographs?* The answer to this question may depend on what one considers to be manipulation. Purists would urge using photos and videotape exactly as they were shot. To change these images is to change reality, and media should be in the business of reporting, not changing, reality. Others might argue that it is appropriate to change something in a photograph or tape to make it more aesthetically pleasing. For example, suppose you took a picture of a friend standing outside a campus building, near a group of trees. It might be that the angle was such that your subject was positioned in front of the trees and that in the developed picture a tree appears to be growing from the person's head. If you intend to use that photo in the campus newspaper, is it ethically permissible to alter the photo and move the tree to one side so that the awkward effect of the tree appearing to spring from the person's head is avoided? Or consider this possibility. Suppose you shot a videotape showing some school-children playing hookey near a local river and the tape clearly shows obscene graffiti scribbled on the concrete supports of a nearby bridge. Is it ethical to electronically eliminate that graffiti before the tape is aired as part of a story on school truancy?

Alteration of photographs and videotape is a common practice. Electronic imaging technology enables technicians to do a variety of things to photos and videotape. In the 1980s, official White House photos of a hospitalized President Ronald Reagan had an IV tube cropped out so that the public would not become alarmed at the sight of their very ill president. *National Geographic* magazine was criticized in 1982 for moving two Egyptian pyramids closer together so that they would fit nicely on a magazine cover. Do aesthetics triumph over ethics? Are some types of alteration acceptable and other types not? How does one make such distinctions?

The postmodern philosopher Baudrillard warns us to neither create nor perpetuate a fiction. However, Schopenhauer might argue that if the action had received due consideration, demonstrated respect for self and others, and achieved a balance in terms of the factors involved, it would be an acceptable action. Nevertheless, purists might argue that too much manipulation of photographs might result in individuals feeling they could no longer rely on photos or tape to depict actual people and events. In order to maintain the credibility of the image, a practical course of action would suggest no manipulation. But, as with most ethical dilemmas, there are "degrees" of manipulation. Some alterations might be harmless; others might significantly change the meaning of the photo or tape.

Postmodern Ethical Concerns

As our culture moved into the postmodern era, additional ethical concerns surfaced. Some of these may have been around for a while, but they seem more easily recognized now because they reflect postmodern characteristics, particularly in terms of stressing victimization and in the cognitive dissonance created by some current journalistic practices.

It often seems that the most important philosophy for most news operations is "If it bleeds, it leads." This phrase reflects the news selection policy of many television stations and some newspapers. An examination of the types of stories appearing on evening newscasts on many local television stations reveals much emphasis on crime news. Some news operations seem obsessed with reporting crime news. A local television newscast that does not lead with a crime story of some sort is a rare find; often the crime story has few or no implications for the audience. For example, on one particular Friday night, one television station in the South apparently ran short of brutal killings and rapes. The station settled on a story about a 7-year-old boy who was accidentally shot in the leg with a BB by two older boys who were harassing him. The camera zoomed in to show the bruise on the boy's leg. Interviews were conducted all around. The investigating police officer called the incident "a shame." The two older boys said they only wanted to scare the boy, and didn't mean to shoot him. The little boy's mother said the two older boys were nothing but bullies. A local television critic called this approach to news "junior high journalism."

Is this a news story? Not if one requires a "hit" on one or more of the news values discussed earlier in this chapter. The boy was obviously distressed by the incident, as was his mother. And he was lucky that the BB did not strike an eye, but this sort of interaction among the young, although not desirable, is fairly routine. Does the story meet the tests of audience, impact, proximity, timeliness, prominence, or unusualness? Probably not, yet it was the lead story on the evening newscast. Weren't there other, more important things going on in the area—a major metropolitan area, the fifteenth largest in the nation? Was there important news at the national or international level? Was it less important than the "bully" story?

If the emphasis on reporting crime news weren't enough, some stations appear to have reporters (or news executives) who would really rather be cops. "Crimestoppers" segments are popular with many broadcast news operations. The notion here is that the station can use its personnel to reenact, or dramatize, an unsolved crime. In doing so, it is hoped that some member of the audience will remember having seen the incident and phone police, providing important information that may lead to a resolution of the case. It should be noted that while newspapers often splash crime news on their front pages, they are much less inclined to let this type of news dominate. Crime news of all sorts can be found in newspapers, but usually it is tucked inside, and often presented in capsule form.

When crime news is emphasized by news organizations, it almost certainly reinforces the postmodern *trend toward victimization.* Mass communication researchers have studied the degree to which television "cultivates" a particular view of crime in viewers. We know that viewers who watch a lot of television consider themselves to be likely victims of crime or wrongdoing to a greater extent than is probable in the real world. Viewers often live in the "TV world" of violent crime. This is not to say that crime is not a problem in contemporary America; it is. But not everyone is guaranteed victim status. Is it any wonder so many trivial lawsuits are filed over things like spilled coffee or hurt feelings? How can the public place the various aspects of life in any sort of context when television news, particularly, reports that the most important news of the day is related to crime. Agenda-setting, indeed!

Another disturbing contemporary journalistic practice is an increasing tendency of news organizations (and personalities) to become *involved with the stories* they are reporting. There is some evidence of this in the "Crimestoppers" news approach. But there is additional evidence. Here, too, television news organizations seem to be more deeply involved than newspapers or magazines, but there are instances where the print media are also becoming involved.

Twice in a period of a year (in February 1996 and in January 1997), "media organizations have paid to fly relatives to retrieve youths at the center of attention-getting disappearance cases." In the 1996 incident, "five Tampa Bay and three Orlando TV stations," as well as the two local Tampa Bay newspapers, "split the cost of an $8,314 Learjet charter to pick up a 17-year-old in New York, where she had been discovered after a five-week disappearance that made national headlines."[19] In the 1997 incident, another television station flew a father to Virginia to reunite him with his 7-year-old daughter who had been taken by her mother in violation of a custody agreement. As a result, the station had an exclusive story because a camera crew accompanied the father on the plane.

These incidents—and they are only two among many—clearly demonstrate the willingness of news organizations to participate in a story. Has the line between reporting the news and making the news been crossed? Indeed it has. Yet this sort of action, in postmodern America, is not causing the cognitive dissonance it should. Few seem to care that news is being redefined by those who most benefit from its redefinition. Can the audience tell the difference between *spontaneous coverage* and *choreographed coverage?* Are media in the business of reporting the news, or serving as charities for those who are sitting on a hot story but are in financial need? The inconsistencies here are clear. News no longer has to meet a set of clear standards. News is simply what news organizations say it is, and they often say it is what benefits them economically. Cognitive dissonance alarms should be going off in the heads not only of the audience but also of those involved in the news process. However, most just shrug their shoulders and, in postmodern fashion, ignore the inconsistencies between what should be done and what is being done.

CBS newsman Ed Murrow, in his 1958 speech, was "frightened by the imbalance, the constant striving to reach the largest audience for everything; by the absence of a sustained study of the state of the nation."[20] Although postmodernism was a barely developed concept in 1958, it is clear that Murrow was troubled by the inconsistencies, by the cognitive dissonance, resulting from news practices in his day. One shudders to think how Murrow would react to news practices today.

Anyone can be a journalist. No examinations are required to enter the field; no licenses must be obtained. No oversight board monitors the work and behavior of journalists. Economic influences, that is, the desire to garner high ratings and more revenue, have made the field wide open to some who wouldn't have even been considered in pre-postmodern times. For example, in the early summer of 1997, the Fox News Channel hired rapper Chuck D to provide news and commentary. Chuck D has made his living as a rap music artist. What qualifies him to provide news and commentary to a cable news operation? Chuck D himself provided the answer: "I'm a 36-year-old black man. . . . I've graduated from college, I'm a taxpayer and I can put sentences together. Why shouldn't I do commentary?" Precisely! Chuck D's response is an excellent example of postmodern reasoning and symbolic of all that's wrong with TV news these days. He sees no conflict between his life experiences as an entertainer and his future work as a journalist. Chuck D, whose real name is Carlton Ridenhour, said he wants to bring something different to the news. "I want to alert younger viewers to the news and knock the older people in the head."

What were Fox news executives thinking when they hired Ridenhour? Were they aware of any inconsistencies between the job he had and the job he was seeking? Were they aware that he may have had an agenda of some sort and how this agenda might impact on the important job of providing accurate and meaningful news reports? Were their cognitive processes undisturbed as they considered a person with no credentials for an important news job? In postmodern America, these questions are never asked and therefore never answered.

This *laissez-faire attitude* regarding the news and those who present it has important ethical implications. Does such action as has been taken by various news organizations reflect poor ethics or merely poor judgment? Durkheim reminds us that we should determine the moral ideal or standard that governs a planned action and explain how society benefits from the action. What moral ideal or standard governs participation in a news story? What ideal or standard allows the employment of an entertainer as a journalist? In point of fact, there are others, nonentertainers, who have jumped from their particular fields to journalism. It is routine for an individual who has been in politics or government to quit that job and become a journalist. President Clinton's adviser George Stephanopolos quit his White House job and went to work for ABC. New York Congresswoman Susan Molinari resigned her House seat to become a weekend news anchor for CBS. Is this more acceptable than giving a news job to an entertainer? Do these individuals have any sort of political agenda they will be advancing in the performance of their news jobs? Schopenhauer urged giving mature and repeated consideration to any plan before carrying it out. He warned that without such serious consideration, the "greedful will" will triumph and your action will lack balance and appropriateness. Has the greedful will overtaken American news organizations in postmodern America?

There is no need to belabor the point beyond the degree to which we have already gone. However, additional questions need to be asked and answered, and ethical positions need to be examined. Consider these items:

- Why do reporters insist on telling us what they *think,* rather than what they have *seen?*
- Just because a story has good visuals, does that make it good news?
- How do media "frame" their stories? That is, from what perspective is a story, particularly one involving conflict, told?
- What impact does the newsroom culture have on the selection and preparation of news stories?
- Are codes of ethics developed by the various news organizations actually practiced in newsrooms, or merely posted?[21]

Do these and similar issues clearly involve ethics? The answer depends on one's definition of ethics, but if there is substantial agreement that ethics involves making judgments between appropriate and inappropriate behavior, then the answer, of course, is yes. More than 40 years ago, Ed Murrow observed that media needed to be reminded that "the fact that your voice is amplified to the degree where it reaches from one end of the country to the other does not confer upon you greater wisdom or understanding than you possessed when your voice reached only from one end of the bar to the other."[22]

▼ Case Studies

Use the following case studies to stimulate your thinking about some of the ethical issues facing journalists. You may wish to use the ethical decision-making model presented in Chapter 10 as a guide to analyzing the ethical dilemma. Review the ethical decision-making tools presented at the conclusion of Chapter 10 to help you provide a rationale for your judgments.

Case Study #1. Supporting Professional Football

The Tampa Bay Buccaneers of the National Football League (NFL) have the worst won-loss record in all of professional sports. Many residents of the Bay area see them as "lovable losers" and support them regardless of their on-field performance. Others are critical of the team's performance, noting that the franchise has been a laughingstock among other team owners and area residents for many years.

Tampa Bay was awarded a professional football franchise in 1976. The team was purchased by Malcolm Glazer in 1994, shortly after the death of original owner Hugh Culverhouse. The team was no more productive under Glazer than it had been under Culverhouse. At one point in 1995, Glazer appeared to be on the verge of selling or moving the team. If sold, the team would likely move to another city; Baltimore and St. Louis were among the top choices. If not sold, the team might be moved anyway. The potential sale and possible move of the Bucs generated much local attention. Some fans wanted them to stay; others were willing to help them pack.

As events developed, it appeared that the Glazer family, composed of Malcolm and his sons, Bryan and Joel, were willing to make a long-term commitment to keeping the Bucs in Tampa Bay if the community would provide the team with a new stadium. There was nothing really wrong with the stadium the team was currently using. It just wasn't new. It did not have luxurious "suites" from which the rich and famous could view the game, and for which privilege they would pay top dollar. In fact, the stadium was acceptable enough to the NFL for the area to be awarded Super Bowl XXV. A problem developed, however, when neither the Tampa City Council nor the Hillsborough County Commission was willing to raise taxes to support the construction of a new stadium. It was decided that the issue would be put before area voters in the form of a referendum, a penny on the dollar sales tax. One-half cent would go toward the construction of a new stadium; the other half-cent could go to a fund for schools and to finance improvements in police and fire protection.

As might be expected, the community was divided over whether this referendum ought to be passed. Some objected to "rich" sports owners leaning on taxpayers for facilities that would make the owners even richer. Others felt the civic pride of having a professional football team justified additional taxes. Still others noted that the stadium tax should not be combined with a school and community services tax; these were, in their view, separate issues.

Tampa Bay area television stations and newspapers followed this story closely. There were daily updates on where things stood with regard to the proposed referendum as well as the proposed sale of the team. Local media took sides in the battle in mid-October, just a few weeks before the referendum. Seven local television stations aired a program titled "Home Field Advantage." The program featured local sports anchors, local politicians, and representatives of the football team in a spirited discussion asking viewers "to pony up for a new stadium for the Tampa Bay Buccaneers before the team is lured out of town." All the stations promoted the program heavily. The *St. Petersburg Times* gave stadium backers a special low rate for a full-page advertisement promoting the broadcast. The broadcast was carried live and at no charge by the participating stations. There was no place for non-cable viewers to go if they wanted to see something else during that time period. The program effectively blanketed the coverage area. Cable subscribers, of course, had other alternatives. One local sports anchor, when questioned about his participation in the event, said he was simply trying to inform the people about an important issue. "This was no different than going on a telethon," he said.

There is no way to determine the precise impact the program had on the attitudes of Bay area residents. Nevertheless, the referendum passed by a small margin a few weeks later.

Key Questions   Is there an ethical difference between television stations providing free time for fund-raising telethons (like Jerry Lewis's Labor Day MDA telethon) and providing free time for supporters of a local sports franchise to argue for public funding of a new stadium? Were Tampa Bay sports anchors acting ethically when they appeared on behalf of the local professional football team? Does a reporter's responsibility to objectivity include those individuals who report on sports?

Case Study #2. Chopper Journalism

Daniel Jones was apparently a troubled man. The 40-year-old maintenance worker from Long Beach, California, was HIV-positive and was angry about the way he had been treated by his health maintenance organization

(HMO). He felt that there was too much bureaucratic red tape and that HMOs emphasized making money rather than caring for the ill.

On April 30, 1998, Jones stopped his pickup truck on a busy Los Angeles expressway overpass and spread a banner out on the ground so that the news helicopters could see it. The banner read: HMOS ARE IN IT FOR THE MONEY!! LIVE FREE, LOVE SAFE OR DIE. By this time, of course, the always vigilant choppers were hovering overhead, and traffic was clogged. Jones returned to his truck and set the vehicle afire. He then placed his chin on the barrel of a shotgun and pulled the trigger. The television newscopters captured it all for live broadcast as *breaking news.*

Suicides like the one involving Jones are common and seem to be increasingly presented as a staple of the news. It is probably true that this was a news story of some sort. As Larry Perret of KCBS-TV noted, "This was a legitimate news story. You got a guy on the freeway closing two of L.A.'s most populated interchanges."[23] True, but the cameras were not focused on the traffic but on a man who was about to do violence to himself. Is this news or voyeurism?[24]

These types of stories are usually ratings winners. Los Angeles is a competitive news market. News is expensive to cover. The lease on a news helicopter can cost upwards of $1 million. Kerry Brock of New York City's Media Studies Center suggested that "if you're a television station and don't have a helicopter, you're not in the game."[25] Nevertheless, criticism of the coverage of the Jones suicide was immediate. Television stations were inundated with phone calls, most complaining about the graphic nature of the broadcast. Of particular concern to some was the fact that the incident was broadcast in mid-afternoon, "just in time to greet kids returning home from school. Two stations actually cut away from children's programming to get in on the action."[26] Cable's MSNBC also carried live video from the scene.

Derwin Johnson of the Columbia Graduate School of Journalism was bothered by the incident. "It's a classic case of technology running the beast instead of a clear editorial process. I don't think there was any reason to go live with this."[27] Although Los Angeles television news directors expressed their regret at showing the graphic violence of the incident—they noted that they had not anticipated its outcome—many stations "stayed on the story for an hour during which time they could have discerned that the man was obviously disturbed and that a catastrophe might have been in the offing."[28] Radio Television News Directors Association president Barbara Cochran said she believed the industry needs to develop some guidelines for live coverage of potentially explosive situations. However, Howard Rosenberg of the *Los Angeles Times* observed that "the media don't tend to learn from mistakes like this."[29]

Key Questions   What ethical responsibilities do television stations have in carrying live broadcasts of breaking news? Are television stations under any ethical obligation to moderate or modify their news programming because children might be in the audience? What is the ethical motivation for live coverage of potentially explosive situations? Are there unethical motivations that might stimulate such coverage? Would Aristotle's Golden Mean be a useful philosophy to apply in this situation?

Case Study #3. A Glass Not So Transparent

Stephen Glass was hot—at least several well-known magazines thought so. The 25-year-old journalist had talent. His stories were compelling, and his work was published in *Rolling Stone, George, Harper's,* and the *New York Times Magazine.* The editors of the *New Republic,* a magazine of political opinion, were particularly delighted because Glass was on the publication's staff and made regular contributions to the magazine. As one editor observed, Glass "could get into rooms other reporters couldn't get into, and come away with quotes and anecdotes the others couldn't get."[30]

Yes, it was clear that Steve Glass had talent, but, as his editors unhappily discovered, his particular talent was in making things up. "Glass concocted story after story and slipped them all past his editors and fact checkers."[31] He often supported his stories with forged notes and interview transcripts.

How clever was he? Pretty clever, actually. He invented a computer association called the National Assembly of Hackers and a special interest group called the Association for the Advancement of Sound Water Policy. He invented the town of "Werty, Iowa," and even created a fake Web site for Jukt Micronics, a nonexistent computer software company. Perhaps fact checkers should have gotten a little suspicious when they read of a George Bush cult group called The First Church of George Herbert Walker Christ, but they didn't. An examination of the 41 stories Glass had written for the *New Republic* revealed that almost two-thirds of them were at least partly fabricated; six were apparently entirely made up.

How could this happen? Two explanations were offered. One suggested that staff turnover at the *New Republic*—four editors in four years and the departure of several skilled staff writers—was to blame. Too little time and effort were assigned to fact checking. The other explanation suggested that journalism is a youth-happy industry and that many reporters land high-profile jobs before they have fully grasped the fundamentals of their craft. Glass rose quickly at the *New Republic,* from an intern in 1995 to assistant editor and then to associate editor.[32] However, it is also possible that Glass was simply a pathological liar. Glass disappeared for a time following his firing at the *New Republic,* but reportedly surfaced again in the spring of 1998 when he took final exams at the Georgetown Law School, where he had been attending evening classes.

Key Questions What responsibilities do newspapers and magazines have in checking the factual accuracy of stories they print? How can young journalists be encouraged to act ethically in the performance of their duties? Could Glass argue that he was only following Machiavelli's philosophy?

Case Study #4. Conflict of Interest

CBS's Walter Cronkite said no; CNN's Bernard Kalb said no; NPR's Daniel Schoor said no. But David Brinkley, formerly of NBC and ABC, said yes! The question put to each of these journalists was whether they would be willing to endorse a product in a commercial message.

David Brinkley had a brilliant journalistic career, one that spanned 50 years. He is probably best known for his Sunday ABC morning program *This Week with David Brinkley,* which began in 1981. Prior to that, he was part of NBC's Huntley-Brinkley evening news team. His face is recognized by millions, and he is easily one of the most respected newsmen of our era. Shortly after his retirement from ABC in October 1997, Brinkley agreed to appear in several commercials for Archer Daniel Midland (ADM), an Illinois-based food processing company. ADM was one of the sponsors of Brinkley's Sunday ABC program. In 1996, ADM paid $100 million in price-fixing fines and had, at the time, charges pending against two company executives for trying to fix the world market in lysine, a food additive.[33] Three company executives were later convicted on the price-fixing charges, each facing up to three years in prison.

Criticism of Brinkley's action came quickly. His appearance in the commercials, some critics said, "created the possibility that the audience might think he still worked on his former program."[34] Joan Konner, former dean of the Columbia School of Journalism, felt the switch in roles was improper. "I think it's awful," she said. "Lines should be distinct and they are not distinct in this case."[35]

Brinkley is not alone in his role as reporter-turned-pitchman. Linda Ellerbe, formerly of NBC, did an ad for Maxwell House coffee. Former CBS morning host Kathleen Sullivan appeared on behalf of Weight Watchers. Other former journalists who moved to the ad world include Deborah Norville, Mary Alice Williams, and Richard Valeriani. Even Chet Huntley, Brinkley's old evening news partner, was a spokesperson for American Airlines after retiring from NBC. Still, Brinkley is viewed as something of a role model, a dedicated journalist with over a half-century of faithful reporting.

Not everyone is bothered by Brinkley's actions. Marshall Loeb, editor of the *Columbia Journalism Review,* noted that there is a significant difference between an active and a retired journalist, and that he was not much bothered by Brinkley's actions. Other critics, however, charged the entire news industry with a kind of cronyism. Many journalists appear to be models of journalistic integrity and independence, yet pocket "hefty fees for friendly lectures to corporate lobby groups."[36]

Key Questions   Since Brinkley was retired and was no longer a practicing journalist, was it really unethical for him to earn a little extra money by appearing on behalf of an advertiser? Are all reporters, retired or not, ethically bound to disclose their connections to those individuals or organizations on which they report? Is it possible for a media employee, journalist or not, to avoid unethical practices in an industry so dominated by economic concerns? Did Brinkley follow Aquinas's four cardinal virtues?

Case Study #5. The Stars Shine in Magazines

Americans have a large appetite for celebrity news. Viewers consume television talk and newsmagazine shows with relish. Newspapers often run celebrity news on their front pages. Now, it seems, magazines, too, are succumbing to the celebrity culture in ways that may not be obvious to their readers. Pop singer Madonna is a good case in point.

Madonna proved that she was indeed a "material girl" by insisting that she have control of the material, specifically material *Rolling Stone* proposed to use in its thirtieth anniversary special issue. The material in question included a cover photo, layout, story photos, and the copyright to the photos.[37]

Did *Rolling Stone* turn over editorial control of the piece to the pop diva? Yes, mostly. It said no to layout approval but agreed to everything else. Madonna appeared with singers Tina Turner and Courtney Love on the cover of the Fall 1997 issue of *Rolling Stone.*

An unusual practice, you might wonder? Not really. These days more and more celebrities are asking for control of how magazines present information about them. Magazines say they have no choice. The magazine market is competitive. Many magazines must compete with television newsmagazine programs. In order to get the cooperation of many celebrities, magazines are caving in to their demands.

Actually, the relationship between celebrities and magazines has always been symbiotic. Celebrities need the magazines for publicity; magazines need celebrities for sales. But now, many feel, the situation is out of control. *Details* magazine editor Michael Caruso feels that the balance of power has shifted. Things that were previously forbidden are now being negotiated. Some publicists even go so far as to give magazines a list of questions that a reporter may and may not ask their clients. Others specify the makeup, clothing, even the camera angles to be used.

One solution to this problem is to eliminate the reporter altogether and have the stars essentially interview themselves. In *US* magazine, for example, actor Mel Gibson prepared an article titled "The Unbelievable Truth about Mel Gibson. By Mel Gibson."[38]

Some observers wonder what happened to journalistic integrity and editorial control. They seem to have been caught between the economic interests of the magazines and the publicity needs of the celebrities.

Key Questions   Can a magazine or newspaper allow the subject of a story to control the story's content and still maintain journalistic integrity? Are the celebrities themselves acting unethically when they try to influence editorial content? Does the ethical philosophy of Ayn Rand support the actions of the magazine? Of the celebrities?

QUESTIONS FOR DISCUSSION

1. Does it make any difference whether journalism is considered a trade or a profession? Why?

2. Look again at the news values presented early in the chapter. On how many of these values should a story "hit" before it is deemed worthy of publication or broadcast?

3. In your own words, state the difference between a public and a private figure.

4. Broadcasters are charged by the Communications Act of 1934 to serve the public interest, convenience, and necessity. Is this part of the law out of date? Explain your thinking.

5. Under what circumstances would the manipulation of a photograph be appropriate? Under what conditions would it be inappropriate?

6. In what ways do contemporary journalistic practices contribute to a postmodern society? Should journalism reflect society or attempt to change it for the better?

ENDNOTES

1. John C. Merrill and S. Jack Odell, *Philosophy and Journalism* (New York: Longman, 1983), 119.

2. Ibid., 120.

3. J. Harriss, K. Leiter, and S. Johnson, *The Complete Reporter* (New York: Macmillan, 1985), 30.

4. B. S. Brooks, G. Kennedy, D. R. Moen, and D. Ranly, *News Reporting and Writing* (New York: St. Martin's Press, 1985), 4–5.

5. Neil Postman, *Amusing Ourselves to Death* (New York: Viking, 1985), 33.

6. Russell Baker, "The Celebrity Consumer Culture," *St. Petersburg Times*, 14 September 1997, sec. A, p. 10.

7. Christopher Reed, "Celebrities Against Liberties," *St. Petersburg Times*, 14 September 1997, sec. D, p. 8.

8. "In Pursuit of Diana," *New York Times* report, *St. Petersburg Times*, 11 September 1997, sec. A, pp. 1, 8.

9. Baker, sec. A, p. 10.

10. A. M. Rosenthal, "The Blood on Journalists' Hands," *St. Petersburg Times*, 3 September 1997, sec. A, p. 10.

11. Richard Folkerts, "When Worlds Collide," *U.S. News & World Report*, 15 September 1997, 40.

12. Charles Krauthammer, "The Great Di Turnaround," *Time*, 22 September 1997, 104.

13. Ayn Rand, *Introduction to Objectivist Epistemology* (New York: Mentor, 1966), 42.

14. Ayn Rand, *The Virtue of Selfishness* (New York: Signet, 1964), 50 and 96.

15. Marshall McLuhan, *The Medium Is the Massage* (New York: Bantam, 1967), 63.

16. Jonathan Alter, "Genuflect Journalism," *Newsweek,* 22 September 1977, 37.

17. Edward R. Murrow, "Lights and Wires in a Box," *Documents of American Broadcasting,* ed. Frank J. Kahn (Englewood Cliffs, NJ: Prentice Hall, 1978), 255.

18. Ibid., 257.

19. Eric Deggans, "Are Media Buying Tickets to Sticky Ethical Morass?" *St. Petersburg Times,* 16 April 1997, sec. B, p. 2.

20. Murrow, 257.

21. Codes of ethics have been developed by the Radio Television News Directors Association (RTNDA), by the American Society of Newspaper Editors (ASNE), and by the Society of Professional Journalists (SPJ), among other news and professional organizations.

22. Murrow, 253.

23. Howard Chua-Evan, "Too Many Eyes in the Sky?" *Time,* 11 May 1998, 30.

24. Rem Rieder, "As Good and as Bad as It Gets," *American Journalism Review,* June 1998, 6.

25. Chua-Evan, 30.

26. Frank Rich, "Coming to You Dead from L.A.," *Tampa Tribune,* 5 May 1998, Nation/World, 7.

27. Chua-Evan, 30.

28. Rich, 7.

29. Debra D. Durocher, "L.A.'s TV News: Pulling Away from Live Shots," *American Journalism Review,* June 1998, 10.

30. Eric Pooley, "Too Good to Be True," *Time,* 25 May 1998, 62.

31. Ibid.

32. Lori Robertson, "Shattered Glass at the *New Republic,*" *American Journalism Review,* June 1998, 9.

33. "Brinkley Goes from Newsman to Adman," New York Times News Service and the Associated Press, 6 January 1998.

34. Ibid.

35. Ibid.

36. Jeff Cohen, "Buying and Selling the News," *St. Petersburg Times,* 31 January 1998, 13A.

37. Robin Pogrebin, "Magazines Bowing to Stars," New York Times News Service, 5 May 1998.

38. Ibid.

CHAPTER 12

Ethical Issues and Case Studies in Advertising and Public Relations

There is an old adage that runs in this fashion: What are the three most important things in having a successful business? The answer? "Location, location, location." True enough, especially if customers must visit a business to obtain goods or services. But the nature of business has changed over the last dozen years or so, and technologically rich American consumers may not have to leave their homes to purchase many of the things they need or want. E-mail, direct mail, and telephone marketing are just some of the practices that have changed the way many firms and their customers do business.

In postmodern America and contemporary culture, one could argue that the three most important factors in a successful business are location, advertising, and public relations. Having a good location helps, but so do having an effective advertising program to promote your product or service and having a successful public relations effort to develop and polish your corporate image. In postmodern America, image counts for a lot, and public relations professionals are accomplished at polishing your image, especially when they team with advertising executives. This one-two punch can leave customers convinced that they must have such-and-such a product or service from that marvelous such-and-such company.

In this chapter we will examine some ethical issues that arise from contemporary advertising and public relations practices.

▼ Advertising

Advertising is not a mass medium. It is persuasive communication placed on radio or television, in newspapers or magazines, as well as elsewhere. It uses media but is not a medium in the strictest sense of the term. Advertising messages are part of the *content* of media in much the same way that news and entertainment are part of the content of media.

Advertising is seen by some as inseparable from marketing and therefore an important business function. On some university campuses, departments of advertising and marketing are housed in schools of business. However, on other campuses, advertising remains in schools of journalism and mass communication. Wherever it is placed in the academic world, it maintains its close connection to media.

As with many aspects of media culture, advertising involves money, and where there is money to be made, whether by individuals, groups, or corporations, and money to be spent (by consumers), the opportunities for ethical problems abound. In this section we'll look at eight problematic areas/practices in advertising and explore the ethical issues involved in each.

Overview

Advertising is everywhere in America—on television and radio, in newspapers and magazines. Ads can also be found in urinals, in taxis, on T-shirts, on grocery carts, on buses, in schools, in doctors' offices, at the beach, in movie lobbies, and attached to utility poles. This list is not exhaustive. Advertising is ubiquitous and, some say, intrusive. However, America is a capitalistic society, and much of what we see from advertisers must be tolerated. Yet many feel there ought to be at least a few places in America where advertising does not intrude.

Influencing buyer behavior is the main purpose of advertising. This purpose may be accomplished in any of several ways, but, generally, advertising's aim is to create customers for products and services. Consumers, on the other hand, purchase goods and services in "an attempt to satisfy some need"[1]—safety, love, esteem, or self-fulfillment, among others. It is widely recognized that some advertising messages push consumers toward positive ends, while others propel them toward negative behaviors.

One troubling aspect of advertising is the notion that advertising creates a consumer culture where the emphasis is on acquiring all the things we want. Many of the goods and services we are urged to purchase are things we *need*, that is, items necessary to life. Among the many things we need are food, clothing, shelter, medical services, repair services, and cleaning products (for both home and body). This list is not exhaustive either. Yet some advertising messages seem intent on getting us to acquire products or services not because we need them but because we *want* them.

There is nothing wrong with buying things we want. Individuals are free to use their disposable income in any way they wish. Nevertheless, an increasing barrage of advertisements, using both subtle and not-so-subtle appeals, seems to have blurred the line between our needs and our wants. Children, especially, are vulnerable to the relentless broadcast of advertising messages. It is easy to make children believe that they *need* an item, when in fact, they may only *want* that item. While it is true that many children do not have toys to play with, many more have so many toys they could not possibly play with all of them in any given week. Children are often convinced that they must have an item they have seen advertised and will nag their parents until the item is purchased for them.

Advertising can have a similar impact on adults. Phrases like "Shop 'till you drop" and "Born to shop" seem to indicate that shopping endlessly is something of a profession, something akin to work, not something one does to meet basic needs. How many pairs of shoes does a woman need? How many ties does a businessman need? Ten, twenty, thirty? In postmodern America, reason has been replaced by the persuasive advertisement. We do not have to think about, reason out, what we need; we simply let advertising determine what we need. Advertisers tell us what we should have, and we go get it.

This creation of a consumer culture, where one is essentially defined by what one owns, is seen by some as dangerous. Americans value the accumulation of "stuff." If I have more stuff than you, I must be more successful. The Spartan life, as led by Socrates and others in ancient Greece, or even the simple life advocated by the American writer Henry David Thoreau, are of little value to most people in postmodern culture. It is true, of course, that even ancient kings and queens measured their power and influence according to what they possessed. The problem is not a new one, but the extent to which it has advanced and taken control of the culture is new and is a significant problem. Here lies the basic postmodern approach to contemporary life. Postmodernism does not say that all phenomena of contemporary culture are new, only that many of these phenomena have reached extremes not previously seen. The movement toward extremes has changed everything about the culture. Our culture is being redefined and pointed in a different direction.

However, it must be noted that advertising does have some positive aspects. Chief among these is that ads generate revenue for media. Media do not have to depend on the government for funding and can thus remain independent of governmental influence and presumably do a better job of informing people about issues that affect their lives. This is an important benefit. Advertisements can also be entertaining. Many ads are creative and easily bring a smile to the face.

The main worry among some observers is not that advertising has few benefits, but that it is out of control to the extent that an "infotainment" culture has been created. James B. Twitchell calls this new enterprise *Adcult.* Twitchell believes that "the culture we live in is carried on the back of advertising."[2] Advertising extracts from us not only our money but also our time. It takes time to read, view, and absorb all those advertising messages. Twitchell asks whether this is the way we want our culture to develop. Is this what we want to be and do?

Historically, advertising has had its problems. Some early ads clearly stereotyped individuals in a way that would be objectionable to current thinking. The *Wall Street Journal* noted that "marketers have long perpetuated ugly stereotypes to sell everything from soap to Scotch over the years.

The difference is that in past decades, the ads, including a 1941 Shell Oil Company ad featuring a black boy eating watermelon, didn't generate a storm of controversy." In 1956, the Philip Morris Company used a young mother cradling a baby to sell cigarettes. A 1945 ad from Shell Oil showed a lab technician injecting fluid into the tail of a mouse encased in a glass vial. Such ads, acceptable to audiences in their day, would certainly generate a chorus of protests today.

Many of the issues mentioned here have ethical implications. In the pages that follow, eight ethical issues relating to advertising will be examined. These are not, of course, all the concerns about advertising practices that an ethicist might have, but they are a representative cross section.

▼ Instructional Case Study

In early September 1995, Clara and her daughter, Jennifer, were shopping in Chicago's Water Tower Plaza Mall when they came across an ad for designer jeans. "The ad showed a very-young-looking girl in a skimpy tank top, her jeans pushed below her bellybutton." The ad, Clara said, was absolutely pornographic. "They're exploiting children," she said. But Jennifer, age 15, thought the model looked cute. "All my friends wear their pants down past their underwear," she said, noting that, in her school, Calvin Klein was the most popular clothing designer.[3]

The ad Jennifer and her mother saw might be considered tame in comparison to others in the Calvin Klein advertising campaign that began in August 1995. These ads featured "pubescent models in lurid poses. . . . One of the most offensive [shows] a young man alone, his face in that numb, deadened look associated with films that can only be bought in an adult bookstore. A man off-camera says, 'You got a real nice look. How old are you? Are you strong? You think you could rip that shirt off of you? That's a real nice body. You work out? I can tell.' "[4] To some observers, this broadcast ad and others in the same Klein campaign represented a trip to "the heart of adult darkness, where toying with the sexuality of young teens is thinkable."[5]

In fact, these "discomfitingly intimate snapshots of very young men and women in provocative states of undress" may have been designed to shock and draw protests. As Bob Garfield of *Advertising Age* noted, "If you make a small amount of the right kind of noise, the media will deliver you tens or hundreds of millions of dollars worth of free publicity."[6] Garfield's words turned out to be prophetic. The *New York Daily News,* for example, ran this headline: "This Ads Up to Porn." The accompanying story dutifully served up one of the offending ads.

Some felt the ads were clearly pornographic; however, Klein said "most of the models are adults, as old as 29." Some retailers rebelled and urged Klein to pull the ads. Klein complied, but the advertising message was already in the cultural stream. The free publicity about the controversy continued, even as Klein prepared to introduce a designer line of sheets, towels, and tableware. Later he would introduce CKone perfume worldwide. In a full-page ad in the *New York Times,* Calvin Klein, Inc., "issued a statement that said it was 'taken aback' that its campaign had been misunderstood. . . . The message of the campaign, it said, was that 'young people today . . . have a real strength of character and independence.' " Klein himself told *Newsweek* magazine that he was "shocked" that other people didn't get it. "My intention," he said, "was not to create a controversy, in spite of what people think." Yet controversy is nothing new to Calvin Klein. In the early 1980s, feminists howled in protest over his "crotch shots of a 15-year-old Brooke Shields cooing that nothing came between her and her Calvins. Later, Klein "eroticized the nubile bodies of Marky Mark and Kate Moss" to sell underwear.[7] The 1995 ads for Calvin Klein jeans were merely an extension of what had gone before and had been successful.

Appeals

Advertising messages may be developed in many different ways. Much depends on the product or service being offered and its target audience. Quite often, the actual structure of an ad is determined by the *appeal* it makes to its target audience. Appeals may be made to one's emotions, senses, or intelligence. Safety, health, home, and fear are common appeals in advertising, although there are many other appeals that can be used effectively.

Two appeals can be easily seen in the instructional case study: sex and ego. It almost goes without saying that sex, as a persuasive technique, is powerful. Ego is also a strong appeal. We all want to be valued for how we look, think, or act. When these two appeals are combined, as they are in the Calvin Klein ads, the impact is sure to be powerful.

So what is the ethical problem here? Is it unethical to use whatever persuasive appeals are at hand to sell a product or service? After all, that is what advertising is all about. To take away an ad's appeal is essentially to render it non-persuasive, just a jumble of words and/or pictures about a product or service; without the appeal, its connection to us as individuals may not be clear. In other words, we might have no motivation to purchase the product or service. True enough. However, ethical concerns arise when the appeal is in poor taste or when the appeal constitutes the total substance of the ad.

Consider this. An advertisement cannot exist without a central idea. The ad's structure and appeal should come *after* the central idea, sometimes called the selling idea. What is the selling idea in the Calvin Klein ads? The durability of the jeans? The wide range of styles and colors of underwear? The price? Are these clothing items easy to care for? The ads give us none of this information. Admittedly, what these questions ask for is rational information, information that will help us think about the utility and economy of owning the clothing. Instead, the central selling idea of the ads appears to be sex, and since the ads seem to involve underage models, not even acceptable sex. The ads seem designed to strengthen a teen's ego by suggesting that exciting sexual adventures are in store for the wearer of CK clothing. Is this a realistic claim? Regardless of the realism of the claim, is this an ethically acceptable central selling idea?

It is not, according to Schopenhauer, Voltaire, Bacon, and a host of other philosophers. Machiavelli doubtless would support Calvin Klein's "flexing of the ethical absolutes" to gain the desired ends, but he stands alone here, overshadowed by others who urge balance, reason, and maturity in dealing with ethical issues. Are the ads balanced? Reasonable? Do they demonstrate a mature approach to selling a product?

Could the ego and sex appeals be used appropriately in the ads? Certainly. This text will not redesign the CK ads on these pages, but it is possible to provide important information about the product and gently suggest that the jeans and underwear provide you with stylish clothing so that you may look and feel your best. When you look and feel good, others notice. Shy glances, broad smiles, and appropriately dressed models, when teamed with a central selling idea, could make for an effective and ethical advertisement.

Advertisers should be careful in the use of strong appeals in their persuasive selling messages. Extreme use of almost any appeal, but especially fear and sex, can create an artificial climate and deprive the consumer of the right to make an intelligent, informed purchasing decision. *Persuasion* can be seen as "an active attempt . . . to change a person's mind" and gathers strength by its use of facts and logical thinking. *Propaganda*, on the other hand, while designed to change a person's mind, presents nonfactual information, especially opinion, as if it were fact.[8] Few people object to genuine persuasive communication; almost everyone objects to propaganda disguised as persuasive communication.

Regardless of whether they are judged to be persuasion or propaganda, ads such as the Calvin Klein ones are almost always seen as offensive. Some might say that, offensive or not, they do sell products. Treating human beings as a means to an end—as the CK ads seem to be doing—violates Immanuel Kant's idea about the ethical treatment of people. Underage models are being used to sell clothing. Kant would not think this appropriate.

More recently, another appeal surfaced and was met with some protest. An ad for Sweden's highly reliable automobile, the Volvo, aired late in 1997. The ad promised "Volvo can save your soul."[9] A religious appeal? Certainly appears to be. Is it ethically acceptable to mix theology and advertising, just to sell a car? Religious appeals are rare but not unheard of. For example, a 1997 Miller Brewing Company television ad showed beer-drinking angels partying in heaven. The three young men featured in the ad wore white clothing and wings and were dancing to music while swilling Miller Lite. When they run out of beer, "they look down on Earth and create a wind gust that drops a tree in front of a Miller truck. The bottles fall off the back of the truck and float up to heaven, and the party resumes."[10]

Some ministers have criticized the ad as showing that God sanctions beer and alcohol abuse. The Reverend Edward Smart, pastor of an African Methodist Episcopal church, gathered 3,000 signatures on a petition and then persuaded the city council of Newark, New Jersey, to pass a resolution condemning the ad. Smart said the ad, in which the head angel is black and the music is hip-hop, was "not only blasphemous but aimed at . . . black children. Why is . . . a black angel in charge of the beer concession in heaven?" he asked.[11] However, a Miller company spokesperson said the ad was meant as a joke and that the company had received a tremendous amount of positive feedback about the ad.[12]

In terms of the Volvo ad, there is nothing wrong with touting the car's safety features. If the car is ruggedly constructed to resist collision damage and injuries to its occupants, then such a claim may be made. But to suggest that the car has properties that have some spiritual or metaphysical benefit is to cross the line separating ethical from unethical claims. Sometimes the product is not objectionable, but what the advertiser says about the product often is.

One more example bears examination. This one is not necessarily unethical, but it does demonstrate bad taste and an inappropriate use of an appeal. Reading a recent issue of *Time* magazine, I was surprised when I turned a page and found myself staring at a personalized advertising message. The ad, for Kinko's copying services, addressed me by my first name and urged me not to settle for mediocrity in my business/public presentations. The ad further urged me to stop by the nearest Kinko's for a demonstration of how to make my next presentation spectacular, primarily through the use of Kinko's transparency, binding, and laser printing services.

Although the ad was harmless enough, it was also overfamiliar and insulting. By what right does the Kinko corporation call me by my first name? This suggests a friendship or familiarity between me and the company that is nonexistent. Most people do not make friends with their copying service. Even if you go to a copy shop "where everybody knows your name," this is not friendship. It is good business technique, but little else. The company is clearly using a pseudo-friendship appeal to promote its services. This sort of thing is probably part of the price we pay for having free and open communication in America—communication that includes ad messages.

Somewhat more annoying was the implication that I had been settling, or would settle, for mediocrity in my public presentations. This sort of approach insults by suggesting that if one has not been using Kinko's products and services, one has been delivering mediocre presentations and doesn't realize it, or if realized, settles nonetheless for mediocrity. Kinko's assumes facts not in evidence. The company has not seen any of my presentations and is in no position to judge their quality. Additionally, a person does not have to be highly educated or overly sensitive to be insulted by the sort of appeal made in this ad. Try telling those with whom you deal—your auto mechanic, your restaurant server, your postal carrier, your minister or priest or rabbi, your dentist—that they are doing a mediocre job and see what response you get.

"Bring your presentations to life," the ad begins, as if all my previous presentations were dead. Whatever my faults might be, delivering a dead presentation is not one of them, an assertion that hundreds of students will gladly support. Humor aside, this ad is clearly in poor taste. It is not unethical, but it does demonstrate the degree to which an advertiser will go in terms of appealing to a consumer. A very narrow line separates poor taste from poor ethics.

Other magazine advertising inserts may be more problematic. For example, in a June 1998 issue of *Time* magazine, FIRSTPLUS Financial Corporation of Dallas, Texas, printed subscriber names and addresses on a voucher certificate that looked very much like a check. The certificate I received was for $42,780. The accompanying copy addressed me by my first name, indicated that I could have the cash in 7 to 14 working days, and that the money could be used to pay off credit cards or car loan obligations. A toll-free number was provided, and I was urged to "call today." No additional details—such as the loan's annual percentage rate (APR), monthly loan payment, loan initiation, or other applicable fees—were given.

Setting aside the problem regarding complete disclosure, this ad could conceivably cause subscribers problems. If you fail to see and remove the personalized ad, it stays with the magazine when it is thrown out. This opens up the possibility that dishonest individuals who sort through trash will find it. Identities have been stolen and financial problems created for innocent individuals with far less information than appears on the voucher certificate. Farfetched, you might say? Not really. Thousands of individuals have their identities stolen annually. At the very least, finding this voucher might inspire someone to visit a person's home when he or she is absent (the address is clearly printed on the ad) and sort through the person's garbage in an attempt to find other documents that might support a claim to identity.

This is not paranoia. It is simply cautious living in a postmodern culture. If you doubt the seriousness of what could happen, ask those whose lives have been wrecked by individuals who have stolen their identities and incurred huge financial obligations as a result. The key question here—to be answered by those who engage in such advertising practices—is whether this sort of personalized approach is ethically defensible. Should advertising messages put consumers at risk?

Puffery

It is widely believed that a little puffery in advertising is acceptable. Puffery may be defined as exaggerating a product's qualities or benefits so that the product appears in a favorable light. After all, Americans themselves use a little puffery in their own day-to-day lives. Some people color their hair to remove the gray, thus making themselves appear younger than they actually are; some people lie about their age for the same reason. Numerous cosmetic products are designed to help us present ourselves to the world in the

best possible light. Few of us want to be seen as we really are, so we dress and act in ways that maximize our positive impact on the world. This is the basic principle behind puffery.

Furthermore, few would criticize the advertising practice of making necessary modifications to products that must be filmed under hot, bright lights. Ice cream would surely melt in just a few minutes. Can mashed potatoes be substituted for the ice cream? The potatoes can be prepared in such a way as to resemble the consistency of ice cream and can rest easily and for longer periods of time than ice cream atop a sugar cone under hot lights. Corn flakes quickly grow soggy in milk, and the milk slides off the flakes easily when they are lifted in a spoon. Can one use a thin, white glue to simulate milk, thus showing that each delicious bite of corn flakes is surrounded by healthful milk? Practices such as these are common in the production of advertisements. Most people do not object to reasonable modifications for purposes of "product mock-up." But at what point do such modifications become ethically unacceptable?

There is a legal point beyond which advertising demonstrations may not go. The Federal Trade Commission Act prohibits advertising messages in which a test, experiment, or demonstration falsely provides a viewer "with visual proof of a product claim, regardless of whether the product claim is itself true."[13] In a case that went all the way to the U.S. Supreme Court, a Colgate-Palmolive commercial for Rapid Shave shaving cream was found to be deceptive. The commercial, as broadcast, showed that the product's super-moisturizing power was such that it could shave tough, dry sandpaper. In the demonstration the shaving cream was applied to what appeared to be sandpaper, and immediately thereafter a razor was shown shaving the sandpaper clean. "Apply, soak, and off in a stroke," the announcer said.

However, the Court found that sandpaper of the type shown in the commercial could not be shaved immediately following the application of the shaving cream. Clean shaving of the sandpaper required a soaking period of about 80 minutes. Further evidence revealed that the mock-up was not, in fact, a type of sandpaper, but loose sand on plexiglass. The Court noted that when a viewer is invited to rely on his own perception for proof of a claim, advertisers should make viewers aware that "the use of undisclosed props in strategic places might be material deception." The Court found no fault in using mock-ups for purposes of illustration (using mashed potatoes for ice cream), but drew the line at using false demonstrations that appear to offer additional objective proof of the claims being made.[14]

In sum, those who construct advertising messages should be careful in the production of product demonstrations. This will avoid both legal and ethical problems.

A more common form of puffery involves the use—or overuse, some would say—of words such as *new* and *improved*. American consumers seem programmed to seek out the new. For most, "*new* is a magic word. . . . Small wonder [advertisers have] learned to slap 'new and improved' on all their products, always promising a cleaner toilet, a brighter shine, better wetness protection."[15]

Does this practice constitute a serious ethical problem? Many would say no. American consumers are a savvy bunch, they say. They know that *new* and *improved* is just one of the many techniques advertisers use to lure buyers; therefore, no one is being led into any sort of behavior that is harmful. Since consumers know advertising tricks, there is little deception here.

Others point to the ultimate advertising defense against criticism of what it does: the doctrine of *caveat emptor,* Latin for "buyer beware." Implicit in this concept is the notion that the buyer, not the producer or advertiser, bears the responsibility for the effects of the product. Did you purchase a carpet cleaning solution that did not perform exactly as advertised? Too bad, but you bought the product knowing full well that conditions in your home were not like the conditions under which the product was demonstrated in the advertisement. It worked in the lab but failed to work in your home. Oh, well, sorry, but that's life. It is not our fault, advertisers say, that the cleaning solution did not do the job to the degree you wished. You must be more careful in your purchasing behavior.

Is the doctrine of *caveat emptor* an ethical one? Should advertisers accept the responsibility for the performance of their products? What is the buyer's responsibility? How much puffery is acceptable in an advertisement? What ethical philosophies support your views?

Sweepstakes

Eighty-eight-year-old Richard Lusk of Los Angeles wandered through Tampa International Airport looking for Ed McMahon. Lusk was sure he had won the October 1997 American Family Publishers (AFP) sweepstakes. After all, the bold print on his letter said: RICHARD LUSK HAS WON IT ALL AND WILL DEFINITELY RECEIVE $12 MILLION CASH GUARANTEED. The elderly Lusk had returned six other such announcements, but since he had no further response, thought they might have gotten lost in the mail. This time, he said, he decided to deliver the entry personally to American Family Publishers. "The Tampa address on the AFP material actually leads to Time Customer Services . . . a subsidiary of Time Warner, which processes sweepstakes entries."[16] Lusk, of course, was disappointed to learn that he had not won, that he had failed to read the sweepstakes message's fine print: "If you have and return the top winning entry, we'll say. . . ."

Airport police were not surprised to see Lusk. He wasn't the first sweepstakes victim to fly into Tampa in search of millions in winnings. "Airport police report at least eight identical incidents over the past few years. . . . They are all elderly and they are looking for Ed McMahon," said Lt. Kevin Perridge of the Tampa Airport Police.[17] McMahon was the well-known sidekick on the old Johnny Carson NBC *Tonight Show*. He is also, along with former teen idol Dick Clark, spokesperson for the AFP sweepstakes. Airport police do not keep official records of such events, but officers on the night shift and airline clerks are all too familiar with the pattern. Airport officials say some people probably fly in and fly out without ever telling their story to an officer or agent.[18]

In January 1998, Lusk came to Tampa again, this time in search of an $11 million prize. His visit seemed strange because an AFP spokesperson had said that after Lusk's autumn trip, the company removed him from all mailing lists. Yet Lusk had the latest mailing in his hand: RICHARD LUSK, FINAL RESULTS ARE IN AND THEY'RE OFFICIAL: YOU'RE OUR NEWEST $11,000,000 WINNER.

This latest Lusk incident, together with several others, resulted in a flurry of lawsuits against AFP. At least 32 states lodged legal complaints against the company. In an attempt to settle the matter, AFP agreed to stop using the slogan *you're our newest winner,* and pay a total of $1.25 million to 25 states. The agreement, signed in early March 1998, did not include Connecticut, Indiana, Florida, South Carolina, and Maryland, states that either have already sued or plan to sue AFP.

The sweepstakes problem is particularly acute in Florida, home to thousands of retirees. John Dennis, Jr., of Palm Harbor, Florida, was obsessed with magazine sweepstakes. "At one point he was spending $600 of his $900 monthly Social Security check for magazines and other sweepstakes-related products."[19] Thomas and Mabel Clark of Clearwater, Florida, drove to a Cadillac dealer one Tuesday afternoon and arranged to purchase a 1998 Deville, white with a blue top. The special showroom price was $51,000. Clark, 91, and his wife, 88, showed the salesperson a letter from United Sales Purchasing Exchange, a catalog and sweepstakes company in California. He would have no trouble, Clark told the salesperson, paying for the car with his $3.6 million prize. The Clarks spent thousands of dollars on gifts from the United Sales catalog: orange peelers, brass-plated hangers, clothes, linen, teapots, organizers. Most of the items were still in the shipping boxes, stacked in a back bedroom of their apartment.[20]

One 83-year-old woman from St. Petersburg, Florida, told her daughter that she had been notified by Publishers Clearing House that she was a winner and that she should be home on a Wednesday afternoon to meet the prize van. Her daughter read the letter and said it did look like her mother had won. They waited all Wednesday afternoon. The van never arrived. Eighty-three-year-old Cliff Patterson of Clearwater, Florida, called the *St. Petersburg Times* to say that "he was surprised to hear that Richard Lusk might be the $12 million AFP winner." Patterson was sure he had won that contest. "I got two letters from them, and I'm waiting for my money," he said.[21]

Are these elderly Americans senile? Have they lost it? Don't they realize the nature of these sweepstakes activities? Most sweepstakes victims, say those who study and care for the elderly, are healthy and mentally sharp. But they come from a generation "that considered it important to answer your mail."[22] In modern America, important things did arrive by mail: birth and death notices, draft notices, tax refunds, and the like. However, in postmodern America, the mail also contains dozens of official-looking documents that are merely disguised sales pitches.

An attorney for AFP noted that the company's sweepstakes contests are entirely legal and always include a clear disclaimer. It is not the company's fault, the attorney continued, if "some people get caught up in the pursuit of sweepstakes millions . . . there are bound to be people who are unable to separate reality from fantasy."[23] Children of the elderly and those elderly who have been misled by sweepstakes pitches say the companies make it very easy to be confused. Recent immigrants may also be caught up in the sweepstakes frenzy, unaccustomed as they may be to this sort of give-away. AFP spokesman Ed McMahon declined comment on the sweepstakes problems, but Dick Clark blamed consumers for any confusion. "I guess they need to read better," Clark said.

Not all sweepstakes contests have disclaimers. In Ozello, Florida, Jim Liles received what looked like a stock certificate proclaiming him a Gold Club Member, "entitled to a special $5,000 INSTANT CASH PRIZE." The certificate contained no disclaimer. There was no mention of the need to return and have a winning entry. Liles sent back the paperwork along with an order for a magazine. He is still waiting for his money. Liles says he has wised up. "To me, this is deceptive advertising," he said, "designed to get gullible people to buy more magazines or the merchandise they are trying to sell."[24]

Are sweepstakes appeals unethical, or does the doctrine of *caveat emptor* hold? An examination of sweepstakes promotion practices reveals that individuals of all ages are lured into purchasing magazines and other products they do not need or want, hoping to win the big prize. So far, only elderly citizens have made trips across country in search of the million-dollar prize. Media value the freedoms provided them by the First Amendment. But many believe that with these freedoms comes social responsibility, and part of this responsibility involves abstaining from misleading advertising and promotion practices. Are sweepstakes contests illegal? Many legal scholars say no. Are they unethical? Many ethicists say yes. They mislead, and they prey upon individuals who are particularly vulnerable to the promise of big money. Sweepstakes companies are not operating on Kohlberg's mature, postconventional level of ethical decision making. Neither is their action supported by John Stuart Mill's "greatest good for the greatest number" philosophy. Sweepstakes promotions create a fiction, something that philosopher Jean Baudrillard notes is a common practice in postmodern culture. But sweepstakes contests do not present reality in a meaningful context, and that is unethical.

Tobacco Advertising

Mark Twain said he did it a thousand times. More than 3 million Americans did it last year, according to the American Cancer Society. What is it? *Stop smoking!* Many more would like to stop, about three of every four who smoke. Nevertheless, almost 50 million Americans still light up; the American Cancer Society reports cigarettes kill about 500,000 Americans a year (almost 20 percent of all Americans who die and 30 percent of all who die from cancer).

The average age of a firsttime smoker in America is about 13. More than 3 million adolescents smoke cigarettes and about 1 million more use snuff, a smokeless tobacco. The American Cancer Society reports the average smoker spends $900 per year on cigarettes. Is it any wonder, then, that advertising is important to the makers of tobacco products? A California survey showed that cigarette advertising is the most influential in drawing children into the smoking habit. There are other influences, to be sure; peer pressure and family members who smoke are two. But a study published in the *Journal of the National Cancer Institute* found tobacco advertising to be the most persuasive in developing the smoking urge in children ages 12 to 17.

In the late 1990s, tobacco companies were the target of a number of law-suits aimed at holding them responsible for the negative health effects brought on by the regular use of their products. Most suits were settled out of court for massive amounts of money; others are still pending. Along with the promised cash settlements, tobacco companies agreed to modify their advertising practices, including the retiring of Joe Camel, a smoking icon among the young. Tobacco companies also agreed to remove billboard advertisements near schools and in selected neighborhoods.

Yet even with these agreed-to changes, huge amounts of money are still spent on tobacco advertising. Since tobacco ads were outlawed on television and radio by federal law in January 1971, much of the advertising budget goes into print ads in magazines and newspapers. These print ads appear to be highly successful. Federal law requires all ads to contain a prominently displayed health warning. For years, these warnings were small and unobtrusively placed. Federal law now requires the "Surgeon General's Warning" to be larger and placed in a position where it can be readily seen. Many full-page magazine tobacco ads place the warning, typically 3/4 inch by 3 1/2 inches in size, in the lower left corner of the ad.

Some cigarette ads have interesting appeals. For example, an ad for Winston cigarettes appeared in a December 1997 issue of *TV Guide.* The ad showed a shy-looking young man with a plain haircut and black-rimmed glasses. On his lap sat an attractive long-haired, blond woman wearing an extremely short skirt and smoking a cigarette. An obvious sex appeal ad, the message was simple: "At least when I wake up, my smokes will be real." The ad implied, of course, that if this rather nerdy-looking young fellow thinks that such an attractive woman would be interested in him, he must be dreaming. By smoking Winstons, the ad suggests, at least he has some grip on reality, something to enjoy. And enjoy Winstons, he can, because, the ad says, new Winstons have "no additives, true taste." What the ad neglects to mention, however, is that when he wakes up from his dream, in addition to "real smokes," he may also have some "real health problems" as a result of his use of tobacco.

In a different magazine, another ad, this one for Virginia Slims, shows an attractive African-American woman, cigarette in hand, apparently speaking of a Christmas gift she has just received. "When we say, 'Oh you really shouldn't have,' we don't really mean it." Is this statement to be interpreted as referring to the gift, or to the practice of lighting up? The ad offers yet another appeal. Next to a picture of a pack of Virginia Slims Lights, we are told, "'Tis a woman thing." This is a clear appeal to gender and to matters of self-image and ego.

One could argue for or against specific ads. A few might be seen as ethically acceptable; others might be deemed unethical. But in terms of real ethics, it is the general principle that is important here, not its various incarnations. The important question is this: Is it ethically acceptable to advertise a product that kills? There is overwhelming scientific evidence that tobacco use—in whatever form—is a deadly habit. When this evidence is placed against industry statements that there are really no serious health problems associated with tobacco use, the industry's claims are flimsy indeed. Not everyone believes in science, but the evidence on this issue is substantial and convincing.

Tobacco's image was not improved in late Spring 1998 when 39,000 tobacco industry documents were released, further revealing evidence of coverups and suppression of scientific evidence that smoking is harmful. The documents clearly show that, to a considerable degree, tobacco company lawyers controlled research into smoking and health and that the companies themselves went to great lengths to conceal what they knew. For example, in spite of company claims to the contrary, the documents reveal that the R. J. Reynolds Joe Camel campaign was specifically targeted to teens. The campaign was successful, increasing the brand's share of the market from almost nothing in 1988 to 33 percent in 1991.

Tobacco products have harmful health effects, yet advertisers continue to market them and consumers continue to buy. To compound the problem, print media readily accept tobacco advertising. Ruth Whitney, editor in chief of *Glamour* magazine, which regularly carries a lot of tobacco advertising, observed that "there's nobody in this country who doesn't know cigarettes kill."[25]

Mirabella magazine took an interesting stand on tobacco advertising some years ago. The magazine was part of Rupert Murdoch's News Corporation. Editor Grace Mirabella established a policy of not accepting tobacco ads. However, in the face of pressure from a major British tobacco company—the company threatened to pull its ads from all Murdoch publications—the policy collapsed; however, tobacco ads in the magazine were limited to no more than three pages per issue. Reflecting on the incident, Grace Mirabella noted that banning tobacco ads "was probably too much to ask," given that Rupert Murdoch was on the board of Philip Morris. Still, the magazine did not soft-peddle health issues and had a reputation for being a strong anti-tobacco voice.[26]

Make no mistake. This book is not suggesting that laws be passed to curb free speech. The preferred ethical course of action is voluntary self-restraint. Just because one *can* advertise a harmful product doesn't mean one *should*. Suggesting that advertisers abolish tobacco product advertising is sure to bring a yelp of protest from those who benefit from the growing, advertising, and sale of tobacco products. This is not a popular position to take. As we have seen, tobacco advertising pumps massive amounts of money into media industries. Tobacco farming makes a significant contribution to the economies of North Carolina, Kentucky, and Tennessee.

What will these farmers grow instead of tobacco? The answer is simple: anything that does not, by its regular, intended use, damage the health of or kill human beings. In view of what we know about the harmful effects of tobacco, one wonders why farmers would want to continue to make their living producing a product that shortens the lives of others. In catering to the consumer's desire for tobacco, aren't they capitalizing on what will eventually be the misery of others? Is this ethical behavior? Obviously, these farmers are not philosophical consequentialists. If they were, they would stop growing and selling tobacco immediately.

Notice the postmodern inconsistency with regard to this issue. The president, Congress, and the American people continue to be concerned about the quality of health care in this country. There are special concerns about the health of children and the elderly. Scientists are working diligently to find new drugs that will kill an increasingly virulent bacteria population; they are trying to find solutions to problems such as AIDS and Alzheimer's. In other words, we want to provide each American citizen with a long, quality life. Yet on the other hand, we encourage the growing, sale, and use of tobacco products, products that science has declared deadly. Where is the cognitive dissonance here? How can we intellectually support these two contradictory practices? Why aren't alarm bells going off in our heads? Do consumers see the obvious inconsistency of belief and practice with regard to this health issue?

Alcoholic Beverage Advertising

Similar questions could be asked about the practice of advertising alcoholic beverages. Doesn't the use of alcoholic beverages, like tobacco use, result in health problems? Why isn't the alcoholic beverage industry under the same sort of attack that the tobacco industry is?

Actually, controversy has always swirled around the use of alcoholic beverages. From the Old Testament to Shakespeare to present day, the use of alcoholic beverages has a rich history in the lives of some individuals and has just as strongly been opposed by some other individuals.[27] "The advertising of alcoholic beverage products is a subject of vehement public debate and prospective policy-making."[28]

A significant body of research shows that excessive alcohol use is tied to major health problems. Too, everyone knows the problems that can result from a drunk getting behind the wheel of a car. While most people acknowledge these aspects of alcohol use, there is some disagreement whether advertising has a significant enough impact on alcohol abuse problems to require legal action restricting, or perhaps eliminating, alcoholic beverage advertising.

In general, research has attempted to link alcoholic beverage advertising to increased consumption and the resulting health or social problems, but the results have been mixed. Current thinking among many policymakers is that "advertising contributes, in a very minor way, to total alcohol consumption and negative health consequences associated with excessive drinking."[29] Nevertheless, advertising's role is seen as minor when placed alongside other factors, such as personal income, beverage prices, and demographics. The result is that alcoholic beverage advertising and use—while still under attack from some quarters—has not yet reached the critical point in the consciousness of the government or the public, a point that would send it down the same road the tobacco industry has recently been traveling.

Direct Mail Marketing

Direct mail marketing generates about $244 billion per year in sales. Millions of consumers order a variety of products from the advertising circulars and catalogs they receive in the mail. Where there is big money to be made, ethical problems usually follow. There are at least two issues related to direct mail advertising that need examination.

Data-base Information   Direct mail advertisers, or direct marketing companies as they are sometimes called, develop and maintain customer information data bases. These data files contain what is often referred to as public information about individuals, particularly those individuals who have ordered something by direct mail. Data-base information may include name, address, gender, age, and estimated income (determined by zip code), among other things. It can also contain a list of products purchased.

"Metromail, a division of publishing giant R. R. Donnelley and Sons, freely advertises a 15 million name list of 'Who's Got What' . . . the world's largest ailment data-base." Do you suffer from digestive problems? Asthma? Diabetes? Your name might be on the list and available to selected mailers. The going rate is about $300 for 1,000 names.[30] But, you might say, I've never ordered anything by mail. I couldn't be on any of those lists. Not necessarily true. If you have ever filled out a warranty card for an item and answered all those lifestyle questions (unrelated to the product you just purchased), or if you have ever used a credit card to purchase something in a store, chances are those data were transmitted somewhere and that someone added that information to your personal data dossier.

Companies engaging in this practice are essentially safe from a legal point of view. They have, after all, only recorded data about you that are either public information or data that you provided by returning a questionnaire or using a credit card. But companies are walking a fine ethical line here. For one thing, these data-base files may contain information that you do not wish to have revealed to strangers or to companies whose main interest is not in you but in your money. While companies may sell the information, there is some question as to whether it is ethically appropriate to maintain files on individuals without their knowledge or without the opportunity for those individuals to examine their files and delete sensitive material. If you subscribe to the philosophy of moral legalism, you probably have few concerns about this practice. After all, if it is legal, it is moral. Individuals adopting a stricter code of ethics may not be so accepting of direct mail practices.

Second, companies get you to return a product warranty card filled with lifestyle and personal information by failing to point out that you do not need to fill out the lifestyle questions to secure the warranty. You may indeed need to return the card with the serial number and date and place of purchase information, but failing to answer the two dozen or more personal behavior and preference questions does not invalidate the product's warranty. No statement to this effect appears anywhere on most warranty cards. The cards cultivate the erroneous impression that without this information, warranties are not valid.

Mail Tricks   Direct mail companies use a variety of techniques in an attempt to generate a consumer response. These tricks, as many call them, include fake handwriting, brown envelopes, vague postmarks, and urgency messages. Computers can simulate handwriting, making the message appear to have been written personally by a human being. Computers can even produce simulated coffee spills on a piece of paper to add realism.[31]

Brown envelopes are used in much government correspondence. The use of this type of envelope by direct mail advertisers, together with official-looking markings, can make consumers believe that the information inside is official government communication. These "official" markings often include the words "priority," "urgent," or "rush." Vague, illegible postmarks are used to conceal the fact that boiler-room operations produce much of the correspondence and may be thousands of miles away from the firm soliciting your business.[32]

Reading what's inside the envelope, consumers may be subjected to an overuse of the word "free"—perhaps a free gift of some sort with a certain dollar purchase. "Buy one, get one free" is a common sales technique. Seen another way, this opportunity is simply asking you to purchase two of the items at 50 percent off the original price. This may not be a bargain if you do not need two of the items, or if the items are similarly discounted at a local store. In purchasing locally, you avoid shipping and handling charges, which can be substantial.

Telemarketing

Telemarketing possesses many of direct mail's characteristics. You know the drill. Your hot pizza has just been delivered. As you are reaching for that first slice, your mouth watering in anticipation, the phone rings. On the other end is a telemarketing representative who may try to sell you a product or service, or get you to accept a credit card with a low, introductory annual percentage rate. Regardless of whether you decline or listen to the pitch, by the time you get back to the table, your pizza is cold.

More and more companies are turning to telemarketing, realizing that while direct mailings can be ignored, phone calls rarely are. One telemarketing executive notes that telemarketing will become even more pervasive because it is a relatively inexpensive form of marketing. For example, one firm found that "if you send 100 pieces of mail, you may get two subscriptions." But with 100 phone calls, you'll get about 15. Consumers can avoid some of these calls by asking to be placed on a "do not call list." There is a charge for this service in some states.[33]

If one adopts the moral legalism ethical theory, then one has few problems with any of these practices. When combined with *caveat emptor*, moral legalism lets the direct mail advertising and telemarketing industries sleep easily at night. However, if one chooses to rise above the conventional level of morality where, Kohlberg says, behavior is often motivated by its legal ramifications, one can see a clear principle at work: deception. Almost everything about the direct mail advertising business is deceptive. Deceptive practices include the following: not informing consumers about how information about them is being placed in data bases, rented, and sold to companies without their knowledge or consent; making direct mail solicitations appear to be urgent, official government communications; using computers to generate letters that appear to have been prepared by real people; making telemarketing calls that are intrusive and often cannot be avoided unless one pays a fee.

These practices constitute a manipulation of the consumer, and, while usually legal, are almost always unethical. People are being used as a means to an end. This violates an important tenet of Kantian ethical theory. These practices are, however, postmodern in that they exist in a laissez-faire environment where individuals accept no responsibility for their actions.

Advertiser Influence on Media Content

Who should have the most influence about what people see and hear on television? Program producers? The television audience? Advertisers? Eighty-seven percent of the respondents in a Roper poll commissioned by ABC, CBS, and NBC, replied "that it ought to be individual viewers themselves, by deciding what they will and will not watch. Almost no one—just nine percent—thought advertisers should be able to shape content by granting or withholding sponsorship."[34]

Yet, in postmodern America, advertisers are exerting more and more control over media content. Advertisers have always been sensitive about having their sales pitches placed in or near controversial material, whether broadcast or print. But in 1996, the Chrysler Corporation generated a renewed examination of this issue by sending a letter to at least 50 magazines. The letter demanded summaries of upcoming articles in issues where the company's advertising was to appear. Editors were essentially asked "to think twice about running sexual, political, social issues."[35] Chrysler's action goes well beyond previous practice. Magazines have for some time regularly provided a "heads-up" warning about articles that might embarrass advertisers, but the Chrysler letter pushed the envelope beyond normal notification. To make matters worse, Chrysler demanded that the letter be signed by an appropriate magazine representative and returned so that the company would have proof of compliance.

Chrysler is not the only company to keep a tight rein on the relationship of its advertising messages to media content. Kimberly-Clark, maker of Huggies diapers, demands that its ads "be placed only 'adjacent to black and white happy baby editorial.' " Colgate-Palmolive, Kmart, Revlon, IBM, and AT&T demand, and get, concessions from magazines on the position of their ads relative to editorial matter.

In many cases, these magazine-advertiser interactions merely result in moving an ad to another location in the magazine or in delaying an ad's appearance until the next issue. However, in some cases, advertisers have been successful in killing an article. The *Wall Street Journal* found this to be the case with *Esquire* magazine. A 20,000-word short story by David Leavitt was scheduled for the April 1997 issue. The story had a gay theme and some raw language. When Chrysler, which had purchased four pages in the issue, objected to the piece, editor in chief Edward Kosner killed it, even though it had already been approved for the issue and was in page proofs. Will Blythe, the magazine's literary editor, could not stomach the decision and immediately resigned, noting that, sadly, "we're taking marching orders (albeit indirectly) from advertisers."[36]

"Corporations and their ad agencies have clearly turned up the heat on editors and publishers . . . some magazines are capitulating, unwilling to risk [the loss of] even a single ad," the *Columbia Journalism Review* reported.[37] Magazines, for their part, face growing competition for ad dollars and not just from other magazines. New media, including the Internet, are searching for advertising dollars, and this could ultimately have a negative impact on print media income. Because there are so many of them, magazines are thought to be particularly vulnerable to changes in print ad budgets.

Another manifestation of the advertiser-magazine conflict can be seen in the publications targeted to teenage girls and young adult women. Magazines such as *Glamour, Mademoiselle, Marie Claire,* and *Cosmopolitan* are being squeezed by advertisers to adjust their content. For example, "food advertisers have always demanded that women's magazines publish recipes and articles on entertaining (preferably ones that name their products) in return for their ads."[38]

Likewise, clothing advertisers prefer their ads adjacent to fashion spreads; cosmetic companies like to be associated with positive coverage of beauty subjects. Only one high-profile magazine is free from such advertiser influence over content: *Ms.,* which went ad-free in 1990 and relies on its cover price to meet its revenue needs. One scholar noted that the collusion between advertisers and women's magazines has this effect: "to perpetuate readers' sense of themselves as defective and in need of improvement—and have got women trying to achieve a level of 'perfection' that is impossible and self-destructive."[39]

These examples illustrate a postmodern dilemma: the power struggle. The philosopher Michel Foucault noted that much in the postmodern world can be explained by examining the power relationships involved in any controversy or even any activity. Advertisers have significant power with regard to the placement of their advertising messages. Magazines have less power in asserting editorial independence. In a postmodern culture, a contest of power interests is a common occurrence, the results of which rarely serve the needs of individuals. "In the long run, everybody involved is diminished when editors feel advertisers' breath on their necks. Hovering there, advertisers help create content that eventually bores the customers they seek."[40]

Applying Ethics to Advertising

Given the economic needs of those involved, can we expect ethical behavior from the advertising industry and the media? The answer to this question is not as elusive as it might seem. Yes, ethical behavior can and should be expected of individuals, groups, and corporations in all walks of life. The following list presents suggestions designed to make advertising a more ethical industry in a postmodern culture. These suggestions are an outgrowth of the Judeo-Christian philosophy and are derived from an official 37-page Vatican text on "Ethics in Advertising." One does not have to be a religious person to see the positive ethical and social benefits to be derived by following these principles.

1. Eschew appeals to greed, guilt, lust, vanity, and envy. These are human weaknesses and exploiting them is unethical. Use advertising appeals that respect the audience.
2. Present products in a realistic light, stressing quality and price as rational bases for choice. This practice minimizes deception and avoids appeals to emotion.
3. Be morally responsible for the effects of the products sold or promoted. Avoid the postmodern trap of shrugging off personal responsibility and placing it elsewhere.
4. Refrain from producing advertising messages that create a consumer culture—that is, emphasize the acquiring of material goods and cultivating a lavish lifestyle. Pandering to excessive consumerism misses the point of what is important in life and can be destructive to the individual.
5. Employ only those who have high ethical standards and a strong sense of responsibility. These sorts of people may be hard to find, but they are out there and they will work hard for you.

In short, "where freedom of speech and communication exists, it is largely up to the advertisers themselves to insure ethically responsible practices in their profession."[41] While some critics condemn advertising as a complete waste of time, talent, and money, others note that, when properly executed, advertising has much to contribute, especially in helping consumers add to the quality of their lives and make responsible choices in their purchasing behavior. Ethical advertising behavior rests on three principles: truthfulness, the dignity of each human being, and social responsibility.[42]

▼ Public Relations

Public relations (PR), like advertising, is not a mass medium. It does, however, use and interact with media in doing its work. If you were to ask 20 PR practitioners for a definition of their field, you'd likely get 20 different answers. Nevertheless, most would agree with this definition: "Public relations is a general term that describes a variety of complex activities, some of which are related to media."[43] PR activities are often placed in the following categories: "(1) opinion research, (2) press agentry, (3) product promotion, (4) publicity, (5) lobbying, (6) public affairs, (7) fund-raising and membership drives, and (8) special events management."[44] It should be clear from this list that some public relations activities involve media. For example, if a PR practitioner or firm has a client who wishes to stage a special event that involves an entire community—say, a local professional sports team's sponsorship of a fund-raiser for handicapped children—public relations activities would likely include planning and managing the event as well as releasing information about the event to the media and even encouraging the media to cover the event as a news or public service story. Note, however, that *public relations* and *publicity* are not synonymous, although publicity may be one of the many activities a PR firm undertakes on behalf of a client.

Public relations has an interesting history. Certain PR activities have been noted in civilizations as old as ancient Greece. Many of the current PR practices are outgrowths of the work of Ivy Lee, Edward L. Bernays, and others whose early experiences and ideas in the field gave it an identity and a mission.

Many public relations practices are implemented to bring about change in the way people act or in what they believe. Some practices have the potential either to help or hurt people. Therefore, a public relations practitioner bears full responsibility for truth and fair play.[45] A look at current public relations practices reveals at least three areas where ethical problems might easily arise. This does not mean, of course, that all PR firms and practitioners are guilty of these or any other ethical violations. Some individuals and firms do their work in a perfectly straightforward, ethical manner. Others may be said to be stepping close to the line that separates ethical from unethical behavior.

Spin Control

Spin control is the name given to attempts by public relations practitioners (or anyone, for that matter) to twist or manipulate facts and/or reality into a form that is pleasing to a client. This is a common practice in politics. For example, White House press secretaries are usually good at "spinning" after a presidential news conference. Often the press secretary, asked to comment on a misstatement or factual blunder by the president, will say, "What the president meant was. . . . " Thus, those being controlled by the spin are encouraged to forget what was actually said and to substitute what the press secretary said the president should have said.

Harmless? Perhaps, but this sort of activity may be seen as a manipulation of the facts, a changing of reality. If the president made a mistake, why not just take responsibility for the mistake and correct the statement rather than try to twist a false statement into something that resembles the truth? Surely in matters of both domestic and foreign policy, clear statements are more easily understood than false statements made somewhat more obscure by the twisting of spin control artists. One can easily see that spin control, whether practiced in politics, public relations, or elsewhere, is an ethically suspect practice.

An extreme of spin control involves the manufacturing of information. Larry Speakes, presidential press secretary for six years during the Ronald Reagan administration, once made up a quote and attributed it to the president. The occasion was the president's attendance at a summit meeting in Geneva, Switzerland. When caught, Speakes said he was merely exercising his "public relations man's license." This implies that being a public relations practitioner entitles one to make up things in order to present one's client in a positive light. Activities such as this cause ethical problems for PR practitioners. Speakes later confessed, "I was clearly wrong to take such liberties." Well, of course, the damage was already done to Speakes's credibility and possibly to the credibility of other PR spokespersons. The public may always wonder whether what a spokesperson says is true or made up. There is certainly nothing wrong with a public relations professional having a dialogue with members of the press. That is often part of the job. If questions are answered truthfully and responsibility taken where necessary, few ethical problems will result.

Another aspect of spin control is the staging of pseudo-events. *Pseudo-events* are defined as "events manufactured for the exclusive purpose of generating publicity, dramatizing an occurrence, or calling attention to something."[46] One could argue that almost all events—from a blood drive by the American Red Cross to the announcement of a new downtown office building—are pseudo-events in that they are all developed for specific purposes and would not occur naturally without human direction. How can one tell a real event from a pseudo-event? It is often difficult, but here is a useful rule of thumb. Ask this question: Who directly benefits from the event? If the event serves the larger, general public welfare, then one could consider it an acceptable, or real, activity. If the event serves to benefit an individual or a corporation, especially financially, the event may be suspect. As always, this is a judgment call. But the "who benefits?" question may provide insight and often provides an answer as to the general acceptability of an event.

Consider this example. Suppose a popular local bookstore invites a well-known fiction writer to visit the store, talk with patrons, and autograph copies of her latest book. Would it be appropriate for the bookstore's public relations director to ask the local news media to cover this "important event"? Who benefits from the event? The author benefits, of course, because of the exposure and sales that will likely result from her appearance. The bookstore, too, will benefit because it will sell copies of the book and get its cut of the purchase price. Is there any contribution to the general public welfare here? Probably not, unless one considers that such activity will stimulate the local economy and in this way benefit the community. But this is a flimsy argument; almost any activity can be tied to the economy. The sale of illegal drugs adds money to the economy, but few would advocate this activity simply because money circulates in the doing of it. The "economy argument" alone does not justify us accepting any activity as appropriate. Other factors must be considered.

Related somewhat to the pseudo-event is the practice of hyping an event or product. *Hype* may be defined as the intentional exaggeration of the importance of an event or product for the purpose of artificially creating an atmosphere of excitement. For example, several years ago, Christmas holiday shoppers were all abuzz over a doll called Tickle-Me Elmo. Although it had been on store shelves for some time, this toy was first brought to the attention of the public on the Rosie O'Donnell television talk show. Rosie showed the toy and demonstrated how it worked, indicating that her child would probably like it. Suddenly, this was a "must-have" toy for Christmas. The doll quickly disappeared from toy store shelves, as shoppers, caught up in the television talk show hype, flew into a frenzy in an attempt to get the toy for their children for Christmas. Some who were lucky enough to purchase the item ran classified ads in local newspapers, offering to sell their Elmo (still in the box) at up to ten times the retail price. Doubtless more than a few parents paid this exorbitant amount just so the doll would appear under their tree on Christmas morning.

Did the demand for Tickle-Me Elmo result from a natural interest on the part of children and their parents, or even from interest generated by a normal advertising campaign? Did the demand depend entirely on the hype given the product on a television talk show? If some public relations person or firm was behind the doll's appearance on Rosie's show, that person or firm would be considered extremely successful and would be handsomely rewarded for serving the client well.

What is unethical about this? That is not completely clear. Much depends on the answers to a few questions. Was there some public relations firm or person behind the Tickle-Me Elmo appearance on Rosie O'Donnell? If so, was the influence of this person or firm revealed? Was Rosie or the production company compensated for the appearance of the toy? If so, was this compensation revealed? Complete disclosure of the particulars would be helpful in judging the ethical appropriateness of the incident. Perhaps the Tickle-Me Elmo appearance was incidental to other things that were going on in the show. If spontaneous, does this minimize the ethical problem one might have with hyping the doll on national television? Often there is no way to get answers to questions such as these. Public relations activities are usually performed out of view of the public, and few outside the organization may know what really did or did not happen.

Fake News

Many people think that public relations is little more than press-agentry. In other words, a public relations person is often seen merely as a press agent, attempting to manage the image of a client (product or event) by influencing the news media to consider the client as news and incorporate information about the client into a news story or broadcast.

It is true that the relationship between public relations and journalism is a symbiotic one; their cooperation has mutual benefits. In any case, the danger here is that material produced by public relations practitioners may go directly on the air or into print as "news." This may be more of an ethical problem for journalism than it is for public relations. One could argue that it is the job of public relations to produce both print and video news releases for use by media. Can the PR firms be blamed if media put these materials into the "news stream" without noting that the information was not prepared by journalists using normal news-gathering methods? The material may or may not meet the public interest, convenience, and necessity that news presumably does, but may instead meet the private, financial needs of a PR firm's client. Some news editors report being overwhelmed by material from PR firms and being annoyed by repeated calls from the PR firms asking whether the materials have been received and when they will be used.

All of this may simply be part of the processes involved in both the news and public relations businesses. One cannot ask news organizations to stop using this material simply because it comes from PR firms. Some of it may, indeed, have broad implications and usefulness to the public-at-large. On the other hand, one cannot ask PR firms to stop working on behalf of their clients. Aristotle's Golden Mean provides a solution. His ethical theory encourages one to avoid extremes and determine the "just right" course of action, a course that usually lies somewhere between the extremes. Solving this problem will take some self-restraint on the part of those involved, together with some additional time and attention to detail, as well as a clear understanding that journalists and public relations practitioners usually have different definitions of what constitutes news.

Loyalty and Truth

Some of the ethical problems that arise in public relations can be seen as manifestations of a postmodern culture. The hyping of an event or product and the staging of pseudo-events are clearly fictions, created for specific financial purposes. The philosopher Jean Baudrillard notes that while the creation of fictions is a common postmodern practice, it is nonetheless ethically suspect. One should strive, rather, to present the truth and to present events in context so that they may be fully understood.

Public relations firms are thus often caught between loyalty to a client and presenting the truth to the public. Is the truth always of paramount importance?

What role does loyalty play in the interaction among PR firms, clients, media, and the public? Is a PR firm's first loyalty to its client or to the public? To what degree may the truth be "flexed" and still be the truth? What are the postmodern power relationships one ought to consider here? Michel Foucault notes that one always has an obligation to the truth, even if power relationships make that obligation difficult.

Ethics in public relations practices arise from the recognition that the work is governed by a philosophy of mutual benefit to the client while at the same time benefiting not only all those involved but also the greater public good.[47] This in no way limits the "fundamental responsibility of public relations to build and maintain a hospitable environment so that an organization can pursue its mission."[48] It does, however, suggest that when the ultimate goal of the public relations professional is to enhance public trust in an organization, "only the highest ethical conduct is acceptable."[49]

▼ Case Studies

Case Study #6. Taken for a Ride?

There are many time-tested ways for an organization to raise funds. Church and school groups are fond of car washes and bake sales. Proceeds from these events normally go to support the groups' social, religious, or educational activities. Many (eleemosynary) organizations, that is, nonprofit charities, often need activities that generate more money than selling cookies and washing cars usually earns. One fund-raising method popular among some charities is the walk-a-thon, or its cousin, the bike-a-thon. For these events, participants solicit donors to pledge money based on how far someone walks or rides a bike. "Among the most high profile [of these events] are the AIDS Rides."[50]

In the summer of 1997, the AIDS Rides events and their entrepreneur-operator Dan Pallotta, together with his firm TeamWorks, came in for some criticism. The chief complaint—from other AIDS groups, AIDS activists, and some law enforcement officials—was that "not enough of donors' money went to the AIDS patients themselves." According to one report, 82 percent of the money raised in the 1996 Florida AIDS Ride "went to overhead instead of directly helping patients."[51] In Pennsylvania, the attorney general's office "recently required Pallotta's firm . . . to pay a penalty to settle charges that it had misled the public in a Philadelphia ride."[52] As a result, several AIDS groups decided to drop their affiliation with Pallotta.

Pallotta, for his part, said that he had lost a number of friends to AIDS and wanted to do something to help. He "copyrighted the term 'AIDS Ride' and offered to set up events . . . for a fee of $160,000 to $180,000." Some AIDS organizations praise Pallotta's events as a creative, effective way to raise funds. Still, the question remains as to how much of the money collected should be directed to administrative costs and how much given to help those with AIDS.

Is this an ethical question or a financial one? That depends. The National Charities Information Bureau acknowledges that any fund-raising organization will incur overhead costs, but recommends that these costs not be more than 35 cents on the dollar. Pallotta says 43 cents of every dollar collected by his firm goes toward overhead expenses, but a *U.S. News & World Report* calculation showed a better estimate of overhead is around 50 cents on the dollar. An investigation by the Pennsylvania attorney general revealed that at least 72 cents of every dollar collected by Pallotta in that state went to overhead costs, leaving only 28 cents for use by AIDS patients. By contrast, the American Lung Association's two-day bike-a-thons earn between 60 and 75 cents for charity. The Pennsylvania investigation also showed that Pallotta's annual income from his AIDS Rides activities was about $270,000.

A spokesperson for TeamWorks noted that the AIDS Rides are costly, but they do raise a considerable amount of money. The logistics of a ride can be a nightmare: rest stops, showers, meals, medical facilities, staging areas, tents, and entertainment. Whatever the costs, the spokesperson continued, "The rides produce a net gain for AIDS charities."[53]

Key Questions Did Pallotta mislead participants in any way? Do Pallotta's AIDS Rides promote the greater good? When economics and ethics collide, which often wins? Is it possible to act ethically and still meet financial obligations?

Case Study #7. Nike Takes a Hit

Nike, Inc., maker of athletic shoes and assorted other sports gear, is a company worth about $9 billion. For a while, Nike's reputation was spotless and its products sold briskly. However, in 1997, it was discovered that Nike's shoes are manufactured in Asia, in factories where low wages and harsh working conditions appear to be the norm. In some factories, there is evidence of physical abuse.[54] The best known incident occurred at a Vietnam plant where several women fainted while being forced to run laps around the buildings in a warehouse complex as punishment for some infraction.

Nike's labor practices drew the attention of the Doonesbury cartoonist Garry Trudeau and the movie director Michael Moore. Trudeau "lampooned the company's operation in Vietnam in his syndicated . . . strip," and Moore, of *Roger and Me* fame, invited Nike's CEO Philip Knight "to move the company's shoe operations in Asia to jobs-hungry Flint, Michigan," Moore's hometown and a city almost abandoned by General Motors' plants. Knight responded that "Americans simply don't want to work in shoe factories," a statement disputed by an unemployed father in Flint.

Time magazine visited Nike plants in China and Vietnam and found that the average monthly wage in China is about $73 and about $40 in Vietnam. The company says this is a fair wage and that any corporation is going to pay the going rate—and little more—regardless of where company plants are located.

In addition to Nike's labor practices, its marketing strategy has come under attack. The price of a pair of Nike shoes has drawn some criticism. At $180 a pair, some complain that Nike exploits inner-city youth who are made to feel that if they wear Nike shoes, they can become stars. Prominent in Nike advertising are the Orlando Magic's Anfernee Hardaway and the Chicago Bulls's Michael Jordan. Nike attempted to divert some of the criticism by providing Jordan with a "point-of-view" statement that he could use to deflect some of the tough questions he might be asked about the Nike marketing/price strategy. The result? When asked to respond to complaints that Air Jordans are too expensive, the professional basketball legend "pointed out that his new Jordan brand shoes will start at a relatively inexpensive $90 or so. He also noted that the launch [of the new product line] is scheduled for a Saturday so that kids don't cut school to be the first to buy them."[55]

Yet even with these controversies, Nike products continue to sell, though analysts say that 1997 U.S. sales were flat, compared with the previous fiscal year's 36 percent increase in business. Part of the decline may be attributed to aggressive, price-cutting campaigns by Nike competitors Reebok and Adidas. Nike's annual report noted: "We are not here to eliminate poverty and famine or lead the war against violence and crime." The company felt it was being unfairly singled out because it is the most visible athletic gear manufacturer.[56]

To its credit, Nike has made some improvements in working conditions in its Asian factories. The company developed a code of conduct "which, among other things, calls for clean and well lit factories and better housing conditions for workers. . . . " Nike is, however, resisting independent third-party monitoring of its labor practices.[57]

Still unresolved is the advertising/public relations strategy of marketing high-priced athletic shoes primarily to urban youth, many of whom are poor and can ill-afford the footwear. Sometimes the Nike trademark—a "Swoosh" symbol—is all that is needed to reach males ages 11 to 17. Young boys are often mesmerized by images of Tiger Woods, Michael Jordan, and Michael Johnson. Although the primary criticism of Nike centered around its foreign labor facilities, some critics see its advertising and public relations campaigns as equally unethical.

Key Questions What aspects of Nike's business and advertising practices do you find ethically objectionable? On what grounds? How would Peter Abelard have judged Nike's actions? What would Immanuel Kant have said about Nike's use of people as a means to an end?

Case Study #8. The 1997 Lemon Awards

In December 1997, the Center for Science in the Public Interest (CSPI), together with a consortium of public interest organizations—including the Center for Auto Safety, the U.S. Public Interest Research Group, the National

Council on Alcoholism and Drug Dependence, the National Women's Health Network, among others—presented "lemon awards" to nine sponsors of "the most misleading ad campaigns of 1997." These sponsors, CSPI said, developed spots that were not only misleading, but also unfair and irresponsible.[58] Selections for 1997 (and the company response) were as follows:

1. A Cadillac Catera television ad showed the automobile "crossing a double-yellow, no-passing line to pass other motorists." This, said an auto safety rep, promotes sales over safety, is dangerous and illegal. A company spokesperson said the yellow line is dotted indicating that it is OK to pass, but that the spot is being reedited to make this clear.

2. Long-distance carrier Sprint developed a misleading "speak free on Monday nights" campaign. The campaign offered free long-distance calling on Monday nights but failed to tell consumers about the restrictions that may apply. Sprint responded by noting that the campaign is aimed at non-Sprint customers, not at current Sprint customers who would face limitations.

3. Visa's check card ad shows various celebrities having trouble making purchases with regular checks. These ads, CSPI said, do not tell users that these check cards, which draw funds directly from an individual's checking account, are not protected by the same liability laws as credit cards and normal checks. Visa responded by saying it would not hold card users liable for unauthorized use of debit and credit cards.

4. The Nutri-System Weight Loss Clinic ran ads promoting a safer alternative to the Pro-fen weight loss pill, which was shown to have the potential to damage the heart. The new drug, Phen-Pro, combined phentermine and Prozac. "Neither the U.S. Food and Drug Administration nor the makers of Prozac endorse this combination for weight loss." Nutri-System did not respond.

5. Anheuser Busch ran ads offering merchandise for customers collecting "Bud Points." This, critics say, encourages irresponsible drinking among college students so that they can earn lots of Bud Points in a short time. Twenty people would have to drink eight beers a day for six months to win a pool table. However, an Anheuser Busch vice president called CSPI "the Grinch out to steal life's little pleasures." She noted that 150 people could win the pool table in six months if each person drank one beer a day.

6. The R. J. Reynolds Tobacco Company's "No Bull" campaign for Winston cigarettes claimed that the cigarettes lacked the additives often present in other brands. However, a list of ingredients was not made available to consumers, so there was no way to verify the claim. An R. J. Reynolds spokesperson said the company's claims were factual and substantial.

7. Lichtwer Pharma U.S. sells its Ginkai brand of an herb, gingko biloba, that the ads claim will improve memory. CSPI said the ads' claims are

bold and misleading. The product has been shown to be effective in improving the memory of those suffering from dementia or other severe memory impairments, but the claims about memory improvement for those not suffering some kind of impairment are suspect. The company said its claims are backed up by more than a dozen clinical studies, and that the customer satisfaction rate is 80 percent.

8. The American Egg Board ads say cholesterol probably will stay about the same in healthy egg consumers on low-fat diets. This claim, a nutrition specialist says, contradicts the advice of every major health authority in the country. Egg Board president Louis Raffel said the group stands by its statements.

9. Abbott Laboratories produces Ensure canned beverages. Its ads say the drink is the "No. 1 doctor-recommended supplement." CSPI put the product in its "Hall of Shame." The National Council of Senior Citizens noted that healthy adults need Ensure about as much as they need a bottle of baby formula. An Abbott Laboratories spokesman declined comment.

Key Questions   What ethical principles are involved in each of the nine lemon award winners profiled here? How might each of these ads be reworked to reflect a more ethical approach? Do the ads violate Bacon's requirement to seek the truth?

Case Study #9. Put on a Happy Face

Law governing securities requires public companies to file detailed financial reports every three months, providing investors with information on revenue, profit, and any unusual financial activity. Companies have 45 days from the end of a quarter to file their reports. In early 1998, Sunbeam Corporation was faced with reporting a first quarter loss. When the announcement was made, the company's stock price fell 25 percent. As is often the case, the company cushioned the blow somewhat by announcing—at the same time—changes in operations. In this case, the vice president for consumer products was fired and a new president of household products was hired.

Many companies with bad news to report resort to an old spin technique: bury the bad news. This usually involves the production of a creative news release, one that mentions problem areas only after the reader has been hit with the good, though often less important, news at the start. For example, Abraxas Petroleum reported record cash flow and revenues for the final quarter of 1997. Further down in the news release, the company reported a net loss for the period. Abraxas released the report on a Friday—an end-of-the-week trick used by more than a few companies. A Friday release usually appears in Saturday newspapers, the least read issue of the week. Financial markets are closed on Saturday, and by the time Monday rolls around, the impact of the announcement is almost certainly to have diminished and is therefore less damaging to the company's stock. A tell-it-before-the-holiday strategy also often works to a company's advantage.

One public relations officer said that sometimes company lawyers stall announcements by manipulating the timing of board meetings, arranging things so that a board signs off on a report at the very last minute. Still, these sorts of activities can backfire. Investors aren't stupid, and the market usually figures out what is going on pretty quickly.

Key Questions   Is it unethical for public relations practitioners to release unpleasant information about a client at a time most advantageous to the client? If companies are not legally obligated to "trumpet" their shortcomings, are there times when it might be ethical to do so? What potential problems can arise with a "creative" news release?

QUESTIONS FOR DISCUSSION

1. Why is it difficult for many people to separate advertised items into two categories: things we *need* and things we *want*?

2. Are some advertising appeals more ethical than others? Which appeals seem to be the most ethical? How appropriate are sex, fear, and guilt appeals?

3. What is the difference between communication that is persuasive and communication that is propaganda?

4. To what extent are you willing to accept puffery in an advertisement? Why?

5. Should the doctrine of *caveat emptor* prevail in all advertisements? Can you think of some ads where this concept would and would not be appropriate?

6. Consider the public relations practice of spin control. Are there instances where this technique is inappropriate? How might it be used in an ethical fashion?

7. How does a pseudo-event differ from a real event? Can a pseudo-event ever be ethical? Explain.

8. How important is loyalty in public relations? Must loyalty always conflict with telling the truth? Can the two coexist in a working relationship between public relations practitioner and client?

ENDNOTES

1. James E. Littlefield and C. A. Kirkpatrick, *Advertising* (Boston: Houghton Mifflin, 1970), 14.

2. James B. Twitchell, " 'But First, a Word from Our Sponsor . . . ,' " *Wilson Quarterly*, 20, no. 3, Summer 1996, 68.

3. Michelle Ingrassia, "Calvin's World," *Newsweek,* 11 September 1995, 60.

4. Margaret Carlson, "Where Calvin Crossed the Line," *Time,* 11 September 1995, 64.

5. Ibid.

6. Ingrassia, 62.

7. Ibid., 63.

8. Richard E. Petty and John Cacioppo, *Attitudes and Persuasion: Classic and Contemporary Approaches* (Dubuque, IA: William C. Brown, 1981), 3.

9. Suzanne Fields, "When Seeking Salvation through Advertising Becomes Offensive," *Tampa Tribune,* 17 November 1997, Nation/World, 7.

10. "Ad with Beer in Heaven Is Sacrilege, Pastor Says," *St. Petersburg Times,* 24 December 1997, sec. E, p. 1.

11. "Beer Ads Provoke Opposition," *Tampa Tribune,* 27 December 1997, Business/Finance, 8.

12. "Ad with Beer in Heaven," 2.

13. *Federal Trade Commission* v. *Colgate-Palmolive Co.,* 380 U.S. 374 (1965).

14. Ibid.

15. Leonard Pitts, Jr., "Suckers for a 'New and Improved' Sales Pitch," *Tampa Tribune,* 22 November 1997, Nation/World, 14.

16. Paul Wilborn, "Would-Be Millionaires Fly to Tampa," *St. Petersburg Times,* 25 October 1997, sec. A, p. 1.

17. Ibid., 10.

18. Ibid.

19. Paul Wilborn, "Florida Looks into Contest Come-ons," *St. Petersburg Times,* 25 October 1997, sec. A, p. 1.

20. Paul Wilborn, "Couple Keeps Hoping as Mail Piles Up," *St. Petersburg Times,* 2 November 1997, sec. A, p. 1, 10.

21. Ibid., 10.

22. Ibid.

23. Ibid.

24. Paul Wilborn, "Reality Gets Lost in Contest Pitches," *St. Petersburg Times,* 25 December 1997, sec. A, p. 20.

25. Russ Baker, "The Squeeze," *Columbia Journalism Review,* September/October 1997, 36.

26. Grace Mirabella and Judith Warner, *In and Out of Vogue* (New York: Doubleday, 1995), 241.

27. D. Kirk Davidson, *Selling Sin* (Westport, CT: Quorum Books, 1996), 33–34.

28. Joseph C. Fisher and Peter A. Cook, *Advertising, Alcohol Consumption, and Mortality* (Westport, CT: Greenwood Press, 1995), 1.

29. Ibid., 146.

30. Susan Headden, "The Junk Mail Deluge," *U.S. News & World Report,* 8 December 1997, 43.

31. Ibid., 46.

32. Ibid., 45.

33. "Telemarketers Ringing Up Big Business," *Tampa Tribune,* 16 November 1997, Business/Finance, 3.

34. Baker, 34.

35. Ibid., 30.

36. Ibid., 32.

37. Ibid., 30.

38. R. G. Reeves, "Lipstick Journalism," *Weekly Planet,* 4–10 December 1997, 25.

39. Ibid., 26.

40. Baker, 36.

41. "Vatican Stresses Need for Moral Advertising," *Advertising Age,* 10 March 1997, 26.

42. Ibid.

43. John C. Merrill, John Lee, and Edward Jay Friedlander, *Modern Mass Media* (New York: HarperCollins, 1994), 294.

44. Jay Black and Jennings Bryant, *Introduction to Media Communication* (Dubuque, IA: Brown & Benchmark, 1995), 454.

45. Kerry Tucker, Doris Derelian, and Donna Rouner, *Public Relations Writing,* 3rd ed. (Upper Saddle River, NJ: Prentice Hall, 1997), 5.

46. Black and Bryant, 466.

47. Tucker, Derelian, and Rouner, 7.

48. Ibid., 6.

49. Fraser P. Seitel, *The Practice of Public Relations* (Columbus, OH: Merrill, 1989), 144.

50. Julian E. Barnes, "Do Some AIDS Events Take Donors for a Ride?" *U.S. News & World Report,* 16 June 1997, 39.

51. Ibid.

52. Ibid.

53. Ibid.

54. William J. Holstein, "Casting Nike as the Bad Guy," *U.S. News & World Report*, 22 September 1997, 49.

55. Ibid.

56. Ibid.

57. Ibid.

58. "Sour Appeal," *St. Petersburg Times*, 5 December 1997, sec. E, p. 1.

CHAPTER 13

Ethical Issues and Case Studies in the Book, Recording, and Radio Industries

Overview

It is widely acknowledged that the radio and recording industries are inter-dependent; that is, each depends on the other to a significant degree in being able to do its work. This symbiotic relationship results from the needs of radio stations for music as program material and the needs of the recording industry for radio to play its product, thereby creating market demand. This long-standing relationship has worked well for both industries. The book publishing industry is included in this chapter because it shares ethical concerns in two areas with the radio and recording industries: business practices and content.

▼ Instructional Case Study

At his trial in March 1994, Michael Diana was convicted of obscenity. County Judge Walter Fullerton sent Diana to jail for the weekend. Fullerton also sentenced Diana "to perform community service, avoid all minors, take a course in journalism ethics, and undergo a psychological evaluation."[1] Diana appealed, and in 1997, the U.S. Supreme Court refused to hear the case. Diana was required to serve his sentence.

The case resulted from Diana's production of a series of comic books called *Boiled Angel*. These comics depicted crude drawings of rape, murder, and dismemberment, among other things. Although the comics only circulated to a subscriber list of about 300, they were nonetheless judged obscene and designed to sexually arouse readers. Diana denied the charges, saying his books were only produced to express his own horror at the sort of acts depicted. However, at the trial, a psychologist testified that Diana's work appealed to "those with a libertine bent."

Publicity about the case led to appearances for Diana on national television. He also published a book, essentially a compilation of his work, titled *The Worst of Boiled Angel*, advertised as "200 pages of shocking fun."

▼ Book Publishing

Statistics from the U.S. Department of Education in 1997 show that the average American adult had a considerable amount of leisure time each week—an average of 39 hours and 24 minutes. How did the average person spend this time? In various ways, of course, but 15 of those hours were spent watching television and only 2 hours and 48 minutes were spent reading. The sorts of things being read were not specified, but it is likely that newspapers and magazines, as well as books, filled that time.

Books are big business. However, "nearly 60 percent of adult Americans have never read a book and most of the rest read only one book a year."[2] Nevertheless, we know that books are more likely to be read by young adults who are educated, have an above-average income, and live in urban areas. Numerous bookstore chains have sprung up throughout the country in recent years, among them Bookstop, Borders, Super Crown, and Barnes and Noble. These stores are designed to appeal particularly to those young adults. Most offer comfortable chairs in which to sit, relax, and read. Some of these stores have a café area where specialty coffees, teas, muffins, and other delectables are available. The evening hours are often filled with concerts, poetry readings, or other special events. Bookstores don't just sell books anymore; they sell a lifestyle. They do this because the competition is intense and the economic issues pressing.

Economic Concerns

About 55,000 books are published each year, but only about 200 or so will sell more than 200,000 copies. Unlike the medieval period when monks and monasteries controlled books and their reproduction, the postmodern American publishing world is open to more people than ever before, both authors and purchasers.[3] The book publishing hierarchy still exists, of course, but the Internet, desktop publishing, and other electronic opportunities have made it possible for many individuals to publish their own work.

Technology has also enabled book publishers to produce both hard and paperback books quickly and at a relatively modest cost. A mass market paperback can be produced in about five days, though most take six months to a year. The markup on books is typically 40 to 50 percent for most bookstores. This might seem a little high, but it appears to be necessary in order for the stores to stay in business. About 40 percent of the hardbacks are returned to warehouses unsold. The publishers, not the bookstores, absorb the loss.

The result of these economic facts of life is that "in both hard and soft cover publishing, 2 percent of the publishers do 70 percent of the titles, and the top third of the industry is responsible for 99 percent of what is printed."[4] Large publishing houses that have diversified holdings are more likely to survive and prosper in this highly competitive environment than are smaller publishing houses without other sources of income.

Against the backdrop of this competitive economic environment, publishing houses, like many other businesses, often seek ways to maximize profits. Business and editorial decisions made with an eye on the bottom line are not always ethically problematic, but they can be.

Content   Although censorship is not a major problem for book publishers, several issues relating to content can cause ethical concerns. In much the same way that tabloid newspapers are not considered part of the mainstream press in America, publishers of pornographic materials are often considered to be outside the book publishing mainstream. From time to time a book or magazine produced by an alternative press is singled out for attention, as was the case with publisher Larry Flynt's *Hustler* magazine. But for the most part, materials from alternative presses reach their target audiences without becoming a regular part of typical bookstore business.

Nevertheless, some books published by mainstream publishing houses have come under fire. This most often occurs when a book, judged controversial by some, makes its way into the public school system. Take, for example, William Golding's *Lord of the Flies,* a novel often assigned as part of a high school English course. Many parents have objected to both the language and some of the situations described in the book. Even a classic like Mark Twain's *Huckleberry Finn* has been the target of some criticism by both parents and outside groups on the grounds that it presents a negative picture of Jim, an African-American slave. One of the most objectionable aspects of the novel, these critics say, is the persistent use of the word *nigger* to refer to Jim. In cases such as these, there is much confusion about what should be done. The epithet is clearly inappropriate in postmodern America, but it was a common term for blacks during Twain's time.

Legal issues and ethical issues seem difficult to separate. On the one hand, the First Amendment prohibits Congress from infringing upon the freedom of the press, which includes book publishers, but, on the other, the courts have often declared certain media materials obscene.

Is it legal to produce suggestive, revealing, explicit books? Is it ethical to produce such materials? The answers to these questions depend on the target audience. If the book is a serious one with an instructional purpose, such as texts for schools or books of classic literature or poetry, then objectionable material should be avoided unless such material is factual in nature and has a clear, defensible instructional purpose. Textbooks should not resemble light entertainment books: popular fiction, self-help, and celebrity works, for example. If the book is produced for entertainment purposes only, authors have much more freedom to write *creatively* and may make their books as explicit as they desire. In either case, a proper ethical position to take would be one that suggests all books, whatever their audience, be in good taste. This presents us with the problem of defining good taste. The philosopher Arthur Schopenhauer would remind us that we need to be very much aware of the greedful will and its tendency to draw us toward the baser aspects of life. Fight the greedful will by acting with compassion and respect for all. Books should, then, avoid appealing to the prurient interest of the culture. *Prurient interest* may be defined as being abnormally preoccupied or obsessively interested in sexual matters.

The case study in this chapter deals with the issue of appropriate content. The comic book *Boiled Angel* contained crude drawings of rape, murder, and dismemberment. A court found the book obscene. Was it? Obscenity has always been difficult to define. Even the U.S. Supreme Court found it so. Justice Potter Stewart's famous statement that although he could not define obscenity, he could recognize it when he saw it,[5] provides little help.

It is a generally accepted notion that the definition of obscenity will vary from community to community. A big city like New York, for example, would have standards about what is acceptable that are different from standards in a small town like Florence, Alabama. Since *Boiled Angel* had a subscriber list of about 300, was its influence such that it violated community standards? Perhaps. The trial was held in Largo, Florida, a small community in itself, but part of a larger metropolitan area.

How much consideration should be given Diana's claim that he was only illustrating things that he personally found abhorrent? Does that claim square with the promotion line—200 pages of shocking fun—for the book he later published? If he were personally opposed to the sorts of things depicted in his book, why was it advertised as "fun"?

While it may be perfectly legal to produce books of a crude or explicit nature, it may not be in the culture's best interest to do so. Just because we *can* publish these materials does not mean we *should*. Much research has been done on the relationship between obscene, pornographic material and human behavior. Results are mixed, at best. Too often the studies have been done on college students, making it difficult to generalize to the population at large. Concern about this issue dates from 1971, when the government released *The Report of the Commission on Obscenity and Pornography*. The report indicated that there was no clear, empirical link between exposure to erotic materials and crime or delinquency. Subsequent studies have failed to generate models that would consistently explain the relationship between exposure to pornographic materials and specific behaviors. Indeed, some studies show violent material to be more harmful than sexual material.[6]

Decisions about the content of books must inevitably be made at the individual level, that is, made by the author first and an editor second. This is not to suggest that books be censored but that mature human judgment and a strong set of moral values play a part in making decisions about what is published. It could be argued that *Boiled Angel* demonstrated neither mature human judgment nor a strong set of moral values. A balance must be maintained between books that reflect Matthew Arnold's concept of "the best that has been thought and said" and postmodern America's desire to have reading material for entertainment.

Author-Publisher Issues   Authors, naturally, wish to receive as much money as they can for their books. Publishers, on the other hand, want to obtain and keep popular writers, introduce new products, and increase their profits. These two often conflicting goals can lead to ethical problems.

Some publishers provide extremely large advances to certain authors, advances that may run into the millions of dollars. When the writer is a proven success, the publisher can usually recover the cash advance and make money on a book. Tom Clancy, Stephen King, and Danielle Steel are writers who have a successful track record of sales. But what about large advances to unproven writers, those individuals, often celebrities, who are writing books about their lives or experiences? Is a large cash advance appropriate in view of the fact that most such books never sell enough copies to cover the advance, much less make the publisher any money? Take, for example, the books written by the lawyers on both sides of the O. J. Simpson murder case. Prosecutor Marsha Clark received a large advance for her book, *Without a Doubt,* but the book failed to meet sales expectations. It sold so poorly that many bookstores discounted it 30 to 50 percent just to get it off the shelves. In some bookstores even this steep discount failed to motivate buyers. A book by Christopher Darden, Clark's co-prosecutor in the Simpson case, fared little better. *In Contempt* began showing up on discount tables a short time after its release.

Should large advances be reduced and the money used to promote or develop a promising new writer? Of course, these sorts of decisions are often business decisions, and publishing houses are entitled to do business within the law any way they see fit. Nevertheless, although the issue of large advances to celebrity authors is not wrong or evil, it may not reflect good judgment and may not, in the current economic environment, be an appropriate use of money. This may be especially true when those involved are second- or third-level celebrities. Vanna White, whose only claim to fame is that she is attractive and can turn letters on television's popular *Wheel of Fortune* game show, wrote *Vanna Speaks.* Trouble was, no one was listening (or reading). Her book soon appeared at discount stores across the country—priced at $1.

In late 1997, the pop singer Jewel signed with HarperCollins for $2 million to deliver her autobiography (all 23 years of it). This sum is believed to be the most ever paid for a pop singer's memoirs. Elton John is said to want $12 million for his, but so far no publisher has taken him up on it. The announcement of Jewel's forthcoming autobiography was followed by HarperCollins's release of a volume of Jewel's poetry: *A Night without Armor: Poems by Jewel.*

A related issue involves the accuracy of royalty statements to authors. Most book contracts specify what percentage of sales will be paid to the author (usually 10 to 15 percent). Royalty payments are typically made annually. Authors receive information from publishers indicating sales, expenses, and the like. These statements also show the amount to be paid to the author as a result of sales. The problem here is that there is no way for an author to check the validity of the royalty statement. The way some royalties are computed puts the author at a decided disadvantage. If the statement shows 10,000 books—or units, as they are sometimes called—sold, how can the author be sure that 10,000 and not 15,000 units were sold?

Falsifying royalty statements would be a violation of a contract, though contracts differ from company to company. Proof of this sort of deception is hard to come by. Most companies will not open their books to authors so that facts and figures can be checked. The Science Fiction Writers of America (SFWA) regularly conducts random audits of publishers (who consent to the examination) to see whether royalty payments are being properly paid. Whatever the legal implications here, there are some clear ethical implications. It is wrong for publishers to lie, deceive, manipulate, or in any other way defraud the authors with whom they have a legal—and moral—contract.

Some publishers avoid the royalty issue by offering a new author a flat, up-front fee instead of royalties. This practice takes unfair advantage of new, first-time writers. These newcomers are often anxious to get their work into print; they might accept, for example, a $2,000 flat fee for a book manuscript and surrender further claim to the book. If the book sells well and the publisher makes, say, $595,000 (100,000 copies at $5.95 each), the royalty would be about $4,760 (figured at 8 percent of gross sales). The publisher keeps the extra $2,760 ($4,760 minus the $2,000 flat fee) that would, under typical royalty arrangements, have gone to the author.

This arrangement can work in a slightly different way, too. In 1997, Bantam Books altered its standard contract for Star Wars novels. "The original terms, an advance plus a 2% royalty, were dropped in favor of a flat fee." Michael Capobianco, president of the Science Fiction Writers of America, described the new contract as "extremely regressive in its treatment of writers."[7] According to Capobianco, SFWA feels the new contracts "do not meet professional standards." However, "Bantam has indicated that it is happy with the new contract and has no interest in changing it." Bantam is "setting a very dangerous precedent," Capobianco said.[8]

Is it ethical for a publisher to offer this flat-fee arrangement to an anxious new writer—or to an experienced writer—knowing full well that the result could be that the writer would end up getting less for the book than would normally be the case? Or is this just good business practice?

Author-Agent Issues   A small but growing problem in the book industry is the rise of specialized agents. An agent is typically an individual who has wide contacts within the book publishing industry and who represents the interests of the author to these companies. Agents work to get their clients the best possible deals with the publishers. The work of agents has long been a part of the industry and most agents do their work honorably. However, some agents are taking a less traditional approach to their jobs, an approach that raises ethical concerns.

Traditionally, agents are paid a percentage when a book is accepted by a publishing firm. However, an increasing number of agents now charge the author a fee to read a book and determine whether it is suitable to be offered to a publishing firm. There are, of course, no guarantees. The author pays the fee regardless of whether the book is offered to a publisher. There is no way to determine whether the agent actually reads the book or merely collects the fee. This practice takes advantage of new, anxious writers and is clearly unethical.

A second questionable practice is the service provided by a *book doctor*. If a book manuscript has been rejected or is in some way not ready for consideration by a publishing house, a book doctor will edit or fix the manuscript for a fee. Again, there are no guarantees, yet many authors are led to believe that a book doctor can heal an injured manuscript. If a manuscript is in any way acceptable to the publisher, chances are the firm, through an in-house editor, would specify what needed to be done to improve it. If the book is rejected outright, no amount of doctoring will likely make it acceptable to that publisher, though it might have been acceptable to another publisher without any changes in the first place.

It should be noted that many writers produce what can only truthfully be called junk. Not everyone who aspires to being a successful writer has the talent to achieve those aspirations. Yet both book doctors and reading agents will accept junk and collect their fees. Is this just good business practice, or is it ethically questionable activity? Do the activities of book doctors and reading agents meet Plato's tests of courage, moderation, respect, wisdom, and justice? They could argue that they are only following Machiavelli's belief that one is allowed to flex the ethical absolutes to the degree needed to gain the desired goal. But they are also operating on Kohlberg's pre-conventional level of ethical behavior. They are being selfish and are not considering the needs of others.

Specialized Books Some ethical concerns have arisen over the publication of some types of specialized books. *Audio books* are books that have been recorded on audiotape and are available for sale at somewhat less than the price of the typical hardback. These audiotapes contain an abridged version of the book, which means that the listener does not get to hear each and every word that appears in the hardback but only the passages that are important to the movement of the plot. Encouraging consumers to buy the tape instead of the book is of ethical concern to those who believe the practice violates the overall purpose of reading. For one thing, it destroys literacy in that it encourages consumers *not* to read. If the main purpose of reading is to get the plot, then audio books may meet that purpose. But if reading has other purposes, such as vocabulary development or stimulation of the imagination, then audio books may not meet those goals. Listening is a passive activity; reading is an active activity. Reading is work; audio books require little work. Is this necessarily a good thing for American culture? There is certainly nothing evil or wrong about audio books, but they may be ethically questionable in that they encourage consumers to take the easy way out by letting someone else do the work of reading for them.

Instant books have also generated some ethical concern. These books are rushed into print, usually within a week or two, following an important celebrity or news event. The thinking is that they will sell like fast food because they are quickly available and relate to an event or well-known person currently making news. Probably the best known example of an event that generated a number of instant books was the death of Diana, Princess of Wales. Prior to that, it was the murder trial of O. J. Simpson. Simpson was accused of killing his wife, Nicole, and restaurant employee Ron Goldman. Simpson's arrest and trial generated much media attention, and a number of books quickly appeared on the newsstands on a variety of Simpson topics ranging from his years as a professional football player to the murder trial itself. Other events in the 1990s that generated instant books include the FBI–Branch Davidian standoff in Waco, Texas, and Tiger Woods's winning of the 1997 Master's golf tournament.

Self-help books have also come in for some criticism. These books often take a popular culture approach to various aspects of life. Many writers of this type of book are not acknowledged experts in their fields, but self-appointed experts. Their advice ranges from the trivial to the obvious. For example, a 1997 book on child raising suggested parents keep a master calendar showing their kids' appointments. For taking long trips, parents were told to stock the car with paper towels and snacks. Are parents so poorly prepared for the job of raising children that they need tips like these? To have a highly effective family, another book notes, one should "think before you speak. Plan ahead. Try to see the other guy's point of view. Tell the truth. If you can't say anything nice, don't say anything. Moderation in all things. To thine own self be true. And so on."[9]

These books seem to play upon the postmodern obsession with the self. They provide simple answers to complex situations and usually contain intellectual contradictions galore. Is it ethical to provide what might be called "pseudo-help"? Many of the problems individuals and families have are beyond the self-help stage. Many people need professional help, yet may not seek it if they get a false sense of security or closure from self-help books. Sometimes even professionals cannot help with a problem. How can we be assured that books will? Warnings are placed on many American products urging consumers to be cautious about using the items. Perhaps some sort of disclaimer should be placed on these self-help books indicating that although the books may not help one to solve problems, they may make the authors wealthy. Is it unethical to create the impression that the books lead to solved problems? Do these books distort or present an accurate picture of reality? The postmodern philosopher Jean Baudrillard points out that individuals are ethical when they resist the negative aspects of contemporary culture and try to present reality in a meaningful context. Do the self-help books do this?

College Textbooks   The college textbook market presents yet another ethical concern—that many college and university bookstores regularly buy back textbooks at the end of a semester and then resell them to new students for the next semester. This practice clearly benefits the students. Many are able to purchase a textbook at a considerably reduced price. Since the cost of books has increased significantly in the last decade or so, it is natural for students to do what is in their best interest and purchase a perfectly good used book.

This practice also benefits college and university bookstores. They can make a tidy profit by selling the same book three or four times. However, this practice is not beneficial at all to either textbook authors or publishers. Neither the author nor the publisher gets a royalty payment for repeated sales. Actors get residual payments when their films or television programs are purchased and repeatedly run on television or cable services. Video production companies also get some of the money that results from repeated sales of a product they produced. But textbook authors and publishers get nothing from the repeated use of their materials because of the legal black market in textbook sales. Is this practice unethical?

Related is the sale of complimentary copies of a textbook, provided to instructors in the hope that the book will be adopted for their classes, to an independent dealer who will then sell them to a warehouser who will eventually sell them to college bookstores. Complimentary copies generate no revenue for either author or publisher. When these free copies get into the textbook mainstream, they rob authors and publishers of their deserved royalty. It must be admitted that many college and university professors are guilty of selling copies of books they got free. The black market prospers while authors and publishers are denied money they have earned and should rightfully have. Thomas Hobbes suggests that ethics requires one to rise above self-interest, promote justice, and strive for mutual accommodation. The black market textbook system is almost totally about self-interest. Justice and mutual accommodation are not characteristics of its operation.

▼ Recording Industry

The recording industry is faced with two ethical issues: *content* and *promotion practices.* Content seems to be the primary concern for most people. Promotion practices are, for the most part, hidden from public view.

Content

Consider the following song lyrics:

I got my 12-gauge sawed off
I got my headlights turned off
I'm 'bout to bust some shots off
I'm 'bout to dust some cops off . . .
Die, Die, Die Pig, Die!

These lyrics are from a song titled "Cop Killer" by the rapper Ice-T from his album *Body Count*. Other songs on the album take up the same anti-cop theme. One song, for example, talks of "smoked pork," ghetto slang for a killed cop. The song has Ice-T "summoning a police officer on the pretext of needing help. You hear the footsteps of the officer and his inquiry. And then you hear the gunshot. These bad dudes have just smoked themselves some pork."[10]

You do not have to be a police officer to object to these lyrics. Any individual concerned with law enforcement should be concerned that this and similar messages are making their way into the culture, and particularly the culture of young urban youth. The syndicated columnist William Raspberry notes that "rap artists are the de facto leaders of a generation of urban youth." Raspberry wonders where our children are being led. There is no particular mystery about the message being conveyed: killing policemen is a good thing. "The danger implicit in all the uproar is of empty-headed, suggestible . . . kids, crouching by their boomboxes, waiting for the word."[11] Whether or not this is the typical street reaction to the song, the issue of music lyrics, and particularly rap lyrics, raises important legal and ethical questions.

Observers of this phenomenon generally are in two camps: the free speechers who favor no restrictions on this sort of media content and the conscientious objectors who think such content is beyond bad taste and significantly destructive to society. Of particular concern to some is the degree to which otherwise well-respected companies are involved in the production and distribution of rap music. For example, Warner Brothers Records produced and released Ice-T's *Body Count* album. Warner Brothers Records is part of the Time Warner conglomerate, an organization that, among other things, publishes *Time* magazine, the respected, leading newsmagazine in the country.

"Of course, Ice-T has the right to say whatever he wants. But that doesn't require any company to provide him an outlet. And it doesn't relieve a company of responsibility for the messages it chooses to promote. Judgment is not 'censorship.' "[12] *Time*'s editors make daily value judgments about what to include and exclude in their newsmagazine. They are paid to exercise their judgment and encouraged to promote and tell the truth as they see it. What sort of judgment is being exercised by those who authorize the production of music that advocates murder?

Rap music is not only about murder. It presents images and suggests actions that make people uncomfortable. For example, black women are often referred to in the music as "bitches" or " 'hos." These sorts of messages are demeaning to women and destructive to the social culture not only of the minority group to which this music is pitched but also of society as a whole.

It should be noted that it is not just rap music that many find objectionable. Several individuals and groups—many of them in the rock music mainstream—have produced ethically questionable records. "One song by the group Nine Inch Nails, for example, describes a violent sex act in the crudest language possible. . . . [Other] artists sing about dismemberment and cutting off women's breasts."[13] In 1997, Meredith Brooks hit the top-ten list with "Bitch," a song that celebrates an in-your-face, let-me-be-me, stay-out-of-my-way, I-don't-have-to-be-nice-to-anyone philosophy. While certainly milder than the songs discussed earlier, it still communicates the message that confrontation, not cooperation, is the preferred approach to human interaction.

Have these songs gone too far? Are they beyond what we are willing to accept as a culture that believes in individual responsibility and simple decency? Have corporations gone beyond the pale in allowing the production of these sorts of materials solely because they sell? Do producers and distributors have a corporate responsibility to the culture to monitor the work produced under their imprimatur? Do such songs qualify as "art," human activity that elevates and inspires the spirit? Or do they simply reinforce an already vulgar, coarse, and violent world? Voltaire reminds us that we should use reason to balance the passions and act for the greater good of society. The recording industry would do well to heed his advice.

It is not our purpose here to suggest that laws be passed or that a government agency be established to oversee media behavior. Ethics cannot be legislated and should not be supervised by the government. As has always been the focus of this text, the key to ethical behavior in society *begins with the individual and proceeds to the corporate or institution level.* Other aspects of society will begin to fall in line once individuals and corporations show leadership. Francis Bacon urges individuals who seek the ethical path to apply the powers of reason, understanding, and will to control the appetites to which life subjects us. The ethical path, Bacon says, is the path to knowledge and truth, and the journey must begin with the individual.

Promotion Practices

Given the interdependent relationship between the recording and radio industries, it has been traditional for record companies to provide copies of new music to radio stations free of charge. Years ago, stations received music on vinyl, either the 33 1/3 rpm long-play album or the 45 rpm single. As technology changed, so did the recording industry, and most music is now provided to stations on compact disc (CD).

No one has much of an ethical problem with this practice. It is seen as beneficial to both industries. Neither industry tries to hide this cooperative arrangement. Some stations use a music subscription service that, for a monthly fee, provides them with new product. However, some record companies provide stations, particularly those in large markets and those near colleges, with gifts in order to inspire the stations to play their music. Much of this activity is hidden from public view. The practice of accepting gifts, even though one might disavow that such acceptance has any influence on what music is played, is ethically problematic.

Are the gifts trivial, or are they valuable enough to have some influence on what is played? One station estimated the value of the promotional items it received in one year, items such as CD's, posters, T-shirts, coffee cups, and the like, at more than $45,000. It could be argued that these gifts are trivial and of so little value that they could not realistically be considered bribes for playing certain songs. Was the material used and enjoyed by station staff? At what point does a friendly gift become a bribe for playing certain music? Is any gift appropriate, no matter how inexpensive or trivial? Shouldn't the music be allowed to stand on its own merits? If the song is a good one with quality production values, then why not play it, regardless of what incentives were or were not received? If the song is not particularly memorable or is poorly produced, why not reject it?

Benedict Spinoza's philosophy might be of some use here. Spinoza suggested that one determine the good, or the ideal standard, against which something should be judged. Set aside emotion, think through the situation, and reach a just, faithful, and honorable conclusion. Is this a good process for determining which records to play, determining whether a particular song meets the standards set by the format or station programmers? In addition to standards for judging music, some standards should be set for the acceptance of free goods or services from record companies. The easiest and most morally defensible position is to accept nothing from the companies. Once a single item is accepted, the question is raised of whether the gift had an influence on music selection.

Many stations, particularly those in large markets, receive promotional material from sources other than record companies. Free tickets to music concerts or new blockbuster movies are often provided to stations, which then give them away on the air to listeners. This practice not only promotes an upcoming event but also gives listeners an incentive to tune to a particular station. Rarely does a station disclose how it came by the tickets it is giving away. Since the station is giving away the tickets, listeners may assume that the station is the source of the tickets when, in fact, it may just be passing them along from the concert or event promoter.

▼ Radio

Radio is not the influential medium it once was. In the 1950s television took some of radio's audience. More recently, the popularity of cable's Music Television (MTV) and VH-1 channels, with their 'round-the-clock presentations of music videos, has further decreased radio's audience. Too, the availability of compact discs (CD's) has encouraged people to build personal music libraries. Still, FM radio is an important part of the lives of many Americans, especially during morning and afternoon drive-times. AM radio has lost almost all of its music-listening audience to FM and now programs news, talk, sports, or other specialty formats.

Content

Like the book publishing and recording industries, radio has a potential ethically troublesome problem in terms of content. Some stations play the explicit, ethically questionable songs discussed earlier in this chapter. Other sorts of program content also can raise ethical questions.

Talk-Advice Dr. Laura Schlessinger's nationally syndicated radio call-in show may have as many as 20 million listeners. Each weekday, Dr. Laura takes calls from across the nation and provides advice to those individuals who have a problem they haven't been able to solve and are lucky enough to have gotten through on the phone. Some critics say Dr. Laura is little more than a pop psychologist, offering instant answers to complex questions. Her in-your-face approach is provocative, just the sort of approach that appeals to some and turns others off. Dr. Laura's disciples "credit her with restoring decency to a wayward world; they describe her as a rabbi, a moral compass, the mother they never had. Her detractors say she's a self-righteous prude capitalizing on shock-jock techniques."[14]

She prefers to be known simply as "Dr. Laura." Her doctorate is not in psychology or counseling but in physiology. Nevertheless, Dr. Laura is a licensed marriage and family therapist. Still, some feel that she is abusing the influence having a nationally syndicated radio program provides her. She is "quick with a one liner, able to rule on the toughest of dilemmas in under two minutes."[15] She cuts callers off if they protest too much about the advice she is giving them. She often interrupts callers who are in the middle of explaining their problem with a "Grow Up!" comment or an admonition to "Stop Whining!" Few callers get to finish their explanations before she serves up a solution to their problem.

Is there some sort of ethical problem with this sort of radio programming? The answer may depend on how seriously one takes the program. Viewed as theater, as a dramatic performance, it can be fairly entertaining. Viewed as expert advice, it may be on thin ethical ice. For one thing, many trained psychologists, therapists, social workers, and counselors believe that most social and behavioral problems are complex, so complex, in fact, that time is required for professionals to understand their clients and to discover the full scope of their problems. One claim, of course, is that counselors keep you coming back so they can continue to bill you. This may be true in some cases, but it is widely acknowledged within the counseling community that it takes time to explore client concerns and to discover reasonable, workable solutions.

How can Dr. Laura, then, even begin to understand a person or a problem in the short time the individual is allowed on the air? A licensed therapist ought to know that real help requires getting to know the client and taking the time to explore all client concerns fully. Can this be accomplished on a call-in radio show? Is it unethical to state, imply, or in any other way make the audience believe that problems can be solved before the next commercial break? Is she really helping callers or merely manipulating troubled adults into actions that may not be psychologically, behaviorally, or morally sound? Should a radio call-in host be telling a caller to move across the country or quit a good job, based on 90 seconds or so of conversation with that person?

Take, for example, a single mother of two who is on welfare and pregnant with twins. "Should she give them up for adoption? Dr. Laura says no: That would damage the older kids too much. The mother, she says, should call Catholic Charities and team up with another single mother to pool resources and responsibilities. Case closed, just in time for commercial break."[16] Even a layperson can see that Dr. Laura has rushed to judgment in this case. She has not interviewed the older children, so how could she possibly know that putting the soon-to-be twins up for adoption would damage the older siblings? She might be right, but she has an equal chance of being wrong. Do callers realize this? Maybe, maybe not. In any case, Dr. Laura is on a slippery ethical slope here. Arthur Schopenhauer urges individuals to give mature and repeated consideration to any plan before proceeding to carry it out. How much consideration does Dr. Laura give callers? Plato urges one to acquire the knowledge necessary to make a good decision and then act in a way that others are served by the action. Has Dr. Laura gathered enough knowledge about her callers' problems to make good decisions? Are her callers well served by her advice?

Callers who need a kinder, gentler approach might tune in another nationally syndicated radio program, Delilah after Dark. The program airs evenings on about 90 FM stations nationwide. Delilah plays love songs and offers soothing advice to callers with romantic problems: the lonely, the divorced, the lovesick, the separated, the engaged, the married. "She's a cross between your psychiatrist, your mother, and your girlfriend," says one radio programmer whose station carries the program.[17]

Delilah has no formal training in counseling or therapy. When asked about her qualifications, Delilah says she got her doctorate "in the school of hard knocks." Probably true. She is married to her second husband and has a child from the marriage as well as a child from her first marriage. She grew up in a dysfunctional family. Her father was an alcoholic and disapproved of her first marriage to an African-American. Her mother died from brain cancer. The same kinds of observations could be made about Delilah's program that were made about Dr. Laura's. As theater, the show can be entertaining. As a source of serious advice, the show joins Dr. Laura's out there on thin ethical ice.

Delilah seems to be a more sympathetic listener than Dr. Laura, but her advice is less expert. At least Dr. Laura is a licensed counselor and therapist.

Delilah is just a disc jockey. The problem with both these programs is that they can be taken seriously by individuals who may be so psychologically or socially vulnerable that they are led by the program's advice to make decisions that can significantly damage their lives.

Of course, one could just shrug these programs off with a *caveat emptor*— let the buyer beware (a concept discussed fully in Chapter 12). One might be inclined to lower one's voice on this issue if a disclaimer were regularly aired during these programs. The disclaimer might say something to the effect that "the program you are listening to is provided to you for entertainment purposes only. Individuals needing social or psychological help should see a qualified counselor."

Talk-Political Personalities   It is easy to find talk shows with a political flavor on AM radio. These nationally syndicated programs typically air each weekday. Some political commentators have shows that are only broadcast regionally and typically reach a significant part of their geographic area but not the entire nation. Most programs feature lengthy commentary by the host, and, if time permits, listeners may call in with questions or comments. The best known of these national political talk show personalities is Rush Limbaugh, a conservative who has made something of a career out of opposing liberal politicians and liberal positions on issues such as abortion. At one time, in the mid-1990s, Limbaugh was said to be one of the most influential conservatives in the country.

Oliver North, on his Common Sense Network, is also a conservative voice that draws many listeners. North, a retired army colonel, was implicated in the Iran-Contra arms-for-hostages scandal during the Reagan administration, but he was never convicted of a crime and now serves as a rallying point for Reagan-era conservatives and retired military personnel. G. Gordon Liddy, a convicted Watergate burglar who served a five-year prison term, is by far the most radical of these in-your-face political talk show hosts. Liddy's program, Radio Free D.C., airs on more than 250 radio stations nationwide and is often about guns, violence, and the overthrow of the Washington elite. Limbaugh and North are highly critical, but neither advocates violence as a means for change. Liddy, or the "G-man" as he is often called, appears to openly advocate violence. For example, in denouncing "federal agents as 'bottom-dwelling slugs,' " Liddy says "shooting back is reasonable. . . . I have counseled shooting them in the head."[18] Whatever the issue under discussion, all three talk show hosts wrap their comments in patriotic rhetoric.

President Bill Clinton, in a speech following the Oklahoma City terrorist bombing that killed 168 people in 1994, said much of the blame for that incident and for many antigovernment groups and activities rests on the shoulders of the political talk show hosts who incite individuals to take destructive action. Clinton did not mention any of these hosts by name, but it was clear to those familiar with this sort of radio programming that he was referring to Liddy and his ilk.

Is there an ethical concern here? These programs are certainly legal, from a First Amendment point of view. Broadcast speech is protected speech under the Constitution. Nevertheless, one could raise the issue of appropriateness, at least in Liddy's case. It could be argued that we need a political dialogue in this country and that both liberals and conservatives deserve to have forums for the presentation of their respective views. Critical comment about those in and out of political power is a necessary part of the democratic process. However, such comment should not advocate violence or any other activity that is harmful or illegal. Perhaps the philosophy of moral legalism is at work here. If the actions of these radio hosts are not illegal, then they are not unethical. However, moral legalism is a philosophy not everyone is happy with. It allows someone to say something that might not be illegal, but which might be unethical. Lying is a good example. It is not illegal to lie on a radio broadcast, but it is certainly unethical not to tell an audience the truth. After all, the radio host is speaking from a position of power; the host controls the airwaves for several hours each weekday. This power must be used responsibly.

Perhaps these and other political talk show hosts would do well to follow John Stuart Mill's admonition to act so that one's actions bring about the greatest good for the greatest number. Émile Durkheim suggested that one examine a proposed action to determine whether it contributes to and reflects the existing social and moral fabric of life. Do these political talk show hosts contribute to the moral, social, and political fabric of American life? Are they using their influence in a socially responsible manner? Often the answer to these questions depends on whether one agrees with what the host is saying. But aside from whether one agrees or disagrees with any particular issue, can there be a moral standard applied to whatever comments any individual might make as a talk show host?

Shock Jocks   In the late 1990s, the two most famous *shock jocks*, radio personalities who preside over programs designed to shock or titillate listeners, were Howard Stern and Don Imus. Both Stern and Imus work in New York City and are syndicated nationwide.

Stern is probably the better known of the two. He has written two books, starred in a movie based on one of his books, and was fined $1.7 million by the Federal Communications Commission for broadcasting indecent material. His broadcasts often feature detailed discussions about oral sex or lesbian sexual experiences. For example, Stern has "played Lesbian Dial-a-Date and Gay Dial-a-Date and Guess Who's the Jew. . . . He even made fun of his wife's miscarriage. . . . He joked about having sex with the puppet Lamb Chop."[19] The *Washington Post* media critic Howard Kurtz says: "Stern builds himself up by trashing others."

Imus is Stern's crosstown rival and, while often suggestive, is not as explicit as Stern. When someone once told him that he was just like Stern, Imus snapped that he was Stern "with a vocabulary. I'm the man he wishes he could be."[20] Imus's show meshes "eighth grade locker-room jokes with fairly serious talk from pundits and politicians. Even those politicians and celebrities who talk with him on the show are fair game for his humor. When talking once with Senator Ted Kennedy of Massachusetts, Imus "played the sound of a car skidding and a person gurgling underwater,"[21] a not so subtle reference to the death of staffer Mary Jo Kopechne in Kennedy's famous Chappaquiddick auto accident.

Both of these radio programs have found space on television. Stern's radio show is regularly videotaped and played later on the E! cable network. Imus's show is carried live each morning by MSNBC, the cable news/talk service. The entertainment value of these shows is thin, some critics say. There is little music, only superficial news, and much "I think, I want, I-this and I-that" from the hosts. Yet both shows have large audiences.

These two are not the only controversial radio hosts in America. Almost every major market has an Imus- or Stern-type individual who is explicit, controversial, and widely listened to. If you scan the dial while traveling, you might find the Greaseman, whose comments regularly get him into trouble. (On the day after Martin Luther King, Jr.'s, birthday—a holiday—he asked if his listeners knew what it would take to get the whole week off. His answer— four more bullets.) In Tampa, you could hear Bubba the Love Sponge, sponsor of wet T-shirt contests and "no panties Thursdays." On the West Coast, you might hear J. Paul Emerson, whose daily vocabulary consists of words like "assholes, buttheads, and slimeballs."[22]

In terms of looking at what is ethically appropriate, we must again walk the fine line between what is permitted by the First Amendment and what is not permitted ethically. One might ask, with Immanuel Kant, whether the audience is being used as a means or an end. If the audience is being used as a means to fame and fortune by the radio personalities, then their broadcasts are inappropriate and unethical. Peter Abelard might ask about their intentions. Is it the intention of these shock jocks to appeal to the prurient interest of the audience and thereby garner ratings and fat contracts? Or are they serving "the public interest, convenience, and necessity" as the Communications Act of 1934 challenges broadcast stations to do? Remember that "public interest" does not mean "what interests the public." Stern often responds to critics who say his program is indecent and offensive by noting that no one is forced to listen to a program on radio. If listeners are offended, Stern says, they should just change the station. *Caveat emptor* again!

An Observation

As is often the case with ethical dilemmas, the problems the book, recording, and radio industries have must be addressed by the individuals in those industries before proceeding to a different level. Ethics begin with individuals. They must examine their conduct to see whether it is ethically appropriate. They must accept the responsibility for their actions and not try to justify their actions by placing the responsibility elsewhere. An important principle that all might consider is Voltaire's notion that one should use reason to balance the passions and act for the greater good of society.

▼ Case Studies

Case Study #10. The Romance Writer

In 1996, romances accounted for 50 percent of all mass market paperbacks sold—$1 billion worth of books. Two major players in the paperback romance industry are authors Janet Dailey and Nora Roberts. At the 1997 annual convention of the Romance Writers of America, Janet Dailey made a startling admission: three of her books had sections that had essentially been lifted from Roberts's books.

Plagiarism? Doesn't all that romance stuff sound pretty much alike anyway? How can you tell something is copied? Plagiarism has been around as long as there have been writers. Its formal definition is the "use of another's writing without proper use of quotation marks . . . without crediting the source."[23] Plagiarism frequently appears in student homework of several sorts. As early as the third or fourth grade, students are often encouraged to "do reports," which often means copying something from an encyclopedia or a reference book. Some elementary school teachers require that the source be cited; others do not. By the time students reach high school, they may not have a clear notion of just how to use the words or ideas of another. Some students take notes poorly and, as a result, unintentionally misuse a source. Others know they are copying directly without citation, but do it anyway. Still, by the time most have graduated from high school, they know what plagiarism is, and that it is against the law. When they get to college, of course, a whole new set of possibilities opens up to them: fraternity and sorority files, term paper warehouses, and the Internet.

There is no question that Janet Dailey, the author of 93 novels, knew about plagiarism. Why did she do it? Industry insiders say it may have been a combination of jealousy and desperation. Nora Roberts was, in 1997, the romance industry's hottest writer. Dailey said a "series of family traumas . . . triggered a psychological problem."[24] But this explanation seems thin.

Initially, Dailey apparently agreed to rewrite the copied parts, apologize publicly, and contribute to the Literacy Volunteers of America. However, the two authors could not come to a settlement agreement. In late 1997, lawyers for Roberts reported that she had decided to proceed with a copyright infringement suit against Dailey.

Aside from the legal issues surrounding this case, what are the important ethical considerations? There are hundreds of romance writers in the world. There may be a limited number of ways to express ideas and describe events, especially in the world of romance writing where so much of the work is formula-driven: the characters are young, vibrant, and physically gifted; the plot is simple—woman meets man, woman loses man, woman regains man; sexual activities are implied but never explicitly described. How many different ways can one say, "His sensual kiss sent waves of electricity through her body"?

Examine these two excerpts:

> Like a rocket the heat tore up her arm. Eden found it was one thing to ignore what she had convinced herself she never needed, and another thing entirely to resist what she discovered she did.

—From *Notorious* by Janet Dailey

> Like a rocket the heat tore down her fingertips. It was one thing to ignore what you'd never needed, and another to resist what you suddenly did.

—From *Sweet Revenge* by Nora Roberts

Key Questions   One longtime writer once observed, "Everyone borrows from everyone else." Do the two passages constitute evidence of plagiarism? How much can be ethically borrowed? If one borrows anything, is it plagiarism? Does the "borrowing" of the work of another violate Judeo-Christian principles?

Case Study #11. Marv Takes a Loss

Marv Albert's voice is easily recognized by sports fans nationwide, but especially in New York where he was the voice of the New York Knicks professional basketball team and the New York Rangers professional hockey team. He also worked for NBC Sports; his assignments ranged from basketball to football to boxing. He was a frequent guest on David Letterman's late night television program.

In May 1997, Albert was charged with forcible sodomy and assault and battery in a case brought by his longtime lover, Vanessa Perhach. According to the suit, Albert became angry during one of their intimate sessions when Perhach would not agree to having another man join them. Albert reportedly bit Perhach on the back several times and forced her to perform oral sex. When the charges became a matter of public record, Albert assured his employers that he was innocent of the charges.

When the trial began in September 1997, conflicting testimony was presented. Albert's defense team found that Perhach had approached a Washington, D.C., cab driver and offered him $50,000 if he would testify that Albert had asked him to procure a young boy for three-way sex. The driver, however, tape-recorded the conversation and gave the tape to Albert's lawyers. Score one for Marv! Perhach's lawyers were busy, too. They found a woman, a hotel employee, who testified that Albert called her to his room and met her at the door wearing women's underwear and a garter belt. "She charged that he tried to force her to have oral sex." She said she yanked off his toupee and escaped.[25] Score one for Vanessa! Albert huddled with his lawyers and decided he would plead guilty to a misdemeanor charge of assault and battery if the forcible sodomy charge was dropped. The settlement was accepted, and the trial was over. Albert was later given a 12-month suspended sentence on the assault and battery charge.

There are several ethical issues here, some not so obvious. No ethical code would support the behavior of either Albert or Perhach. Nevertheless, their activities, however sordid, were part of their personal lives, not their professional lives. What Albert did or did not do in his interactions with Perhach did not have an influence on how he performed his sportscasting duties. Essentially, his sex life had nothing to do with how he called a Knicks or Rangers game, or how he reported a boxing match or a football game. His broadcasts were not unethical. He used no unacceptable language, made no racist, sexist, or disparaging comments, and never mentioned sexual matters or his personal life.

What is the relationship between one's personal and professional ethics? Must they be one and the same? Does the fact that an individual is a celebrity—even a second-level celebrity sportscaster—mean he or she is held to a higher standard of conduct than you or me, or a local radio or television sportscaster? Should all those employed in broadcasting have their personal life examined, or should one's life only be examined when one gets into some sort of trouble? What are the ethical issues here, and how can they be satisfactorily resolved?

A related issue arising from the Albert incident involves his good friend David Letterman. As a frequent Letterman guest (almost 100 appearances through the years), Albert often brought clips of humorous sports incidents to the show. They were usually marked by Albert's trademark "Yesss!" outburst at a remarkable play or unusual turn of events.

When Albert's trial began, the media followed it closely. News about the trial led the network evening news broadcasts several nights. The trial naturally led to a number of jokes at Albert's expense. The tabloids had a field day: "Marv Wigged Out," blared one; "Marv Bites Back," trumpeted another. *The Tonight Show*'s Jay Leno, Letterman's late night ratings rival, made Albert the butt of frequent jokes, 43 by one count.[26] Letterman, however, did not tell a single Albert joke and was criticized for protecting his friend. Leno, however, agreed with Letterman's approach. "I understand completely," Leno said. "If it were . . . a close friend of mine, I wouldn't make jokes about him, either."[27]

Key Questions What role does loyalty play in ethics? What sort of sacrifices are ethically appropriate for a friend? Is it inappropriate for Letterman to ignore the Albert incident? Should he have made fun of his friend? Would that have been ethically acceptable?

Case Study #12. Jay Tells a Joke

The Tonight Show with Jay Leno is the undisputed leader in the late night television talk show ratings wars. Although Leno's show was second to David Letterman's *Late Show* for several months following Letterman's move

Did Jay Leno make an ethical choice? *AP Photo / Mark J. Terrill*

from NBC to CBS, it wasn't long before Leno regained the top spot, a position held for years by *The Tonight Show*'s previous host, Johnny Carson. Following the lead of other television comedians, including Jerry Seinfeld, Paul Reiser, and Kelsey Grammar, Leno wrote a book. Leno's was an autobiography titled *Leading with My Chin.*

In his autobiography, Leno tells the story of his life and especially of his rise to fame in television. At one point in the book, Leno reports that one of his early television appearances was on Dinah Shore's syndicated daytime talk show. The plan was for Leno to come out and deliver a comic monologue. The talent coordinator asked him what his outcue was, that is, the last line of the monologue, so that the band could jump right in with music to cover his exit from the stage. Leno pondered a moment and finally said his outcue was "Thank you, thank you very much."[28]

When he was introduced, Leno came on stage to a rousing ovation. Feeling pretty good about himself, Leno began with a rather weak joke. "I'm from the United States! Are there any United States people here?" The audience responded with a huge ovation, much more than such a lame joke deserved. Surprised by the response to such a poor joke, Leno said, "Thank you, thank you very much," at which point the bandleader, recognizing the outcue, struck up the band to play him off stage. Leno "stood there, stunned. . . . Dinah said, 'Come on over here, Jay.' " He walked over to the couch and sat down. Dinah continued, "That's some of the freshest material I've heard in a long time." Leno responded, "Well, thank you very much. At this rate, I could do this show eighty, ninety times a year." In looking back on the experience, Leno noted that "it was the most ridiculous shot of my career."[29]

Amusing story. So what's the problem? The problem is that it isn't true. The incident described did not happen to Leno. "It happened to another comedian, Jeff Altman. Leno liked the story so much he paid Altman $1,000 for the right to publish the tale as his own."[30]

Like a biography, an autobiography is assumed to be a truthful account of a life. Was Leno truthful? Not exactly. He claimed that "something similar had happened to him on the same show, but he wished to 'meld' his story with Altman's to acquire a better ending."[31] Is it ethical to include false incidents about one's life in an autobiography? Like biographies, autobiographies are considered nonfiction and are shelved separately from the fiction in bookstores and libraries.

Key Questions What responsibility to the truth does an individual have in writing an account of his or her life? Is truth something that exists in itself, or, as some postmodernists claim, is truth merely socially constructed? Is there a danger in reaching a time "when nothing can be said to be objectively true, when consensus about reality disappears"?[32]

Case Study #13. Reading Can Be Instructive

James Edward Perry had never been much of a reader, yet a book listed in the Paladin Press catalog interested him. It was only 130 pages long, and it cost $10, but he ordered it. The information he found in the book was apparently quite useful to him on the evening of March 3, 1993. That night, in Silver Spring, Maryland, Perry killed three people: Mildred Horn, her eight-year-old quadriplegic son, Trevor, and his nurse, Janice Saunders. Perry used at least 20 of the specific instructions contained in the book *Hit Man,* a step-by-step guide for contract killers.

Rex Feral, the book's author, insists that the manual "provides a public service," because sometimes hiring a hit man is "the only means of obtaining personal justice."[33] Peder Lund, the founder of Paladin Press, noted, "As a publisher and a pragmatist, I feel absolutely no responsibility for the misuse of information."[34] Paladin Press's catalog contains other interesting titles: *Winning a Street Knife Fight: Realistic Offensive Techniques* and *Advanced Ultimate Sniper,* as well as *Homemade C4: A Recipe for Survival.*

Free speech advocates were quick to claim that even the most objectionable writing is protected by the First Amendment. Others noted that "people cannot openly traffic in information that has as the sole purpose of assisting others to commit murder."[35] Although the legal arguments pertaining to this case have flown fast and furious, little has been said about the ethical aspects of the case, particularly whether it is ethical for a publisher to disseminate materials such as *Hit Man.*

For the record, James Perry and Lawrence Horn, Mildred's ex-husband and Trevor's father—who was apparently after a $2 million insurance settlement his son had received—were convicted of first degree murder. Family members sued Paladin Press, claiming "the company is liable for the murders because it provided the blueprint."[36] A federal appeals court in Richmond, Virginia, has allowed the suit to go forward, noting that "the Constitution does not protect books that aid and abet in the commission of a crime."[37] This case may be tied up in the courts for some time, but the ethical issues involved may not be so difficult to decide.

Key Questions   Is an individual ethically responsible for information transmitted to others, or are the receivers of the information ultimately responsible for its proper use? When it comes to objectionable material in the media mainstream, should the First Amendment or ethical principles prevail? What philosophy could Paladin Press advance in support of its actions?

QUESTIONS FOR DISCUSSION

1. Is it possible to control the content of books when the economic pressures are so great on publishing houses? What if a particular segment of the audience *wants* a book with questionable content?

2. Is it ethical to condemn a book because its language does not meet contemporary standards, even though the language met the standards of the time during which it was written?

3. Is there a point where music lyrics cross the line from protected speech to inflammatory, inappropriate speech? Who should make the judgments in such cases? What sort of ethical standards could you suggest for the music industry?

4. Can you suggest some ethical standards for talk radio shows? Is there a point on those shows beyond which a host should not go?

5. Shock jock radio shows are popular. How do you account for their popularity? Do you think most listeners have ethical problems with the content of these shows? Why?

ENDNOTES

1. Craig Pittman, "High Court Won't Hear Obscenity Case," *St. Petersburg Times,* 2 July 1997, sec. B, p. 4.

2. James B. Twitchell, *Carnival Culture: The Trashing of Taste in America* (New York: Columbia University Press, 1992), 268.

3. Ibid., 81.

4. Ibid., 86.

5. *Jacobellis* v. *State of Ohio*, 378 U.S. 184, 197 (1964).

6. Daniel Linz, "Exposure to Sexually Explicit Materials and Attitudes toward Rape: A Comparison of Study Results," *Journal of Sex Research*, 26, no. 1, 1989, 50; Augustine Brannigan and Sheldon Goldenberg, "The Study of Aggressive Pornography: The Vicissitudes of Relevance," *Critical Studies in Mass Communication*, 4, 1987, 262.

7. Press release, "Writers Deserve Royalties," Science Fiction Writers of America, 8 September 1997.

8. Ibid.

9. Andrew Ferguson, "Now They Want Your Kids," *Time*, 29 September 1997, 64–65.

10. Debbie M. Price, "To Make Money, Rap Star's Album Carries Free Speech Too Far," *Tampa Tribune*, 13 June 1992, sec. NW, p. 11.

11. Barbara Ehrenreich, "Is It Creative Freedom?" *Time*, 20 July 1992, 89.

12. Michael Kinsley, "Ice-T: Is the Issue Social Responsibility," *Time*, 20 July 1992, 88.

13. William J. Bennett and C. DeLores Tucker, "Responsibility Requires Silencing Vulgar, Violent Music," *St. Petersburg Times*, 3 June 1995, sec. A, p. 12.

14. Joannie M. Schrof, "No Whining," *U.S. News & World Report*, 14 July 1997, 48.

15. Ibid., 51.

16. Ibid.

17. Jeanne Malmgren, "Listener for the Lovesick," *St. Petersburg Times*, 6 October 1997, sec. D, p. 1.

18. Howard Kurtz, *Hot Air* (New York: Basic Books, 1996), 13.

19. Ibid., 273, 276.

20. Peter Laufer, *Inside Talk Radio* (New York: Birch Lane Press, 1995), 107.

21. Kurtz, 13.

22. Laufer, 137.

23. James D. Lester, *Writing Research Papers, A Complete Guide* (Glenview, IL: Scott, Foresman, 1972), 47.

24. Marc Peters and Yahlin Chang, "The Queen of Hearts Gives Up Her Throne," *Newsweek*, 11 August 1997, 74.

25. Matthew Cooper, "Marv Goes to the Showers," *Newsweek*, 6 October 1997, 40.

26. "While Leno Laughs, Letterman Spares a Friend," *St. Petersburg Times*, 11 October 1997, sec. B, p. 2.

27. Ibid.

28. Jay Leno, *Leading with My Chin* (New York: Harper, 1996), 192.

29. Ibid., 193.

30. John Leo, "This Column Is Mostly True," *U.S. News & World Report*, 16 December 1996, 17.

31. Ibid.

32. Ibid.

33. Adam Cohen, "Murder by the Book," *Time*, 1 December 1997, 74.

34. Ibid.

35. Ibid.

36. Ibid.

37. Ibid.

Ethical Issues and Case Studies in the Television-Entertainment and Film Industries

Overview

The television-entertainment and film industries are not totally dependent on each other, but they often work closely. Television needs major motion pictures for network movie nights; some networks produce their own movies and often work with major production houses to develop movie product. In any case, both television-entertainment and film share some of the same concerns, particularly in terms of content and ratings.

▼ Television-Entertainment

Television's Golden Age is considered by many to be the 1950s when *I Love Lucy, The Honeymooners, Texaco Star Theater, Strike It Rich, The Life of Riley,* and at least a half-dozen other shows provided the audience with both quality and variety. By those standards, some critics say, current television-entertainment programming pales. Others say that it is just as good, if not better, than the early shows. They point to *The Simpsons, Seinfeld, Frazier, ER,* and *NYPD Blue* as programs from the 1990s that are as well produced and entertaining as anything from the 1950s. Still others say comparing shows four decades apart is not a useful activity. It is not a level playing field. The culture has changed in the last 40 years and so have production capabilities. Nevertheless, most admit that plot lines are just as sound and character development is just as good as ever.

Overall, however, television's track record for producing good shows has not been dramatic, particularly if one defines a good show as one that is renewed for two or more seasons. From the mid-1980s to the early 1990s, about 80 percent of each autumn's new shows failed to attract a large enough share of the audience to be renewed for a second year. This failure rate is about 10 percent higher than for the 1970–1984 period.[1] To compound the problem, network viewership has been declining over the past decade. In the face of increased competition from cable services and video rentals, the networks have seen their share of the audience decrease significantly. For example, the networks lost 10 percent of the viewing audience (from 75 to 65 percent) between 1993 and 1996. Network shares dropped another 4 percent in 1997.

▼ Instructional Case Study

During the Spring 1997 sweeps, "Ellen DeGeneres, the star of the ABC comedy *Ellen,* revealed that she was a lesbian, and so did her character on the show. . . . The coming-out episode became the highest-rated regular program on ABC for the entire season."[2] *Ellen* became the first television series to have a main character who was gay. Controversy about the program diminished somewhat during summer reruns, but flared again when the new fall season began. Vice President Al Gore "praised *Ellen* . . . saying it had forced Americans 'to look at sexual orientation in a more open light.' The Christian Coalition immediately responded by saying Gore was 'way out of the mainstream.' "[3]

The gay theme also caused ABC programmers some discomfort. Before one new episode, the network ran a parental advisory message. ABC was concerned about a scene where Ellen kisses a straight female friend. DeGeneres publicly threatened to quit the show if ABC persisted in giving the show a parental advisory warning. ABC continued to post ratings for the show. DeGeneres said little about it thereafter, but the network chose not to renew her show for the 1998–99 season.

Entertainment Content and Program Ratings

The term *ratings* typically refers to the percentage of the potential audience that a specific television program attracts. In the late 1990s, for example, *Seinfeld* and *ER,* two NBC shows, regularly had the highest ratings—that is, their share of the audience was greater than that of other programs in their given time periods. However, in 1997, the term *ratings* took on a slightly different meaning. Now the term also refers to the designation given a program by a network, a designation that indicates something about the program's content and functions much like the ratings given to films.

On January 1, 1997, the television industry, at the urging of Congress and children's advocates, implemented a program ratings system designed to be of particular use to parents in screening programming for their children. TV-PG designates a program urging parental guidance. The TV-14 rating is given to shows deemed unsuitable for children under 14. A rating of TV-MA is assigned to programs that are for mature audiences only. These designations

appear as icons in the upper corner of the television screen during the first 15 seconds or so of a program. This system lasted only six months. By July 1997, Congress was suggesting additions to this system. After some discussion, the networks, with the exception of NBC, agreed to add four additional designations to the existing system: L (for coarse language), D (for suggestive dialogue), S (for sexual content), and V (for violence). This brought the television ratings system more in line with the system used by the film industry.

Not everyone is pleased with the ratings system. NBC, for example, refused to be dictated to by Congress and dug in its heels. The network uses the original ratings system, but has declined to add the L-D-S-V notations. NBC cited freedom of the press issues in its refusal to adopt the additional designations, ones that were developed and promoted by Congress, specifically by Senator John McClain (R–Arizona) and the Senate Commerce Committee. NBC said, "There is no place for government involvement in what people watch on television."[4] One of the problems stems from the fact that no specific criteria have been developed for the L-D-S-V notations. The system appears entirely arbitrary.

Studies of viewer opinion of the ratings system, conducted about five months after the revised system was implemented, revealed that viewers do not seem to care much how television shows are rated. There have been few complaints, network officials say. A spokesperson for the National Association of Broadcasters (NAB) noted, "We have heard nothing from our audiences on this issue. The silence has been deafening."[5] Subsequent research revealed that parents say they are using the ratings to help them monitor what their children watch, but many survey respondents could not name any of the ratings used for shows. A Kaiser Family Foundation poll showed that 54 percent of parents surveyed said they used the ratings, while 46 percent said they did not. These results seem to contradict earlier findings that showed the ratings system to have been largely ignored. In any case, the Kaiser survey did find that "parents did not have a good understanding of what some ratings meant, particularly the ratings designed for children's shows."[6]

The degree to which television provides appropriate programs for children has long been a concern for parents, teachers, and children's advocacy groups. Researchers have known for some time that, in many homes, television functions as a baby-sitter. One study showed that for children ages 2 to 12 television was used to keep the child occupied while the mother engaged in household tasks, an average of three and a half hours per day.[7]

For a time, parents were urged to set their television dials on a public broadcasting station where their children could see such educational shows as *Sesame Street* and *Mr. Rogers' Neighborhood*. Many children did, indeed, watch these and other Public Broadcasting System (PBS) children's shows, but ultimately dials were turned and other programs found. When the Nickelodeon children's channel joined many cable systems, youngsters began to enjoy *Inspector Gadget, Roundhouse,* and *Ren and Stimpy*.

As the culture changed, so did the American family structure. It wasn't long before an increasing number of homes were single-parent ones, and in many of the two-parent homes, both parents had outside jobs. The result was that America became a nation of *latchkey children*—children who come home after school to an empty house and nothing to do. These children often plopped themselves in front of the family television set and watched whatever interested them until their parents came home. This may not have been much of a problem when program choices were few. But the television world rapidly expanded. Music Television (MTV), movie channels, and other specialized services were added to the list of programs available for viewing—viewing without parental supervision.

Parents, teachers, and children's advocacy groups soon became alarmed at what children were watching. Truth be told, children's programming on anything other than public television has never been of high quality. Saturday morning cartoon shows, long a staple of children's lives (while parents sleep in) have always had lots of violent action. Research shows that "there is considerable violence in television, particularly in programs that children are likely to watch."[8] Not only is violence present, but it can have a significant impact. "Children can learn new and complex aggressive acts simply by observing those acts performed once by a model."[9]

An impressive body of research, together with the concerns of parents, teachers, and others, explains, to a great extent, the continuing interest in providing acceptable programs for the young. Congress has been slow to act, due in some part to the restrictions placed on it by the First Amendment. Nevertheless, when elected officials see an opportunity to endear themselves to the voters, they often pounce on it. Through the Federal Communications Commission (FCC) and various congressional committees, Congress managed to become involved in the discussion of this issue. The result has been the program ratings system described earlier.

Another approach was championed by President Bill Clinton and Vice President Al Gore. They urged the development of a computer chip, called the v-chip, which allows parents to prevent objectionable shows from being tuned in on their television sets. The FCC approved technical standards for the chip in early 1998, and manufacturers say that the blocking technology will likely be available on televisions (and computers) sometime in 1999, although the official deadline for having the device installed on new sets is January 1, 2000.

Along with violence, coarse language, suggestive dialogue, and sexual content are also of concern. These content problems are all of a piece. There are simply a number of programs that are not appropriate for children. How do we manage what children watch without infringing on the First Amendment or without blatant censorship?

The instructional case study raises ethical questions about both program content and program ratings. Does *Ellen* dramatize situations or issues that are inappropriate or troublesome to some viewers? Is the program appropriate for viewing by children? Should it carry a parental advisory warning? Of course, as is often the case with ethical issues, there are no clear-cut yes or no answers to these questions. Some viewers believe that a homosexual lifestyle is immoral. Others see a gay or lesbian orientation as simply an alternative lifestyle and find it just as acceptable as a heterosexual one.

No one could successfully argue that most adults are incapable of handling the controversial nature of *Ellen*. But what of the children? Assuming one does not want to censor programs with which one may disagree—after all, we do have freedom of expression and our country has always welcomed a diversity of opinions about most everything—is it unreasonable to provide a parental advisory message? Is it important to inform viewers about program content so they can make a decision about whether they want to see the program or want their children to see it?

Communication professor Thomas Nilsen's philosophy of *significant choice* can be helpful in determining what should be done here. Although Nilsen's philosophy was not one of those covered in the philosophy discussions of Section II of this text, its usefulness in this case requires us to consider it. Nilsen believed that one's most ethical course of action is providing others with a "free, informed, rational, and critical choice." The opportunity to make a significant choice "can be regarded as an important element of respect for individuals. This respect typically requires treating people as rational human beings with aims and purposes of their own, about which they are capable of making significant choices."[10]

This philosophy actually works well on both sides of the *Ellen* issue. As far as the program itself is concerned, the star and the program producers are allowed free, informed, rational, and critical choices in their selection of issues or situations to dramatize on the program. Additionally, the parental advisory warning provides viewers with the same sort of significant choice in determining whether to watch the program themselves or to allow their children to see it.

Aristotle would likely agree with this sort of solution. He urged finding the mean, the just right position between two extremes. The mean can be determined only after one has examined the full complexity of the situation and considered all relevant factors.

What about DeGeneres's claim that there should not be an advisory message attached to the program? The postmodern philosopher Michel Foucault reminds us that we have an obligation to the truth, and that most problems, including ethical ones, are usually reflections of the power relationships that exist. What power relationships are involved in the *Ellen* debate? DeGeneres might feel that the network is exercising its power to label her show in a fashion she considers inappropriate and this diminishes the program and perhaps attacks her image or self-worth in the process. On the other hand, some viewers might feel that DeGeneres is using her power as the star of the program to promote an alternative sexual lifestyle that many consider immoral. Power versus power! Who wins? There may be no real winners in a contest such as this.

What about truth? Foucault reminds us that our truth obligations require us to discover the truth, be enlightened by the truth, and, of course, tell the truth. Determining the truth from the *Ellen* situation is not all that difficult. It is true that some Americans live a gay or lesbian lifestyle. Ignoring this truth does not seem to be a realistic course of action. On the other hand, it is also true that many Americans oppose this lifestyle and may not wish to have it presented to them or their children on a television screen without some advance notice. Ignoring this truth does not seem to be a realistic course of action, either. How does one reconcile these two truths?

As noted, Aristotle's Golden Mean suggests the just right position is somewhere between the extremes. In the case of *Ellen,* the extremes seem to be (1) censorship of content and (2) freewheeling, unrestricted, unlabeled content. Kohlberg's notion that an ethical decision ought to reflect logical reasoning and sound moral judgment is useful here. If one is to reach the mature, postconventional level of ethical decision making, one must critically reflect on the issues of a moral dilemma and base a judgment on considerations of universal human rights and dignity. In other words, each side in the *Ellen* conflict must respect the other and, as Voltaire suggested, balance the passions.

Television Talk Shows

Through the years many television program types, or genres, have been both profitable and durable during prime time hours: sitcoms (situation comedies); action-adventure series; police, medical, western, and family dramas; and science fiction shows. Each type has experienced some degree of success as television program offerings have expanded. Broad-based variety shows such as *The Ed Sullivan Show* in the 1950s, *The Smothers Brothers Comedy Hour* in the 1960s, and *The Carol Burnett Show* in the early 1970s essentially disappeared in the 1990s. The variety show format—music and comedy—does not appeal much to contemporary tastes.

Daytime television has survived on a combination of game shows, soap operas, and talk shows. Game shows seem to generate considerable viewer interest, but, for the most part, do not appear to raise significant ethical questions. Soap operas have always generated some critical comment, especially about the amount of suggestive sexual activity on these shows. For example, research studies in 1985 and in 1994 reveal that the 1994 soaps contained more frequent sexual incidents than those analyzed a decade earlier. The incidents centered "on physical intercourse, primarily among partners who are not married to anyone, and . . . the sexual activity is visual as well as verbal."[11] Nevertheless, most soap opera viewers are adults, and many critics do not single out the soaps for special criticism regarding their appropriateness for children. Television talk shows, however, are another matter.

Television talk shows differ in significant ways from the radio talk shows discussed in Chapter 13. The most important difference is that television talk shows have a visual component that is lacking in radio. The television shows are usually taped before a live audience, members of which are often allowed to participate in the program. After the program's guests are presented on stage and after their problems are exposed or their stories told, the program host often seizes a microphone and gallops into the audience. Individuals are singled out here and there for their comments about what they have just seen and heard. Two key ethical issues raised by these talk shows are *content* and *procedures.*

Content   Geraldo Rivera, Sally Jessy Raphael, Montel Williams, Rikki Lake, Maury Povich, Jenny Jones, and Jerry Springer are among those who have television talk shows available via syndication in almost every major market. Among the topics discussed on these programs on a typical autumn Friday in 1997 were the following: gossip, plastic-surgery woes, crime stories on television news, hair makeovers, and paternity tests. As long as the gossip isn't malicious, an ethicist could not find much to strenuously object to in this collection of programs. However, on Tuesday of the following week, the overall nature of the program content had changed. Viewers were able to tune in programs on serial killers, drugs, former lovers, a sex survey, erotomania, dangerous teens, fulfilled wishes, and lovers. Talk show critics argue that this latter list of program topics more accurately reflects the overall nature of these programs.

As is the case with radio talk shows, the television "talk culture is spectacularly ill-suited to dealing with complicated subjects."[12] Therefore, "the plot is always the same. People with problems—'husband says she looks like a cow,' 'pressured to lose her virginity or else,' 'mate wants more sex than I do,' 'boy crazy,' 'dresses like a tramp'"—are subjected to relentless preaching by the host and the studio audience.[13] "With few exceptions the guests are drawn from trailer parks and tenements."[14] The result is that the subjects under discussion are often lurid, if not bizarre. Some critics feel that this sort of public humiliation of guests borders on class exploitation and has important ethical implications. Should these programs be capitalizing on people who are "so needy—of social support, of education, of material resources and self-esteem—that they mistake being the center of attention for being actually loved and respected?"[15] Rousseau's philosophy advocates treating others with compassion and seeking to promote harmony among all those involved. Do television talk shows of the sort described promote that goal?

As theater, these talk shows are fairly entertaining, but as serious program material—and they are taken seriously by many viewers—they fail to provide much positive benefit to either participants or audience. Although television talk show guests have more on-air time than radio call-in participants, there is still precious little time to present a problem in its full context before advice is shouted to the guests by audience members, all of whom are strangers and none of whom is a qualified advice-giver. On television talk shows, on-stage guests do get Andy Warhol's 15 minutes of fame, but selected audience members get only about 15 seconds. What positive outcomes result from such exchanges?

A Pennsylvania State University researcher who studied daytime talk shows concluded that they "do more harm than good." Most of these shows "are simply mouthing mantras of pop-therapy. . . . Strangers get to give advice without being responsible for its effect. The central distortion that these shows propound is that they give useful therapy to guests and useful advice to the audience."[16] St. Thomas Aquinas reminds us that the best actions are those guided by prudence, justice, temperance, and courage. Can any of these virtues be said to be at work on television talk shows?

The content of these television talk shows, then, is an important ethical issue. Why must private lives be made public? Of what use are these programs to participants if no sound, reasonable, problem solution is offered them? Why are commercial breaks inserted at precisely the moment someone in the audience begins to question the whole process or takes the issue in a direction not approved of by the host? It is not difficult to see how "the national conversation has been coarsened, cheapened, reduced to name-calling and finger-pointing, and bumper-sticker sloganeering" by television talk shows.[17]

Procedures If the content of television talk shows were not troubling enough, the way some of these shows "ambush" their guests raises additional ethical concerns. A 1995 study by the Kaiser Family Foundation found that "America's television talk show hosts score an average of 16 'ambush disclosures' an hour on guests. . . . Often guests have little or no control about the disclosure."[18] The study analyzed 200 videotapes of daytime talk shows and found what most already know: "Hosts and guests talk mostly about family, personal relationships, and sex."[19] The study found that "the most common disclosures per hour were: five of a sexual nature, four about a personal attribute such as addiction, three about abuse, two about an embarrassing situation, and two about criminal activity."[20]

Ambush disclosures can sometimes have decidedly negative consequences. One legendary talk show moment featured a brawl between white skinheads and the black civil rights activist Roy Innis. On another show, this one about domestic violence, chairs were thrown, and the host, Geraldo Rivera, suffered a broken nose. Another famous talk show moment came when a male guest on the *Jenny Jones Show* was told he would meet a secret admirer. The guest "was humiliated when the admirer turned out to be a homosexual man. The guest was charged with murdering the admirer following the taping."[21] Clearly, the "ambush" nature of these programs raises serious ethical concerns. Lawrence Kohlberg's moral development philosophy notes that the most mature level of ethical decision making is one where all involved are treated with dignity and are recognized as having certain rights, especially when actions involve them as individuals and concern personal matters. Do television talk shows operate on Kohlberg's highest level of ethical decision making? Is the dignity of each guest respected? Are guests properly informed about what might happen on the show?

For his part, Geraldo Rivera took steps in early 1998 to clean up his journalistic image. After 11 seasons of serving up "daily dosages of urban blight and occasional fisticuffs," the *Geraldo Rivera Show* was scheduled to leave the air.[22] Rivera struck a deal with NBC that was reportedly worth $40 million. He planned to return to the mainstream of network news, but, as of early 1999, had not done so. Before his syndicated talk show, he spent some time as a journalist with ABC News, but was fired in 1985.

Jenny Jones remained unrepentant. In her autobiography, *Jenny Jones, My Story*, published in 1997, she was unapologetic for her syndicated talk show, "a favored target of critics, part of the . . . trash TV trend where family feuds, makeovers . . . dominate daytime."[23] Jones says her detractors "never want to write about how the show, and she personally, helps many people." Critics often take an elitist view of her show, she says, noting that she does not exploit her guests or look down on them. "They're the same people I run into when I go shop Kmart, which I do," she says.[24]

Public Television

Education television programs are generally defined by the Federal Communications Commission as material serving the intellectual, cognitive, social, and emotional needs of children, age 16 and under. Traditionally, public television, by way of the Public Broadcasting Service, has been home to many of the programs deemed appropriate for children. Adults, too, have found public television shows to be worthwhile and generally of high quality. However, public television has its own set of unique problems, problems that raise several ethical concerns.

Is Sesame Street Really Educational?   The claim that public broadcasting's programs for children—programs such as *Mr. Rogers' Neighborhood* and *Sesame Street*—are educational and therefore beneficial to children has largely gone unchallenged. There is no question that these and similar shows are nice programs and better for children than programs filled with violent or sexually suggestive content. However, there is little evidence that these programs do much to prepare young children for school.

Sesame Street really does not prepare young children for school and the challenging world of learning; it grooms them only for more television. A close examination of the program itself reveals that it doesn't actually glorify learning at all. It glorifies television and the youth culture. The program looks very much like a commercial, with fast cuts, jazzy music, and very, very short segments. This is not the way material will be presented in the elementary school grades. There is no doubt that the program is clever and well crafted, but it bears little resemblance to reality. Children on the show do not pout, hit, or engage in other cruel or behaviorally inappropriate acts as many children in the real world do. The most egregious act on the part of a child on the program is wasting water.

It is not politically correct to criticize Big Bird, one of the program's main characters, or to threaten PBS funding as congressional budget slashers did in the late 1990s. Nevertheless, when one looks beyond the shiny, public broadcasting image and examines programs like *Sesame Street* in some detail, it becomes clear that postmodern thinking has blocked the cognitive dissonance that should exist concerning the actual contribution these shows are making. They may keep children away from more violent and suggestive programs, and that is certainly a positive contribution, but they are not programs with high educational value in terms of preparing preschoolers for the kinds of academic experiences they will actually have.

Is there an ethical problem here? Yes, if one is inclined to accept conventional wisdom about certain programs, especially about the benefit of PBS shows. It should be noted, however, that researchers have found that programs like *Sesame Street* do help with "the development of cognitive skills among disadvantaged and advantaged preschool children. The gains in learning are greatest when children are encouraged by teachers or other adults who watch the program."[25] Other researchers have disputed some of these claims, noting that without encouragement from adults, children learn very little from these programs. The danger, then, is in making too broad a claim about the benefits of watching these programs. One has an ethical obligation to the truth. Respect for the truth ought to make one careful about the claims made regarding the educational benefits derived from watching children's programs on public broadcasting stations.

Funding   A second concern about public broadcasting is the continued encroachment of commercial messages on public stations. "Ever since Congress changed 'educational' TV and radio into public broadcasting in 1967, public stations have been gradually getting more and more commercial. From strict sponsorship rules that prohibited moving logos and the mention of anything besides a company's name, we have gone to enhanced underwriting guidelines that allow public broadcasters to describe a company's products or services and give addresses and phone numbers."[26]

There is much discussion about what sorts of commercial messages ought to be allowed on public television. Some people support full-fledged 30-second commercials on public television. Others say that is too extreme, but it might be acceptable for PBS to "go commercial on weekends to support non-commercial programming" during the week.[27] Still others favor maintaining the status quo. Other suggestions include charging commercial users an annual rental fee for spectrum space, with the money going to support noncommercial users; imposing a surcharge on new television sets; or treating public stations as premium channels and charging cable subscribers a modest fee to have the service available on home cable service.

New concerns arose in mid-1998 about PBS member stations and their commitment to increased commercialism. Since 1995, PBS has been forming "alliances with some of the most powerful media companies in the nation—often the very ones it was designed to be an alternative to."[28] Warner Home Video now handles the PBS Home Video label; Warner Brothers Records provides companion recordings to PBS programs; Microsoft has a deal to use PBS material on its WebTV Internet service.

Is this an economic issue or an ethical issue? Clearly, economics are involved. It takes money—and lots of it—to provide the sorts of programs one finds on public television. Over the last decade or so, Congress has reduced the amount of money provided to public broadcasting from government coffers. Corporate sponsorships still exist, of course, but this revenue source alone is not sufficient to support all that public television wants to do. All public stations conduct their own fund-raising campaigns every so often. Most declare a subscription week or a pledge drive activity and broadcast special programs. These programs are frequently interrupted so local celebrities and station personnel can beg the public for money. Some viewers find this practice annoying; others find it sad, but necessary. Public broadcasting's economic problems have no clear solution, at least not one on which there is consensus.

The ethical issue here is the influence commercialization of public broadcasting would have on program content. Who will have the real say about what is produced and aired? Corporate sponsors? Public broadcasters? The audience? Under commercial systems, no sponsor usually means no program. But public broadcasting operates under different criteria, "emphasizing quality, educational value, and social usefulness."[29] Will the criteria change when increased commercialization takes hold? What has commercialization done to mainstream public television program content? Are heavily commercialized network programs, by and large, quality shows or mediocre ones? In a postmodern world, what power relationships will result from a pairing of commercials with public television's specialized content? Will such a practice promote John Stuart Mill's ethical notion that one should promote the greatest good for the greatest number. What is the greatest good here? Is it the continuation of public broadcasting under the present underwriting guidelines? Is it the modification of public broadcasting to fit the needs of its advertisers? Is it maintaining a clear distinction between what network television offers and what public television offers? Is the greater good served by the establishment of yet another advertising medium?

It is obvious that these and other issues relating to public broadcasting challenge us to understand issues of power and influence clearly. The challenge also includes determining what quality television is and how it is to be financed. To make things more complicated, all this must be done with a keen sensitivity to the ethical issues involved.

▼ The Film Industry

Film occupies a unique place in mass communications. Films, or movies as they are commonly called, do communicate with a mass audience but not in the same way that television, radio, newspapers, magazines, and advertising do. Film is often considered an art form and not in the same category as other, fact-based media. This notion comes from the idea that most media have a journalistic foundation. Journalism drives the media machine. Without journalism, media content would be strikingly different. Newspapers and magazines would be most directly affected, but so would television.

Filmmakers have flexibility in regard to their product. Presenting a movie with little relationship to the truth—some critics would point to

Oliver Stone's *JFK* as an example—is not much of a problem. We do not expect the truth from movies; we do expect movies to be highly entertaining. However, if television, radio, newspapers, magazines, or advertising messages stray too far from the truth, the audience is apt to be less forgiving, expecting something close to the truth especially from the broadcast and print media. Audiences are more likely to use materials from what might be termed the journalistic media rather than film media to construct their views of reality.

This argument rests on the "basic assumption . . . that the media can determine our perceptions about the facts, norms, and values of society through selective presentations and by emphasizing certain themes,"[30] a view supported by research data. In contrast, films are *not* the "main source of information about the social and political environments"[31] in which audience members live and make decisions. Nevertheless, if the ability to communicate with a mass audience is a definitive quality of a mass medium, then including film in the mass communication field makes sense. Films should not, however, be seen as merely longer versions of 30- to 60-minute television-entertainment programs. Almost everything about films, from budget to acting to how they are commonly viewed (in theaters), puts them into a category all their own.

Character and Content

Not everyone subscribes to the notion that movies are less influential on individual character than television programs. One critic suggests that "movies are a part of culture, and like literature and music, they shape character."[32] Jimmy Stewart, John Wayne, and Gary Cooper, among others, were movie actors whose on-screen behavior sent a clear message: there is no "taking the easy way out and no excuse for misbehavior."[33] Presumably, this notion is important to the entire film industry; the Motion Picture Production Code has as one of its general principles that "no picture shall be produced which will lower the moral standards of those who see it."

Ken Auletta, media critic for the *New Yorker*, responding to readers' concerns about movie presentation of graphic violence and pornography and the glorification of junk culture asked several filmmakers this question: "What won't you do?" Most did not answer the question directly but launched into a defense of free speech. Oliver Stone, however, did answer the question. He said, "I'd pretty much do anything," a conclusion most would draw after seeing Stone's *Natural Born Killers.* Actor Debra Winger, noting that filmmakers go from being devoted to their families to glorifying on-screen killers, said, "They're doing things out in the world that are very, very questionable. . . . It's almost as if they never paused and looked at the whole picture."[34]

In terms of content, movies have almost always been more extreme than television. If an explicit movie is shown on a premium cable channel, such as

HBO, Showtime, or Cinemax, it is never edited. But if the same movie is shown on network television or on a local independent television station, it is almost always edited for content. Television programs are never judged obscene; movies frequently are. For example, in the summer of 1997, police in Oklahoma City knocked on Michael Camfield's front door and demanded he give them a movie he had rented. The movie, *The Tin Drum*, was a 1979 Academy Award–winning film. It included an oral sex scene between a boy and a girl. "The officers had used video store records to find Camfield," and they demanded the tape on the grounds that it was obscene under Oklahoma law, "which says that any depiction of a person under 18—or anyone portraying someone under 18—having sex is obscene."[35]

This case certainly has legal implications, especially with regard to privacy and free speech issues. In terms of ethics, its importance is less clear. If one considers film an art form, then who is to say that it has or does not have artistic merit? Since the film was foreign-made, it did not bear the MPAA movie rating "R." It was not playing to a mass audience; it was being viewed in the privacy of an individual home. No ethical codes favor censorship; almost all require the exercise of good judgment. Was poor judgment used in any aspect of the Oklahoma City case? Is it ethical to rent the movie for private viewing? Is it ethical for "Big Brother" to invade one's home and confiscate it?

If one follows the philosophy of moral legalism, then the police action may have been justified; the movie appears to be against the law in Oklahoma. However, in confiscating the movie, police intrusion into a private home raises other, serious legal questions. On the other hand, a postmodern culture would argue that such a law is ridiculous and that individual rights ought to prevail. This case appears to have no clear-cut, ethical solution. One could persuasively argue that the unedited film is not appropriate for network television. Is it not appropriate for private viewing?

Political Involvement

No aspect of our culture is immune to the influence of politics. The term *politics* does not refer only to the art or science of government; in its broadest sense, it can refer to a variety of activities within any organization, activities that involve policy, power, influence, and leadership. When the politics of the film industry meet the politics of government, one hardly knows what to expect.

What is the proper relationship between media industries and the government? Normally, one expects the media to avoid close relationships with anyone in government service. This expectation derives largely from the notion that the media serve as watchdogs on government activities, and if they get too cozy with politicians or other government service employees, conflicts of interest could result. So, ethically, media and their employees have traditionally avoided such entanglements. That tradition, however, is under attack, according to the critic James Fallows. Fallows believes that the walls that have traditionally restrained media, particularly journalists, from entangling relationships are coming down. He notes many prominent media figures have joined the lecture circuit, accepting large speaking fees from all sorts of institutions and individuals. Furthermore, these media figures have failed to disclose this information in their broadcasts or in their columns.[36]

If film is a mass medium, should the industry avoid close relationships with politicians? If film is an art form, what harm is there in building relationships with a variety of individuals, including politicians, who might have an impact or influence on the industry?

In 1997, several high-profile Republicans, including Senators Fred Thompson of Tennessee and John McClain of Arizona, and Representative Billy Tauzin of Louisiana, made trips to Hollywood to meet with movie moguls. Not only were these politicians wined and dined by the likes of Steven Spielberg, David Geffen, and Jack Valenti, but they also returned to Washington with "their campaign accounts fattened." Tauzin, at the time, was chair of the telecommunications subcommittee.[37] Movie insiders described these meetings as "a strategic reassessment dealing with the new realities of Washington." That, of course, can mean almost anything. The record shows, however, that Senator Arlen Specter of Pennsylvania, for example, "championed a bill that gave Spielberg's project to record oral histories of Holocaust survivors a grant of $1 million."[38]

Is this relationship between movie moguls and Washington politicians ethically acceptable? Is it good politics or just poor judgment? From a postmodern perspective, such activity is expected. Foucault's theory of power relationships holds here. Hollywood and Washington both possess powerful institutions: the film industry and the government, respectively. It should come as no surprise that these two powerful segments of postmodern culture actively seek to maximize their power and influence in the current political and cultural environment.

Editing Techniques

It could be argued that the rapid progress of technology has outpaced our ability to make sound judgments regarding its use—an idea developed further in Chapter 15. However, the issue is raised here to introduce a problematic ethical situation. In the movie *Contact*, starring Jodie Foster, quotes from President Bill Clinton were inserted into key segments of the film. These quotes were taken from presidential news conferences but placed in the film out of context so that the quotes took on an entirely different meaning. For example, one quote featured Clinton asking "the American people to remain calm in the face of some minor provocation from Saddam Hussein." In the movie, Clinton appears to be reassuring a nervous public about the possibility of life in outer space.[39] This use of the presidential image gave a "seal of approval" or at least a "sense of credibility" to the film and amounted to a presidential endorsement of the movie.

The ethical issue, of course, is whether quotations—any quotations, but especially those of a sitting president—should be used out of context for the simple purpose of propelling the plot of a movie. Is this an ethical use of someone's words? Not so fast, some might say. Remember *Forrest Gump*? That movie had the actor Tom Hanks shaking hands and speaking with Presidents Kennedy, Johnson, and Nixon. All three presidents were made to look rather silly. Nobody complained much about that. Well, of course, there is a difference. "JFK, LBJ, and RMN are all safely dead and fair game for movie gimmickry."[40] Technological tricks with a sitting president is another thing altogether. Jean Baudrillard reminds us that we should neither create nor perpetuate a fiction. It is ethically important to resist the negative aspects of contemporary culture and to present reality in a meaningful context? Did the producers of *Contact* cross Baudrillard's ethical line?

Business Practices

The Hollywood film industry has an iron-fisted grip on its business practices. By some accounts, the industry is the most tightly controlled of any in America, revealing little about how its revenues and expenses are managed. Neither is much revealed about how a host of other industry decisions are made. This is not to suggest that everything done is illegal; nevertheless, outsiders speculate that not much of what happens in the industry is perfectly aboveboard. This speculation is based on the few bits of information that have leaked into the public arena. At the very least, some of the industry's practices have ethical implications.

Take, for example, the issue of screenplays. The industry is hungry for fresh material. In 1996, according to one observer, studios paid more money for screenplays than in any previous year. Of course, not all screenplays purchased will be made into films. Yet the cost is staggering and the appetite for new material unsatisfied.

This heightened need for fresh scripts has given rise to both legal and ethical problems. For example, in the late 1980s, the syndicated humorist Art Buchwald filed a $20 million suit against Paramount, charging that the studio had plagiarized his work in the 1988 production of *Coming to America*, a popular film starring Eddie Murphy. Buchwald won the suit; the court awarded him $900,000 plus $150,000 in court costs, but it was unclear how or even whether he would receive any money since studios use creative bookkeeping practices. By some accounts, this means that studios tend to inflate the cost of everything, from soup to janitorial services, in an effort to demonstrate that such-and-such a film made no money. In this way, the studios can often avoid paying actors or others contingency salaries or royalties based on a film's profitability.

Forbes magazine reported that *Coming to America* grossed $350 million worldwide, but according to Paramount, it is yet to show a profit.[41] In fact, the studio reported an $18 million loss for the film. *Business Week* reported that the loss "came after deducting such costs as the interest the studio would have earned if it had banked the $58.4 million film budget instead of spending it on moviemaking." The studio's balance sheet was quite detailed, showing, for example, an expenditure of $256 to a McDonalds for Egg McMuffins for the film's extras.[42]

Another plagiarism suit surfaced in late 1997. The author Barbara Chase-Riboud filed a $10 million suit against Steven Spielberg and DreamWorks, charging that the film *Amistad* was based on her historical novel, *Echo of Lions*. Chase-Riboud said Spielberg stole her work and used it as a basis for his film about an 1839 mutiny aboard a Spanish slave ship. Spielberg denied the charge, saying his film is based on history and another book about the slave revolt, *Black Mutiny*, by William Owens. Chase-Riboud's lawyer called it "pure piracy, conspicuous copying, and rank plagiarism." I am astounded, he continued, "by the arrogance of power by the Goliaths of Hollywood. This is the most compelling case of plagiarism I have seen in 25 years."[43] Spielberg's lawyer, however, said that Chase-Riboud simply wanted money and indicated that if she really had principles, she would be applauding the film, "not trying to stop it for money." A federal judge refused to block release of the film, saying that it did not appear to be plagiarized, but the judge allowed Chase-Riboud's lawsuit to proceed. The film opened in theaters across the country two days after the judge's ruling. A couple of months later, Chase-Riboud dropped the lawsuit, noting that she and her lawyers had reviewed Dream-Works's files and concluded that Spielberg had done nothing improper.

There may be more such suits or threats of suits that are settled. The mass audience rarely gets a glimpse of this aspect of the film industry. It is only when an individual takes a complaint public that the moviegoing audience gets to see this part of the industry.

Let's return to the issue of the film industry's creative bookkeeping. A good example of how the system works is the financial report on the blockbuster hit *Forrest Gump*, a film released in July 1994. The film grossed more than $650 million worldwide. Soundtrack sales and videocassette sales were not included in this figure. Neither were licensing fees for such items as Forrest Gump wristwatches, Forrest Gump Ping-Pong paddles, and Forrest Gump cookbooks. By one estimate, these fees could amount to as much as $350 million. But, believe it or not, the film lost money. Six months after its opening, the studio reported a net loss of $62 million. The studio listed "negative costs," "interest on negative costs," and "overhead," among other mysterious items on the balance sheet. One accountant noted, "With this kind of bookkeeping, anyone can lose money."[44]

The ethical implications of these financial manipulations are clear. Studios are using thinly disguised false expense techniques to deprive writers, actors, and others of earned, rightful income. It is patently absurd, for example, to deduct as an expense the interest one would have earned had production money been banked. This kind of creative bookkeeping would not be allowed by the Internal Revenue Service for individual citizens. This "what if" deduction is one among many that are designed to lighten the pockets of industry workers and fatten studio coffers. These practices are most certainly unethical. Michel Foucault believes that, even in a postmodern society, individuals have a responsibility to the truth. This responsibility presumably extends to corporations. How truthful is Paramount?

Two other film industry issues are worth mentioning. One relates to the distribution and exhibition practices of the industry, and the other to the racial and ethnic diversity within the industry. In terms of distribution and exhibition, the tightfisted control the industry maintains over its product is much in evidence. The studios rigidly regulate the number of prints made of a film and often insist that theater chains guarantee box office receipts before a film will be released for showing in that chain's theaters. If the film does not generate the guarantee, the chain must make up the difference. This sort of business practice has generated millions of dollars for the film industry, and although this and similar practices have been declared illegal in several states, studios have found ways to accomplish much the same thing without doing exactly that which has been declared against the law.[45] These practices certainly have ethical implications.

In one way, insisting on a box office guarantee can be seen as a type of extortion: a studio has a film; a theater chain needs to screen the film; the studio twists every single dollar of revenue it can from the theaters, then claims that the film was the top revenue-producing movie in the country in the week it opened, generating $X million. This, of course, implies that Y million people went to see the film, which might not be the case. Studios do not distinguish actual ticket sales revenue from other opening week revenue (collected from the theaters as a guarantee). This practice can make a film seem more popular than it actually is. Misleading? Certainly. Unethical? Yes, unless one subscribes to the postmodern practice of substituting fiction for reality. Jean Baudrillard warns against creating fictions, but acknowledges that a host of fictions populate contemporary life.

The issue of racial and ethnic diversity has been a concern in American culture for more than 50 years. Laws have been passed, suits filed, policies challenged and changed, and sensitivities heightened, all in an effort to make our cultural and social environment more reasonable and more equitable. Progress has been made in many areas, but some observers believe there is still much to be done. The Hollywood film industry is one industry that has not progressed much with regard to racial and ethnic diversity. It is true that blacks, other minorities, and women are in evidence in many films. More than a few industry personalities have become rich. Nevertheless, Hollywood is seen as one of the last refuges of resistance to a more equitable society. Many in the industry support racial and ethnic initiatives in government and education but refuse to demonstrate that support in their own industry by working toward changes in the way the industry does its business. Many races and ethnic groups are still stereotyped in films or, at the very least, not shown in the same light as whites. Few make their way to top management positions within the studios.

▼ Case Studies

Case Study #14. Offering Advice to Postmodern Teenagers

It almost goes without saying that teenagers in postmodern America face a set of problems more challenging than any recent generation. Contemporary culture hands young people problems that are highly complex and often quite disturbing. How do teens cope? Do they seek out their peers for advice? Sometimes. Do they ask their parents for help? Sometimes. But, increasingly, postmodern teens seem to be turning to media, and particularly television, as a place to get ideas for problem solving.

Take the case of Jeff. He met a girl at a party and ended up sleeping with her. One-night stands are certainly nothing new. However, as it turned out, the girl was the daughter of his dad's fiancee—in other words, he slept with his future stepsister. This would certainly seem like a problem that cries out for professional help, and Jeff did seek help—from MTV's *Loveline*.

Loveline is one of MTV's most popular shows, garnering about 500,000 viewers per night. Program hosts Drew Pinsky and Adam Carolla stand ready to provide advice to teens who are unwilling to ask Mom and Dad about their problems. Pinsky, a 39-year-old father of triplets and director of chemical-dependency services at a Pasadena, California, hospital, is a practicing internist who believes that the show does good work. "The point is to create a coast-to-coast peer counseling session, where listeners can learn from the consequences of the callers' actions," he says.[46] Carolla, on the other hand, is a former carpenter and stand-up comedian. His purpose on the show is apparently to add humor to the proceedings, to be the "spoonful of sugar that makes the medicine go down." One 14-year-old from Las Vegas notes that Carolla is so funny, "you actually pay attention when he gets serious."

The dynamic duo claim a 3 million listener audience for the syndicated radio version of *Loveline,* and they stay busy. They plan to publish an advice book, and each is working on other projects: Carolla has a pilot for a variety-comedy show, and Pinsky wants his own daytime talk show.

No one seems to question their motives or the quality of advice the two dispense. It has apparently become accepted that one condition of the postmodern media culture is that when teens need help or information, they turn to television or other media. For example, the 14-year-old boy charged with killing three classmates after a prayer meeting at a Paducah, Kentucky, high school in late 1997 was reported to have told a teacher: "It was like I was in a dream, and I woke up." The boy told investigators that he had recently seen *The Basketball Diaries*, a 1995 movie in which the main character dreams about mowing down five of his classmates.

Media's influence on behavior is still not clearly understood, but researchers who have studied the issue say that individuals often confuse the television world with the real world. Tragic consequences often result.

In terms of MTV's *Loveline* program, what assurances do viewers have they are getting competent advice? Of course, the advice is often entertaining, but as the media critic Neil Postman notes, combining information and entertainment is not always a beneficial way to learn. Rather than improving discourse, television often presents discourse as visual images, often devoid of context. The myth that no problem or issue is so complex or so personal that it cannot be solved in a few minutes on television is widely believed.

Key Questions Is *Loveline* doing good work, as Pinsky claims, or is it just another bit of visual fluff that ultimately corrodes the lives of those who watch it uncritically? What ethical concerns arise from programs such as *Loveline*? Do such programs serve a greater good?

Case Study #15. Annie Sprinkle Goes to College

Many universities have student codes of conduct. These are needed, many say, to help students determine what is and is not appropriate on a university campus and by extension, in real life. One such code, at Sarasota's New College, prohibits the display of sexually explicit material. Yet students were both surprised and angry when "campus police stopped a late-night outdoor projection of ex-porn star Annie Sprinkle's 'Sluts and Goddesses Video Workshop' during an October, 1996 party of college students and minors, and seized [the] videotape."[47]

Senior Amy Andre, to whom the tape belonged, challenged the university's actions on the grounds that it violated the free speech provisions of the First Amendment. Andre said she was threatened with arrest and that police refused her repeated requests to return the tape. Andre's lawyer, George K. Rahdert of the American Civil Liberties Union, said, "The wall [on which the movie was being shown] . . . is its own First Amendment forum within that community." The exterior wall of the dormitory on which the film was projected had "been host to other graphic films depicting heterosexual sex and violent rape scenes— with no restriction from university officials," Rahdert noted.[48]

Andre had shown the tape earlier in the year at a New College tutorial on lesbianism, where students selected the class material. The movie is an "all female film with explicit sexual scenes including sex toys and group sex."[49] Sprinkle described her film as "an artistic, conceptual, experimental look at female sexuality." She added, "It's meant to be a work of art . . . it's a film to provoke thought and conversation on the subject of sex. My objective was . . . to stimulate minds."[50]

The university began disciplinary proceedings against Andre, and her lawyers immediately asked for an injunction barring the university from disciplining her on the grounds that the seizure of the tape had violated the student's constitutional rights. In January 1997, a federal judge issued a temporary injunction preventing the university from proceeding with any disciplinary action against Andre. The judge noted that "constitutional law requires a judge to view questionable material in its entirety, determine it is obscene, and then issue a warrant before it can be seized by law enforcement."[51] The university followed none of those procedures, the judge said. The university appealed the decision, but the ruling was allowed to stand.

There are thorny legal issues here, to be sure, but additional concerns arise from the ethical issues it involves. Apparently still to be decided is whether film is an art form or a mass medium, and whether the public showing of an erotic film is ethically acceptable. Many observers objected to the showing of the film on the grounds that minors were present. Others simply disapproved of the film's strong sexual content.

Key Questions   Assuming it was legal to screen the film, was it ethical? On what ethical grounds could one justify showing the film? Are there ethical philosophies that would argue against its showing? What is the postmodern view on the showing of such films?

Case Study #16. Exploring South Park

Satire has a long and rich history in Western culture. Many works of literature and art have poked fun at the folly or wickedness that human beings often engage in. But whatever the subject of ridicule, the overriding purpose of satire is to point the way toward improvement of the human condition. In English literature, the works of John Dryden and Alexander Pope stand out as models of good satirical writing. In American literature, H. L. Mencken's work has a biting edge that few writers, except perhaps Dorothy Parker, have been able to match. Does satire work outside of art and literature, say, on television? One could argue that television's *All in the Family* was clearly satirical, poking fun as it did at Archie Bunker's prejudices. For the most part, however, television has not historically been a medium that lends itself well to satire.

During the 1997–1998 television season, *South Park* was the most popular show on cable. It was certainly the most talked-about show in all of television. The program aired at 10 P.M. Wednesdays and was rated TV-MA, but almost a quarter of the program's audience was under 18. In the last two weeks of the February 1997 sweeps period, almost 5.5 million viewers watched the show, an extremely large audience for a cable program.

South Park, shown exclusively on the Comedy Channel, features four dirty-talking third-graders who live in South Park, Colorado. These youngsters (Stan, Cartman, Kyle, and Kenny) lead violent, flatulence-filled lives. Episodes have shown them poisoning Grandad; promoting a boxing match between Jesus and Satan; and talking with Mr. Hankey, the Christmas Poo, a stool specimen dressed in a sailor hat and speaking in a high-pitched voice. In other words, in *South Park*, "if it ain't bordering on the obscene, it ain't happening."[52]

The program's creators, 26-year-old Matt Stone and 28-year-old Trey Parker, make no apologies for the raunchy nature of the show. There is no question that the show goes beyond simple innuendo. Herewith some *South Park* highlights:

- In one episode, aliens insert a huge anal probe into Cartman.
- In another episode, titled "Big Gay Al's Big Gay Boat Ride," Stan follows his dog to an amusement park for homosexual pets, prompting a character to chant the line, "Stan's dog is a homo!"
- In the famous "An Elephant Makes Love to a Pig" episode, an eight-year-old tries to mate an elephant with a pig, but when the two animals show no sexual interest in each other, they ask an adult what to do; the adult responds, "Get them good and drunk."
- In every episode, Kenny, one of the continuing characters, is murdered. He has been shot, run over, stabbed, and decapitated. Each time, the other characters say, "Oh my God, they killed Kenny. You bastard." Yet Kenny returns unscathed for the next episode, and the next killing. In another episode, after Kenny's demise, one character observes, "Everybody has somebody they want to be killed."
- The co-creators of the series were asked why Kenny is killed each week. Stone responded, "Trey and I created Kenny. So we can kill him. Leave us alone."[53]

Is *South Park* satire, good comedy, or obscene programming? Opinions differ, of course. *Spin* magazine observed that the program is "probably truer to the kid experience than any other program on TV. It has the familiar sadism, the shameless greed, and the exuberant curiosity—in spades. *South Park* may be one of the realest social worlds on TV."[54] Both *Newsweek* and *Time* ran lengthy stories about the program, but neither was very critical of its content. Parents, educators, and other professionals who deal with children worry about the program's influence. The show's violence has had at least one tragic consequence. A 12-year-old boy in Ocean City, Maryland, committed suicide and left a note for his parents. The note told them to watch *South Park* to learn why he killed himself. He specifically mentioned Kenny, the character who is murdered in every episode.[55]

Both Stone and Parker acknowledge the controversial nature of the program, but seem not to care much about what critics say. You can't argue with success. Stone admits that they are not following any of the rules and that "we've become so successful because people out there are hungry for something different."[56]

Key Questions   Does *South Park* qualify as satire? What cultural values does the show communicate to its viewers? Is success or popularity a reliable measure of a program's ethical acceptability?

QUESTIONS FOR DISCUSSION

1. Who bears the greater ethical responsibility for what children see on television, parents or television stations and networks? Explain.
2. Is it enough that television networks provide ratings for their shows as a means of informing viewers about program content? What else could be done?

3. In what ways are television talk shows, like those of Jenny Jones and Jerry Springer, positive contributors to entertainment programming? In what ways do these programs engage in ethically questionable practices?

4. What are some ethical concerns raised by the programming and money-raising practices of public broadcasting stations?

5. Could it be argued that the controversial content of some films is less corrosive to society than the controversial content of some television programs? Explain your thinking.

6. Is it reasonable to ask film studios and television networks to provide ethically appropriate entertainment programming? Why? What ethical philosophies might one use to encourage them to produce movies and programs of higher quality, regardless of the resulting economic impact?

ENDNOTES

1. Susan Tyler Eastman, Sydney W. Head, and Lewis Klein, *Broadcast/Cable Programming* (Belmont, CA: Wadsworth, 1989), 155.

2. James Collins, "Yep, She's Still Gay," *Time,* 27 October 1997, 110.

3. Ibid.

4. Nat Hentoff, "McCain's Idea of Voluntary Ratings," *St. Petersburg Times,* 20 October 1997, sec. A, p. 11.

5. "Reactions to Ratings Proves Nil," *Tampa Tribune,* 2 March 1998, Baylife, 3.

6. "Study: TV Ratings Are Misunderstood," Associated Press report, 28 May 1998.

7. Walter Gantz and Jonathon Masland, "Television as Babysitter," *Journalism Quarterly,* 63, no. 3, 1986, 534.

8. Alexis Tan, *Mass Communication Theories and Research* (Columbus, OH: Grid Publishing, 1981), 213.

9. Ibid., 226.

10. James A. Jaksa and Michael S. Prichard, *Communication Ethics* (Belmont, CA: Wadsworth, 1994), 74–75.

11. Bradley S. Greenberg and Rick W. Busselle, "Soap Operas and Sexual Activity: A Decade Later," *Journal of Communication,* 46, no. 4, Autumn 1996, 159.

12. Howard Kurtz, *Hot Air* (New York: Basic Books, 1997), 15.

13. Barbara Ehrenreich, "In Defense of Talk Shows," *Time,* 4 December 1995, 92.

14. Ibid.

15. Ibid.

16. Kurtz, 69.

17. Ibid., 4.

18. Associated Press, "Talk Shows: 'Ambush' TV," *St. Petersburg Times,* 17 November 1995, sec. B, p. 2.

19. Ibid.

20. Ibid.

21. Ibid.

22. Walt Belcher, "Geraldo Gone," *Tampa Tribune,* 28 November 1997, Baylife, 6.

23. James Endrst, "Jenny Jones Makes No Apologies," *St. Petersburg Times,* 3 December 1997, sec. D, pp. 1, 3.

24. Ibid., 3.

25. Tan, 251.

26. Fred Flaxman, "Commercials Aren't What PBS Needs," *St. Petersburg Times,* 21 July 1997, sec. A, p. 6.

27. Ibid.

28. Dan McGraw, "Is PBS Too Commercial?" *U.S. News & World Report,* 15 June 1998, 42.

29. Flaxman, 6.

30. Tan, 264.

31. Ibid., 253.

32. Paul Craig Roberts, "Movies Shape Character—For the Worse," *Tampa Tribune,* 20 July 1997, Commentary, 2.

33. Ibid.

34. John Leo, "Media Moguls Can't Make a Moral Connection," *St. Petersburg Times,* 19 August 1997, sec. A, p. 8.

35. "Film Ruled Obscene; Police Raid Home," Associated Press, *St. Petersburg Times,* 28 June 1997, sec. A, p. 3.

36. James Fallows, *Breaking the News* (New York: Viking, 1997), 113.

37. Susan Estrich, "Hollywood Cuddles Up to the GOP," *St. Petersburg Times,* 12 June 1997, sec. A, p. 22.

38. Ibid.

39. Philip Terzian, "Hollywood's First Fan in Presidential Pique," *Tampa Tribune,* 19 July 1997, sec. Nation/World, 14.

40. Ibid.

41. *Forbes,* 19 February, 1990, 145, 179.

42. *Business Week,* 14 January 1991, 35.

43. *New York Daily News* story, in *St. Petersburg Times,* 30 November 1997, sec. B., p. 2.

44. *Forbes,* 6 June 1995, 155, 42–43.

45. Garth Jowett and James M. Linton, *Movies as Mass Communication,* 2nd ed. (Newbury Park, CA: Sage, 1989), 43–44, 51.

46. Sarah Van Boven, "The Doctor Is Always On," *Newsweek,* 15 June 1998, 62.

47. Jacqueline Soteropoulous, "Judge Blocks USF from Punishment," *Tampa Tribune,* 25 January 1997, Metro, 1, 3.

48. Ibid.

49. Ibid., 3.

50. Ibid.

51. Ibid.

52. Greg Orlando, "Going South," *Wizard: TCM # 80,* April 1998, 134; Lawrie Mifflin, "The Victory of Vulgar Television?" *St. Petersburg Times,* 18 April 1998, 1D.

53. Mike McManus, "Puzzled about Teen Violence? Have You Seen 'South Park'?" *Tampa Tribune,* 31 May 1998, Commentary 6.

54. Chris Norris, "Welcome to South Park, Fat-Ass," *Spin,* March 1998, 68.

55. McManus, 6.

56. Orlando, 136.

CHAPTER **15**

Ethical Issues and Case Studies in New Media Technology

In his 1970 book *Future Shock,* futurist Alvin Toffler observed, "We are racing toward 'overchoice'—the point at which the advantages of diversity and individualization are canceled by the complexity of the . . . decision-making process." Toffler may have been a true visionary because his words accurately describe the postmodern technological condition. In much the same way the Industrial Revolution ushered in the modern age, the technological revolution has ushered in the postmodern age. Americans now have access to more technology than they can possibly use—or understand.

Decision making in a postmodern culture is difficult. There are so many factors to consider: individual rights, ethnic and racial sensitivities, a global economy, changing social norms, the influence of politics, the growing influence of corporations, the decline of education. Additionally, one has to consider whether, and often how, to incorporate current technological advances into one's personal and professional lives.

In this chapter we will look at some areas of technology, particularly those related to communication and media, and examine some of the ethical problems that have come to be associated with them. This chapter differs somewhat from the others in this section of the text in that it essentially combines interpersonal and mass communication into a category that might be called *new media communication.* Strictly speaking, there is a clear difference between interpersonal communication and mass communication, but new technology is blurring this line. For example, a chat room conversation may initially begin as discourse involving only two individuals, but as others sign on and join the chat room, the discourse rises to the group level, at least, and maybe beyond. As technology advances, the labels we place on certain types of communication become more problematic. Few watertight types of communication are left in postmodern culture.

▼ Overview

For purposes of this chapter we will define new media as those aspects of communication that enable us to communicate electronically with other individuals, groups, or a mass audience. This means, specifically, the various kinds of interpersonal, group, and mass communication available to us through our computers. Included are local and regional computer networks, as well as national and international systems. Of course, the element with the highest profile in this broad collection of electronic activities is the Internet, but the new media category includes other electronic and telecommunication elements that represent a convergence of communication devices. For example, Nokia's 9000 Communicator Phone is a do-it-all piece of hardware that is part computer, Web terminal, and digital cellular phone. Its keyboard allows one to type memos, send e-mail, or fax messages. It can store up to 2 megabytes of information. Then there's net television, developed by, among others, Oracle, Inc., in cooperation with RCA. A "net-top" box, about the size of a cable television converter box, connects your television to the Internet. With Web TV, as it is sometimes called, you can surf shows and sites. It has a remote control and a wireless keyboard, enabling you to send e-mail, chat, and customize your television viewing.

Even something as simple as keeping a daily schedule can be technologically complex. For example, in 1997, the Palm Pilot personal organizer captured about two-thirds of the hand-held computer market. About the size of a postcard, it used a simplified alphabet (no dotted i's, no crossed t's), and was capable of storing addresses, phone numbers, e-mail, and calendar entries. It also provided two-way paging. A new, thinner model (Palm Pilot III) arrived early in 1998. At the same time, two other companies announced that they were producing hand-held units. Philips offered the Nino 300, and Casio developed the Cassiopeia E-10. Each unit had its advantages and disadvantages, prompting industry observers to note that selection was essentially a matter of personal taste, since all performed essentially the same kinds of tasks. Not to be outdone, Seiko announced a short time later that it was producing the first watch-size PC, called the Ruputer, to be worn, of course, on the wrist.

We do indeed live in a complex, technology-rich world. It is not surprising to note that as electronic technology has developed, so have our ethical problems. Had Aldous Huxley been writing his futuristic novel *Brave New World* today, he might have titled the work *New Postmodern World*.

▼ Electronic Communication: The Internet

For years, Americans heard about the coming of the information superhighway. "It is the future of communication," we were told, "and all it requires is a home computer." Well, yes and no. There is now little doubt that the information superhighway—the vast electronic chain of communication options—will be important to future communication, but some say that the highway is still under construction and that it presently is little more than a narrow two-lane road. And, as more and more people are finding out, it may require something more than just a home computer. It will require the basic hardware, of course, but many peripherals may also be needed in order to be able to communicate effectively, and nothing in the world of electronic communication is inexpensive.

It will, above all, require an understanding—a literacy, if you will—of the nature of electronic communication. Users may not be required to know how a Pentium II chip processes 500 million instructions every second, or that IBM has crammed 11.6 gigabits of data into one square inch of disk space, but they will certainly have to know how to use such capability effectively. A computer keyboard is not your father's typewriter anymore. It is much more—a gateway to the world. Interestingly, IBM's miniaturization process is roughly equivalent to "storing an 18-story stack of double-spaced, typed pages on your thumbnail" and will likely make computers more energy efficient.[1]

Many Americans have little interest in communicating electronically. However, large numbers do, and their numbers are growing. "In 1992, just two percent of the U.S. population enjoyed e-mail access . . . [but] by 2000, more than 135 million people—half the U.S. population—will be doing most correspondence via the Internet."[2]

A 1997 Roper Starch Worldwide poll found that barely 2 percent of the 2,003 adults interviewed in a survey "mentioned the Internet and other online services as a potential source of news." With a 3 percent margin of error, it is actually possible that no one is using online services for news. This survey notwithstanding, we know that some people do access online services, especially during working hours, to get up-to-date news and weather information. Still, in the late 1990s, television was the leading news source for most Americans. In terms of credibility, online services ran dead last, with only 1 percent of those interviewed finding them a credible news source.[3]

So what are millions of Americans, and millions more people of every race and nationality worldwide, using online services for, if not for news? That depends, but most uses can probably be found among the following: personal communication (electronic mail or interactive communication); non-news information, such as may be found in libraries or data bases; purchasing, such as making airline reservations or ordering an item from a Web site or catalog; entertainment; and browsing. Some may be using the Internet for business purposes. The possibilities are as varied as the sites on the World Wide Web.

For purposes of discussion here, it seems appropriate to focus on the use of the Internet. Certainly the Internet is not the whole spectrum of electronic communication, but it is a large part of it. When appropriate, reference will be made to other electronic communication options, but a look at the Internet will provide the opportunity to examine some ethical problems common to all electronic media.

▼ Instructional Case Study

William White was extremely concerned. The 18-year-old University of Maryland undergraduate student had "heard some allegations, apparently secondhand, about parental mistreatment of a girl in suburban Washington."[4] He decided to do something about it. "He posted the allegations on the Internet, along with the family's home telephone number, and sent the information along to 11 interested news groups with the suggestion that users call the girl's mother at HOME and tell her you are DISGUSTED . . . and will no longer tolerate these outrages."[5] White, a publicist for the Utopian Anarchist party, knows something about improper behavior. The previous year he briefly faced criminal charges for possessing deadly weapons and for distributing obscene materials.

Response to White's Internet message was overwhelming. The girl's family received many threatening telephone calls, and the mother had a nervous breakdown. Although White thanked his cyberspace colleagues and said there was no longer any need to call because the message had obviously been received, the calls did not stop. In an interview with the *Washington Post*, the girl's father was distressed that no one could "stop anything that goes over the Internet. . . . It's like a virus. How do you stop it?"

Electronic Communication: Privacy

One of the most sensitive issues relating to the use of electronic communication is privacy. *Privacy* may be defined as the right to be left alone, to have your personal property and affairs free from unwanted intrusion. At one point in our history, Americans enjoyed a significant amount of privacy. But the population has grown and the technological revolution has taken hold. These and other changes in the political and social cultures have resulted in a gradual decline in the amount of privacy individuals have. Some feel that the decline has been more than gradual. One writer has even gone so far as to say that "privacy is dead. We are all buck naked before the information providers of this world."[6]

It is now fairly easy for almost anyone—"a congressional committee, a credit agency, a bank, an insurance company, an employer, or a curious hacker"—to access information about us. Any or all of these can check our credit card purchases, "drool over our histories, [and] cackle malignly at our embarrassments."[7]

The case study reveals a negative aspect of electronic communication. Actually, such communication has more than one negative aspect: "no rules, secrecy, mass access, anonymity." The system is capable of much more mischief than the case study illustrates. Problems will almost always surface in any system that is as loose as the Internet.

Is electronic communication via the Internet just another one of life's little nuisances for those whose lives are intruded upon? After all, other annoying practices exist: junk mail, telemarketing calls, door-to-door solicitation, and the like. But these nuisances have a few laws governing them; not so with the Internet. There are no laws and few self-regulating mechanisms to tame the Internet. It can do what it wants. The result is that it is something like a virus. It can't be stopped. There is no way to stop people like William White from getting online and causing turmoil in a family. White, using hearsay information, apparently set himself up as judge and jury, convicting a set of Washington, D.C., parents of child abuse. No proof was required, either by White or his Internet disciples, who gleefully sped along the information highway to a predetermined destination.

Notice the postmodern contradiction here. White blithely ignored his own brushes with the law and orchestrated a campaign against a family he did not know, using information of which he had no firsthand knowledge. Where was *reason* and *common sense* in this process? Shouldn't they have told him that he had no business taking such action against the girl's parents? He had neither legal nor, given his own background, moral standing on the issue. Of course, in a postmodern culture, this is not a problem: full-speed ahead with what "I" want to do; I'll do it because I *can*, never mind what I *should* do. Consequences? Forget it. No one is concerned about consequences in postmodern America; no one accepts responsibility.

It goes without saying that Aristotle is not resting comfortably in his grave over White's excessive pursuit of behavioral extremes. Where is the just right course of action? Where is Aquinas's prudence? Bacon's control of life's appetites? Voltaire's balance of the passions? Rousseau's compassion? They are missing in the White case, and, many would argue, they are also missing in our postmodern culture.

Some information about us is considered public information. For example, real estate transaction records and some court documents—as well as other sorts of official records—are kept by city, county, and state governments. Much of this information is available through city, county, or state Web sites. Want to know the assessed value of Mr. Jones's property next door, or Ms. Smith's across the street? Easy. Call up the city or county tax assessor records. Voilà.

Other kinds of information are gathered by online companies. Computer users often leave information behind at Web sites. This can include "buying preferences, hobbies, income and medical data, Social Security numbers, addresses, previous addresses, even sexual preferences." This sort of information gathering has just begun. The Internet is still very young. "We have not yet imagined some of the purposes . . . to which people will put it."[8]

If you use a personal computer tied to a LAN (local area network) or to an online service provider, you are leaving electronic footprints when you use that computer. These footprints may be easily followed. Even something as routine as e-mail leaves significant footprints. So you think hitting the delete key is all you need do to remove a message? Wrong! Your employer, for example, may have a complicated system that stores e-mail and other data in a different format and with backups. If you hit the delete key, the message on your screen may disappear, but "it is still somewhere, and usually in multicopies." One industry president noted that he had found "deleted" data that was eight years old.[9]

You may be somewhat surprised that employers are keeping such information on their employees. Hard to believe, perhaps, but true. "Nearly two-thirds of 960 employers surveyed by the American Management Association say they keep a close eye on their workers' e-mail, phone calls, voice mail, and computer files." Employers justify their actions by noting that "what is done on company time belongs to the company." The best advice? "Never put anything in your computer that you wouldn't want broadcast on your company's PA system."[10]

This information-gathering activity goes well beyond employers. A survey of the Internet's 100 most popular Web sites found that "about half collect personal information from users who click on their sites or through mailing lists or other means."[11] One particularly disturbing practice is the creation of *cookies*. These nuggets of information can be placed in users' computers and accessed without their knowledge. The worry is that this technology "can track which Web sites are visited, what pages are looked at, even a user's hobbies, then link the data to people's names and addresses. This information can then be sold to advertisers or other interested parties."[12] Most Web sites fail to disclose adequately what they are doing, especially explaining why they are collecting this information about users, how it may be used, and what steps a user can take to limit its use. Many officials are urging self-policing, but there is little indication that Web sites are doing much about it.

Many adults find the decline in privacy as a result of new media technology more than a little troublesome. But most people become even more concerned when their children's privacy is violated. A survey by the Center for Media Education found that "about 40 percent of 38 major children's Web sites . . . gather personal information . . . from young users. Only one in five of the Web sites asks children to check with their parents before releasing personal details. Also, 40 percent use incentives, such as free gifts and sweepstakes, to encourage kids to tell about themselves."[13]

Positive changes may be on the way. "Lexis-Nexis, the nation's largest seller of detailed information about Americans, plans to let people easily examine the personal data it keeps on file about them." The Federal Trade Commission sees this action as a very positive step. "Access is critical to consumers' ability to determine whether there are errors in their file and they have an opportunity to correct them."[14] A nominal fee may be required to access information a company has on file.

Still, even this action rankles. Some people may feel that this plan does not go far enough. Many would like the opportunity to delete their file completely. After all, they argue, if it is personal information, who should have ultimate control over it? The person or some computer data gatherer? Isn't there something of a postmodern inconsistency here? If personal information about an individual is being used by a company to make money (and the company does make money when the information is sold to advertisers or others), shouldn't the company be paying the individual for the use of this information instead of the other way around? To be charged a fee to correct errors in personal data merely adds insult to injury. The money seems to be flowing the wrong way, a postmodern phenomenon visible in other parts of the culture.

On the heels of the Lexis-Nexis announcement, Microsoft said it would join Netscape and Firefly Network "to create a software standard that will place limits on how managers of Web sites can collect and reuse information about consumers who visit their sites."[15] Some observers say these actions come as a preemptive strike against efforts to pass laws that crack down on the release of data about users by Internet companies. Many would like to avoid new laws if possible. But as things stand now, "everything you want to know is for sale. . . . It's a question of how much risk you want to take and what your personal morals are."[16]

Nevertheless, despite arguments to the contrary, new laws may eventually be passed. Given what we know about the slippery slope of ethics in our postmodern culture, one cannot realistically expect personal morals to do the job of protecting privacy. So few people have personal morals these days. One scholar suggests new legislation that would "establish for all citizens property rights over the merchandising of data on one's self." The principle would be simple: "No sale or trade of such data for any commercial purpose would be legal without express permission from the person concerned."[17]

There are no easy solutions to problems involving privacy and electronic communication. Some people hold that the First Amendment requires the Internet to be a mechanism for free and open information; others say that some have taken the freedoms provided by the First Amendment and used them as license to engage in all sorts of questionable, unethical behaviors. Still others think they have the last word: you can't stop progress. The Internet and electronic communication represent progress, technological progress at any rate. But has our moral progress—our ethical sense of what is and is not appropriate, what is right and what is wrong—kept pace with technological developments? Many would say it has not. Still, these issues must be addressed and many of our problems solved before technology grows into an 800-pound gorilla.

Electronic Communication: Sex on the Internet

Sex sells. Almost anywhere and almost anytime. It should come as no surprise, then, that money is to be made by placing certain "sexual services" on the Internet. We're talking about more than mere pocket change. Beth Mansfield of Tacoma, Washington, created an "adult content" site on the

Internet's World Wide Web. Within a few months, she had advertisers and expects to gross $1 million annually.

"There is an insatiable demand for sexual entertainment online. . . . Sex related searches make up 10 to 20 percent of requests by visitors to search sites on the Web . . . sex also is widely considered to be the Web's current top moneymaker."[18] How widespread is the "adult content" Internet phenomenon? Probably about 6,000 sites out of half-million or more total sites are sex-related, said one Internet marketing expert. Not all of them are explicit enough to be called pornographic. CyberErotica is one of the largest Web sex sites. A member has access to more than 10,000 sexually explicit pictures. New pictures, sometimes as many as 1,000, are added each week. A quarter-million people visit the site daily. The site owner grosses about $800,000 a month.[19] Some adult sites sell a variety of sexual potions and lotions, as well as vibrators, bondage gear, and other sexual items. Most site entrepreneurs make their money through membership fees. In many instances, nonmembers can visit a site for free and perhaps see a few photos, but to see more, they would have to take out a membership, selling sometimes for as little as $10 a month.

As you might expect, these adult Internet services have raised a chorus of protests from several different segments of society. While many find the notion of online sex services distasteful, most are willing to admit that adults can handle the material that is available and that they have the maturity necessary to make judgments regarding their own behavior toward the material. The problem comes, many say, when children are exposed to the online adult sites. To the minds of more than a few Americans, it is unwise for a child to be able to call up a site proclaiming "Sexy Nude Babes!" Parents who hold strong religious beliefs often object to the several pro-Satan home pages available on the Web. Children often lack the intellectual and emotional maturity required to place controversial material in its proper life context. Of course, "what one group claims as guardianship of public morality strikes another as unconscionable, not to mention unconstitutional, interference."[20]

In response to complaints about sexual material on the Internet, Congress passed the Communications Decency Act, which prohibited the posting of indecent material over the Net. However, the U.S. Supreme Court ruled the act unconstitutional and voided it in June 1997. Still, the problem of sexual, suggestive, indecent material on the Internet persists.

More recently, several large media and technology companies joined to promote "a wide-ranging set of voluntary actions . . . to prevent children from accessing adult-oriented material."[21] Some say the companies may not be all that concerned about children, but that they are very much concerned that Congress will enact a new law of some sort, one that would regulate Internet content; many fear licensing restrictions and the kinds of regulations placed on radio and television.

Whatever their motivation, the proposal provoked interest and comment. The plan was to develop software "filters" that would let young children surf the Web but prevent them from having access to sexually explicit Web sites. However, not everyone is happy with the proposal. Some antipornography groups believe that filtering is no substitute for "new laws that criminalize the transmission of adult material to minors." Some free speech organizations feel that "filtering mechanism(s) prevent children from obtaining a great deal of useful and appropriate information."[22]

Some companies have already moved to limit child access to suggestive material. When a customer creates a new AOL screen name, America Online asks "whether the parent wants to block access to chat rooms and Web sites. . . . The service also intends to expand its offering of parental control options . . . adding a new category for 'young teens.' "[23]

The ethical issue here is clear: Is it ethically appropriate for children to have access to adult-content sites on the Internet? Since the Supreme Court ruled these sites may legally exist, we need not consider removing them completely. But shouldn't parents have the option of controlling what their children have access to? The age of majority in this country ranges from 18 to 21. Individuals who have reached that stage of development are presumed to be sufficiently mature intellectually and emotionally to make decisions for themselves. About the only things one can do before age 18 is get a driver's license and get a job, but even these activities carry restrictions.

Why don't we issue driver's licenses to teens age 13 and 14? Why don't we allow 11- and 12-year-olds to work full time in factories? The answer, of course, is that it takes time for youngsters to prepare for the adult world. Before age 16 (except in certain hardship cases), one is judged insufficiently prepared for the world of adult traffic. Child labor laws protect children from being exploited on the job. Even when they do start to work, some teens find themselves unable to cope with the complexities of the workplace. How is it, then, that a 12- or 13-year-old can be deemed capable of handling the even more complex world of postmodern sexual affairs? Given what we know of teen pregnancy rates, one could argue that what is already out there is a bad enough influence on today's youth, even without the Internet.

Still, the question remains: Is it ethically appropriate for children to have access to adult-content sites on the Internet? The easy answer, and one that is ethically defensible, is that parents should make this decision for their children. Some children may be ready to surf the various adult sites on the Web; others may not be ready. Whose responsibility is it to make this determination? The parents. If one is seeking a broad ethical principle to apply here, Durkheim's ethical theory works well: determine the moral ideal or moral fact that governs a planned action, then explain how society (or one's child) benefits from the action.

In a postmodern culture, a laissez-faire attitude prevails. A postmodern response to the problem might run something like this: sex sites exist on the Internet; get over it! However, in a modern culture—or in the culture that may follow the postmodern period, a culture I have termed *neo-modern*—reason and common sense prevail. Each segment of the culture has a stake in other cultural segments; each practices self-restraint and takes responsibility for its actions.

Education and the Internet

When one enumerates the positive benefits of computer technology and Internet use, education almost always appears at the top of the list. In recent years, faculty members at every educational level—from elementary schools to the universities—have been under pressure to use electronic technology in teaching. The conventional wisdom of the practice has great appeal: computers produce better-educated kids, more students can be taught at lower cost, and teachers will become more productive.

Educators' Views   Many educators have rushed to embrace the use of new technology in the classroom, but others remain skeptical. Those who have resisted the wholesale rush to technology have been accused of being lazy, obtuse, or simply Luddites.[24] But those who have dared to criticize academia's latest sacred cow (computers in education) are not taking the denunciation of their position passively. At least two national conferences were convened to examine the issue. In December 1997, a conference titled "The Computer in Education: Seeking the Human Essentials" was held at Teachers College of Columbia University in New York City. In the spring of 1998, Harvey Mudd College of Claremont, California, offered a conference touted as "a second look at information technology and higher education."[25] There were many lively discussions at each conference as the believers and the skeptics squared off with their best arguments. As it turned out, many skeptics were individuals who were seeking a balanced approach to computer use, not individuals who completely rejected the practice. What everyone found out was that there are significant arguments on each side of this issue.

Meanwhile, faculty members at the University of Washington campus at Seattle were drafting a letter to Washington Governor Gary Locke, "protesting what they say is a 'frightening' and potentially 'disastrous' drift toward replacing instructors with computerized teaching tools."[26] Eventually 850 faculty members signed the letter, which noted that more than faculty jobs was at stake, though that was certainly a concern. Also of prime importance, the letter said, was the quality of higher education. The letter emphasized learning as "a human and social practice, an enrichment of soul and mind" and should not be turned into a profit-making activity by computer hard- and software manufacturers.[27] One faculty member noted, "We have an awful lot of signatures from the computer science department. . . . They think this is a nightmare, and they are in a position to know."[28]

Student Views   Virginia Tech in Blacksburg has always prided itself in being on the cutting edge of technology. It came as no surprise, then, when the university transformed an abandoned discount department store into a "large classroom with 250 networked computers on which students take introductory mathematics classes."[29] Professors roam the floor seeking students who need individual attention.

Many people say the new system is doing a better job of teaching math than did the old lecture-type sessions. Failure rates are down and professors can offer more one-on-one teaching. But many students are dissatisfied with it. They say they'd rather learn from a human being. One freshman noted, "It gets kind of boring just sitting in front of a computer screen."[30] Some students feel ripped off by the university, but math department chair Robert F. Olin says it's only natural for students to be a little uncomfortable with the change. "They haven't had mathematics like this before," he says. They'd rather "sit back and let it come to them."[31]

Other Views   Educators are not the only ones speaking out on this issue. Engineers, scientists, even technology industry insiders are not all that convinced that computer-assisted instruction helps students learn more, better, and faster. Studies show that computer use raises student motivation for a time, but the novelty soon wears off. It is true that "certain students in certain subjects . . . learn as well, if not better than, students conventionally instructed." Therefore, some say, "the unthinking rush to wire schools and buy machines within the last decade" may have provided more positive benefits to high-tech computer makers than it has to students.[32] A key problem, one educator notes, is that it is often difficult for teachers to integrate computers into their daily classroom activities. Available software does not match the curriculum. The variations in software "make it difficult to figure out what works, with whom and when."[33]

It is true that much information exists on the Web. However, more than one educator has pointed out that "our children are barely able to handle the data they already have—the databases and computer CDs and videotapes at many public libraries, the newspapers they don't read, the 24-hour news channels and C-SPANs they don't watch, the old-fashioned books they ignore. Couldn't we teach them to use what they've got before favoring them with three orders of magnitude *more*?[34]

Here is another potential problem. In early 1998, the *Wall Street Journal* reported on a study published in the journal *Science*. The study revealed that even the most thorough search engines find only about one-third of the pages on the Web. Some popular sites cover 10 percent or less of the material. If you lack a specific Web address, a search may not turn up the document you are looking for. C. Lee Giles, the study's co-author, said, "I don't think people realize how little coverage of the Web the search engines provide." To complicate the problem, millions of new pages are added to the Web annually. Finding a specific document or piece of information will not get any easier. Perhaps just as startling was the study's conclusion that it is probably impossible to index the entire Web. Having a giant data base is of little benefit if search engines are unable to scan it all. Yet many politicians and school officials tout computers as the bridge to the twenty-first century.

Whatever problems education has, and it has many, will not be magically solved by the introduction of computers into the classroom. Our postmodern culture lacks context, and computers provide information without context. The real storehouse of humankind's knowledge is available—in books. Getting a grip on that knowledge, which is in large part determining how much one doesn't know, is a lifelong process that takes time, in-depth study, thoughtful analysis, challenging dialogue, and experience. How do computers, as currently used in most American classrooms, address those goals?

Equally to the point are these questions: "What did the students learn, and how well did they learn it? Did they simply acquire factual information, or did they learn to analyze, synthesize, and exercise critical judgment about the subject matter? Did they learn to write clear, grammatical, logical prose? Did their learning last beyond the end of the course?"[35] These are questions that ought to be asked of every course, not just those using computer-assisted instruction.

Other Classroom Technology What about other sorts of technology-assisted instruction? Several states have used technology-assisted instruction with varying degrees of success. At one university, 30 students had a typical experience. They sat in a darkened room watching a videotape of a professor teaching a class, last year's class on the same subject. On screen, the professor stands and talks. Once in a while the camera pans to show an illustration on an overhead screen. Sometimes a student—from last year—asks a question, but the student is off-camera and is neither seen nor heard. If today's students have any questions, there is no one in the room they can ask. The students in the class hate this method of instruction. "You'd think for all the money we pay in tuition, we might get a real teacher," said one.[36]

Many states are trying to educate more and more students for less money. But it would be unfair to characterize technology-assisted instruction, or distance learning as it is sometimes called, as a failure. It works at many universities. Even where it works, there is still limited interaction between students and faculty, and often the low-budget quality of the instructional videotape pales in comparison to the high-quality television pictures students are used to.

Like computers and the Internet, video is still just a tool, and like any tool, it must be properly used for maximum benefit. To use a tool just because we have it is to risk using it inappropriately. Ethical problems spring up easily from inappropriate behavior.

▼ Economic Issues

As you have seen elsewhere in this text, money often complicates an issue and usually results in some ethically questionable actions. America Online hatched a plan in mid-summer 1997 to increase its revenue. It announced plans to sell the telephone numbers of its 10 million subscribers to certain companies that would use those numbers for telemarketing purposes. This was expected to generate a financial windfall for AOL. About all it did was anger many subscribers. Within a day or two, AOL backed away from its plan. Not only were customers angry, but privacy advocates felt that providing customers' phone numbers to telemarketers was a violation of privacy. A quick compromise was reached. AOL customers will, via prior consent, have a yes or no option in terms of the release of phone numbers to telemarketing firms. Still, AOL stands to make millions in releasing the numbers of those who do not opt out.[37]

Even as AOL and other online services rake in millions, the cost of subscribing to these services is rapidly increasing. One industry analyst noted that "in the next five years, between one-third and one-half of U.S. households will not be able to afford Internet services."[38] From the provider's point of view, a substantial investment is required just to upgrade the Internet infrastructure. Costs will, of course, be passed on to users who will soon see an end to flat-rate pricing and unlimited access. Even at today's prices (AOL charges $21.95 a month for unlimited access, and other providers have similar charges, but not all the others provide unlimited access), "roughly one-third of America's 100 million households can't afford the $240–$260 a year it costs for Internet access, never mind $1500 to $3000 for a home computer, the primary method of accessing the Internet."[39]

It has been a long-standing assumption among many communication scholars that as the flow of information to the public increases, so too do the differences in knowledge acquired by different socioeconomic groups. This does not mean that individuals in the lower socioeconomic groups are completely uninformed, but that the growth of knowledge is somewhat greater among those in higher socioeconomic groups, thus creating a knowledge gap. It has been suggested that this knowledge gap could be further widened by increasing dependence on electronic technology as a means of getting information. The lower socioeconomic groups would be less likely than the higher ones to be able to afford the electronic hardware required to put them in touch with the world through the Internet. Thus, the knowledge gap between classes would widen.

Lest anyone doubt that electronic technology is as much about money as it is about information, consider the case of Microsoft. Early in 1998, the U.S. Justice Department filed an antitrust suit against Microsoft, charging it with breaking a 1995 agreement by "forcing computer makers to pre-install its Internet Explorer Web browser as a condition of licensing the Windows operating system upon which their businesses depend."[40] Microsoft chairman Bill Gates rejected the charges. Negotiations between the government and the company began, but no agreement was reached, and court action on the issue seemed likely. Although there were still some issues to be resolved as this chapter was being written, the court did allow Microsoft to proceed with the release of its Windows 98 software program in late June 1998.

▼ Other Concerns

There are other issues relating to the use of new media that raise concerns. One such concern, and this one may be more of a psychological than an ethical concern, is the notion that Internet use can become addictive. Can someone actually become "hooked" on the Net? Yes, according to some mental health professionals. Internet dependence, sometimes called Internet addiction syndrome, has been grouped "with addictive disorders like gambling, alcoholism, and drug abuse."[41] One woman who spends 30 to 50 hours per week online said, "When my computer breaks, I just freak out." "You have to go online to talk to people," the 20-year-old said. Like this woman, most Net addicts "concentrate on interactive areas of the online world, predominately chat rooms where they can exchange instant messages with other users around the globe."[42]

What sorts of negative consequences do such an addiction have? That depends on the person. Some people stare at the screen for hours, ignoring sleep, family, food, and finances. The 20-year-old woman quoted above saw her academic career slip away. Because she spent so much time online, her grades went from A's and B's to C's and D's. In Cincinnati, a woman was placed on probation and ordered to take parenting classes after a judge learned that she was letting her three children live in squalor while she spent up to 12 hours a day online. In one southern county, a woman lost custody of her two children after a judge ruled that she was addicted to the Internet.[43] Admittedly, these may be extreme cases, but many people who spend a great deal of time online admit to having complications in "RL," online shorthand for real life. Three major clinics have opened to treat computer-related disorders: McLean Hospital (affiliated with Harvard), Peoria, Illinois's, Proctor Hospital, and the Intervention Center near Washington, D.C. Computer-addiction support groups are springing up all across the country. Yet not all mental health professionals agree about the validity of Internet addiction. One psychologist said, "People no more suffer an addiction to the Internet than someone who reads books all the time suffers from 'book addiction disorder'."[44]

Many businesses voice a different concern about heavy dependence on the Internet. Sometimes a simple error can throw the entire Internet system into chaos, creating worldwide problems. One such incident occurred on July 17, 1997. Data traffic on that mid-summer morning was thrown into chaos when a computer operator in Herndon, Virginia's, Network Solutions, Inc.—the company that assigns the widely used dot.com Internet addresses—"ignored automated alarms signaling problems with the computer that routinely updates Internet address information." The result was that, for most of the day, Web sites were inaccessible and millions of e-mail messages were returned to senders. Individuals and businesses who use the Internet in their work found it impossible to communicate or conduct business.[45]

Could one little mistake do all this? Yes. The Internet is a fragile structure and when the Herndon, Virginia, computer sent "corrupted data to 10 other computers around the United States and abroad that handle the Internet's global network address directories," the problem spread.[46] One scientist noted, "This is just the tip of the iceberg . . . the infrastructure is totally dependent on this weak link." A business executive added that the problem illustrates the need "to have more than one central keeper of Internet addresses." "This was really serious," said a network administrator in Springfield, Virginia. "A lot of things were broken."[47]

Another technical glitch silenced many beepers for several days in late May 1998. Early on a Tuesday evening, the Galaxy IV communications satellite, in geosynchronous orbit above Kansas, turned away from the earth when the on-board computer apparently failed. When the bird tilted away from the earth, it was unable to beam signals to about 80 percent of the 45 million pagers in the country. However, the problem was not confined to beepers. Since the Galaxy IV also served as a relay station for dozens of other signals, some broadcasters and data networks went down. For example, the glitch caused National Public Radio's feed to disappear and delayed some airlines for a time until weather reports were received from other sources. Most of those affected were able to get up and running fairly quickly by shifting to other satellites while a backup satellite was moved into the old Galaxy IV orbit. Some data networks were required to switch to another satellite in a different orbit. This required manual dish orientation for most users. Everything appeared to be back to normal by Friday of that week, but questions remained about the degree to which everything from automated teller networks to air-traffic controllers depends on the growing number of communications satellites (about 100) in orbit, and vulnerable, above the earth.

An additional concern are the scams, cons, and hoaxes that are a regular part of Internet activity. The Illinois attorney general filed civil charges against a 22-year-old man for violating consumer fraud laws. The man was accused of running an illegal online raffle. He was soliciting donations, usually about $10, for a chance to win a Dodge Viper. In Las Vegas, a man lost almost $6,000 to an online auto buying service. The service took his money, but failed to purchase a car for him.[48]

Cons and scams have been around for a long, long time. Nevertheless, "a new generation of hucksters has made the Internet the latest tool for carrying out all sorts of schemes." Much of the fraud on the Net is of the "time honored variety—pyramid schemes, chain letters, questionable business opportunities, bogus franchises, merchandise and services promised but not delivered, overpriced scholarship services, work-at-home scams, and phony prizes and sweepstakes."[49] For example, one work-at-home scheme advertised that you can make lots of money designing graphics on your home computer. But you must first send in $300 to $500 for the software. Once you have the software, the rest is up to you. There were no additional suggestions or helpful hints about using the software in developing an at-home business.[50]

Although it probably doesn't qualify as a con or a scam, many computer users are increasingly annoyed by the practice of *spamming*—the mass sending of advertising or other promotional-type messages. These messages usually end up in individual e-mail boxes. Similar messages may be sent en masse to fax machines. Many of the messages appear to be from legitimate business or service organizations, but some consumers see them as intrusive. These unsolicited messages take up computer space or use expensive fax paper.

Early in 1998, the Southern Law Poverty Center, a Montgomery, Alabama, organization that tracks hate and paramilitary group activity, reported an increase in the number of hate groups operating in America. The Center found this particularly alarming and pointed to the 163 Internet Web sites advocating racial hatred. The first such site was created less than three years ago. The growth exhibited by these hate organizations may be the result of Internet information about them. The Center observed that this sort of public visibility makes it easier to recruit young people.[51]

Special Issues for Journalists

Much of the discussion in this chapter has focused on an individual's use of computer technology to communicate with others via the Internet. There are, however, some special technology issues that concern journalists. Dianne Lynch does an excellent job of discussing some of the ethical dilemmas journalists face in cyberspace in the January/February 1998 issue of *American Journalism Review.*

Lynch's article deals with many of the issues already discussed in this chapter, issues such as privacy and online tracking devices ("cookies"). However, she raises other issues that are worth mentioning. In terms of the work journalists do, Lynch is concerned about *immediacy, corrections, archiving,* and *plagiarism.* Can journalists meet around-the-clock deadlines, which is a reality for online news services? Will the need for immediacy influence a story's accuracy and balance? And what about corrections? Most newspapers run corrections regularly, but most online news sites have not adopted the practice. Is it unethical to ignore factual errors in one's online story? How long should an online news service keep information for access by consumers? Is downloading information a form of plagiarism if the "copying" of the work or ideas of others is not somehow acknowledged? Consumers copy and use information without attribution from the Internet all the time. Is it ethical for journalists to do the same?[52]

The *Dallas Morning News* is a good case in point. One of the benefits of the Internet is that users have rapid access to information. But what if the information is erroneous? As the *Dallas Morning News* found out in January 1998, it not only can cause embarrassment but also cause other information providers to compound the mistake.

The *Dallas Morning News* incident involved a report relating to the alleged affair between President Bill Clinton and Monica Lewinsky, a former White House intern. On Monday night, January 26, the newspaper reported on its Web site that investigators into the alleged Clinton-Lewinsky affair had found a Secret Service agent who was willing to testify that he had seen the president and the intern in a compromising situation. The story was also carried in the paper's first on-the-street edition.

Shortly after midnight, the newspaper retracted the story. On the paper's Web site, the story was called "inoperative." The paper explained that its source for the story was not accurate and was not in a position to know facts about the case. Nevertheless, the story was the lead story on ABC's *Nightline*, on cable networks, and on local radio and television broadcasts—all of which picked it up from the Internet. Both Knight Ridder and the Associated Press carried the story but sent out kill notices later. Howard Kurtz of the *Washington Post* noted that "the national impact of the bogus story underscores once again the impact of the Internet, [and] the incident also illustrates the dangers of relying on a single source who lacks firsthand knowledge."[53]

Lynch, in her AJR article, notes that "while most journalists contend that traditional values remain relevant online, they disagree sharply about how those values play out in a medium defined by immediacy, interactivity, burgeoning competition, and unflagging pressure to produce revenue."[54]

Journalists face challenges not related to the Internet in the use of electronic technology. The quality of our electronic tools has improved in the last several years, and some tools such as cameras, microphones, and recorders are small enough to be concealed in clothing. Thus, they may be used to gather information surreptitiously. This practice is illegal in some states, but may be used in certain circumstances in some others. Regardless of what the legal issues on the use of such devices might be, there are important ethical issues to be considered. Is it deceptive to use these tools without informing those who are being recorded or videotaped? Does the use of these tools damage or destroy relationships of trust between individuals? Would you want your conversations secretly taped or your activities clandestinely videotaped? Does such behavior contribute to the greater good? Is it ethical to invade someone's privacy in this fashion?

▼ Ethical Considerations

What is a good ethical position to take on the issues discussed in this chapter? How can one avoid becoming addicted to the Internet? Is it possible to escape the various online scams and cons? Can business avoid the chaos brought on by an Internet glitch? A good ethical stance to take with regard to these issues, and the other issues relating to the use of new computer technology, is this one: maintain a balance. In other words, do not embrace new media unreservedly. Consider it a tool—and only one tool among many— that can add to the quality of both personal and work life. This position is supported by several ethical philosophies with which you are familiar. Of most immediate note is Aristotle's Golden Mean, avoiding extremes and selecting the middle course. Spinoza suggests using reason to determine the proper course of action. Aquinas reminds us that ethical behavior rests on the virtues of prudence, justice, temperance, and courage.

The postmodern tendency is to embrace all things new, labeling them as progress. However, just because something occurs later in time than some other event does not necessarily mean it is as good—or better—than what went before. The good, thus, does not necessarily progress in linear fashion. Avoiding extremes and using reason and prudence to help you reach a solution to an ethical dilemma is a decidedly more modern than postmodern approach, but it certainly has benefit in many instances.

▼ What Lies Ahead?

No one knows what the future holds—a cliché, perhaps, but nonetheless true. Predictions about the future are often wrong. Today's new media are still so new that we don't know what kind of adolescence they will have, much less what kinds of adults they will become. Microsoft's Bill Gates believes that "someday, kids will spend more time on a PC connected to the Internet than in front of the TV. It will be a much richer experience."[55] Gates may be right. The key word in his statement is "someday." That day has not yet arrived and may not come unless we get a better grip on new technology and on our own behavior. In the face of this uncertainty, the most ethical course of action would seem to be avoiding the extremes and reasserting reason and prudence into human activities. Doing so would perhaps be a first step in overcoming the incongruities of the postmodern world. Perhaps one day soon, we can look at the world around us and proclaim it (with apologies to Aldous Huxley) "brave neo-modern world."

▼ Case Studies

Case Study # 17. Online Therapy

Martha Ainsworth is in therapy. Although she never sees her counselor, she communicates with him daily. On the phone, you might ask? No, online. Ainsworth is one of a rapidly growing number of people who are turning to online therapy for help with their problems. Is counseling in cyberspace possible? Yes and no. It's being done, but not all psychologists support the practice.

There may be as many as 100 counseling sites on the World Wide Web, up from about half a dozen in 1996. "Most sessions are done by e-mail, though some counselors offer interactive chats. Fees range from a few charging nothing to up to $90 for a 30-minute chat."[56] Is it really therapy? No, say some psychologists. The Internet, whether via e-mail or interactive chat, is not a viable medium to address complex problems. "You can't diagnose and treat disorders by computer contact," said one clinical psychologist. "Too many powerful cues are missing."[57] When counselors meet clients in a normal office face-to-face setting, they watch for facial expressions, eye contact, coloring or breathing changes, and the nature of vocal tones. None of these important indicators shows up on a computer screen.

The practice of online counseling has raised concerns at meetings of the American Psychological Association, whose task force on the issue promises new guidelines for online psychologists soon.[58] Still, some counselors admit that some simple problems may be solved online. They frequently point to common relationship problems as an example of issues that have been successfully dealt with in cyberspace. For example, a client might be upset about the end of a romantic relationship or about the loss of excitement in a current relationship. Often the counselor can ask a few questions and suggest ways for clients to cope. "Clients gain new insights after one or two e-mails. In some cases, in-person therapy is advised if the problem seems particularly serious. What we do is similar to the work of radio therapists," observed one psychologist.[59] Online therapy does not afford the client much privacy. E-mail is not secure; hackers can eavesdrop on therapy sessions. Software to protect privacy is not widely used.

Of particular concern is the fact that some online counselors are not licensed therapists. Of those responding to a California survey, one out of five admitted they weren't licensed, but survey researchers say the true number could be much higher. Although there's no evidence that anyone has been seriously harmed by following advice received online, the advice is not always appropriate. Consider this example. "A worried teenager was nervous about her budding attraction to other girls; the therapist advised spending more time with boys, and the 'problem' would solve itself."[60] Yet even seemingly harmless advice can be problematic if offered by an individual who speaks authoritatively from a position of power, as therapists often do. The opportunity for significant abuse of this influence is considerable.

Online counseling raises a number of serious ethical and legal dilemmas. Issues of liability, professional behavior, counselor credentials, quick fixes, and the like are still to be solved.

Key Questions   Is it ethical to provide simple online answers to complex client problems? Are online counseling services designed to help the clients or merely to be economically enriching for the counselors? How can one be sure of the qualifications of those who run online counseling services? Would Machiavelli approve of online therapy?

Case Study #18. Touching a Nerve

Log on and you might see a picture of a nude woman lapping water from a bowl. An adult-oriented Web site? Bondage and discipline, perhaps? A site for people with pet fetishes? Actually, none of the above. It's *Nerve*, an online magazine. *Nerve* is the brainchild of Genevieve Field and her boyfriend Rufus Griscom. It appears to be "the only intellectual publication that trades in smutty stories and pictures of naked women."[61] *Nerve* is part online sex magazine and part literary journal. Literary figures such as Norman Mailer and John Hawkes have contributed stories to the magazine; Joycelyn Elders and William T. Vollman have contributed essays, on masturbation and venereal disease, respectively. The magazine pays $1 per word. One writer said she contributed "because there is not a hip, general-interest sex magazine around."[62]

Field and Griscom have convinced some big-time photographers to contribute to their online publication. One such photographer who has agreed to provide photos is Andres Serrano, famous for his artistic rendering of *Piss Christ,* a crucifix in a beaker of urine. Nevertheless, the magazine is attracting some legitimate advertisers. "The site has been able to attract a 25 percent female readership. 'A woman feels more comfortable looking at this stuff than going to a newsstand where a man is going to give her a sneer,' says Field."[63]

By most accounts, *Nerve* really isn't pornographic. "The Webzines sexual high jinks are more a ploy to get surfers to stop and read. A University of Washington female sociologist noted, "There are pictures of, like, naked accountants. . . it was strangely unerotic. Willing as I was to get aroused, it wasn't even close."[64]

Key Questions   What ethical responsibility does an online magazine or newspaper have with regard to the information it transmits? Should market factors alone, such as advertiser support, be the main justification for continuing to present sexual material on the World Wide Web? Voltaire argued for "balancing the passions." Does the *Nerve* Web site provide any sort of balance? Does it address a greater good for society?

Case Study #19. Is There a Problem with My Term Paper?

Whatever might be said about the academic inadequacies of today's college students, one thing is for certain. Most know how to use computer technology to their advantage. For many, this means using a computer to prepare a term paper, but not in the conventional manner. Some students ignore a computer's word processing capability and go straight to the Internet. They access sites such as The Source, Nate's Free Reports, Other People's Papers, and PaperSure (formerly the PaperShack). These are among the sites that offer opportunities to download ready-made term papers and reports.

The Evil House of Cheat is a popular site. It pulls no punches in terms of what the papers may be used for. The site notes that it has more than 8,000 essays online in more than 40 categories. "This is perfect," it notes, "if you are doing research or you are just late with an assignment." There is often a charge for the term papers, ranging from $5 to $35 per page. For a higher fee, some companies will prepare papers on request. At the Evil House of Cheat, clicking on certain icons will give a student access to "the best ways to cheat on an exam" and "how to cheat in school."[65]

It is true most sites post a disclaimer stating that the term papers are for "research" purposes only and that they should not be submitted as a student's own work. It is also true that other people's term papers were available long before the Net, primarily from the informal files of fraternity or sorority

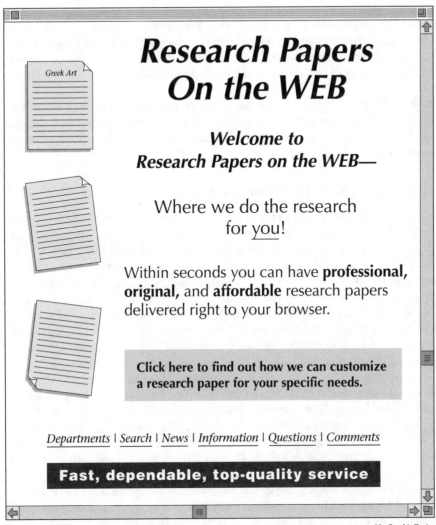

Nu Graphic Design

houses or other campus groups. Yet many educators feel that the use of information from Internet term paper sites is damaging to the educational process.

Boston University took action against many of these term paper Web sites. It sued eight online term paper providers in seven states, accusing them of wire fraud, mail fraud, and racketeering in the selling of papers over the Internet for students to turn in for credit.[66] Although a federal judge dismissed the suit in late 1998, Boston University has said it will refile its case in state court.

One site owner does not see what all the fuss is about. "The typical uproar about the Net is unjustified," he said. "Anybody can find most of what they want in a public library . . . it's no different than a freshman getting a senior's paper and turning it in, only you can do it cross-country." Boston University's president disagrees. "It is an insidious game that results in harm to all students and to the public, which expects that a diploma represents a genuine achievement," he said. "We will take whatever steps are necessary to preserve the integrity of the academic process."[67]

Key Questions   Define *honesty* and *integrity*. Who faces the greater responsibility for the misuse of term paper Web sites: the Web site owner or the student user? Is it ever ethical to even partially use the academic work of others without attribution?

Case Study #20. An Unusual Confession

Five-year-old Amanda Froistad was delighted. Her father was letting her watch all her favorite videos. It wasn't long, however, before the youngster grew tired and fell asleep. As Larry Froistad, her father, tells the story, here is what happened next. "I got wickedly drunk, set our house on fire, went to bed, listened to her scream twice, climbed out the window and set about putting on a show of shock and surprise and grief to remove culpability from myself."[68] Part of that show, Froistad continued, was "climbing in her window and grabbing her pajamas, then hearing her breathe and dropping her where she was so she could die and rid me of her mother's interference."[69] At the time of the incident, Froistad was embroiled in a bitter child custody battle with his ex-wife.

One might imagine that such a confession shocked the courtroom. Only the confession was not delivered in court but to an online support group called Moderation Management. The group advocates dealing with alcohol abuse through moderation, not abstention. The group has more than 200 members, though it is unclear how many were online at the time of Froistad's admission or how many might have read it later. In any case, only three people called police to report the incident.

Dr. Frederick Rotgers, the group's founder and a psychologist, felt that since the child was already dead, nothing much was to be gained from individuals rushing off, engaging in emotional, poorly thought-out action. Rotgers did not call police, but e-mailed Froistad, urging him to see a therapist and work things out. Another group member wrote, "Please, don't blame yourself."[70]

Not everyone was willing to accept Froistad's actions. One group member told him his behavior was "completely unacceptable." Yet few people seemed to focus on what had happened to Amanda. Some were critical of those who turned Froistad in. One person called the informer a "meddlesome rat fink." Syndicated columnist Debra Saunders posed an interesting question. "Are they [members of the Moderation Management online support group] really any different than the rest of America—reluctant to make moral choices and raging and resentful toward those who do?"

Key Questions   Why do you think so few computer users reported Froistad to the authorities? Can you cite ethical reasons for turning him in? Are there any ethical principles that would support a decision not to turn him in? How much responsibility should one individual take regarding another individual's behavior?

QUESTIONS FOR DISCUSSION

1. Can you think of three or four ethical principles that could be established as an Internet code of ethics?

2. In what ways does popular use of the Internet illustrate the basic characteristics of postmodern culture?

3. What is a defensible ethical stance to take on the issue of privacy and electronic communication?

4. What is a defensible ethical stance to take on the issue of sex and electronic communication?

5. In your opinion, which argument—pro or con—relating to computer use in education is the more persuasive? Are there ethical dangers on both sides of this issue? Explain.

6. How can one balance the economic realities and the ethical responsibilities of the world of electronic communication?

7. Are there instances where it would be ethically appropriate for a journalist to carry a hidden microphone, audio recorder, or video camera? What ethical philosophies might support such action?

8. What are some of the special concerns journalists have regarding the use of the Internet in their work?

ENDNOTES

1. "Thinking Small," *Newsweek,* 12 June 1998, 8.

2. "Many More Using Internet," *Tampa Tribune,* 28 December 1997, Business/Finance, 1.

3. "Poll Finds TV Tops, Internet Last, for News," *St. Petersburg Times,* 19 June 1997, sec. B, p. 2.

4. Philip Terzian, "Welcome to the Global Sewer," *Tampa Tribune,* 23 February 1996, Nation/World, 13.

5. Ibid.

6. Robert Reno, "Big Brother Has His Computer Watching," *Tampa Tribune,* 14 June 1997, Nation/World, 14.

7. Ibid.

8. Carol Kleiman, "Computer Is Not Your Confidante," *St. Petersburg Times,* 17 August 1997, sec. G, p. 1.

9. Ibid.

10. Ibid.

11. David Kalish, "Privacy Stolen on Net," *Tampa Tribune*, 9 June 1997, Nation/World, 1, 6.

12. Ibid.

13. "Kids' Online Privacy a Concern," *Tampa Tribune*, 14 June 1997, Nation/World, 10.

14. "Lexis-Nexis Plans to Allow People to See Personal Data," *St. Petersburg Times*, 25 June 1997, sec. E, p. 6.

15. "Web Browser Arch-Rivals Unite to Aid Net Privacy," *Tampa Tribune*, 12 June 1997, Business/Finance, 1.

16. Nina Bernstein, "High-Tech Sleuths," *Tampa Tribune*, 17 September 1997, Nation/World, 6.

17. James B. Rule, "You Should Own Your Own Data," *St. Petersburg Times*, 9 October 1997, sec. A, p. 19.

18. Vic Sussman, "Small Operators Can Make Big Killings on the Web," *USA Today*, 20 August 1997, sec. A, p. 1.

19. Ibid., 2.

20. Michael Krentz, "Censor's Sensibility," *Time*, 11 August 1997, 48.

21. "The Plan: Keep Adult Internet Sites from Kids," *St. Petersburg Times*, 1 December 1997, sec. A, p. 1.

22. Ibid., 6.

23. Ibid.

24. Ed Neal, "Using Technology in Teaching: We Need to Exercise Healthy Skepticism," *Chronicle of Higher Education*, 16 June 1998, B4.

25. Jeffrey R. Young, "Skeptical Academics See Perils in Information Technology," *Chronicle of Higher Education*, 8 May 1998, A29.

26. Peter Monaghan, "U of Wash Professors Decry Governor's Visions for Technology," *Chronicle of Higher Education*, 19 June 1998, A23.

27. Ibid.

28. Ibid., A26.

29. Jeffrey R. Young, "Students Dislike Va. Tech Math Classes in Which Computers Do Much of the Teaching," *Chronicle of Higher Education*, 20 February 1998, A32.

30. Ibid., A33.

31. Ibid.

32. Larry Cuban, "Wired to Learn?" *Tampa Tribune*, 31 August 1997, Commentary, 6.

33. Ibid.

34. David Gelernter, "Melange," *Chronicle of Higher Education*, 29 November 1996, sec. B, p. 7.

35. Neal, B5.

36. James Harper, "Educators Find TV Teaching a Turnoff," *St. Petersburg Times*, 31 March 1996, sec. B, p. 1.

37. Doug Stanley, "America Online Drops Data Sale," *Tampa Tribune*, 25 July 1997, Business/Finance, 8.

38. Jean Gruss, "Business as Usual?" *Tampa Tribune*, 28 December 1997, Business/Finance, 1.

39. Frank Ruiz, "Times May Be Changing for Internet Access," *Tampa Tribune*, 4 November 1997, Baylife, 2.

40. "Action Stations," *The Economist*, 16 May 1998, 70.

41. Doug Stanley, "Hooked on the Net," *Tampa Tribune*, 10 November 1997, Nation/World, 3.

42. Ibid., 1.

43. Ibid., 3.

44. Ibid.

45. "Internet Chaos Sends Warning to Business," *Tampa Tribune*, 18 July 1997, Business/Finance, 1

46. Ibid.

47. Ibid.

48. Margaret Mannix, "Have I Got a Deal for You!" *U.S. News & World Report*, 27 October 1997, 59.

49. Ibid.

50. Ibid.

51. Kevin Sack, "Hate Groups in U.S. Are Growing, Report Says," *New York Times*, 3 March 1998, A10.

52. Dianne Lynch, "Without a Rulebook," *American Journalism Review*, January/February 1998, 41–42.

53. Howard Kurtz, "Dallas Paper's Story Traveled Far before Being Shot Down," *Washington Post*, 28 January 1998, D1.

54. Lynch, 42.

55. "Verbatim," *Time*, 23 June 1997, 19.

56. Marilyn Elias, "Concern over On-Line Counseling," *USA Today*, 14 August 1997, sec. D, p. 8.

57. Ibid.

58. Ibid.

59. Ibid.

60. Ibid.

61. Joel Stein, "They've Got Some Nerve," *Time*, 29 September 1997, 46.

62. Ibid.

63. Ibid.

64. Ibid.

65. Chris Getzen, "For Students Who Cheat, There's a Web of Deceit," *St. Petersburg Times*, 7 November 1997, sec. B, p. 5.

66. Julianne Basinger and Kelly McCollum, "Boston U. Sues Companies for Selling Term Papers over the Internet," *Chronicle of Higher Education*, 31 October 1997, sec. A, p. 34.

67. Ibid.

68. Debra J. Saunders, "Indifferent to a Child's Death," *St. Petersburg Times*, 11 May 1998, A5.

69. Joshua Hammer, "A Chilling Cyberspace Confession," *Newsweek*, 18 May 1998, 36.

70. Saunders, A5.

▼▼▼

CHAPTER 16

Facing the Postmodern Maelstrom

▼ A Call to Action

So now what? The answer largely depends on you as an individual. Simply taking an ethics course or reading an ethics text is not enough. In order to get the maximum benefit from this, or any other, text, you must do something with what you have learned. If you have no personal, formal ethical standards, you should develop some, and right away. If you already have a clear concept of what your ethical standards are, you should use what you now know to refine or polish those standards, making them more useful for life in contemporary culture.

What this really means is that you are on your own to do whatever you wish with the information you have at hand. You can forget what you've learned, or you can use what you've learned. Neither your course instructor nor your text author will know precisely what use you will or will not make of the knowledge you have acquired. No one will check on you, so no one but *you* will know.

From ancient times, philosophers have been seekers of wisdom. The word "philosophy" comes from *philein* (love) and *sophia* (wisdom). Philosophers, or "lovers of wisdom," have long sought the answers to basic questions: What is the meaning and purpose of life? How should we live? What is the right way to live as a human being?[1]

It is impossible to get through life without encountering problems. Some problems are personal; others are professional. In large part, the degree to which we experience success in life is the result of our ability to solve the problems that face us, learn from them, and grow both personally and professionally. It is important for you, therefore, to have a solid life philosophy—a vision of what kind of life you would be most comfortable leading. This vision will likely have social, economic, political, and spiritual components. One aspect of your life view should be a set of ethical standards that you use to make decisions and undertake actions in matters of moral importance.

Contemporary culture will certainly present you with a variety of problems to solve. The difficulty often comes in deciding how to solve these problems, especially in deciding what standards of morality to apply. Contemporary culture also calls you to judge, or at least form opinions about, the problems of others, particularly those in public life. Although you may not be directly affected by their problems, understanding the situations faced by others can be helpful to you as you seek to shape your own life vision.

Consider the following:

- In the spring of 1997, 20-year-old Melissa Drexler of New Jersey gave birth and dropped her baby into a bathroom trash can at her senior prom. She then returned to the dance floor. The child was discovered, and Drexler was arrested. She pleaded guilty to aggravated manslaughter. Prosecutors sought a 15-year jail term, making her eligible for parole in three years.

  Questions to ponder. What value does contemporary culture place on human life? What consequences accrue to those who take the life of another? What value do you, as an individual, place on human life?

- In the summer of 1998, Diane and Mike, two 18-year-old virgins, announced that they would have sex for the first time, August 4, live on the Internet. They called the event "OurFirstTime." They gave users an Internet address and encouraged them to log on and witness the consummation of their relationship. In anticipation of the event, thousands of computer users visited the Web site at the address given. A couple of weeks before the scheduled date, the event was discovered to be a hoax. "Diane" and "Mike" turned out to be Michelle and Ty. Both are actors and neither, apparently, is a virgin.

  Questions to ponder. Is intimate behavior between two individuals appropriate in a public media forum? What role has the Internet had in shaping current cultural and moral values? What role should media have in the shaping of values? How can personal freedom, freedom of speech, and personal responsibility be balanced in a free, broad media environment?

- A research study, conducted for the National Constitution Center in late Summer 1998, found teens, ages 13 to 17, to be more in touch with popular culture than with the nation's history and current affairs. For example, the study found that only 2.2 percent of the teens could name the chief justice of the Supreme Court (William Rehnquist), but a whopping 94.7 percent could name the actor who played the Fresh Prince of Bel Air on television (Will Smith). About 21 percent knew that the U.S. Senate is composed of 100 members; however, more than 81 percent knew how many brothers there are in the musical group Hanson (3). A mere 12.2 percent of the teens could identify the town where Abraham Lincoln spent most of his adult life and which he represented in Congress (Springfield, Illinois), but 74.3 percent knew the name of the town where cartoon character Bart Simpson lives (Springfield).[2]

  Questions to ponder. What value do you think a traditional education has for an individual? What value does contemporary culture place on a traditional education? What role have the media had in shaping what young people know and what they should consider important?

▼ A Backward Look

This text began with a discussion of postmodernism, or more specifically, a discussion of the postmodern condition of contemporary culture. The purpose of this early discussion was to describe the environment in which we live so that some context would be available for us to consider some of the ethical problems faced by those who work in media. By this time, you are most likely familiar with the characteristics of postmodern culture: lack of common sense, declining ability to use reason to solve problems, the presence of a multitude of ironies and incongruities, and an unwillingness to take responsibility for one's actions, among others.

The other early chapters in this text pointed out that ethics—moral guidelines used to guide human behavior—are important if a culture is to maintain a sense of order and come close to getting a grip on truth and reality. There is an inherent good in *doing the right thing*, but one must *be the right thing* in order to act consistently in an ethical fashion.

Of prime importance is sound, systematic, ethical decision making. Such decision making requires common sense, reason, logic, a willingness to take the time to determine the ethical course of action, and then the courage to implement that action. In the philosophy section of this text, you were given the opportunity to study some important philosophers, their lives and their thought. Numerous ethical decision-making tools were developed to aid you in making sound ethical choices. A decision-making model was presented to illustrate how systematic, thoughtful decisions could be made. Finally, ethical issues and concerns in each media area—from advertising to new technology—were analyzed and discussed and case studies presented for further analysis.

▼ A Look Ahead

Acting ethically at any time is difficult, but particularly so in postmodern culture. In John Barth's novel, *The End of the Road*, one of the characters notes that "the more sophisticated your ethics get, the stronger you have to be to stay afloat . . . you really have to flex your muscles and keep your eyes open, because you're on your own. It takes *energy*: not just personal energy, but cultural energy, or you're lost." And it is so, in postmodern culture.

Still, there are other arguments that support the incorporation of the material in this text into your daily life. George Eliot, another novelist, but writing in an earlier historical culture period, made an equally important observation. Eliot concludes the novel *Middlemarch* with these words: "For the growing good of the world is partly dependent on unhistoric acts; and that things are not so ill with you and me as they might have been, is half owing to the number who lived faithfully a hidden life, and rest in unvisited tombs."

Of course, neither Barth nor Eliot was thinking specifically of ethical issues in the media, but they were both very much aware of the importance of ethical behavior in real life. Engaging in ethical behavior in both one's personal and professional lives will take effort, and it may go against the grain of the culture, but unless some are willing to take that sometimes rugged course of action, the culture may be unable to support the kind of growth and development it needs. In any case, you ought not to do good for the recognition it may bring, because, as Eliot notes, you probably won't be recognized for it. Much of the good of the world is the result of the work of unknown individuals who lived faithful lives. We can thank such individuals for their past contributions and hope that there are enough of this sort left in the world to make the future a better place.

You have an exciting and challenging future in mass communications. What sorts of ethical problems will you face? How will you solve them? How long will the postmodern period last? What lies beyond it? We have no answers to these questions, but there is little doubt that the future will present you with all sorts of interesting dilemmas. Some of these situations will involve issues of ethics; some will not. It might be useful to remember what the philosopher Frederich Nietzsche once observed: "Whoever fights monsters should see to it that in the process he does not become a monster. And when you look long into the abyss, the abyss also looks into you."

Sure, it is a little scary contemplating the future, anticipating unknown personal, professional, and ethical delights and dangers. It will be easy to jump the track, to lose your focus, especially in a postmodern culture. But remain calm, use your knowledge of ethical philosophies, and determine a proper course of action. As Charles Dickens wrote in *Martin Chuzzlewit*, "What never ran smooth yet, can hardly be expected to change its character for us; so we must take it as we find it, and fashion it into the very best shape we can."

▼ Real-Time Case Studies

The 20 case studies in Chapters 11 through 15 of this text are designed to generate discussion and comment in a classroom setting. But once you are in the real media world, you may not have much time in which to make an ethical decision. After you have practiced analyzing and responding to the case studies in the previous chapters, try your hand at solving the four ethical dilemmas presented here under time constraints. Each situation is described and a short time allotted in which to make a decision. This roughly approximates the time you might have to reach such a decision in the real world. Hopefully, many of the dilemmas you will face in your media work life will not be so urgent as to require a rapid response, but some situations will likely require you to be fast on your ethical feet.

Real-Time Case #1. Divulging Information

Situation. You have been working for a local public relations firm, Competent Public Relations (CPR), for almost a year. You were delighted to get the entry-level job fresh out of college. Your duties include various sorts of writing and promotional activities on behalf of your company's clients.

On a particular Friday morning, you arrive at work first and discover that the company safe has been broken into and the contents removed. Some vandalism is also evident around the office. You phone your boss first, and she tells you to call the police, but no one else. The boss and the police arrive at the same time, and the police do their job (questions, fingerprints, etc.). Other workers arrive and learn of the break-in. After the police leave, the boss calls everyone into the conference room and says she does not want information on the break-in to be given out. It could damage the image and reputation of the firm and might cause clients to feel that their interests were not being safeguarded. "It makes us look sloppy," she says. "If they can steal from the safe, they can steal from our client files. If our clients know this, we'll be hurt."

At 12:30 P.M., when everyone else is out to lunch and you are alone covering the phones, a local newspaper reporter enters the office and observes the remnants of the vandalism (some of it has not yet been cleaned up). He begins to question you about the incident. "I saw something on the police blotter," he says, "about a break-in. What happened here? Was anything taken? What was the extent of the damage? Do you have any disgruntled former employees?"

The Problem. What do you say in response to the reporter's questions?
Time Allotted before Response Required. 15 seconds.

Real-Time Case #2. Making the Call

Situation. Although competition for jobs in broadcast news was stiff when you graduated with an undergraduate degree in broadcasting two years ago, you were lucky enough to be hired by KNEW, a 50,000-watt all-news and talk radio station at 1570 on the AM dial. You quickly established yourself as an excellent reporter and writer and soon landed a spot as the station's afternoon drive-time news anchor.

Your Tuesday begins much like any other day. You arrive for work at 9 A.M. and set about performing your daily, routine news tasks. Shortly before 10 A.M., chatter on the police scanner in the newsroom has everyone abuzz. Your news director dispatches a reporter to the scene of an apparent murder. By early afternoon, it is clear that the police have a 30-year-old man in custody. He reportedly will be charged with shooting his 4-year-old son in the head. KNEW's reporter on the scene reports that he is on his way back to the station.

About 15 minutes later, the scanner is busy again, this time with news that the suspect has escaped the police. He apparently released himself from the handcuffs, grabbed a detective's pistol, and killed both the detective and the detective's partner. The newsroom is stunned by this development. Further reports reveal that the suspect, now identified as Hank Earl Carr, has taken the detectives' police cruiser and is now heading north on the interstate.

You have been busy for the past 30 minutes or so writing story updates that were read almost immediately on the air, but now your news director tells you to prepare to go on the air live with the details of this breaking story. As you make your way to the news booth, you are handed a story that says Carr has shot and killed a state highway trooper who attempted to stop his flight. On the air, you are calm and articulate, relating what is known of the story to your audience.

The story continues to develop as the afternoon wears on. About 30 minutes later, you learn that Carr has left the interstate highway and taken refuge inside a gasoline service station. He is apparently holding the station clerk, a woman, hostage. Your news director decides he ought to go to the scene. He leaves you, as afternoon news anchor, in charge. Reports continue to come in, but apparently Carr has barricaded himself in the service station and the police are having no success in convincing him to release his hostage and turn himself in.

For the next hour or so, the standoff continues, and nothing much happens. You are just about to go on the air with a summary of the events up to the present time, when an enterprising student intern from the local university strides into the news booth and asks, "Would you like an interview with this Carr fellow? I called the service station pay phone, and it is ringing. He might answer. Wanna take the call right here, live on the air?"

The Problem. Do you take the phone and attempt to speak with the suspect?

Time Allotted before Response Required. 10 seconds.

Real-Time Case Study #3. The Jumper

Situation. Your work in the news department at network affiliate Channel 4 has been widely recognized in the community as quality, unbiased, honest reporting. You have become something of a local personality. You are active in a number of civic organizations; you have hosted fund-raising telethons for a variety of well-known service organizations; you even write a weekly column for the local newspaper.

On this particular day, you arrive in the newsroom and find your colleagues discussing a 40-year-old man named Larson Bruce. You are familiar with Bruce. He has been the subject of a state-wide manhunt since he snatched his children, ages 5 and 8, from his estranged wife's car two weeks ago. You were not assigned the story but have followed developments with interest. Your colleagues inform you that Bruce has surfaced and is currently standing on the railing of the Tenth Street Bridge, just above the deep, swift river that flows through your community. He is apparently prepared to jump if authorities come near him. No one knows where the children are, and Bruce isn't saying.

As you settle down for your first cup of newsroom coffee, you receive a call from your city's police chief asking you to come to the scene. You tell the chief that another reporter is covering the story for your station, but the chief says he wants you there because Bruce has requested your presence. Apparently, the chief says, Bruce wants to tell his side of the story and has indicated he will trust no one but you to tell the story. The chief asks you to hurry, indicating that Bruce has said he will jump if you aren't there in 15 minutes. Your station is located about 10 minutes away from the bridge. The chief says a police cruiser is on its way to the station to pick you up and should be there in about 5 minutes.

The Problem. Do you assist the police by going to the scene and talking with Bruce, perhaps persuading him to come down from the railing or at least to tell authorities where his children are?

Time Allotted before Response Required. 5 minutes.

Real-Time Case Study #4. The Profile

Situation. As a freshman student in mass communication, you like to consider yourself on the cutting edge of the discipline. You make a concerted effort to keep up with a wide range of media issues. In your studies, you are proud of your writing skills. Your professors have told you that your writing is crisp, clear, and compelling. You are particularly proud of an interview you conducted with the mass communication department's most popular professor. You spent more than an hour with her earlier in the term and turned out an excellent profile for your media writing class. The class instructor told you it was one of the best pieces he had read in a long time.

As you are leaving class today, you overhear a conversation between two of your classmates. One is the features editor for the school newspaper; the other is a staff writer for the paper. The editor is trying to get the writer to produce one more faculty profile piece for tomorrow's special edition of the school newspaper. The writer notes that she has a big economics exam tomorrow, that she has already written three profiles, and that she does not have time to do another. You remember your profile on mass communication's most popular professor. With apologies, you step into the conversation and offer the editor your profile. He agrees to take a look at it and asks you to bring it to the newspaper office before 6 P.M. "I'll make a quick decision on it," he says. "We have an early 8 P.M. deadline tonight."

Shortly before 6 P.M., you arrive at the newspaper office and hand your profile to the editor. He reads it quickly and says, "Pretty good. We'll use it." Excited about seeing your work in print, you thank the editor and head for the door. "Oh, by the way," the editor calls, "this prof knew that she was speaking 'on the record' and that her comments could be published?" You pause a moment and think back to the interview. You recall telling the professor that the interview was for a class assignment only. "Well, I'm not sure," you say, "I guess she knows it could be published." "Can't guess about this," the editor says. "Call her."

You step to the newsdesk phone and call her school office. The answering service picks up and informs you that the professor is out of town at a scholarly conference and will not return until next week. "Our deadline is just a little more than an hour away," the editor reminds you.

You rush from the office and head for your apartment. You grab the phone book, find the professor's home number, and dial it. No answer. You phone your writing instructor and ask him if it is OK to publish the profile. You argue that there is really nothing controversial or embarrassing in the piece. It is, in fact, rather flattering. He suggests you talk with the profile subject and get her OK. After all, he notes, you did say the interview was for a class assignment only.

You rush back to the newspaper office, arriving at 7:45 P.M. The editor asks, "Is it a go?" You point out that you have been unable to reach the professor and that perhaps the piece could run next week. The editor nixes this idea, noting that faculty profiles run only once a year and that if your piece does not run in tomorrow's special edition—with the other profiles—it will not run at all. "I'm going to give you the responsibility here," he says. "Do we go with the piece?"

The Problem. Do you agree to let the faculty profile piece run without talking to the professor?

Time Allotted before Response Required. 10 minutes.

ENDNOTES

1. Robert C. Solomon and Kathleen Higgins, *A Short History of Philosophy* (New York: Oxford University Press, 1996), 1–2.

2. "Teens Know Bart, Fuzzy on Abe," Associated Press report, *Tampa Tribune,* 3 September 1998, Nation/World, 2.

Glossary

absolute an ethical principle or concept that is strong, firm, unchangeable, and universally applicable

aesthetics an area of philosophy concerned with the nature and expression of beauty and that which humans find pleasing

agape unconditional, Christ-like love, the basis for Fletcher's Christian situation ethics

amoral neither moral nor immoral, behavior based on no moral standards

appetite in Bacon's philosophy, the human power that causes emotional, nonreflective actions

axiology an area of philosophy concerned with the study of ethics and aesthetics

bravery in Plato's philosophy, a quality resulting from courage, the knowledge of what is to be feared and what is not to be feared

categorical imperative in Kant's philosophy, the notion that one ought to act only on those principles that one would be willing to become universal law

caveat emptor Latin for "let the buyer beware," a common concept in advertising that places product performance responsibility on the purchaser, not on the maker or distributor of the product

character a person's attributes, traits, or abilities, especially as these qualities demonstrate moral or ethical strength

checkbook journalism the practice of paying for interviews with newsmakers

cognitive dissonance in human experience, the notion that two inconsistent concepts or ideas cannot comfortably exist in the mind and that individuals become uneasy until they are able to resolve the conflict and restore consistency

compassion a quality of character resulting in an individual having feelings of sympathy or benevolence for others

conflict of interest an ethical dilemma created when media employees engage in any outside activities that might influence the way in which they do their media jobs

conscience a quality of character that motivates an individual to strong moral behavior and self-discipline

consequentialism the idea that it is ethically important to consider the possible consequences or results of an action as an important factor in decision making

courage in Aquinas's philosophy, a cardinal virtue and a quality of character that enables one to stand up to and bravely face opposition, hardship, and danger

deism a religious viewpoint, especially popular during the Enlightenment, based on the idea that belief in God is clearly reasonable to the human mind and that the existence of God need not be complicated by religious institutions; also interpreted as the belief that God created the world and then withdrew from it to see what man would make of it and how he would comport himself

deliberation in Aristotle's philosophy, thinking, that is, the use of reason as a means to the truth

dialogues in Plato's philosophy, the conversations between Socrates and others designed to provide insight into a variety of issues, including proper ethical behavior

end commonly thought of as the result of an action, particularly political, ethical, or social action; the goal one has in mind that leads one to certain actions

Enlightenment a historical culture period (c. 1650–c. 1850) characterized by the awakening of the human spirit and mind, chiefly as a result of the development of science and the human ability to reason

epistemology an area of philosophy concerned with the acquisition of knowledge and with the knowing process

ethics moral principles for living and making decisions

existentialism a philosophy popularized by Jean-Paul Sartre and others, though thought to have been originally conceived by Kierkegaard, opposed to the rationalist view of the universe as an ordered system, one that can be understood by a thinking person; thus, each of us is condemned to something of a solitary life, faced with little real meaning in existence, and totally responsible for the choices we make

fin de siècle literally, "end of the century"; also, occasionally used as a term referring to a range of behaviors often resulting from changing cultural conditions as a society finishes one century and begins another

Golden Mean Aristotle's notion that the proper ethical response to a problem lies between two extremes; hence, the just right or mean response is best when it avoids excess or defect

good in Plato's philosophy, that which man finds useful or that which man finds pleasurable; in Aristotle's philosophy, the object of all human striving

habituation in Aristotle's philosophy, the repeated doing of acts that have a similar or common quality, especially when the common quality is deliberation, or thinking

hype an intentional exaggeration of the importance of an event or product for the purpose of artificially creating an atmosphere of excitement

hyperreal world in Baudrillard's philosophy, a term referring to contemporary society and characterized by the domination of images and fictions that have little meaning

instant books paperbacks, usually, rushed into print following an important celebrity or news event

intention in Abelard's philosophy, the purpose or motivation behind an action and the primary grounds on which an action may be judged for its ethical merit

journalist an individual whose job it is to gather, prepare, and report the news

know thyself a Greek philosophical notion suggesting that self-knowledge is important in any human action, including ethical action

laissez-faire generally, a term meaning noninterference, especially in political, economic, or social affairs

logic an area of philosophy concerned with the nature of reasoning and with the rules for correct thinking

means commonly defined as the actions taken to achieve a certain goal, result, or end; in Machiavelli's philosophy, means are of little ethical import; in other philosophies, means are very important ethically

moral agent an individual who is capable of acting on his or her own thinking, particularly as it relates to ethical decision making

moral fact in Durkheim's philosophy, a statement that directs an individual's action—action based on an obligation or a duty

moral ideal in Durkheim's philosophy, a standard of behavior set by society for its members, embodying the values that the society wishes to be preserved and transmitted to the next generation

morality from the Latin *moralis* meaning customs and manners; a system of ideas of right and wrong conduct

moral legalism the notion that proper ethical behavior is based on the law; hence, that which is legal is moral (or ethical) and that which is illegal is immoral (or unethical)

moral relativism the notion that all ethical systems are equal and that everyone is free to choose his or her own regardless of how others might be affected; also, the belief that moral principles are not absolute, but conditional or contingent on the situation we find ourselves in

metaphysics an area of philosophy concerned with the nature and functions of reality

modernism a term describing the historical culture period (c. 1850–c. 1960) characterized by a faith in reason and science; the development of strong religious, educational, and family institutions; and advances in art, literature, and technology

new media in this text, a term used to represent those aspects of electronic communication that enable us to communicate with other individuals, groups, or a mass audience

nonconsequentialism the idea that one need not consider the possible consequences (or results) of an action as part of the ethical decision-making process

nothing in excess a Greek philosophical notion suggesting that avoiding extremes or excessive behavior is the way to a successful and ethical life

objectivism in Rand's philosophy, the belief that man ought to live for himself, use reason to determine his own moral codes, then use those codes to guide his actions; sometimes called *rational self-interest*

ought part of the ought-implies-can philosophy, whereby there are certain actions one is required to take out of a sense of obligation or duty

paparazzi a term for photographers who pursue celebrities in an attempt to get intimate or revealing photos

persuasion as an advertising technique, the attempt to change a person's mind about a product or service in order to motivate the purchase of the product or service

plagiarism the copying of the work of others—without proper source identification—and presenting it as one's own original work

postmodern a term describing the conditions of contemporary culture, characterized by a discontinuity and ambiguity in all aspects

of life; also, as a historical culture period (c. 1960 to present)

pragmatism generally, a philosophy stressing decision making based on the practical, the most useful, the most realistic thing to do

prominence as a news value, the degree to which well-known individuals are principals of a story

propaganda communication designed to change a person's mind through the presentation of nonfactual information—especially opinion—disguised as fact

proximity as a news value, the closeness or nearness of the event, geographically, to the audience

prudence in Aquinas's philosophy, one of the cardinal virtues and a quality of character that results in an individual selecting a sensible course of action

prurient interest abnormally preoccupied or obsessively interested in sexual matters

pseudo-event an event created for the exclusive purpose of generating publicity or dramatizing an occurrence beyond its natural impact

public's right to know a phrase used as justification by some media for their intrusion into sensitive areas and based on the notion that individuals in a democracy need information on which to base life decisions

puffery in advertising, exaggerating a product's qualities or benefits so that it appears in a favorable light

ratings a term that may refer either to the percentage of the audience a specific radio or television program has or to the program-content designation system developed by the television networks

rationalism a philosophy based on the notion that individuals can derive knowledge of the world around them through the use of reason and that such knowledge reveals a larger system

reason in numerous philosophies, the ability to think and reflect in the consideration of any problem

relativism a philosophy stipulating that there are no universally true or valid moral judgments or principles; hence, those principles that do exist must of necessity be flexible and variable

right to privacy historically, the right of American citizens to be let alone, to have their personal property and affairs protected from unwanted examination, especially examination by the government or the media

simulation in Baudrillard's philosophy, the substitution of the false for the real; may result in a collapsing of the real and the image together in a *simulacrum*

spin control the name given to attempts by public relations practitioners and press spokespersons to twist or manipulate facts or statements into a form that is pleasing to a client

tabloids half-size newspapers that publish stories of a sensationalistic nature; may also refer to some pseudo-news television programs

telemarketing the selling or promotion of products or services using the telephone to reach potential customers

temperance in Aquinas's philosophy, a cardinal virtue, the avoiding of extremes in behavior, thought, and emotion

timeliness as a news value, the relative importance of a story to the audience, especially the degree to which the story is or is not time-bound

un-Golden Rule in Machiavelli's philosophy, the notion that you should do unto others what they would do unto you—that is, do things to others before they do things to you

un homme sensible Voltaire's "sensible man," that rare individual who has combined deep feeling with reason in the service of humanity

utilitarianism in the philosophy of Bentham, Mill, and others, the idea that one ought to act by following the moral rule that will bring about the greatest good for the greatest number of people

virtu in Machiavelli's philosophy, the ability to understand, accept, and adapt to change; this notion differs markedly from the common definition of *virtue* or moral goodness

virtue in Plato's philosophy, the correct knowledge of things

will in Bacon's philosophy, conscious behavior, the inclination to control inappropriate behavior; in Schopenhauer's philosophy, all emotions and passions that motivate human actions

Index

Abelard, Peter, 159, 180, 247
    biographical elements, 38–39
    philosophy, 39
    use of hidden cameras and, 184
absolute, *vs.* relative principles, 154, 317
accuracy, checking for stories, 191–192
advertiser, influence on media content, 215–217
advertising. *See also* direct mail marketing; spamming; telemarketing
    alcoholic beverage, 212
    application of ethics to, 217
    case study, 200–201
    description, 197–198
    message's appeals, 201–204
    overview, 198–200
    puffery, 204–207
    sweepstakes as deceptive, 207–209
    tobacco, 209–212
agape, in Fletcher ethics, 121, 317
agent, author's issues with, 236–237
Albert, Marv, 249–250
Albertus Magnus (Albert the Great), 41
alcoholic beverage, advertising, 212
Alexander the Great, 30
American Family Publishers, 207–209
America Online (AOL), 294–295
appetite, in Bacon's philosophy, 44, 317
appropriation, 166
Aquinas, St. Thomas, 159, 194, 264, 300
    biographical elements, 40–41
    philosophy, 41–42
Aristotle, 41, 92, 112, 159, 299
    biographical elements, 29–30
    Golden Mean applied to *Ellen*, 262–263
    paparazzi and, 176, 180
    philosophy, 30–32
Atlas Shrugged, Ayn Rand, 112, 113
audience, news, 164
audio books, issues with, 237–238

Autobiography, John Stuart Mill, 79
axiology, 19, 317

Bacon, Francis, 159, 202, 241
    biographical elements, 42–44
    philosophy, 44–45
Baker, Russell, 172
balance, 92
Barney, Ralph, 155
Barth, John, *The End of the Road*, 311
Baudrillard, Jean, 127, 160, 221, 272
    alteration of photographs and, 185
    biographical elements, 133–135
    philosophy, 135–137
Beauvoir, Simone de, 104–106
behavior, postmodern, 7–12
Being and Nothingness, Jean-Paul Sartre, 105, 107
Bentham, Jeremy, 79, 81
Bernays, Edward L., 218
Bivins, Thomas, 155
Black, Jay, 155
book publishing
    author-agent issues, 236–237
    author-publisher issues, 235–236
    case study, 248–249
    content, 233–235
    economic concerns, 232–233
    overview, 232
    responsibility, 252–253
    specialized books, 237–239
Boorstin, Daniel, definition of celebrity, 171
Bradford, William, 119
bravery, according to Plato, 27, 317
breaking news, television responsibilities with, 191
Brinkley, David, 193
Buchwald, Art, 272

Calvin Klein, advertising, 200–202
Carey, James, 5

categorical imperative, Kant's, 76, 317
caveat emptor doctrine, 206–207, 317
celebrity, 171–173
Center for Moral Development and Education, 115
character, Schopenhauer on, 92
Chase-Riboud, Barbara, 273
checkbook journalism, 183, 317
Child Psychology Training Program, 115
children
    advertising and, 198–199
    Internet and, 290–291
    television programs content and. *See* latchkey
      children
Christianity, 121
Chrysler Corporation, 215
Clooney, George, paparazzi and, 177
cognitive dissonance, 8–9, 317
Colgate-Palmolive, advertising, 206
college textbooks, 239
common sense, postmodern loss of, 8, 287
Communication Act of 1934, 181
Communication Decency Act, 290
computer-related disorders, 296
conflict, news about, 164
conflict of interest, journalists, 183, 193, 317
Confucius, 55
conscience, 317
    Rousseau and, 62
consequentialism, 154, 317
consumption, postmodern, 7
content
    advertiser's influence on media, 215–217
    book publishing and, 233–235
    film industry, 269–270
    issue for radio, 243–245
    issue for recording industry, 240–241
    journalism integrity and story, 194
    program ratings and entertainment, 258–263
    television talk shows, 263–264
cookies, computer, 288
Copernicus, 69
courage, according to Aquinas, 42, 317
Critique of Pure Reason, Immanuel Kant, 76–77
Cruise, Tom, 172

data-base information, direct mail marketing, 213
decision-making
    ethical. *See* ethical decision-making
    real-time, 156–157
decision-making model, 146
    problem solving and, 147–154
decision-making tool, 28, 32, 40, 42, 45, 52, 56, 59, 62, 72,
    77, 82, 93, 97, 109, 114, 118, 122, 132, 137
DeGeneres, Ellen, 258, 261–263
deism, 58, 61

deliberation, for Aristotle, 31, 317
Delilah after Dark, 244–245
DeMille, Cecil B., 111
Descartes, René, 69
Dewey, John, 116
dialogues, Plato/Socrates, 27, 317
Diana, Michael, *Boiled Angel*, 231–232, 234
Diana, Princess of Wales
    media coverage of death, 178–185
    media star after divorce, 168–169
direct mail marketing, 213–214
    mail tricks, 214
Discipline and Punish: The Birth of the Prison, Michel
    Foucault, 131
Durkheim, Émile, 87, 160, 246
    biographical elements, 94–96
    laissez-faire attitude and, 188
    philosophy of, 96–97
duty, concept of, 113

economic issues
    book publishing, 232–233
    definition of, 150
    Internet, 294–295
education
    ethical problems, 16
    Peter Abelard and, 38
    Renaissance moral, 44
    technology and, 292–294, 302–304
Edwards, Jonathan, *Sinners in the Hands of an Angry
    God*, 119
Egyptian period, 3
electronic communication, 284–285
    instructional case study, 286
    privacy, 286–289
Eliot, George, *Middlemarch*, 311
Émile, Rousseau, 61
end, 318. *See also* means
English or Philosophical Letters, Voltaire, 57
Enlightenment period, 3, 57, 67, 87, 318
entertainment. *See* television
epistemology, 19, 318
Essays in Moral Development, Lawrence Kohlberg, 115
ethical decision-making, 145
    tools for, 159
ethical problem, definition of, 150–151
ethics. *See also under* specific names
    current concerns in America, 15–16
    definition, 16–18, 318
    in journalism, 18–19
    philosophy and, 19–20
    standard-based *vs.* duty-based, 113
Ethics, Spinoza, 70–71
Eudemian Ethics, Aristotle, 31

evil
   choice *vs.* good choice, 151
   Spinoza's definition, 71
existentialism, 318
   foundation and essence of, 106–109, 318
   Sartre's, 102, 105
experience, Schopenhauer on, 92

false light, 165
Federal Trade Commission Act, advertising and, 206
feminism, 11. *See also* women
film industry
   business practices, 272–274
   case study, 276–277
   character and content, 269–270
   distribution practices, 274
   editing techniques, 271–272
   political involvement, 270–271
   racial and ethnic diversity within, 274
fin de siècle, notion, 6, 318
FIRSTPLUS Financial Corporation, advertising, 204
Fletcher, Joseph, Christian Situation Ethics, 121
flowchart, use for decision-making model, 147
football, journalism and professional, 189–190
Forest Gump, 272, 273
Foucault, Michel, 127, 160, 216, 262, 271, 274
   biographical elements, 128–131
   philosophy, 131–132
freedom, existentialism, 106, 109

Galileo, 69
Goethe, Johann Wolfgang von, 58
Golden Mean, 31–32, 55, 92, 318. *See also* Aristotle
   applied to PR, 221
Golding, William, *Lord of the Flies*, 233
good
   Aristotle's concept, 31, 318
   Spinoza's definition, 71
Greek period, 3. *See also* Aristotle; Plato

habituation, 32, 318
happiness, Schopenhauer on, 92
Hearst, William Randolph, 173
Hegel, Georg, 22, 90
Heidegger, Martin, 106
Heinz dilemma, 117–118
hidden cameras, 183–184
Hobbes, Thomas, 159, 173, 180, 239
   biographical elements, 53–54
   philosophy, 54–55
hype, 220, 318
hyperreal world, Baudrillard's, 136, 318

impact, news, 164
individualism, radical, 107–108
individual responsibility, existentialism, 106

information/misinformation, 11
instant books, 238, 318
integrity, journalism, 194
intention, according to Abelard, 39, 318
Internet, 284
   case study, 300–301
   concerns with, 296–298
   economic issues, 294–295
   education and, 292–294, 302–304
   sex on, 289–292, 301–302
intrusion, 165

Jenck, Charles, 5
Jewish tradition, 120–121
Johnson, Derwin, 191
journalism
   ethics in, 18–19, 182–189
   integrity and story's content, 194
journalist
   conflict of interest, 183, 193
   definition, 161, 318
   technology issues for, 298–299
   work of, 162–164
Judeo-Christian tradition, 101–102, 160. *See also*
      Christianity; Jewish tradition
   rationale, 119–120
justice, according to Aquinas, 42

Kant, Immanuel, 67, 113, 145–146, 159, 202, 247
   biographical elements, 72–76
   influence on Schopenhauer, 91
   philosophy, 76–78
Kierkegaard, Soren, 106
Kimberly-Clark, 215
Kinko's, advertising, 203–204
Kohlberg, Lawrence, 102, 160, 215, 237, 265
   biographical elements, 115
   philosophy, 116–118
   philosophy as decision-making tool, 153

laissez-faire attitude
   ethical implications of, 188
   postmodern culture, 291, 318
latchkey children, television programs content and,
      260–262
Lee, Ivy, 218
Lee, Spike, *Do the Right Thing*, 147
Lemon Awards, 224–226
Leno, Jay, 250–252
Liddy, G. Gordon, 245
Limbaugh, Rush, 245
logic, 19, 318
loyalty
   case study, 249–250
   public relations and, 221–222

Machiavelli, Niccolò, 159, 192, 202, 237
  biographical elements, 48–49
  philosophy, 50–52
Madness and Civilization: A History of Insanity in the Age of Reason, Michel Foucault, 131
Magna Moralia, Aristotle, 31
manipulation, of photographs, 184–185
mass communication. *See* journalism
Mather, Cotton, 119
McClain, Senator John, television programs' rating issue and, 260
McLuhan, Marshall, *global village* notion, 178
means, 51, 318
media coverage, 177–178
  spontaneous *vs.* choreographed, 187
Merrill, John, 163–164
metaphysics, 19, 318
Microsoft, 295
Middle Ages, 3, 37
Mill, John Stuart, 67–68, 113, 160, 246
  biographical elements, 78–80
  philosophy, 81–82
  philosophy as decision-making tool, 153
Miller Brewing Company, advertising, 202–203
Modern age, 3, 127
modernism, 319
moral fact, according to Durkheim, 97, 318
moral ideal, according to Durkheim, 97, 318
morality, 318
  application of personal standards, 309–310
  ethics and, 17
  Kant's concept, 76
  Kohlberg's definition, 116–117
  Rousseau and, 61
moral judgment, 116
moral legalism, 18, 318
moral relativism, 18, 318
Mother Teresa, 178
Murphy, Eddie, *Coming to America,* 272–273
Murrow, Edward R., 181, 187, 189

National Press Photographers Association, Code of Ethics, 172
new media communication, 283–284, 319
news
  definition of, 164
  journalist and, 162
  values, 163–164, 172–173
Newton, 58, 69, 74
Nicomachean Ethics, Aristotle, 31
Nike, Inc., 223–224
Nilsen, Thomas, philosophy of *significant choice,* 262
nonconsequentialism, 154, 319
North, Oliver, 245

objectivism, 102, 319
  Ayn Rand, 112
  premises, 113
Onassis, Jacqueline Kennedy, 173, 175
online counseling, 300–301
On the Fourfold Root of the Principle of Sufficient Reason, 90
On the Freedom of the Human Will, Arthur Schopenhauer, 92
openness, postmodernism, 7
organizer, personal, 284
ought-implies-can concept, Kant's, 77, 319

paparazzi, 319
  Diana and, 169–171
  tabloid and, 173–177
persuasion, 202, 319
philosophy, 19, 22–23. *See also under* specific names
  decision-making and, 155
photographs. *See also* hidden cameras
  manipulation of, 184–185
Piaget, Jean, 116
plagiarism, 248, 272, 273, 319
Plato, 30, 159, 237, 244
  biographical elements, 25–26
  five cardinal qualities, 27
  philosophy, 26–28
pleasure, Schopenhauer on, 92
polarization of views, 10–11
politics, film industry and, 270–271
pornography movie, 276–277. *See also* Internet
Postman, Neil, 167
Postmodern age, 3
  ethical concerns of, 185–189, 311–312
postmodernism
  characteristic elements, 7–12
  definition, 5
  inconsistency regarding tobacco issue, 212
power, Foucault's notion of, 131–132
pragmatism, 319
privacy
  celebrity and right to, 172
  definition of, 165
  electronic communication, 286–289
  principles of rights to, 165–166
  violation of rights to, 165
profession, journalist's job as, 162–163
prominence, news, 164, 319
propaganda, 202, 319
proximity, news, 164, 319
prudence
  according to Aquinas, 42, 319
  according to Kant, 77
prurient interest, culture, 234, 319

pseudo-events, 219–220, 319
public/private figures, 166–167
    death and ethical concerns, 171
public relations
    case studies, 222–227
    definition of, 218
    fake news and, 221
public's right to know, 167, 319
public television, 266–268
    funding, 267–268
puffery, 204–207, 319
Pulitzer, Joseph, 173

R. J. Reynolds, Joe Camel advertising campaign, 211
radio, content issue, 243–245
Rand, Ayn, 102, 160
    biographical elements, 109–112
    paparazzi and, 176–177
    philosophy, 112–114
ratings, television programs, 258–263, 319
reason, 97, 287. *See also Critique of Pure Reason; On the
        Fourfold Root of the Principle of Sufficient Reason*
    Enlightenment and, 145
    existentialism and, 107
    role in postmodern era, 145
recording industry
    content issue, 240–241
    promotion practices, 241–242
relativism, 320
    cultural ethical, 96
    moral. *See* moral relativism
religion/religious beliefs, 119–120. *See also* Christianity;
        Jewish tradition
Renaissance, 37. *See also* Machiavelli, Niccolò
Report of the Commission on Obscenity and
        Pornography, 234
Republic, Plato, 27
respect for others, Schopenhauer on, 92–93
responsibility, personal, 10
Rivera, Geraldo, 265
Roman period, 3
Rousseau, Jean-Jacques, 159, 173, 264
    biographical elements, 59–61
    philosophy, 61–62
royalty
    college textbooks' author, 239
    issue of statements' accuracy, 236

salary, journalist, 162, 181
Sartre, Jean-Paul, 102, 113, 130, 160
    biographical elements, 102–106
    philosophy, 106–109
satire, 277–278
Schlessinger, Dr. Laura, 243–245

Schopenhauer, Arthur, 22, 87, 160, 202, 234, 244
    alteration of photographs and, 185
    biographical elements, 88–91
    laissez-faire attitude and, 188
    philosophy, 91–93
science, philosophy and, 70, 76
scientific naturalism, 96
Scito te ipsum, Peter Abelard, 39
self-formation, Foucault's concept of, 131
self-help books, 238
selling idea, advertisement, 201
Sesame Street, merits of, 266–267
shock jocks, 246–247
simulation, Baudrillard's concept of, 137, 320
Social Contract, Rousseau, 61
social issue, definition of, 149
society, Durkheim's philosophy and, 96
Socrates, 26–27
South Park, 277–278
spamming, 297
Speakes, Larry, Reagan's press secretary, 219
spin control, public relations, 218–220, 320
Spinoza, Benedict, 67, 159, 242, 299
    biographical elements, 68–70
    philosophy, 70–72
staged news event, 183
standard, Rand's concept of, 113–114
Steele, Bob, 155
subjectivism, radical, 107
suggested media application
    Abelard's ethics, 40
    Aquinas's ethics, 42
    Aristotle's ethics, 32
    Bacon's ethics, 45
    Baudrillard's beliefs, 137
    Durkheim's philosophy, 97–98
    Foucault's ideas, 132–133
    Hobbes's ethics, 56
    Judeo-Christian tradition principles, 122
    Kant's ideas, 78
    Kohlberg's theory, 118
    Machiavelli's ethics, 52
    Mill's utilitarianism, 82
    Plato's ethics, 28–29
    Rand's ethical philosophy, 114
    Rousseau's ethics, 62
    Sartre's philosophy, 109
    Schopenhauer's philosophy, 93
    Spinoza's ethics, 72
    Voltaire's ethics, 59
suicide, as news story, 190–191
Summa Theologiae, St. Thomas Aquinas, 41
Sunbeam Corporation, 226
sweepstakes, 207–209

tabloids, 167, 320. *See also* paparazzi
 paparazzi and, 173–177
talk shows
 political personalities radio, 245–246
 radio-advice, 243–245
 television, 263–266
Taylor, Edward, 119
Taylor, Harriet, 80
technology. *See also* electronic communication; Internet
 issues for journalist, 298–299
telemarketing, 214–215, 320
television
 case study, 275–276
 instructional case study, 258, 261–263
 programs ratings, 258–263
 public. *See* public television
 talk shows' content issue, 263–264
 talk shows' procedures issue, 265–266
temperance, according to Aquinas, 42, 320
The Fountainhead, Ayn Rand, 111
The History of Sexuality, Michel Foucault, 131
Theologia, Peter Abelard, 39
The Prince, Machiavelli, 49–51
The World as Will and Idea, 90
timeliness, news, 164, 320
tobacco advertising, 209–212
Toffler, Alvin, *Future Shock,* 283
trade, journalist's job as, 163
truth, 132

case study, 250–252
Ellen and issue of, 262
public relations and, 221–222
Twain, Mark, *Huckleberry Finn,* 233
Twitchell, James B., 199

un-Golden Rule, Machiavelli's, 51, 320
usualness, news, 164
utilitarianism, 79, 81–82, 320

Van den Ende, Franciscus, 68
v-chip, 261
victimhood, postmodern, 9–10
victimization, postmodern trend toward, 186
virtu, Machiavelli's philosophy, 50, 320
virtue, according to Plato, 27, 320
Voltaire, François Marie Arouet, 88, 159, 202, 248
 biographical elements, 56–58
 philosophy, 58–59

Warner Brothers Records, Ice-T's *Body Count* album, 240
will, 320
 in Bacon's philosophy, 44
 Schopenhauer's concept, 92
women, position in Greek society, 31

Yeats, W. B., 6
Yes and No, Peter Abelard, 39